THE

SPORTSMAN'S BOOK

FOR INDIA

Owing to the antiquity and rarity of this book, certain pages are regrettably absent, and readability is compromised due to the blurring of the original text. If you possess any insights regarding the availability of these missing sections, kindly inform us. Your assistance is crucial in ensuring the completion of this significant work for the benefit of future generations.

THE
SPORTSMAN'S BOOK
FOR INDIA

EDITED BY

F. G. AFLALO, F.R.G.S., F.Z.S.

GYAN

Published by

Gyan Publishing House
5, Ansari Road
Daryaganj, New Delhi-110002
Phone: 011-47034999, 9811692060
E-mail: books@gyanbooks.com

Distribution Network
gyanbooks.com
India, USA, Canada, UK, Australia

ISBN: 978-93-6208-000-4 (PB)
First Published, 1904

2nd Impression 2024

Printed at: Gyan Press, Delhi.

THE SPORTSMAN'S BOOK FOR INDIA
Author: F. G. AFLALO

THE
SPORTSMAN'S BOOK
FOR INDIA

THE SPORTSMAN'S BOOK FOR INDIA

WITH CONTRIBUTIONS BY LIEUT.-GEN. SIR MONTAGU GILBERT GERARD, K.C.S.I., C.B.; GEN. A. A. A. KINLOCH, C.B.; LIEUT.-COL. P. R. BAIRNSFATHER; MAJOR C. H. CLAY; MAJOR NEVILLE TAYLOR; CAPT. A. G. ARBUTHNOT; W. BURKE (Editor of the *Indian Field*); F. O. GADSDEN; AND HARRY STOKES

EDITED BY

F. G. AFLALO, F.R.G.S., F.Z.S.

JOINT-EDITOR OF "THE ENCYCLOPÆDIA OF SPORT"

ILLUSTRATED
WITH PHOTOGRAPHS AND MAPS

LONDON:
HORACE MARSHALL & SON
1904

To

HIS EXCELLENCY

GENERAL VISCOUNT KITCHENER OF KHARTOUM,

G.C.B.,

COMMANDER-IN-CHIEF OF THE INDIAN ARMY,

THIS BOOK IS, BY PERMISSION,

RESPECTFULLY DEDICATED

BY THE EDITOR.

EDITOR'S FOREWORD

NEARLY a century has elapsed since the first appearance of "Oriental Field Sports," dedicated to His Majesty King George the Third by Captain Williamson of the Bengal Army. Some of the original plates of that now rare work having recently come into the Editor's possession, he was prompted to refer to the book itself and was much struck by the wonderful opportunities for sport which must have come in the way of those whose career took them to India in the early years of the nineteenth century. Hundreds of books on Indian sport have been published since then, one of the most recent and most practical being Mr Russell's "Bullet and Shot in Indian Forest, Plain and Hill," which, however, as indicated by the title, deals with one sport only. What Mr Russell and many others have done for Indian shooting, Mr H. S. Thomas and one or two other angling enthusiasts have done for Indian fishing; but there has not up to the present been any one manual essaying to offer sound, practical information, advice without anecdote, on any and every outdoor pastime that may in that country fall to the lot of the official, military or civilian, planter, or even bird of passage.

As regards sport with gun and rod, India always has been a grand playground. With some allowance for the inevitable effect of a more firmly established European occupation on the status of the wild beasts of the jungle, it always must be so. We must discount, as the individual standpoint of a gifted historian not entirely free from eccentricity, the peculiarly discouraging estimate of the country's sporting resources offered by Colonel Malleson in his prefatory apology for the somewhat misleading title of his "Recreations of an Indian Official." Quoting a passage from another of his works, in order to contrast India with home, he says: "In "Europe, where there is so much to tempt a man "into the sunshine and open air; where the "streams invite the angler; the slopes of the "mountains, the botanist; the forest, the sports-"man; and where the merry laugh and innocent "smiles of the daughters of the land invite all, it "must require the virtue of a St Anthony to "persevere regularly in indoor studies." India, he goes on to say, holds out none of these temptations. The handbook now offered for the consideration of Anglo-Indians does not pretend to catalogue the beauties of either the flora or the ladies of Hindostan; but, with regard to the possibilities of its jungles and rivers, it may perhaps serve to show that the gallant chronicler of the Indian Mutiny was a little less than kind to the country which furnished the occasion of the literary and fighting occupation of his life.

And if the India of to-day may still claim to be reckoned very high among the sporting countries of the world, its opportunities forty years ago must have been fourfold.

Swift, who, with all his virtues, could scarcely have been a joyous playmate, was wont to describe the majority of our sports and games as imitations of fighting; and it is certain that the greater part of Indian "sport," as it is understood to-day, is made up of shooting, fishing, hunting and polo, in all of which some faint semblance of warfare might perhaps be traced by an essayist skilled in such exercises. The present handbook, however, ranges over an even wider field of recreation, taking cognisance of all manner of minor sports, games and physical exercises on land and water which help not only to redeem the monotony of station life, but also to fortify the European constitution against the ravages of a climate for which Nature never intended it.

As a first attempt at covering a somewhat appalling geographical area, ranging horizontally over a million and three-quarter square miles and vertically from the playing of bahmin on sunlit seas to the stalking of wild sheep in the eternal snows of the Himalaya 15,000 ft. higher, the book must offer its own plea for lenient criticism. Should future issues be called for, the editor will gratefully avail himself of any suggestions which may reach him on the subject of either useful abridgment or necessary amplification.

One offence, in respect of which the editor

anticipates adverse criticism, is his want of reverence for the new school of Indian spelling, the "Hunterian" way of writing place-names. The official style of accentuating Arabic names like Pŭna and Mórăt seems particularly unsatisfactory, and in the following pages the names will for the most part be found in the phonetic spelling. The editor desires to take the responsibility of altering to this end the spelling used by at any rate one of the contributors.

Another aspect in which this first edition is without doubt open to censure is the want of absolute uniformity of geographical range included under the different sports. Thus, while India proper, with the Himalayas and Kashmir, has been regarded as the region of paramount importance, outlying dependencies, such as Ceylon and Burmah, are here and there alluded to, where any interesting information on the subject was volunteered, without, however, being adequately dealt with throughout. In this, as in other respects, a first attempt may perhaps plead extenuating circumstances.

Until such a book has been in the hands of many readers and reviewers, it is hardly possible to give more than a small measure of satisfaction to everyone; but it is hoped that even in its first edition it may prove useful at any rate to those who are for the first time about to take up their residence, in whatsoever capacity, in India. The errors made, even in these days of frequent communication, advertisement and universal knowledge, by the Griffin, in the purchase of his kit, the moment he has successfully passed the C.S.I. final or secured a post of trust on a plantation, are an endless joy to those already established in the land, but not at all to himself. The sportsmen who have so diligently helped in condensing into this volume so much of counsel and of warning should at any rate have the satisfaction of knowing that their advice has saved their juniors both trouble and expense. Their names are in every case a guarantee of the value of the information they give; and the great pains which they have been at to make that information full and essentially applicable to the conditions of to-day must be evident at a glance. Editing the work of men with so much to say, and so proper a knowledge of how to say it, has been an easy and agreeable task indeed.

The omission of elephant-shooting from the section on big game may, at first sight, seem singular, seeing that, as recently as February 1904, the *Indian Field* contained an account of elephant-shooting in the Mysore jungles. The sport is, however, practically confined to such jungles as those of Mysore and Travancore, in which the Rajahs from time to time permit distinguished visitors to shoot elephants. Doubtless, there are still wild elephants in the East, towards the Bay of Bengal, but the animal is preserved in all British territory, and, for the purpose of this book, may be ignored. Sir Montagu Gerard writes that he remembers, about the year 1872, seeing twenty or twenty-five wild elephants at Rewah, which the Rajah of Rewah (between Allahabad and Jubbulpore) had captured, and he also recollects reading accounts of elephant-shooting in the Pahang Hills, in the south of Madras, forty years ago. All this, however, belongs to a vanished past.

As some assurance that much of the information is the most recent procurable, it may be mentioned that Major Taylor's hints on pigsticking were actually delayed through a pigsticking accident that befell the author, while Captain Arbuthnot's detailed introduction to ways and means in the Himalayas were posted to the editor from a camp thousands of feet above sea-level. Indeed, it would have involved so much further loss of time in the appearance of a book already more than once unavoidably postponed that the editor was unfortunately compelled to omit sending out the proofs for Captain Arbuthnot to revise. He has done the best he could for them, and he desires to take the whole responsibility for any errors in the spelling of place-names not to be found in Hunter's or any gazetteer in common use. For such misprints Captain Arbuthnot is in no way responsible.

Lastly, he has to thank Messrs George Philip & Son, Ltd., for permission to use their admirable blank map of India in the preparation of the sporting chart given in this volume.

BOURNEMOUTH, *Easter*, 1904.

CONTENTS

PART I.—SHOOTING

PAGE

THE TIGER, PANTHER AND BEAR 3
By Lieut.-Gen. Sir MONTAGU GILBERT GERARD, K.C.S.I., C.B.

INDIAN RHINOCEROS SHOOTING 59
By General A. A. A. KINLOCH, C.B.

BISON SHOOTING IN CENTRAL INDIA 67
By Captain A. G. ARBUTHNOT (R.F.A.)

NOTE ON THE "BISON" OR GAUR 79
By General KINLOCH

HIMALAYAN SHOOTING 80
KASHMIR SHOOTING 131
By Captain ARBUTHNOT

THE DEER AND ANTELOPE OF THE INDIAN PLAINS . 193
SMALL GAME SHOOTING 207
By Lieut.-Col. P. R. BAIRNSFATHER (late 14th Bengal Lancers)

PART II.—FISHING

CHIEFLY ABOUT THE MAHSEER 223
WHERE TO GO FOR FISHING IN INDIA 259
By Lieut.-Col. BAIRNSFATHER

COMMUNICATIONS FROM CORRESPONDENTS . . . 268

SEA FISHING 289
By F. O. GADSDEN (late Royal Indian Marine)

ADDITIONAL NOTE ON SEA FISHING 303
By Captain GIBSON (Durham Light Infantry)

PART III.

SPORTS AND GAMES WITH HORSES

PAGE

Pig-sticking 309
Polo 381
Hunting 407
By Major Neville Taylor (14th Bengal Lancers)

Racing and Steeple-chasing 424
Paper-chasing 463
By Harry Stokes (sometime Secretary of the Calcutta Turf Club)

PART IV.

SOME MINOR SPORTS AND GAMES

Training, Condition and Diet 477
Cricket 486
Football 492
Golf 499
Hockey 512
Tennis and Racquets 516
Miscellaneous (Athletics, Badminton, Bicycling, Boxing, Bowls and Croquet, Motoring, Pigeon Shooting and Swimming) 519
Yachting 523
By Harry Stokes

Rowing and Boating 528
By W. S. Burke (Editor of the *Indan Field*)

Gymkhanas 541
By Harry Stokes

Cheetah Hunting 548
By Major C. H. Clay (43rd Gurkha Rifles)

Index 553

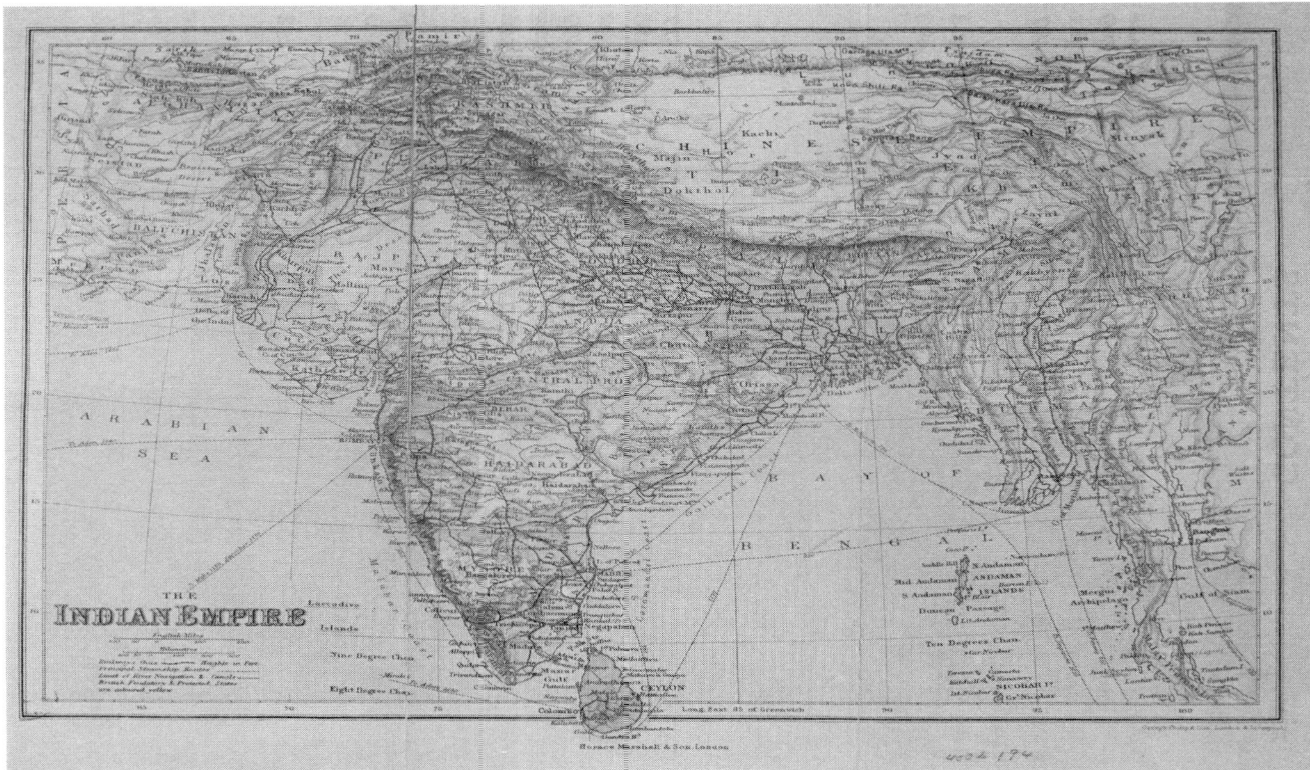
THE
INDIAN EMPIRE
ARABIAN
SEA
BAY OF
BENGAL
CENTRAL PROV.
HAIDARABAD
BALUCHISTAN
KASHMIR
CEYLON
ANDAMAN ISLANDS
NICOBAR I.
Laccadive Islands
Nine Degree Chan.
Eight Degree Chan.
Ten Degrees Chan.
Gulf of Siam
Long. East 85 of Greenwich
Horace Marshall & Son. London

LIST OF ILLUSTRATIONS

FACING PAGE

Buffalo (Cooch Behar) 80
A Typical Kashmir Camp: in the Scinde Valley 138
A Kashmir Shikari en route to the Wardwan Range 140
Ovis ammon (Altai Mountains) . . . 146
Ovis ammon 148
Yak (Thibet) 148
Thibetan Antelope 150
Kashmir Stag or Bara Singh . . . 150
Ibex 154
Bara Singh 154
Burhel (or Narpu) 160
Ibex 160
Markhor 174
Sharpoo (Ovis vignei) 174
Bara Singh (Kashmir) 178
After Bara Singh in the Pulwar Nullah in October 180
Camp in December: after Markhor . . 182
Leopard Shot by Capt. Arbuthnot . . . 182
Black Buck (N.W. India) 196
A Typical Indian River 224
A Good Mahseer 230
A Native Fishing 246
View in the Liddar Valley 280
Bahmin 290

FACING PAGE

Seer or Surmi 294
Three Fish caught outside Port Blair Harbour 300
A 34-inch Boar 312
Australian Horse 316
A Good Australian Hunter 320
Australian Pony Hunter 328
Arab Hunter 344
An Ekka drawn by Mule 372
A Trotting Bullock Car 372
Calcutta Race Course 426
Plan of Steeple-chase Courses at Tollygunge 458
First Over 462
An Historic Finish 466
Naini Tal Lake and Boat House . . . 526
Opposite Bund Hill, Poona 532
Naini Tal 536
Cheetah Hunting 548

MAPS

FACING PAGE

India . . . . . . *Frontispiece*
Route Map: Chamba, Zanskar and Rupshu . 110
Route Map: Srinagar to Leh and Baltistan . 168
Map of Astore and Boonjie, Markhor Ground 172
Map of Pig-sticking, Hunting and Racing Centres in India 309

PART I

SHOOTING

THE TIGER, PANTHER AND BEAR

INDIAN RHINOCEROS SHOOTING

BISON SHOOTING

HIMALAYAN SHOOTING

KASHMIR SHOOTING

THE DEER AND ANTELOPE OF THE INDIAN PLAINS

SMALL GAME SHOOTING

THE TIGER, PANTHER AND BEAR

I.—THE TIGER

WHILST the tiger (*Felis tigris*) and India seem to be inseparably linked together in popular imagination, every real sportsman bound for that country is cheered by the hope that this form of compensation awaits the exile in the Sunny East.

Most people unacquainted with Hindustan, not only picture to themselves that this species of big game is still fairly plentiful within our dominions, but also fancy that the tiger is regarded as the direst scourge of the hapless "rayat." It is therefore generally assumed that the advent of a British sportsman is eagerly welcomed, that he will enjoy every possible assistance, and that his bag will depend solely upon himself and his knowledge of woodcraft.

Such dreams, alas! nowadays, are mere *Châteaux en Espagne*, and the keenest and best shot, not backed up by influence or the indispensable introductions to those who can help, may spend a dozen years in the country without being rewarded with a single chance at a tiger.

To begin with, this, the king of Indian game (as also are bears and to some extent panthers) is now restricted to comparatively limited areas, and is practically extinct in districts where it abounded half a century ago.

Railways, with other facilities for communication, and improved firearms are chiefly responsible for such a state of things; and if tigers yet exist in any quantity anywhere, it is solely because they are protected by physical conditions, or strictly preserved by native chiefs.

Although in some districts increasing cultivation may be the assignable cause for the disappearance of big game, in other parts of the country, one can now beat through the ruins of fortresses, temples, or of what must erstwhile have been populous towns.

I remember upon one occasion our shooting four tigers who had been lying up under the shade of the huge cupola of a palace, which dominated the surrounding jungle.

Present Distribution. Taking a north-easterly line from the Gulf of Cutch to Simla there are precious few tigers to be found out of a menagerie in this, the north-westerly quarter of India; and yet we know that in the sixteenth century even rhinoceros once roamed in the Peshawar valley.

A very few of the former may still exist at the foot of the Himalayas, towards Nagerkot and Chamba, carefully preserved by the local rajahs; and twenty years ago some specimens of the breed were to be found in Sind, jealously guarded by Ali Morad.

In Kattiawar, the last home of the Indian lion, which, but for the nawabs of Joonaghur, would now be extinct, the tiger is absolutely unknown, as it likewise is in Bikanir, Jodhpore and other more or less desert tracts. In Ceylon it does not occur. By far the largest number in the country would now be found in the belt between the river Ganges and the Himalayan mountains, including the Terai and the Soonderbuns. Thence east and southwards, through Assam and Burmah to Singapore, tigers will probably to the end of time continue to abound, swallowed up as they are in the security of dense and practically endless jungles.

The wooded and scantily populated tract between Orissa, the Godavery and the Central Provinces, only recently opened up by a railway, has also as yet been but lightly shot over; and some of the large forests south of the Krishna, are too extensive to lend themselves to the efforts of sportsmen.

The number of tigers there, which is, however, inconsiderable, will probably remain at its normal level for all time.

Elsewhere, throughout Rajputana, Central India, the Central Provinces, Deccan and Bombay, shooting being accessible and jungles, during the hot weather at least, being of manageable dimensions, the best sport for the past three-quarters of a century has been obtained. For this very reason, game has been everywhere enormously reduced, and in some parts practically exterminated.

Even in British territory, a sportsman cannot wander away at his own sweet will without going through any further formalities. Without an order from the local magistrate, one would be absolutely boycotted by the villagers, and simply starved out, having no possibility of purchasing food or hiring beaters.

Difficulties of Supplies, &c.

Once the traveller quits the high road, with its regulated police stations and bazaars, he will find that the small villages, where he would have to move his camp in search of sport, are able to supply little more than grass for his animals. The inhabitants also as a rule much prefer your room to your company, and would far sooner not have any dealings at all with Europeans and their retinues. Villagers often say that the damage done to their cattle by tigers is more than compensated by their keeping down wild pig, which otherwise ruin their crops.

Their objections also are very much due to the prevalent fault of sahibs entrusting all payments to their native servants who would not be true Orientals if they did not systematically defraud their humbler brethren.

As there are always far more sportsmen than there is room for in a district, it is absolutely necessary to limit the number of parties in each, in view of the interests of both the villagers and the sahibs themselves.

The district collectors—*anglicè*, magistrates—having therefore to discriminate between the applicants, naturally prefer to accord the permits only to acquaintances or, at all events, to persons specially recommended.

This is absolutely necessary in their own self-defence, to obviate the very common string of complaints as to ill-treatment or under payments, which too often follow in the wake of a shooting party.

I once marched through a village where four officers of a British cavalry regiment had been encamped for a week shooting. Not one of these gentlemen could speak Hindustani, and their entire "shoot" was being run by a mess contractor, at so much per head per month, including not only food, but also shikaris, beaters, transport and all pertaining to sport. According to the story of the villagers, they had received something like ten per cent. only of their dues and were a hundred rupees out of pocket by the visit of the sahibs, besides having been considerably bullied and ragged by their native following.

I could quote a dozen similar cases within my own experience. When it comes to projecting a trip into independent native territory, it is absolutely essential to be provided with a "Parwana" or passport from the Minister of the State in question. This can be obtained only through the medium of the resident or political agent

Shooting in Independent Territory.

attached to the rajah. Since the rajahs have realised that the surest means of propitiating a visitor of distinction, and the easiest way of earning a star or other form of official approbation, is to show sport to the arbiters of their destinies, they seldom care to admit outsiders.

In the large state of Hyderabad, which extends over some six degrees of latitude by four of longitude, the Nizam after keeping a considerable area as a private preserve, throws the remainder of his extensive territory open to a limited number of parties of British sportsmen. Precedence is, however, very properly reserved for officers quartered in this area, and as, even then, the demand far exceeds the supply, this already restricted number must draw lots for the allotment of beats.

Although the native cavalry regiment to which I belonged for twenty-five years was habitually quartered in independent territory, and although I was personally acquainted with every one of the native rulers and their political agents, I had invariably to commence negotiations to obtain parwanas several months prior to the opening of the shooting season.

The Nepaul Terai. The vast tract of the Nepaul Terai, purposely retained as a waste since the war of 1814 to impede the advance of a British force, is jealously preserved, and a very few favoured guests only are invited across its border. From here down to the Brahmaputra, jungles consist of enormous stretches of giant reeds, growing in some places to a height of 16 or 18 feet high, intersected by sluggish streams that abound in quicksands, and interspersed with impassable morasses.

The grass is tunnelled by regular "smeuses" made by wild animals, and, as man on foot is powerless therein, the success of a shooting party is in proportion to the number of elephants its members can contrive to muster. What with Howdah and Pad elephants, some fifty would be required for a party of half a dozen guns; and these can never be hired but must be ordered, begged or borrowed, according to one's authority or the opportunities such as are enjoyed by officials or resident indigo planters. The nearest approach to hiring I heard of was by one petty rajah who, when absent himself, practically admitted paying guests. I knew a couple of English travellers who were offered by this chief's manager a ten-day shoot at two thousand rupees apiece.

Shooting from the Howdah.

This was really excessively moderate, and would barely cover the expenses of the elephants and other accessories for that period.

Before he fell into financial difficulties, this same rajah gave annual and somewhat overcrowded shikar parties. A friend of mine, who formed one of a dozen guns present at one of these, afterwards described it as "a most satisfactory shoot; we bagged fourteen tigers, and every soul in the party had shot twelve of these himself."

In Assam and Burmah more are perhaps

Assam and Burmah. got by sitting up over a "kill" than by other methods. This is necessitated by the enormous amount of jungle, and is, as a rule, possible only for residents in out-of-the-way corners, such as tea planters, or isolated officials, such chances being very occasional only.

The Soonderbuns. The feverish swamps of the Soonderbuns are so inimical to human life, and so intersected by innumerable creeks and channels that, although tigers here abound, there is no getting at them. Some few are occasionally shot by night watchers, but they have such quantities of wild hog and deer to prey upon that they are not easily lured by a "tie up."

I have heard that the lighthouse keepers at Diamond Point used to shoot several tigers annually, the brutes being attracted by the bright glare of the beacon, to within easy range of the building itself.

In the forests of Southern India one hears of only a very occasional tiger being bagged, more or less by accident, when out stalking bison or other game.

The Neilgherry Hills. Near Ootacamund in the Neilgherry hills, where the cool climate renders the employment of dogs possible, a few, which have wandered up from the jungles below, are from time to time got by sojourners in those parts, but no regular bag is possible in that district.

I trust that the enumeration of these difficulties in the way of sport will not altogether prove a deterrent to the keen novice. They are disagreeable facts which have to be faced, and are better provided for beforehand than ascertained by experience after a considerable waste of money and loss of time and temper.

"Where there is a will, there is a way" holds as true for success in this as in other objects of our ambition, and if a man lays himself out with this one object, he is pretty sure to succeed. He must, however, fully realise the difficulties in the way of its attainment, and must not imagine that opportunities will fall in his way as an alternative to polo or hill station gaieties. To obtain one, he must sacrifice other forms of amusement. As to the exact quarter in which to try his luck, he must be guided by the locality of his headquarters or the facilities for becoming acquainted, whether by letters of introduction or otherwise, with some of those from whom he may obtain the absolutely necessary local assistance. Having, however, obtained this, the sportsman can nowadays, thanks to railways, transfer himself to almost any part of the Continent. Officers quartered in the Punjab often shoot in the Central Provinces a thousand miles distant, whilst others, crowded out in India, now prefer to spend their leave in Africa.

Furthermore, a man must bear in mind that until he is conversationally familiar with Hindustani, the language spoken throughout India, he will only be able to shoot as a guest in someone's party, or, still worse, be in leading strings to his native servants and shikaris. No matter what he pays in the latter case, they will ruin his chances through their own rapacity.

Preparations for a Trip. To come now to the great question of preparations for a trip, almost as many details have to be provided for as are required on a larger scale for the conduct of a campaign. Throughout all the central and southern parts of India with which I am acquainted, a two months' shoot involves your marching in all from three to four hundred miles, zig-zagging about as you hear reports of tigers having killed cattle, and moving camp on an average ten or a dozen miles every alternate day.

I have seen the ludicrous statement by a writer in a sporting magazine, that he and a friend went to such and such a village "where there is good tiger shooting!" as if describing a snipe marsh, or a rabbit warren; and which conclusively proved the purely imaginative nature of his narrative.

As a matter of fact, there may be in these times a pair or in extremely rare cases a family party of three, four, or even five tigers, to a district of two or three hundred square miles in Central or Southern India. I am not alluding to a few regular preserves. There are perhaps only half a dozen spots within that locality where they would be likely to "lie up" during the hot weather—April and May—when shade and water are limited to the vicinity of villages and a few quiet corners elsewhere. It is for you or your shikaris to find out in which of these they may be then located, as a dozen things may occur to induce them to shift their quarters twelve or fifteen miles in the course of a week, and you may have to change camp several times before you get them finally marked down.

Rifles and Ammunition.

Foremost of all considerations must be the battery to be adopted. Improved models follow one another in such rapid succession that the perfect weapon of half a dozen years back is probably now worthy of only a second place.

Of course, a useful all-round weapon is the one usually adopted for choice, or to which most people are restricted by necessity, something between the ·500 Express of the past and the ·265 Manlicher of the present day.

For howdah work in the Terai, and where you have elephants to follow up wounded beasts and thus incur no risk, the handiest weapon with which you can snap shoot is preferable; as the worst which can befall is having an elephant comparatively as much scratched as a fox terrier is in killing a cat.

It is a very different story indeed when you come to select a rifle, specially intended for tiger shooting *under all conditions*, and one to whose stopping power you must, when following up a wounded beast on foot, entrust your life.

As to the best for this purpose, opinions differ widely, but one can unhesitatingly say, that, no matter what calibre you may adopt, a double barrelled weapon is alone admissible, and that your rifle should be as absolutely flush sighted, and the stock have exactly the same length and "cast off" as the shot gun to which you are accustomed.

I have seen twelve bores turned out by some of the first London makers which had a nominal point blank of 150 yards with a charge of only five drams of powder. It is needless perhaps to mention that this was obtained by ornamenting the rib with a standing back sight, having a minute nick to aim through, excellent for target peppering, or even for stalking, but altogether misguiding for practical purposes.

It is scant satisfaction to know that you can hit an egg with it at a measure of 150 yards, when there is a trajectory of about six inches at some unrecorded intermediate point. What you do want to be assured of is that, if only you hold straight, you can hit a charging animal by a snap shot through bushes or grass, within anything from three score to a dozen yards of you.

Rifle makers will not realize that shots in an Indian jungle are fired under very different conditions from those which obtain in a Highland deer forest; and that the ticklish shots are just those at close quarters. The hollow rib with the foresight perched upon a raised lump of metal at the muzzle is also an abomination, and suitable only for pot shots. All quick work must be dependent upon one's familiarity with a shot gun, and you should be able to chuck up and pull with your rifle at a galloping chance between trees as quickly as if firing at a woodcock in covert.

For you to be able to do this, there must be nothing upon the rib to distract your eye. The most that is admissible is a very wide **V** cut down to the rib, which serves to define the centre line for a deliberate aim when you have time to dwell upon it, but which does not obtrude itself upon your vision when taking a quick snapshot.

I do not like bottle cartridges, as the extra thickness of the breech is equivalent to a standing back sight, and tends to make a man shoot high. It is well to bear in mind that a tiger's brain is only a two-inch mark. Even with a rifle chambered for the cylinder cartridge, a certain amount of elevation is perforce given, but the divergence of the line of fire from the line of sight, should not exceed an inch or thereabouts.

For sporting purposes one does not want folding sights for any fixed number of yards—150, 200, or 250. What you require to know is at what range the bullet will have fallen an inch or so below the line of sight, and up to which you can aim as with a shot gun. It is beginning from this point, whether it be 75, 90 or 100 yards, that you want the first raised sight. In the case of a tiger one only fires at above a hundred yards under very exceptional circumstances, such as at an already wounded animal crossing over open ground.

As to the calibre selected, I do not at all hold with the advocates of the very small bores. These with the Jeffrey's or the Dum-Dum bullet may be very deadly and they are extremely handy ;

but they have not the necessary knock down blow and the stopping power of a heavier bullet. It is just the difference between a rapier and a sledge-hammer. I have seen a tiger, shot practically through the heart with a 450 Express bullet, gallop 300 yards before falling. Indeed the man who had fired at it, believed he had missed clean, as the animal did not even wince at the shot.

For similar reasons, a solid bullet should be eschewed for such soft-skinned beasts as tigers, panthers, and bears. Broadside shots are the rule and a solid bullet passes through a tiger and wastes at least half of its energy on the ground beyond; whereas either a shell or an Express bullet expends the whole force of its momentum on the animal itself.

I remember hitting a tiger and a tigress almost right and left, the former with a solid spherical ten-bore ball, and the latter with a Meade shell.

The former which had had a generally vital spot traversed from side to side was not bagged for a couple of days and was then full of fight, whilst his mate, hit too low down in the shoulder by the shell, lay down within a hundred yards and was got without trouble. For an end-on shot the solid bullet is undoubtedly at its best, as you rake the brute from end to end, and may smash a thigh as a wind up. It is also the most reliable projectile when you have to fire through bushes; and I have sometimes employed solid in lieu of expanding bullets with Express rifles under such circumstances.

As to the desideratum of obtaining a knock down blow with a rifle of manageable size, from a theoretical point of view a tiger of from 400 lbs. to 450 lbs.—which would be an extreme weight—is unlikely to exceed a speed of twenty paces a second when charging in his wildest rush. I think that its "energy," thus developed, is represented at something like 3600 "foot pounds." Against this the ·303 Lee Metford delivers a blow of about 1800, and ten and twelve bore rifles attain from 3000 to 4000 "foot pounds," according to the charges employed.

After for years using a 10-bore with 7 drams, and a Calvert shell of 2¼ oz., which was certainly very much of a "devil stopper," I finally adopted a ·577 with 200 grains black powder, and a 540 grain hollow tip bullet, which gave a "shock" of about 4000 "foot pounds."

Although mere theory must be largely discounted when applied to sporting conditions, it is certainly a great sedative to one's nerves, when walking up a dangerous beast, to entertain the comfortable assurance that you have the physical conditions in your favour, and that you have only to hold straight to stop the most vicious rush of your opponent. It is, however, worse than useless to overweight yourself with an unmanageable rifle, with which you will probably miss at a critical moment.

The ·577 above alluded to was built by Dickson of Edinburgh, weighed 11 lbs. and was absolutely flush sighted. Its trajectory nowhere exceeded an inch above the line of sight when aimed "like a gun," and at 200 yards the bullet had fallen about eight inches below the point aimed directly at. Whilst a soft lead hollow bullet smashed the skull or largest bone of the biggest tiger, it absolutely broke up into chiefly minute fragments in the body of anything save the small-sized panthers. It of course required a solid or hardened projectile for bison or other thicker skinned and heavier game.

Special three and a half inch cartridge cases to contain the necessary seven or seven and a half drams of Curtis and Harvey's No. 6 can be obtained through many gun-makers.

Although cordite has successfully stood the test of experience of an Indian climate, still I mistrust the action of chemical powders under the conditions of an Indian hot weather "shoot" when your gun-barrels often become so hot as to blister the hand.

I have myself seen two rifles burst by using rifleite, and I have heard of half a dozen other instances of similar accidents.

I have read of, but not seen, a new ·400 Express which is advertised to develop an energy of over 4100 foot pounds; and this, which must necessarily possess an even flatter trajectory than a ·577, may be a preferable weapon. This depends however, entirely, so far as tigers are concerned, on whether the "pitch" of rifling is not so "steep" as to render a soft lead bullet liable to "strip."

If a nickel-cased one has to be used, then half of the energy of the projectile will in the case of the feline tribe, be wasted upon the ground beyond. But, as already mentioned, I have not had the chance of examining this rifle.

A broad web sling attached, not by swivels which rattle annoyingly, but by a noiseless screw, makes all the difference in the world both for comfort in carrying and for hanging up a rifle in a tree when posted.

One should never stir in the jungle without a rifle in hand; the gun-bearer is certain to be out of immediate reach just when a gun is required. As my ·577 was a bit too much for a long tramp in a scorching day, I generally carried a ·500 Express myself, which, when there was time to change, served as my second gun. With the sling passed over the left shoulder, and the rifle carried almost horizontally, butt to the front, the weight is imperceptible either on foot or horseback, and you can come to the "ready" in a moment. I have known many animals let off, and seen one or two pitiable panics, which greatly lowered the "izzat" of the sahibs in native eyes, caused solely by would-be sportsmen finding themselves weaponless in the presence of a tiger, and this entirely thanks to their own laziness.

There is nothing to be gained by having too light a rifle. Apart from the question of mere safety with heavy charges, after a stiff climb, or a run to cut off an animal, a light weapon dances about, whereas a heavy one steadies itself and is conducive to good shooting.

If a sportsman employs a single barrel, even as his second gun, he should use a sporting and not a military action such as the Lee Metford, as the clatter of the bolt when reloading is hopeless in a quiet corner.

If unprovided with a second rifle, I recommend one's ordinary shot gun, provided it is not a choke bore, for jungle work, in preference to any single barrel. For convenience of walking and posting yourself in a tree, this should be fitted with a sling, like all Continental guns. The spherical Meade shell, filled with detonating powder (equal parts of chlorate of potash and sulphate of black antimony) is better than solid ball, being lighter and admitting of a larger charge of powder. A No. 13 and not a 12-bore shell should be employed, enclosed in soft leather to prevent windage. I generally used the fingers of my old kid gloves for the purpose. This, with a charge of 3½ to 4 drams, is very effective, and will not hurt your gun, as it is only very occasionally employed.

The projectile, whatever it may be, should be "set" with melted wax poured in upon it, and the cartridge case must on no account have its end turned down or a wad in front of the bullet. One can shoot well enough for all practical purposes up to seventy or eighty yards with such a bullet from a smooth bore.

To come now to the subject of dress and equipment I strongly recommend the young sportsman to procure this entirely in India, where it can be got at a tithe of the cost and of far more suitable materials than he would find at home. **Dress and Equipment.**

There is a branch of the Army and Navy Stores at Bombay where English articles may be purchased cheaper than they can be brought out by a private individual, and reliable ammunition can be obtained from English gunmakers such as Rodda or Manton of Calcutta. Beware however of cartridges retailed by native and other second-rate dealers, and which may have been for years in stock.

Shikar Kit, on the other hand, from head-gear to foot-wear, can be got just as good, and for a fourth of the cost from native rather than from European establishments.

The novice should remember that all shooting in India involves more riding than walking, and he should therefore adopt such a style of knickerbocker or of riding breeches as he personally finds the most convenient for such dual work. The best way is to bring out from London one good pattern of Norfolk jacket and walking breeches, buy or choose your material, and have your suit copied by a native "durzi" (tailor). These men can never cut clothes properly, but will duplicate a model so exactly that, unless specially warned to the contrary, they will even insert any patch, with which it may chance to be ornamented.

I here refer only to clothes such as are required

for tiger shooting and similar jungle work, as proper riding breeches, as well as boots, are only procurable from London makers.

Suitable materials are to be obtained everywhere, from any of the large British mills at Cawnpore, from all large central jails, from the Basel Mission at Cannanore, and from most tailors in India. A shikar suit, which would cost five guineas at home, comes to just one-tenth of this sum when thus manufactured on the spot.

The solah topee, or pith helmet, certainly combines a maximum of sun protection with a minimum of weight, but it becomes a pulp with heavy rain, rarely met with save at the beginning of the monsoon, and is easily smashed up by a fall, or an unexpected bang against a stiff branch. There is a very good pattern named after the Cawnpore Tent Club, and a chin strap should always be used when riding, or working your way through thick jungle. There is usually a very strong, hot wind during the day, and a tight-fitting helmet is most tiring to the head. The enormous mushroom-shaped pith hats, about the size of a lady's parasol, are fit only for old women.

Whatever pattern or material may be adopted, there should be no encircling puggree to catch upon thorns. If a turban is necessary, a stout cover, preferably of fine leather, should be worn over all, as sometimes one must bore a way through bushes with both hands fully occupied by the rifle. A pad of quilted cotton should be worn inside the jacket to cover the whole of the back, and a cummerbund or sash is also very advisable. It is useful to have at the very least a couple of receptacles for rifle cartridges sewn on the right breast of your blouse or jacket à la Tcherkess, so as always to have a "reload" handy. Any dull neutral tint will do, but all bleach lighter by exposure to the sun and a single, unbroken colour is more easily distinguishable than when helmet, coat and breeches are of different shades. Gaiters should invariably be worn both for thorns, and on the chance of snakes in some localities, and the best kind of ankle boots are made of thick, but extremely soft, sambhur leather—with stout, heelless plaited cotton soles. Ours were usually made up in the regimental workshops, but can be got in many bazaars for five rupees a pair. They are of no use for wet walking and are soon ruined by water, but for all dry work they are simply perfect, as they are noiseless to walk in, excellent over rocks, and even in the hottest sun they never draw the feet. A broad leather waist-belt, with a pouch for eight or ten cartridges, and a shikar knife should be worn, but it is useless burdening yourself with anything more, save perhaps a leather drinking cup, and a folding pocket saw, the latter useful for pruning off a branch noiselessly. Indian-made hunting knives are preferable to English ones, of which the steel is too hard, and difficult to get re-sharpened in out-of-the-way places. Bodraj, of Aurungabad, and

Boput, of Nagpore, used to be the two best known makers of these as well as of hog spears.

Tent, Camp Furniture, &c. The Kabul tent of 7 ft. to 8 ft. square, with jointed poles, semicircular bathroom, and "durrie" or carpet, is ample for all sporting requirements. Such a one can be bought at any of the big makers, such as the Muir Mills at Cawnpore for about a hundred rupees (£7) and weighs about 100 lbs., the smallest size weighing only 80 lbs. Plenty of second-hand ones may be seen advertised in the columns of the *Pioneer*, at from half to a quarter of that price. It is better to have a couple of smaller tents rather than one large one. They should be provided with tapes to loop up the sides and admit the breeze, as well as with plenty of pockets for small articles, and hooks for the poles upon which to hang up rifles, clothes and other impedimenta. There are some who believe that yellow, whether for clothing or tents, has a great power to neutralise the effects of sun rays. One requires a couple of tents; one to go on overnight to the next camping ground, with a similar or smaller one to be kept back in the case of a thunderstorm—not at all uncommon towards the end of the hot weather. Your servants are spared considerable labour in pitching and striking tents by having duplicate ones, a matter of some importance when moving camp, as you generally have to do several times a week. You should also have a couple of "rowties" for your servants. These weigh about 30 lbs. apiece and cost as many rupees.

For camp furniture—bed, table, chair, wash-hand stand and canvas tub, all of which it is advisable to have in duplicate—by far the best patterns are to be got from Messrs Luscombe of Allahabad.

Chaguls—water bags of porous leather or permeable canvas—are indispensable, both out shooting and for use in camp, and may be bought cheaply in any Indian bazaar. In them the water is automatically kept cool by evaporation, at a much lower temperature than any of the expensive and unsatisfactory patterns of service water bottles yet invented.

Similarly, narrow canvas water buckets, just large enough to cool one bottle in at a time, are a positive necessity in a dry hot climate when out of reach of ice and other appliances of modern civilisation. A man may go for hours in the sun without drinking, but, once he tastes water he feels compelled to continue. The golden rule, however, is never to taste anything stronger than tea until sunset. At dinner one can take wine or whisky and soda, as usual.

The four tents for yourself and servants, with the requisite amount of camp kit, above enumerated, should cost about Rs.600—say £40—and form just a camel load, which, nominally of 320, is generally of about 400 lbs.

To do things fairly comfortably for a two months' expedition, each man requires five camels; as not only do your numerous servants drag about with them a considerable amount of lumber, but you also have to carry a supply of soda water to supplement your gazogenes, necessary to guard against bad water—besides other stores. There are also all sorts of stable requisites, and occasionally you have to carry some days' corn for your horses and food for followers.

Camels and other Transport. Camels may be hired for from 10 to 12 rupees apiece per mensem in Northern and Central India; but for the eastern and southern portions one is largely dependent upon wheeled vehicles, pack bullocks, or coolies. The last-named are the most expensive of all forms of transport, about eight being required per camel load at four times their cost. Forage and the wages of attendants (one to every four) is included in the hire of pack animals, as also are the necessary loading ropes; but suleetahs or saddle bags, and "khajawahs" or panniers, must be provided by the hirer and would cost about £1 per animal.

Servants. For a party of four, or even of two guns, you further require some sort of mess tent and establishment, say a cook and his assistant, khitmatgar, or butler, "bheestie" (water carrier) and a sweeper, for which a resident in the country would pay about Rs.60 to 80 a month —say £5,—and a visitor, requiring English-speaking servants, something like treble that sum. If one attempts to do with a very small establishment, the one certain result is that utensils are never properly cleaned and that water is obtained from the nearest stagnant puddle; whilst, if you try to make your personal servants assist for the common welfare, each one shirks the work and leaves it to his neighbour.

As you must generally carry the whole of your stores, in addition to cooking utensils, six or eight camels are required for your mess.

A suitable tent and *Batterie de Cuisine* will cost say, £40, and the monthly hire of camels, £7. Officers quartered in India and other residents bring their own personal servants; khitmatgar or butler to wait at table (and who cooks after a fashion in case of need), bearer (valet), water carrier, dhobie or washerman, sweeper, gun-bearer, and a couple of syces or grooms, required for the minimum of two ponies or horses, which are indispensable for a trip. The wages of these vary from about 20 to 8 rupees a month apiece, for which they "find themselves," and they generally cost a resident say £7 or £8 a month (taking £1 as equivalent to Rs. 15); but if obtained only for a temporary job, their pay would most probably come to £15 or £20 per mensem.

The number of servants sounds superfluous but they are indispensable if only to help in the almost daily pitching and striking of tents, packing and unpacking things, and loading beasts of burden.

In the usual camp life you dine and sleep in the open air. When marching, the mess, with most of your own belongings, start as soon as possible after dinner, and you keep behind one tent, a servant and a camel each to bring on your effects. You commonly march ten or twelve miles, though here and there you have to accomplish double that distance. Mounting soon after sunrise, you canter on to your next camp by eight o'clock, sending on your rifles perhaps another half dozen miles to where you are to beat; you breakfast and ride out there afterwards, and you continue beating for deer, etc., and seldom return before sunset when you tub, array yourselves in light flannels, and dine. You turn in early, as you have to be up with the sparrows, to march again, watch for bears, or go round the paras with the shikaris.

Each sportsman would have to bring or buy his own saddlery, and a couple of ponies, which cost anything from £10 apiece for a light weight who is not particular, to £40 each if he wishes to be fairly well mounted.

Expenses of Trip. It will thus be seen that the preliminary expenses for each man to take the field for a two months' shoot, exclusive of guns, clothes and saddlery, would come to about £100 besides a fourth share of the mess, and his monthly expenditure in wages and transport hire to another £15. Adding on to this £10, for the forage of his ponies, his wine and soda water and miscellaneous items, a sportsman's personal requirements exclusive of food and shikar will average something like £1 a day. Wine and aërated waters must be kept separately, and each sahib's khitmatgar be made responsible for his own master's supply. When there is a common stock kept in the mess, this is drunk by all the servants, each of whom ascribes the leakage to someone else.

In all of the many expeditions that I have undertaken, one of the party acted as secretary, and the expenses both of messing and shikar were equally divided amongst us all. Although we usually enjoyed exceptional facilities, had a guard of our regiment out to collect supplies and beaters and to act as shikaris, and generally received great local help, the cost of these two items usually came to from 3000 to 4000 rupees a month for a party of four, or at the rate of Rs.300 for each tiger bagged. Taken all in all, I fancy that, considering the immense number of blank days, so far as tigers are concerned, and the many others when you individually do not get a shot yourself, each one killed costs the sportsman about £25 under the most favourable circumstances. I do not of course allude to rare and exceptional chances occurring in out-of-the-way places or when an animal is shot by sitting up over water, a tie-up or a "kill."

My last shoot before leaving India, in Hyderabad territory was, all things considered, the cheapest, as I was out entirely alone, bagging twelve tigers in six weeks of actual shooting, while my total expenses did not exceed Rs.3000, say £200. I was, of course, already provided with every requisite in the way of tents, horses and servants, nor had I any elephants, which, even when you have not got to feed them, run away with a good deal of money in the way of rewards.

It will be seen therefore that, when the difficulties in the way of obtaining permission and hiring reliable shikaris have been overcome, tiger shooting is almost as expensive an amusement as renting a Scotch deer forest.

One may confidently state that a party of sportsmen arriving in India have no earthly chance of obtaining tiger shooting, no matter how ready to pay for it, unless through the medium of friends in that country; and that a subaltern quartered in a sporting district will have, if he goes the right way to work, infinitely superior chances to those of any ordinary visitor.

Season. Taken as a general rule the hot weather months, March, April and May, are the only ones when any regular shooting trip can be undertaken with a reasonable prospect of success. One hears of a Christmas tiger being occasionally bagged, but usually under exceptional circumstances. Perhaps about a tiger a week is the most a party could hope for in most localities, between January and March. I have never seen the Terai country in the cold weather, but have been told that at this season it is in most parts a hopeless sea of grass and green reeds. Until this vegetation becomes partially withered, or burned down, sport is impracticable.

When our present King shot in Nepaulese

territory in 1876, Sir Jung Bahadur had a mass of 500 elephants collected to ensure sport. As one can only assist at any of these parties as a guest, it is superfluous to enter into details of the preparations requisite. The procedure generally is simply to form line, the howdah elephants being interspersed with the pad ones; and perhaps a couple of the former guard some open spot ahead. The most likely strips of reeds, pointed out by the cattle herd, are naturally selected, and neither wood-craft nor particularly good shooting is requisite, as one often fires merely at the moving grass.

You may perfectly well wear a suit of white drill, with tennis shoes, and many men use umbrellas going to and from the beats, and have baskets of ice and drinks underneath the seat of the howdah. There is not the smallest risk incurred by any, save possibly the mahouts or people on the pad elephants, and ladies frequently accompany such parties, with no more fatigue than is inseparable from the heat, and the monotonous jolting of the elephant.

It is altogether a thoroughly Oriental rather than English form of sport, but decidedly interesting, as those reed beds contain a greater mass of wild animals than does any other Indian jungle.

In the broken, timbered tracts, which generally prevail in the central, southerly, and western portions of India, game is infinitely scarcer, and elephants are not only almost unprocurable, but also of very little use for hilly and rocky ground.

Throughout native states, villagers are mostly armed, and an immense lot of game get spotted by night watchers who probably wound far more than they kill. The most of these tracts remain jungle, simply because they are too arid to cultivate, and for this reason most timber is poorly grown and stunted.

With the commencement of the monsoon, or rainy season (June to September), grass springs up everywhere as if by magic, and is in a few weeks waist high; trees and bushes become clothed in verdure; and wild animals may be lying about almost anywhere. Except that with the advent of the cold weather from October onwards, the grass dries up to a yellow ochre tint, and gets daily more and more grazed down, and that the leaves of many kinds of trees begin to fall, there is but little improvement in one's sporting chances for the next four or five months. There is still sufficient water and shade everywhere, and wild animals may be scattered about on all sides, whilst if a tiger should be disturbed, he may travel for miles across ground where it is impossible to track him, before again lying up.

By February, thanks to cattle and jungle fires, grass is rapidly disappearing, and by April an undisturbed tract of this is quite a rarity. I have seen a fire, started by woodcutters, continue for three days, and extend for twenty or thirty miles to leeward of the spot where it originated.

As already remarked, there are nowadays but

very few tigers to a large extent of country, and for eight or nine months in the year, these may be lying up anywhere.

It is moreover decidedly dangerous to use beaters in high grass. A tiger will often squat as close in this as a hare does on her form and allow men to pass him by; but if one actually stumbles on to the brute, a fatal accident is almost inevitable.

By the month of March, what with the disappearance of the grass, the fall of leaves and the drying up of all the smaller supplies of water, game becomes concentrated near the banks of rivers, or other water sources, deer and pig to procure food and the large cats to prey upon them.

There are always half-a-dozen well-known spots in each district—islands covered with green jaman, willow, and tamarisk; or quiet, rocky glens, with deep pools of water and thickets of oleander bushes and wild arrowroot, or sometimes masses of rocks overshadowed by creepers at one or other of which any tiger in that part of the country is certain to lie up during the hot weather.

Local Information.

Much may be learned from woodcutters, cattle herdsmen and other villagers, whose avocations take them daily to the jungle, and who invariably know every tiger in their district, sometimes by sight, and certainly by their "pug," or footprints.

The chief difficulty is, however, to induce these men to give correct information; and a sahib who can talk with them direct, and not through the medium of an interpreter, has a far better chance of learning the truth, as natives have then more confidence of really getting any promised gratuity.

The sportsman must above all beware of relying upon the village shikari where a professional one exists. In most British districts there is a Government reward of Rs.50 for each tiger killed, and this is regarded as the shikari's peculiar perquisite. It is a *sine quâ non* to promise this sum to the local man for each of "his" tigers that you may bag; and as your own shikaris expect a similar amount likewise, the cost of sport rapidly mounts up.

Tying-up. Having more or less localised the whereabouts of your animal—from the reports of villagers, or the tracks found in the river bed, and, along the dusty jungle roads largely used by them at nights—you have half a dozen bull buffalo calves tied up at some of the most likely watering-places close to a tempting thicket.

As buffaloes cannot work in the sun, they are valueless save for their milk, and, being sufficiently related to the sacred cow to have their flesh tabooed for food, the males are practically superfluous and are priced at about a rupee for every year of age up to a maximum of five or six.

As a rule, a rupee is paid to the owner should his calf not be touched, but for everyone killed by a tiger (and for which you generally give five rupees) three or four fall victims to panthers, wolves, hyenas, or wild dogs. I have also known a single tiger kill nine "paras" in one night, from sheer devilry, as the last was the only one eaten. Cruel as the procedure of tying-up sounds, I believe buffaloes are absolutely callous, and I have seen one after snorting for a minute at a passing tiger, resume feeding the moment it had passed.

These baits, termed "paras," are watered and fed three times a day, and are fastened up at spots where they can be seen from some little distance. It is seldom advisable to visit them until an hour after sunrise, as, in the cool of the morning, a tiger, if he suspects anything, may travel a mile or two before lying up for the day. It is just at this hour that the village shikari, if so disposed, may upset all your calculations. A very little talking, or coughing within earshot of the scene of the kill will suffice to make the beast decamp. Occasionally wild dogs drive a tiger from the para, and in such cases the brute goes clean away to some distant jungle.

A tiger usually breaks the rope and drags off the carcase of the buffalo into the nearest patch of thick covert. Here he will, unless disturbed, and if not previously beaten for and missed, be found to a certainty lying up to protect the remains from vultures and jackals. I was always very fond of going the rounds with the shikaris in the early mornings, and have, when out alone, more than once been able to stalk and shoot the tiger there and then, when he happened to be favourably placed for the purpose. When, however, as is commonly the case, you find that the rope is broken and the "para" has been dragged off, you quietly approach the spot, and judge by the "pug" of the size of the slayer, and as to whether there is more than one tiger implicated. One can generally know by many jungle signs of the presence of the beast. If vultures are perched on the trees around it is a sure omen of the presence of the tiger, whilst if they have ventured to descend to the carcase, it is an infallible sign that he has left that piece of covert. Langoor monkeys also, which are occasionally about, evince by their restlessness, the sentries they have posted aloft, and by not descending to the ground, that the common enemy is in close proximity. While any movement of his is signalised by the most voluble "swearing" and shaking of branches on the part of the entire troop. Peafowl likewise, which generally abound, utter a peculiar, hoarse clucking note when they see a tiger, and when the latter is on the move rise with a terrified kuk-kuck-ck-ck-k.

When you have none of these guides to help, it is better to wait until it is pretty sure from the height of the sun that the animal has settled down for the day, and then make a few casts around the patch of covert which is supposed to harbour him. There are nearly always some sandy, or dusty, paths, which he must cross and where his pug will be visible.

Having successfully marked down your game, **Beating.** the next thing is to collect beaters up to one hundred, if you can only get them. In some cases this is the work of hours, and you are obliged to make one half of that number suffice. I have even had successful "drives" with only a dozen men, but this is exceptional.

In no case is it advisable to commence beating much before 11 A.M., by which hour animals are generally asleep, and the stones and rocks so hot that a tiger will scarcely ever face the sun, and even should he break away at first, will probably not travel a quarter of a mile before lying up again.

The direction of a beat is regulated entirely by the configuration of the ground and not by the direction of the wind. I have twice known a tiger escape through winding me, but this was in the cool of the evening. In a beat the beast is usually too done by the heat to take heed of anything, and it lolls along with tongue hanging out, oblivious of all but the noise in its rear. A tiger must, however, be humoured and headed towards some natural line of retreat. In a broken country he will, as a rule, break up hill and, like a blue hare, cannot be forced downwards.

Neither will he face an open if there is contiguous covert in any other direction; nor will he be driven up a "kho" (precipitous ravine) when, as frequently happens, the only exit is narrow and easily guarded.

Water he takes to readily, and swims strongly

and well. Village wood-cutters, bheels and seriahs always know what other parts of the jungle an animal affects and will readily break for; and their information, combined with that afforded by old tracks, indicates the line to be guarded. When one knows a jungle, one can tell within a few yards where the animal will break, and in some Central Indian beats there is some historical tree from which a tiger has been shot almost annually throughout the past half century.

Lots are usually drawn for the sequence of places, and it saves trouble to adhere to these for the day. Whilst the central posts are best in an ordinary river beat, the flank ones are the more likely when these rest upon rocky scarps.

Always take post in a tree or on a rock whenever you possibly can do so. Apart from the inadvisability of incurring any avoidable risk, a sportsman is far more likely to be winded, or to be seen when on the ground level, where also he commands far less space, and is unable to see over grass or bushes. Even in a deer drive one thus gets far more shots. Animals, however carefully they may glance around them whilst stealing away, very seldom look up, and the result of being even 6 or 8 feet above the ground level is to get an easy walking shot instead of a difficult snap one through trees. There is the further risk of the animal spotting you, fancying that he is surrounded, and charging back through the beaters.

In some instances, notably in shoots in native

states, regular "machāns," or platforms to shoot from, are erected beforehand in the trees, and light bamboo ladders are provided for the unwieldy sportsman to mount aloft. Such contrivances are most unsportsmanlike and limit beats to one or two previously prepared localities. **Shooting from the Machān.**

Other sportsmen have leather seats with ropes carried about with them. The worst of these are that they involve taking an extra man to carry them, that they take an unconscionable time to fasten up, and that a man seated thereon is much hampered and quite unable to shoot to the right hand side. A small coil of thin and strong cotton rope, and a folding pocket saw are really all that is required. With these and the indispensable gun-bearer who can bring also your chagul (water skin), you can post yourself quickly and quietly, and dispense with the coolies to carry leather seat, chagul, gun, and too often a basket of soda water and other refreshments. Many an animal is lost by the noise occasioned by this superfluous train, and very great delays are the inevitable result.

One should be able to choose for one's self a suitable tree, slip quietly up this to a height of 8 or 10 feet, saw off a few small branches, on the stumps of which you hang rifles and water skin, and attach the rope to form a waist-high balustrade around you. A standing position to fire from should be always adopted, as, with the secure barrier of the rope to prevent overbalancing, you can swing round to either side to shoot. If the tree be at all cramped, one should stand with the **Shooting from a Tree.**

left shoulder facing the beaters; and once you have settled upon the position to preserve during the beat, await its commencement in some other one, so as not to tire your limbs by adhering to a possibly uncomfortable posture.

The gunbearer should never be kept with you, but he should be sent to climb a tree a hundred yards or so, in your rear, to mark any animal passing behind.

It is generally advisable particularly when posted on the ground not to fire until the tiger is abreast of or past you, there being then no risk of driving him back upon the line, the tendency of a wounded animal being to throw up his head and dash blindly forwards; but if he sees himself headed, he will either charge

Other Posts you or turn on the beaters. Where no trees exist, I have obtained a most excellent post by throwing a few sticks, and a "kummal" or native blanket, on to the top of a corrinda bush, and getting a leg up thereon. Kneeling upon this your weight sinks you down under the shelter of the surrounding leaves. A small screen of branches is advisable upon a bare rock, as you are otherwise somewhat conspicuous against the sky line. When on the ground, one should have a tree trunk or other obstacle to step behind in case of need, as a wounded tiger in his blind rush may crash through any bush. When the stem is sufficiently massive, it is better to post yourself in front of, rather than behind it; as, with a small screen of leaves, one is thus apparently less visible than when peeping round the trunk.

It is also advisable to place a dozen men in trees as an outer circle some hundred yards back, to mark any animal, whether wounded or not, which passes the line of guns. It is sometimes also advisable to post some flankers or "rokhs" to guard possible exits not commanded by the guns. The prevalent mistake made by these is to make too much noise, and they shout and yell at an animal, sending him off at a gallop, either past them or back at the beaters. A tiger is always suspicious of a subdued and unaccustomed noise ahead, and is effectually turned by knocking two stones together, by tapping a branch, or by occasional low coughs. He seemingly suspects some trap, and turns to steal off elsewhere. I have successfully used flanks of cord of about 100 yards in length with parti-coloured stuff pennons, such as the "lapi" used in Russian wolf beats, strung along the bushes 3 or 4 feet from the ground.

A tiger will not pass under this, but I have known one charge it roaring and jump it at a low place. I have also improvised a flank, where there were no trees to place "rokhs" in, by tethering my baggage camels at 40 or 50 yards interval through the bushes—their chewing and stamping sufficing to deter the tiger from breaking in that direction.

All being posted, the beat is conducted much as all beats are, save that the greatest noise attainable, by drums, horns and the human throat is indulged in as it encourages the beaters and seems to cow a tiger. Should the latter be seen by them to break away, and should there be no reason to believe that there is a second one on foot, all noise should cease, but the advance be continued up to the "moules" or posts, the party merely tapping the trees and talking quietly. The animal which has broken off is then more likely to lie up near at hand. Whether the tiger breaks away or not, it is as well to continue beating in the neighbourhood up to four or five o'clock, if only on the chance of a panther or bear. A "silent" beat throughout would really be preferable to a "noisy" one, save for the danger to beaters; there is always the risk of a gorged tiger not waking up until the men are all about him, when, seeing himself surrounded, he breaks his way out with the probable loss of human life. Even with a vicious or suspicious tiger, men are quite safe if they will only keep together. It is best to form them into groups of ten or twelve, each under the charge of a sowar or other responsible person. These should advance with all possible noise, and, keeping 40 or 50 yards apart and thoroughly pelting with stones all intermediate thick patches.

If there are any elephants, these should, in all tiger beats, cover the line and one of your shikaris from a howdah can best direct the beaters. It is cruelly dangerous for the latter when the sportsmen post themselves in the howdahs, and then expect footmen to drive a savage beast up to them. The animal must see or hear the elephant in front, and the result is frequent accident. It is altogether a mode of sport uncongenial to an Englishman, although much in vogue with native chiefs, who wish to shirk all form of fatigue and are supremely indifferent to loss of life. It should be a stringent rule when beating for a tiger, that nothing else should be fired at until it is known that the former is killed, or has broken clean away. When beating the same patch of jungle on some succeeding day for an animal which has previously been fired at, you should always drive it in a different direction, the reverse way if possible, or "*oolta hanka*," as natives term it.

In any case the beat should invariably halt at the first shot, nor should it again advance until signalled to do so by the man who fired. We always used whistles, the sound of which after a shot signified that the tiger was dead or had broken off and that the beat should continue. If nothing was heard, one of the shikaris advanced upon an elephant, if you had one, or a few men came round by a flank to ask for orders. It is of course imperative to follow up the wounded beast from a howdah if practicable, and, failing that, for the guns to unite and do so on foot. One should never under any circumstances allow beaters to continue whilst there is even a suspicion that the animal may be wounded. Neither should he be left alone when once hit, or some wretched native woodcutter will probably pay the penalty. When you go out for a tiger, you must be prepared to go right through with the business at any hazard. On no account incur any avoidable risk, but shoot him somehow.

Failing an elephant to follow up with, a "bobbery" pack of dogs is sometimes even better; but there are scarce half a dozen places in India where it would be worth while nowadays to keep any up, and they knock up so easily in the sun that it is often impossible to employ them. In fairly cool weather mine more than once have brought an unwounded tiger to bay, and they so bothered a wounded one that you could dodge up unnoticed on some vantage ground, or behind a tree, and deliver a finishing shot. A herd of village buffaloes driven *up wind* in front of you is also excellent, and they, unlike other cattle, will combine and charge a tiger. They, however, get so excited that you must keep a tree handy to step behind, or they may stampede over you. Even a flock of goats is very useful, as they graze along through the bushes, and by scattering out when they wind your antagonist—disclose his whereabouts. I have seen a wounded tiger successfully lured out of a cave by dangling a white native sheet in front which he mistook for a man and charged. He has sometimes the objectionable habit of doubling back on his trail and crouching to one side of it, and, whilst puzzling over the lost track you may hear a roar on flank or rear. The more noise a tiger makes when charging, the less he is to be feared; and if you stand firm, he swerves off when a few paces distant. The silent ones alone really mean business. Although a tiger instantly localises the position of the human voice, he seems incapable of detecting from whence a shot or a whistle comes.

When you find the earth torn up by the claws of an apparently missed animal, for even a few strides, you will find it dead not far ahead.

Beaters, who receive as a rule two annas a day, should invariably be paid by one of the sahibs with his own hand. They are ranged in rows by villages, hand back the wads issued as counters before the beat, and a rupee is given over to each group of eight, small change only being required for odd numbers. When there had been a particularly hard day's work, I usually gave a rupee amongst five, and double or treble pay when two or three tigers were shot in a day.

It is also very necessary to give a reward to the head-man of the village on which you have been chiefly dependent for supplies and beaters, of ten to fifteen rupees for each tiger bagged from that particular camp, and a similar amount shared amongst the villagers through whose information animals have been got. The "chumars" also, who feed and water the "paras" thrice daily, should get four annas a day for the period of their employment.

All these sums must be paid directly into the hands of the recipients, or they will never get them, and furthermore the "pateil," or head-man, should be asked personally by the manager of the party if everything has been settled up and should be made to sign a receipt to this effect.

Sitting up. Sitting up at nights over a buffalo for a tiger is by no means the poaching style of sport which some people profess to consider it. It is, I think, far superior to simply waiting in camp, as many do, until the shikaris have marked down one's game, and then, with the least possible fatigue, posting one's self in the *machān* allotted, without the smallest idea of "the lie" of the jungle or of anything connected with the sport. With a charpoy tied up, a blanket, pillow, "chagul" and a few biscuits, one can pass a most interesting night, and especially towards sunset and sunrise study a great deal of animal life. It is altogether different in the larger jungles of Assam and Burmah, but in Rajputana and Central India this kind of vigil is very rarely indeed successful. This is probably due to the fact that all kinds of game are so much shot at by native shikaris at nights, that they are very wary. Still, when the extent of the jungle is unmanageable, or when tigers are accustomed to lie up in caves, and beating proves absolutely useless, I have time after time watched at nights, if only as preferable to sleeping in bed.

I have five times only had shots in some hundred vigils, and only thus bagged three tigers in all, although I always sit up quite alone to minimise noise, and also take every precaution. My theory is that, unless a beast is particularly hungry, he circles sometime round the bait before approaching and thus gets your wind. I have sat up with a full moon at a spot where on three successive nights a "para" had been killed, without result, and next morning have found the pug of the tiger within fifty yards on both sides of me. They likewise have a curious instinct to await the setting of the moon before coming forward. I have known, for instance, one which, to judge from the cries of monkeys and pea-fowl, must have been within a hundred yards of the "kill" at sunset, yet did not come forward until three in the morning when the carcase was in deep shade.

Use of Lantern.

I personally believe that a bright light, such as that of a bicycle lamp, might attract rather than frighten a tiger, and I have heard of a Calcutta sportsman employing an electric light when sitting up in the Soonderbuns. When this was switched on, the beast, instead of bolting, always stared up at the glare. Personally, I never yet tried any form of lantern.

A Native Method.

In some of the southern forests, some tribes of natives net and spear tigers for the sake of the reward, but it is a long and tedious affair, the animal being sometimes enclosed for days, the circle of the nets being gradually diminished.

Weights and Measurements.

An average full-grown tiger measures 9 ft. 4 ins. to 9 ft. 6 ins. from nose to tip of tail, stands 38 to 40 ins. at the shoulder, girths some 50 to 54 ins. and weighs about 30 stone. The exceptional sizes I have known were 10 ft. 1 in. in length, 60 ins. in girth and 450 lbs. in weight. Tigresses run about a foot less in length, with proportionate diminutions of girth and weight; although I once saw one of 9 ft. 4 ins. in length.

They usually have two or three, but occasionally as many as five cubs, and I on one occasion saw six in a litter.

According to native shikaris, one may live up to five-and-twenty years. In the vernacular, they are generally termed "Bagh" in Western and Southern India, and "Shere" or "Singh" in other parts. The lion is termed the "Oontia Bagh," "the camel-coloured tiger" in Kattiawar, and the "Shere bobar" in central parts. Maneaters are nowadays very rare indeed. They probably become so accidentally, and although often very cunning and changing their ground frequently, can be got in a beat as easily as any others of their species.

In most large parties the beast belongs to the man who first wounds it; even although this may have been a shot in the paw, and one of his comrades may have had to face and stop its charge.

II.—THE PANTHER

WITH a few minor exceptions every word written above on the subject of tiger shooting applies equally to the pursuit of panthers and bears, which inhabit the same jungles, and all three species of which are often found in the same beat.

All pertaining to camp life and equipment, outfit and weapons remain the same, save and except that it is not necessary to employ as heavy metal for such animals as panthers and bears, *e.g.* a ·500 Express suffices. As the rewards are also on a much lower scale expenses are commensurately less. Panther bears about the same relation to tiger shooting as does trout to salmon fishing.

The *Felis pardus*, termed leopard in Bengal and Ceylon, is, however, responsible for more accidents to sportsmen than is the tiger; entirely because he is more despised and fewer precautions are therefore taken. A friend of mine, a fairly powerful man who was thus tackled, told me that he tried to stand up against the beast, but that its weight appeared to him irresistible. Although people mauled do not seem to suffer from the "shock" generally noticeable in the case of tiger accidents, yet mortification more commonly results, probably from putrid carrion contained in the sheath of the claws.

Several of my pack were wounded by panthers at different times, yet I never knew gangrene to occur in the case of dogs, which almost invariably recovered.

Panthers are far more familiar animals and less afraid of man than tigers, and I have shot one lying up in a cactus hedge, on the side of the main road, within fifty yards of a large village. Many are found in comparatively open country, with but scanty patches of isolated bushes; and they are much more addicted to going to ground than are tigers, even using porcupine and jackal earths for the purpose.

Difficulty of Beating Panthers. They are less easily driven in a beat, generally turn up at the very end of it, and I believe that in the majority of cases they squat in some hole or bush and allow the beaters to pass them by. I remember once beating the same patch of corrinda jungle four times back and forwards, either the panther or his track being seen each time although he never came up to the guns. In our fifth attempt I walked with the beaters and shot him not five paces in front of the line trying to steal round the flank. He was a fairly big animal, as he had killed a camel.

In some parts of Western India native shikaris assert that there are three distinct species of panther, and certainly there is a great difference, in both size and colour, between the large, sleek, and tawny "Tendwa" of the plains, and some of the small, rather long-coated and pale-coloured specimens occasionally found amongst rocky and hilly country. **Panthers and Tigers.** Although panthers frequent the same jungles as tigers, still the disappearance of the latter from any tract is signalised by a very marked increase of the former. I once found a panther which had been killed by a tigress beside a para, and on another occasion I saw a panther spring up a tree to avoid a couple of tigers, which, during a beat, appeared on the pathway. I do not however suppose that the larger species habitually attack their smaller kindred, although they would annex any game killed by their weaker cousins.

Probably owing to its greater familiarity with man, a panther is very much easier drawn by a bait—a goat for choice—than is a tiger; and far more of them are shot over a "tie-up."

Favourite Hiding-places.

One often knows of a panther living on some isolated rocky hill, or rather knoll, such as are common in the Deccan and in parts of Kattiawar. As these contain any number of caves and out-of-the-way retreats underneath the huge granite boulders piled promiscuously together, it is futile attempting to dislodge them, and neither dogs nor fireworks are of any avail.

I heard of two officers who, upon interrogating a shepherd as to the whereabouts of game, were told that for ten rupees he could produce a panther for them. Desiring the sahibs to hide behind a bush near the foot of one of these rocky knolls, he drove his flock past the foot, tethering up one of their number about thirty yards from the sportsmen.

As its companions receded the goat began to bleat piteously, and within a few minutes—it was late in the day—a panther appeared, stealing down the rocks. The friends thereupon tossed up for first shot, and the skin. Presently their quarry approached and springing upon rolled over the goat in a cloud of dust when they banged away their four barrels. As the smoke cleared, the pard was seen bolting up the hill, and the goat, which was merely slightly scratched, was none the worse for the adventure. This was an instance of the use of standing back-sights with rifles.

When proceeding to sit up, which in a quiet jungle it is advisable to do a couple of hours before sunset in the hot weather, it is in very many cases desirable to make no secret of it, and for the party to chat as they come. The sahib having been posted in his *machān*, his attendants should depart for the village talking loudly and this often draws a panther, who fancies that the coast is clear. Native shikaris often, on a dark night, place an oil "bhutee" beside a kill, and aver that this nowise deters the animal. As an

Boldness of the Panther.

instance of the animal's boldness, a friend of mine out in camp, seeing his dogs fed before dinner-time, perceived a panther crouched in the shadow of his own tent watching them. He then picketed a goat within 150 yards, and before he had finished dinner this had been killed. Immediately behind the rifle butts at a station in the Deccan, a panther frequently emerged from the rocks, and lay out on one of them at dusk, within a few minutes of the cessation of the firing, and the removal of the danger flag from the summit. I have also seen a pony killed in camp on a moonlight night, and the panther, although fired at three times, return to eat it.

Although terrified by a pack, panthers prey largely upon single dogs, and sometimes carry these off from under the eye of their owners. I have heard of one tied up to the leg of his master's bed thus snatched away; and a favourite one of my own was snapped up betwixt me and a friend whilst chasing a wounded deer through a belt of covert not fifty yards wide, which lay between us.

Unlike a tiger, a panther will never face water, not at least if this involves swimming.

I have known two or three instances of their becoming man-eaters, and when they do so they seem to be endowed with preternatural cunning.

Remember that no animal can so well conceal his presence, or more frequently remains behind in a beat, and that up to the very last moment that you must be on the look-out for him. I have even heard the thud of a stone against one, without his moving in the bush.

Fear of a Pack of Dogs.

Excellent sport may be had with a few fox terriers backed up by two or three big Polygar, Brinjarra, or selected Pye dogs; which suffice to bring any panther to bay, or force him to take refuge in a tree. Their terror of a pack is probably due to acquaintance with wild dogs, which undoubtedly attack them.

Weight and Measurements.

A full-grown male panther averages 7 ft. 4 ins. in length (of which the tail is usually 3 ft.), 38 ins. in girth, and weighs 12 to 15 stone, *i.e.* about half that of a tiger. Occasionally panthers exceed these measurements, and I have more than once seen 7 ft. 10 ins. and one animal of very close upon 8 ft. in length. The skin measures quite a foot more. I have generally seen two, and occasionally three cubs.

The Hunting Leopard. The cheetah, or hunting leopard, is totally distinct. It is not in the least formidable and has only semi-retractile claws. It is lean and lanky, like a greyhound, rarely measures over 6 ft. 8 ins. tail and all, and weighs under 8 stone—at least a coolie can carry one over his shoulders single-handed. Cheetahs are very rarely seen wild, and then only in open "black buck" country. Their skin is of a lighter ground-work, with solid, distinct black dots, while that of a panther is more orange, with rose-shaped clumps of dots—as if one had dipped the tips of four fingers in ink, and dabbed them on. There are some instances of wild ones being speared in open jungle, which, however, requires a good man and horse. The trapped ones, enlarged on a polo ground for this purpose, are too cowed to show real fight.

III.—THE SLOTH BEAR

THE Indian black, or sloth, bear (*Ursus torquatus*) is found almost wherever jungle abounds, from Ceylon to the Himalayas. He is a purely vegetable feeder, although he has a great partiality for white ants, scorpions and honey-combs, bees and all, which are apparently great delicacies in his estimation.

Jungle fruits, especially that of the mowa tree, and in Kashmir the mulberry, which attract him from considerable distances, are his staple diet, and, except that he occasionally raids the mangoe trees, or Indian corn patches attached to small villages, he does little harm to property.

More wood-cutters and other jungle frequenters are, however, perhaps mauled by bears than by any other kind of animal.

I think this is due rather to their being stupid, heavy sleepers, than to malice prepense. They rely more upon smell than hearing, and sometimes do not realise that anyone is anywhere near, until they start up to find a man within a few paces, and fancying themselves attacked they go for him. The worst is that they have a propensity to attack the face, and I have seen some ghastly instances of disfigurement thus inflicted.

Bears Heavy Sleepers.

Once during a "mogam" beat, *i.e.* when you fire at anything big enough to use a rifle upon—the advance was stopped and word was sent that there was some wounded animal in a bush. Walking up with a brother officer to the spot, we saw a patch of bear skin in a small corrinda clump, and from the smell imagined that the beast was dead. Approaching nearer, we could however see the hair moving with the regular breathing of the creature, so, placing the muzzle of a rifle almost against this, one of us fired, and two bears bolted out, howling dismally. One of these fell dead after a few strides, and the other was also shot. I have also seen a bear tickled up by a spear through a cleft in the rocks, before he would bolt, and I have known two or three very awkward shaves through sportsmen entering a cave on all fours in search of a supposedly dead animal. This, by the way, I have never known even the pluckiest native attempt to do.

As above remarked, bears are frequently met with, and are generally shot in ordinary beats as they lie up in precisely similar jungle to that frequented by tigers. They are, however, often found in rocky hills—even those destitute of rocks—miles from any water, where no tiger or panther would stop.

In Caves. There are, however, in some districts numerous caves which form their natural strongholds, and where perhaps they will remain secure unto the end of time. These are not generally caverns in our acceptation of the word, but more frequently huge masses of rocks of all sizes up to some hundred tons piled upon each other in wild confusion. I have seen these extend for a couple of hundred yards in length by fifty in breadth, one chaos of basalt columns, where the overhanging cliffs above had given way—and which were matted over in places by thick creepers.

It is only by watching these retreats at daybreak that a shot is obtainable, and this is, I think, a most interesting form of sport.

Bears, once disturbed in a jungle, abandon the bushes and betake themselves to some of these underground retreats out of which, after a shot or two in their proximity, they will not stir, except after dark, re-entering in all probability before dawn.

In undisturbed jungles, however, they often do not return from their ramble in search of food until an hour after daybreak. To forestall them, one must sally forth about 4 A.M. in time to reach the crest of the hill or of the scarp whilst it is yet dark. A lantern may perfectly well be used, as it is sometimes rather trying to have to struggle upwards through thorns and climb rocks in a perfectly unknown locality. Once, however, seated on the top, the trouble and fatigue of your early start are soon forgotten, and it is most fascinating watching the appearance of dawn, wondering what kind of a view daylight will disclose, and listening to the jungle sounds and the twittering of the awaking birds. A stray hyena, or a few pigs or deer some hundred feet below, first meet your gaze, and presently, just as the sun mounts with a rush over the neighbouring hills, a couple of black spots slowly sauntering towards the foot of the hill, and occasionally stopping to scratch at a white ant's nest, or pick up some fallen berries, rewards your watch. **In the Jungle.**

Beware, however, of giving them your wind, they will scent you from as far off as a red deer, and I have seen them turn when fully a quarter of a mile distant, and go clean away for miles.

A bullet in the white horse-shoe of the chest is instantaneously fatal, but with a side shot one **The Fatal Spot.**

is very apt to tailor them, as they offer such a round, ill-defined target, and, not distinguishing the shoulder, you fire promiscuously into the centre of the black ball of shaggy hair.

A couple of cubs seem the usual allowance, and these, when small, are carried on the mother's back. I once saw a bear with a cub blunder up to a wounded tiger, who gave her one comb with his claws down the face, when she turned and bolted howling dismally, with her infant kicking up an even more ear-piercing wail of alarm. I once also saw a bear which had apparently been killed by a tiger, but this must be a very exceptional incident.

A wounded bear generally attacks its companion, and I have seen a slightly hurt one go for a buffalo grazing near, but the result of a minute's scrimmage left it a drawn battle.

Measurements. A male bear measures about 6 ft. 6 ins. in length, and the female half a foot less.

More wounded bears get off than any other animal I know, and a profuse blood track often soon dies out. Altogether, they give excellent sport, and you do not feel yourself in for a serious business as you do in the case of a tiger. I know several instances of spearing them on horseback, and it is capital fun chasing them with dogs in the early mornings or at the commencement of the rains.

The Kashmir Bear. The Kashmir brown, or red bear, as it is termed—is a flesh eater and kills both cattle and ponies, but, strangely enough, it is considered not in the least dangerous and never charges a man, as does its congener the black one. It is usually got when out stalking, and it should be classed rather with the Himalayan than with Indian animals of the chase.

INDIAN RHINOCEROS SHOOTING

It is difficult, in fact nearly impossible, to give reliable information such as will enable the ordinary sportsman to be successful in the pursuit of these huge animals. The great Indian rhinoceros (*Rhinoceros unicornis*) is now only found in the Nepaul Terai, in the Bhútán Dúárs and in Assam. To hunt it, most elaborate arrangements have to be made; and no one but a millionaire could afford to organise an expedition without assistance. I doubt whether a Crœsus would be willing to incur the vast expenditure that would be required for the chance of a shot or two at an animal which, although interesting and comparatively rare, does not, in my opinion, afford a very high form of sport.

The Great Indian Rhinoceros. Present Distribution.

Inhabiting, as it does, immense expanses of giant grasses and reeds, often from 20 to 30 feet high, it is generally impossible to obtain a view of it, much less to shoot it, except from the back of an elephant. Progression on foot is

Elephants Indispensable. slow and difficult in its usual haunts; and, in short, without elephants, it is useless to attempt to shoot this rhinoceros. Even if the sportsman *could* walk, he would require two or three elephants to carry his baggage and supplies. Really good elephants are not procurable for lower prices than at least 2000 or 3000 rupees. Staunch Shikárí ones are much more expensive. To their cost must be added that of howdahs, pads, tents and other gear, besides the pay of mahouts and other servants, and the provision of food both for men and beasts—no small item.

The most certain way, and that most generally practised, of obtaining a shot, is to have a large number of elephants to act as beaters, and a sufficient additional number of highly trained ones to carry the howdahs of the shooting party.

Another less certain, but more economical, and perhaps more interesting method is, to take only one or two elephants and move as quietly as possible through the jungles, looking out for fresh tracks, and when found, silently following them up. Under such conditions, a rhinoceros may occasionally be found feeding in an open space, or wallowing in a mud-hole; and it may be feasible to dismount and shoot him on foot. This I have done. Premising that no one would be willing to incur the heavy expense above indicated, the only way to have a chance of shooting a rhinoceros is to obtain introductions to native nobles, commissioners, forest officers, and other officials who have the command of elephants and are willing to lend them, or will give invitations to join their own shooting-parties. I should ill requite the kindness and hospitality that I have received by mentioning names and sending strangers to invade my former hosts; so I must leave my readers to obtain their own introductions.

Commissariat officers, however, are sometimes able to lend Government elephants, on condition that their food is paid for, and any casualties made good; but of late years, Government has greatly reduced the establishment, and there are few military stations within reach of the jungles where rhinoceros are found.

The Nepaul Terai.

I may add that shooting in the Nepaul Terai can only be obtained by special invitation, which is confined to a privileged few.

Indiscriminate Shooting.

Forty years ago rhinoceros were extremely numerous, and several might easily be killed in one day. Owing to indiscriminate slaughter of both sexes and all sizes, their numbers have been terribly reduced; but there are enough left to enable a well equipped sportsman to be pretty sure of obtaining one or two specimens. With these, I think that he ought to be content, although I must plead guilty to having shot six. Even if I had the chance, I would never shoot another, unless it had an extraordinarily good horn.

Of course, in heavy jungle, it is quite impossible to recognise the sexes, and a novice will be unable to distinguish between a full-grown and an immature animal; but anyone with any idea of size will be able to refrain from killing mere calves, which, I am sorry to say, has frequently been done.

Season. February and March are about the best months for this sport. Large areas of heavy grass jungle have then been burnt, and much withered; so that the ground to be hunted over is considerably restricted. The weather is still comparatively cool; and there is not much risk of malarial fever.

Outfit. With regard to outfit, it is again impossible to give more than general suggestions. Anyone who is fortunate enough to be the guest of a Rajah or high British official, will find himself treated with the most lavish hospitality, and will only have to take his usual personal luggage, bedding, of course rifles and ammunition, and two or three native servants.

I may as well put the idea of buying a large stud of elephants, and the corresponding scale of camp equipage, etc., quite out of the question; but the man who cares to buy, or succeeds in borrowing or hiring two or three elephants, need not incur very much additional outlay.

Tents will be required for himself and his followers, but for a short trip there is no necessity for having large ones, which are troublesome to pitch, and heavy to carry.

The Elgin Mills Company at Cawnpore make excellent light tents of various patterns: I prefer my own, which they have manufactured for me,

Tents are best made of strong cotton drill, which does not absorb much water. The colour should be *fast-dyed* "khákí," which is less conspicuous than white. Messrs E. Spinner & Co. of Manchester and Bombay, supply the best.

In these days it is unnecessary to give advice about sporting-dress, the style of which is so thoroughly understood; so I need only mention that clothes should be made of some strong cotton material, either "khákí," or some greenish mixture. For shooting from the howdah, canvas shoes, with india-rubber soles, will be found coolest and most comfortable.

As regards food, the supplies taken should be procured in Calcutta, where everything that can possibly be required may be purchased. Nothing is obtainable in the scattered villages in the jungles, except coarse flour and rice, milk, ghee, and occasionally fowls and eggs. For fresh meat, the sportsman must depend upon his gun and rifle. A small supply of simple medicines should always be taken, such as quinine, chlorodyne, Cockle's pills, etc., also some carbolic oil, bandages, and lint in case of accidents. For the preservation of trophies, carbolic acid, alum, and arsenical soap will be required.

Last, but not least, we come to the important question of a choice of weapons. There are now so many powerful rifles of nearly equal efficiency, that the selection must depend upon individual tastes. For many years I used nothing, in jungle shooting, except a 12-bore rifle on the "Forsyth" principle, with a charge of 7 drams of black powder, and a hardened spherical bullet. The rifle weighed 11 lbs. and there was no inconvenient recoil. It was extremely accurate up to 120 yards, which is a far longer range than one often fires at in the jungle. With it, I killed most species of Indian "Large Game" from rhinoceros downwards, and seldom lost a wounded beast. In justice to the maker I must mention that it bore the well-known name of John Rigby. I have no experience, at game, of the modern small bore high velocity rifles, with nitro powders. From all accounts they are very deadly; but had I again to stand up to the charge of a dangerous beast, I should prefer to stick to my old love.

A shot gun is an absolute necessity on any expedition, to supply the larder; and a miniature rifle is a most useful accessory for the same purpose. A hatchet, a meat saw, and several good butchers' knives, with a steel to sharpen them on, are also indispensable.

I advise anyone who shoots a rhinoceros to preserve the head, feet, and the whole of the hide. Most interesting trophies, and a variety of useful articles, such as tables, cigar boxes, lamp pedestals, trays, etc., may be made from them. Rhinoceros have often been described as having almost impenetrable hides, and being only vulnerable in certain parts. This is entirely a mistake; no animal that I know is more easily killed; and with modern rifles the vital parts may be reached from any point, provided that the direction is right. The brain and heart are, of course, the organs, the shattering of which, insures instant death; but a shot through the lungs, though not so quick in its effect, is nearly equally fatal. The lungs are very large, and when they are penetrated the animal generally soon chokes—usually uttering loud grunts and squeals. I have killed three rhinoceros with single bullets.

The Lesser Indian Rhinoceros.

The Java (*Rhinoceros sondaicus*) or, as it is commonly called, the "Lesser Indian Rhinoceros" (although little inferior in size to the other), may be easily distinguished by the different folds and conformation of the hide, and by the absence of the horn in the female. This species exists in small numbers in the Bhútán Dúárs, where I once saw one shot by a friend. Although it frequents grass jungles, like its congener, it appears to be more of a forest-loving animal; and its favourite haunts are the thickets at the base of the low hills where the thorny cane forms a refuge which hardly any foe can invade. I have followed the tracks in such localities, on foot—but never with success.

This rhinoceros is, I believe, much more plentiful in the "Soonderbuns" (properly *Sún-drában*) or Delta of the Ganges, and is to be found within a few miles of Calcutta. Few Englishmen ever go after them; and I have only met one who had shot any.

When quartered at Calcutta I often intended to try for them; but somehow or other my duties as a Staff Officer always prevented me. As my readers are probably aware, the Soonderbuns consist of low lying land, covered with stunted forest, and intersected by innumerable tidal creeks. The only possible way of visiting them is by water, and for a sporting expedition it would be necessary to engage a sort of house-boat, known familiarly in Calcutta as a "Green boat," which serves as a dwelling-place, and also a "dinghy" of shallow draught in which to explore the smaller creeks. Local pilots and guides would of course be required, and I understand that shikaris are to be obtained. It would be useless to go for only a few days; as progress would be slow, and the game is undoubtedly difficult to find.

All stores, including a supply of fresh water, would have to be taken from Calcutta, and replenished from time to time by special arrangement. Possibly a steam launch might now be hired; if so, it would be a great convenience.

"Mutatis mutandis" my recommendations as regards shooting in the Dúárs and Assam would hold good here; but some extra precautions will have to be taken. Tigers are numerous in the Soonderbuns, and bear a bad reputation as man-eaters. A sharp look-out must therefore be kept, and no straggling allowed, The mosquitoes are an awful pest, and good curtains an absolute necessity. I regret that I cannot give any estimate of the cost of an expedition, but it certainly would be very moderate. A steam launch, if engaged, would probably be the heaviest item.

BISON SHOOTING IN CENTRAL INDIA

Big game shooting of every description in Central India has changed to a considerable extent during the last ten or fifteen years. The hilly forest-clad country, familiar to the many readers of Forsyth's excellent book "The Highlands of Central India," still exists, and still holds game of every description. Many parts, in particular the outlying jungles of the Mandla district, are still as wild and undesecrated by roads and railways as they were fifty years ago. Hidden in the huge jungles there are still to be found the quaint huts of the *Gōnds* and *Bygars*, who retain their aboriginal features and much of their aboriginal skill in stalking and tracking. Bison[1] unfortunately appear to have suffered more by the opening of the country than any other game. There is no compromise for them. They must have absolute freedom from all signs of man. The crack of a rifle, the noise of the woodcutter's axe, a whiff from a distant encampment and the marks of a trodden path are all equally abhorrent to them, and they must shift and march and march till they find

[1] This is the name given by sportsmen to the gaur (*Bos bubalis*).—Ed.

a secluded tract of jungle where none of these objectionable conditions obtain.

The Forest Department has now laid its grasping hands on nearly all the large jungles in Central India. The forests are all marked out with boundaries, game laws have been made, and work smoothly or roughly, are useful or are abused, according to the administration of the immediate district and the personality of the local officials. In a wise moment many years ago certain tracts of jungle were marked out as "Reserves" and kept as free as possible from man, woodcutting, native fires and such like annoyances to the animal race. As foretold by Forsyth fifty years ago, these reserves are now the favourite haunts of the secretive bison, and he is seldom found elsewhere.

The gist of the Central Province game laws is as follows: a map of the different jungles with their boundaries may be seen in the office of the forest officer, and any of these jungles may be hired, or leased, at Rs.7 (9s. 4d.) a month. A shooting pass is given, on which is detailed the number of animals of various species which the holder is allowed to shoot during the month in that jungle. For instance, a shooting pass for Block No. 100, Kalpe jungle, Jubbulpore, or Mandla District, might allow the holder to shoot: sambhur, 2, cheetal, 2, bison, 1; tigers, panthers, bears, nilghai, four-horned deer, etc., without limit.

For tigers there is a Government reward of

Rs.50 sometimes raised to as much as Rs.500 for a man-eater. For a panther, Rs.15. For a wild dog, Rs.5 to Rs.15.

No one is allowed to shoot or "tie up" in your jungle when you have obtained a pass, excepting district civil officers passing through on duty. And of course they are always on duty. Should you be "tying up" for a tiger, however, the laws of sport would, or should, prevent even the district officer disturbing your jungle.

A forest guard is placed at your disposal to act as guide, and to report any breach of forest laws.

These rules appear fair enough and should carry out the idea and purpose for which they were framed, namely, that every one should have a fair chance of obtaining good sport, and at the same time the preservation of the game should not be neglected. In the Mandla and Nagpur districts of the Central Provinces they work very well. In some places they are rendered useless by the individual jealousies of officials. Where the commissioner, district superintendent of police, and forest officer are genuine sportsmen —*no* jealous sportsman can be classed as genuine —there I would recommend the reader to make his shooting expedition. Otherwise, he may find himself unable to obtain coolies; unable to get provisions; or perhaps, after several tedious beats, he will even realise that the game is being driven away from him instead of towards him.

Two good centres for bison-shooting are Nagpur and Jubbulpore. From Nagpur a short distance by rail to Warora, and then about 25 miles by tonga brings you to Chanda, a small civil station. At Chanda you are in the neighbourhood of several excellent bison jungles and may come across buffalo as well. There are several Forest Department bungalows conveniently situated near some of the best jungles from 10 to 20 miles from Chanda, and in the latter place there is a "Dâk," or traveller's, bungalow, with cook, furniture, crockery, etc. All arrangements should be made from Nagpur, and a tent, stores, and all camp kit taken with you. Soda-water can be obtained in Chanda, but it adds very largely to your baggage, and it will be found far more convenient in all Central India shooting to be content with "sparklets." From Warora station send your luggage by bullock cart to Chanda Dâk Bungalow, taking your bedding, kit-bag, rifles and lunch with you by tonga.

Having previously ascertained that you can obtain a pass in a jungle known to hold bison, you should, on arrival at Chanda, call on the district forest officer at his office and select your block of jungle. Then call on the deputy commissioner and invoke his aid in the matter of transport, bullock cart, ponies or coolies, according to the route you are going to take.

As regards rifles and ammunition for bison-shooting you *must* have something with stopping power and penetration. Personally, I consider a ·500 Express, firing cordite cartridges with steel-pointed bullets, sufficient for any dangerous game ; but many prefer a ·577 rifle. Should you expose yourself in an unfavourable position to a charge at close quarters from a wounded bison, buffalo, or tiger, I do not believe there is any weapon that may be depended on to save you, *if* the animal really means bringing his charge right home. A solid lead bullet, placed low behind the shoulder, should prove most effective for a first shot. Then, when following up a wounded bull, take your heaviest rifle and steel-pointed bullets. A shot through the body of a bison is about as useful as a shot fired into a hay-rick ; and I have before now made three holes in a bison's forehead without any fatal effect.

The best season for general shooting in Central India is undoubtedly February, March and April. It is then not too hot, and sambhur, cheetal and swamp deer (the Bara Singh of the plains) should all have their horns in good condition. The jungle will be easy to beat and easy to see through, and the risk of fever should be at a minimum. For bison alone perhaps the beginning of the rainy season is the best, about August and September. It is then close time for all deer, but bison can be tracked and stalked more easily, as the ground is soft and noiseless, and the tracks are unmistakable. Even then, however, it takes an experienced eye to unravel cross tracks through the long grass and to determine which is the most recent trail. It is most fascinating work, as the trail becomes fresher and fresher and you expect to see the huge monster every moment. Probably all you will see of him is an enormous head and pair of massive horns, with the eyes staring straight at you over some bushes, or round a clump of bamboos. Then, if you have a friendly tree beside you, you can risk a shot between his eyes and it will at any rate disconcert him, and perhaps give you a chance of another shot; perhaps it may drop him, but, even then, beware of him! If you are in an open space when you suddenly sight your bison, you may be able to reach some cover by *slowly walking backwards.*

In July, August and September bison must be sought on the high plateau, where they are free from the attacks of a species of horse-fly which infests the jungle during the rains. Their favourite food is the young sprouting bamboo and young green grass. At night they lie out on the grassy hill-tops, and by day they wander through the adjacent jungle, seeking bamboos, or sometimes pools of salt water and mud. But they are travelling nearly always. A herd will perhaps frequent a plateau for a few days and then march steadily on, 15 or 20 miles in a day, to some other ground. As the flies die off or disappear, they come lower down again. High ground, bamboos and fresh grass have at all times, however, a fascination for them. Forsyth relates many a stiff climb after an old bull on the wild Pachmarhi hills. Now alas! Pachmarhi, discovered and founded by Forsyth, and one of the prettiest spots in India, is a civilised station, and the bison has departed from its neighbourhood for ever.

Shooting in the rainy season, however, has its drawbacks. Fever is an almost certain consequence, but, in my opinion, *le jeu vaut la chandelle!* Plenty of quinine and plenty of work should keep off fever, so long as you are in the jungle; say ten grains twice a week, and an extra dose any day you are tired out, or have had to remain long in wet clothes. Your servants should also be dosed regularly. Return to life in a house, and the unwholesome atmosphere of civilisation is almost certain to produce an attack of fever, but then your discomfort is over, and with the memories of good sport to recompense you, what matter a few days in bed? Lindsay Gordon's words are very true, and very comforting:

> "No game was ever yet worth a rap
> For a rational man to play,
> Into which no accident, no mishap,
> Could possibly find its way."

The Mandla district is perhaps the best shooting country in Central India within reach of the ordinary sportsman nowadays. There are many large tracts of country in native states which contain as much, or more, game, but they are not open to everyone, and the "sport" is of a different kind. Armies of beaters, long lines of elephants, jealously preserved jungles, elaborate Machans, and a gorgeous encampment combine perhaps to produce in a few days a phenomenal bag, comparing almost favourably with a record pheasant shoot in England; and some rajah feels himself a step nearer his next decoration. But these are the preserves of viceroys, high civilian officials and gilded globe-trotters.

To shoot in Mandla, make Jubbulpore your headquarters, and call on the commissioner and obtain permission to shoot, as well as any information you can. Get all your stores and camp requisites, and hire a bullock-cart for your baggage and a tonga for yourself. Jackson's Hotel is close to the station and the only one in the place. It is 60 miles, along a good road, to Mandla, and there are very comfortable Dâk bungalows about every 12 miles with "khansamas" (cooks) and furniture in each. Your bullock-cart will take three days, and your tonga, with one pair of ponies, two days. It is an interesting drive, passing for 30 miles over a high plateau, about 2000 ft. above the sea, with dense jungle stretching far on either side. Fourteen miles from Jubbulpore the small bungalow at Dhobi is reached, at the commencement of the plateau. The jungles on either side of the road hold sambhur, and frequently harbour a travelling tiger. Further on, near the twenty-fifth milestone, you pass, on your left hand, the Barangda Reserve jungle, which always attracts bison during the early part of the rains. It is on high ground, contains plenty of bamboos, is comparatively free from flies, and boasts but two tracks through it, which do not appear to have been used for many years; hence the attraction for the bison. There are a few Gōnds in the village below the forest who can find their way about in it; and a guide is absolutely necessary, for without one you might with ease lose yourself every day for a week before getting to know the lie of the land. An old, disused, overgrown cart track runs to what is shown on the map as the village of Sagonia, and the best bison ground lies N.E. of this place, along a ridge with open grassy plains at intervals. There is no village at Sagonia, nor has there been for twenty years, but it may be recognised by a clearing in the jungle and the wild remains of what were once fields of Indian corn. Whether you would find a good bull or not in the Barangda reserve during July or August it is impossible to say, but in 1903 there were tracks of many bison in the jungle.

At 30 miles along the Mandla road you begin to pass through Kalpe jungle, which nearly always holds a tiger or two and sambhur as well. Soon after the road descends from the plateau, till you reach the plain below, and the town of Mandla 15 miles on.

There is a Dâk bungalow at Mandla, as well as a club and about half a dozen civilians. Stores can be obtained there, but it is better to bring your own. South and east of Mandla lies a large tract of jungle-covered, hilly country, 60 miles or more from any railway and only skirted by a couple of roads. Everything seems primitive, and civilisation appears to have laid a far lighter hand than usual on this densely wooded land in the centre of India, so different from any other part of the burning plains.

Bison are by no means plentiful even here, but there are several jungles that may be trusted to hold them. The South Phen country is the best, and Motinala jungle, about 40 miles from Mandla, may be relied on to give good sport.

Rampore jungle, 12 miles from Mandla, has generally a herd of bison in its neighbourhood. The remains of an old fort form a most picturesque and comfortable dwelling there. Another excellent jungle for shooting of every description is the Bunjar Valley reserve. There is a very nice forest bungalow on the northern edge of the jungle, about 30 miles south of Mandla. Five miles further south, by a good forest path, is a wooden shelter, a charming site for a camp. Here you are in the very heart of a beautiful forest of sâl trees, with game of every kind all round you. In front of your tent, enclosed on every side by trees, lies a small, undulating, grassy plain, through which the swamp deer love to roam morning and evening. On the outskirts of the plain you may catch a glimpse of the beautiful spotted deer, or cheetal. In the denser parts of the forest beyond are the favourite haunts of the rugged-horned veteran sambhur.

The nights are no less perfect than the days. The hoot of the owl, the sharp cry of the startled cheetal, the occasional bark of the wild dog pack chasing some poor sambhur to his death, and the weird "conk" of the tiger stealthily patrolling the jungle tracks in search of a dinner, all sound at your very tent door, as you lie awake listening to the voices of nature.

The Bunjar reserve is nearly 20 miles across, and the bison are for ever trekking from one part to another. In the spring perhaps the best place is to the south-west. In the rains Bamnidadar plateau, the high ridge on the southern border, attracts most of them. The great charm of this Mandla shooting is that it is all stalking. Coolies are hard to obtain in any number, and "beating" is but poor sport compared with stalking, and is here quite unnecessary. Tigers are numerous, and, when wandering about the jungle, you are sure to come across several freshly killed sambhur or swamp deer. Should you find them in the morning it is worth while to sit in a tree over the kill at once for an hour, for a tiger will often come to his kill about ten o'clock, just to have a look at it, or to move it a little further into the jungle, before settling down for his heavy mid-day sleep. He will probably return for another feed about an hour before dusk, or earlier in cool weather.

There are several small villages of Bygars in the neighbourhood, and two or three good trackers can easily be obtained from them. The trail of a really big bull bison is unmistakable, and he is generally alone. The younger bulls often go about in small herds, and their tracks will be all of much the same size. Where small tracks are found mixed with bigger ones, the herd is scarcely worth following, as it probably only consists of cows and calves. The bison's sense of smell is surprising even in dense jungle, and it is labour thrown away to attempt to stalk him with the wind.

A map of the Mandla forests may be seen in the forest officer's office in Mandla, and a shooting pass must be obtained from him. A word from him to his forest guards will be an untold help in many ways, for these latter have it in their power to make matters run very smoothly for you or very much the reverse. In the winter and spring there are camels in Mandla, and they are the best form of transport by most tracks. Bullock-carts and baggage-ponies can also be hired. Information as to what transport will be most suitable to the route you intend taking, and their rates of hire and the cost of all provisions, can be obtained from the Thesildar. In these matters, again, the kind offices of the deputy commissioner will be found to expedite arrangements considerably.

A railway is in course of construction connecting Nagpur, Seoni and Mandla, and when this is completed, it will be easy to combine a bison shoot in Mandla and Chanda. At present (Jan. 1904), trollies, and an occasional engine with a few trucks, run for 70 miles or so on this line as far as Nainpur, 20 miles short of Mandla and 30 miles from Bunjar reserve. With the permission of the engineer in charge of the construction, the line might now be a help to reaching Chanda, as the route viâ Jubbulpore to Nagpur is very circuitous.

In addition to the game already mentioned, there are in the Mandla jungles khakur, four-horned deer, panthers and bears. In 1903 the combined rewards offered for a man-eating tiger, tigress, and panther at one time reached Rs. 1200! In the rains transport is a difficulty, as many dry ravines become impassable rivers, and the rice-fields are flooded for miles. Ponies or an elephant would then be the only means of progression, but the best advice is to go in the early spring.

Note on the "Bison" or Gaur by General Kinloch.

[The gaur, largest of its family, occurs in the Terai and in the lower spurs of the Himalayas, from Nepaul eastwards, including the Bhutan Duars and Assam, as well as in the Soonderbuns, within a few miles of Calcutta. Within its range it is common enough, and I have shot it in Chota Nagpur, in the Central Provinces, and in the Nerbudda Valley. It is also found in the Neilgherrys and in Kanara, while Travancore is said to yield the finest heads and Burmah the heaviest animals. Teak, bamboo and high reeds afford the favourite cover of this forest-dweller, which climbs into the rocky hills. The gaur is misnamed by sportsmen "Bison," in the same way as the American bison was called a buffalo. The most sporting way of shooting it is by stalking and tracking. A few are shot from elephant back in the reed jungle of the Duars, the haunts of the rhinoceros and buffalo. In certain tracts of open jungle, as in the Satpura Range, south of the Nerbudda river, the gaur may sometimes be seen far off and stalked, even during the dry weather, when every leaf and stick trodden under foot gives its warning to the animal. For tracking, however, it is better to wait until the rains, when it is easier to tread silently. The risk of fever in the jungle at that season, though not wholly imaginary, has probably been exaggerated. Though the gaur is not ordinarily a dangerous animal, great care should be exercised in following it up when wounded. I myself have been charged by one, and two of my sons were on other occasions knocked over and narrowly escaped being killed. A 12-bore spherical bullet, with 7 drams of black powder, served me so well that with it I killed 9 gaur within a week, and that without losing a single wounded one. I have no doubt that one of the modern small-bore rifles with nitro powder would be equally effective.]

HIMALAYAN SHOOTING

My chief object in these notes is to give as much useful and necessary information as possible to the stranger to India who contemplates shooting, and also to correct a mistaken idea, which exists among many who have known India far longer than I have, that a shooting trip to the Himalayas is, of necessity, a long, expensive and difficult undertaking. I can thoroughly sympathise with the "stranger in the land," for, when I came to

Photo] BUFFALO (COOCH BEHAR) [*P. S. Van der Byl*

India, I was told if I wanted any leave I must go at once. I made up my mind to go, and when I had been just over a month in the Punjaub I started to shoot any animals I might find in the mountains north of Dalhousie, with a servant and shikari who could not speak a word of English! I was recommended to go after black bear, but I refrained from making any definite statement of my plans, as I had a suspicion in my own mind that these animals no longer existed, having been "shot out" many years ago. However I soon found they were a reality, and I thoroughly enjoyed my two months' leave, although my bag only consisted of a red bear, a small black bear, and a goural. I was, on that occasion, totally dependent on my shikari, as I knew nothing of the country, or of the animals of which I was in pursuit; consequently I remained, as I afterwards discovered, somewhere in the vicinity of my shikari's native village all the time, thereby enabling him and my coolies to live practically free of charge.

The two best routes that I know, by which the ordinary sojourner in the plains of India may reach good shooting country in the Himalayas, are through Srinagar and Dalhousie. It is quite possible to start from other places, such as Mussoorie or Simla, but, excepting for one route into Thibet, I think Dalhousie is a better base than any other in the south-eastern ranges of the Himalayas.

The selection of route depends of course on the time available and the description of shooting required. I should recommend the Dalhousie route to anyone who intends leaving civilisation behind him and striking off the beaten track for the first time, or to anyone who has but two months' leave or less. Excellent sport may be obtained in Chamba in one month's marching and shooting from the time of leaving Dalhousie to the time of returning there. In six weeks the little frequented territories across the northern boundaries of Chamba can be reached, and the route has many other advantages, which will soon be apparent to the reader. My best plan will perhaps be to give in the following pages all the useful information I can to the sportsman, or sportswoman (the latter will find no insuperable obstacles in these parts), who intends to penetrate into the Himalayas, with Dalhousie as a base. The details regarding tents, kit, rifles, stores and food may be taken as a fair guide to what will be necessary in any expedition by any other route east of Kashmir.

I shall then endeavour to describe the routes, and the necessary preparations, leading through Kashmir to such sportsmen's paradises as Chilas, Astore, Baltistan and Ladakh.

SHOOTING IN CHAMBA AND ADJACENT STATES

THE first question to be considered is the kit, which it is necessary to have with one on arrival at Dalhousie, the proposed base. Excellent stores can be obtained in Dalhousie, but nothing else made. Tents and camp kit should be sent by goods train at least a fortnight ahead, and, as it is a great advantage when crossing difficult passes or making long marches, to have light loads, I will give particulars of what I found to be the best and lightest camp equipment consistent with comfort.

Tents.—One 80-lbs. Kabul tent without bathroom for myself. One 30-lbs. servants' tent for my cook and shikari, and for cooking in whenever it rains or snows. An extra tent will be required for coolies when going far afield.

Furniture.—One camp bed, one chair, one folding-table, one tripod for basin, one folding Willesden canvas bath, and some matting.

Kit.—One Wolseley valise containing four blankets, one pillow, one suit of flannels, a pair of slippers and a "British warm coat."

Onc kit-bag, containing one spare shooting suit and putties and boots, a few flannel shirts, silk handkerchiefs, underclothing, etc., a warm Norfolk jacket and leather waistcoat for crossing passes. A few books and odds and ends such as revolver, skinning-knife, writing materials, maps, tobacco, etc., may also be added. Here also I may mention my medicine-chest, a very important item, that was also to be found in the depths of the invaluable kit-bag. It contained quinine tabloids for myself and two bottles of quinine-sulphate for servants and natives; one bottle of carbolic lotion in case of accidents with bears;

vaseline, chlorodyne, Cockle's pills, and a few bandages. Another very useful article of my kit was an enamel basin with a leather cover; this contained everything necessary for washing, also razors, brushes, towel, tumblers, candlestick, looking-glass, diary and matches.

Cooking utensils.—The Indian cook or "Khitmatghar," though he has his drawbacks and seldom bears close investigation, certainly does not expect or require any very elaborate outfit to enable him to produce a dinner in the jungle. The following articles alone are really necessary and should be obtained before reaching Dalhousie:—One frying-pan, a tin for baking bread, a nest of four aluminium degchies (a species of cooking-pot), one kettle, one saucepan and a chopper. Two or three old kerosene oil-tins, dear to the heart of every native servant, will complete the "kitchen." These kerosene oil-tins are put to all manner of uses, from thatching temples to boiling bath-water and baking the species of dumplings termed "Scones," which must serve as a substitute for bread from the day on which civilisation is left behind. In addition to the cooking requisites, of course, a few enamel plates, a large teapot, knives, forks and spoons, a small lunch basket and a regulation water-bottle must be taken.

Rifles. Next comes the very important question of rifles. At the present day, the question of small-bore versus heavy rifle is as vexed a one as ever, and when the opinions of men who have spent the greater part of their lives big game shooting remain as divided as they now are, everyone is entitled to judge by his own experience, great or small as it may be. I have no hesitation whatever, therefore, in recommending the ·303 as an ideal weapon for Himalayan shooting. Its lightness, its flat trajectory, its accuracy, and its marvellous killing power *when the right bullet is used* make it, in my opinion, by far the best rifle for the dangerous climb, careful, exciting stalk, and eventual shot, from perhaps a strained position, at a red bear, thar, ibex, or markhor, at any range from 50 to 350 yards. The first year in which I went to shoot in the Himalayas I took a ·500 Express rifle with me, but never again! It is a heavy, unwieldy weapon for any stalking, and no more deadly than the smallest rifle unless you hit your bear in the right place; and its trajectory is too high, and its accuracy insufficient, for the ranges (200-400 yards) at which you must be prepared to risk a shot at markhor, ibex or thar. I had perfect confidence in my little ·303 Martini-Metford carbine, provided that I had my favourite bullets. I tried many different kinds and found that the most deadly and accurate of all for big game was one with an unsplit case showing ⅓ inch of soft solid **Ammunition.** lead at the tip.[1] If more lead was exposed, the accuracy was sometimes affected. In different Himalayan wanderings I have given the ·303 a fair trial, having shot over twenty red and black

[1] These can be bought from Manton & Co., Calcutta.

bears with it; and when using that particular bullet, I don't think I have ever lost an animal that had been hit. I well remember the day I experimented on a very fine red bear with Jeffrey's split bullet, which is so useful for buck-shooting. My first shot stunned him; my second woke him up, and he came straight for me. I got in three shots as he came, the last at about 10 yards, and fired three more as he, thinking better of it, shied off down the hill into some bushes. Then, finishing him off with a revolver shot behind the shoulder, I found it had taken three holes in the head and three holes in the body to make him retire into the jungle. Another rifle that I saw in Holland and Holland's shop a few months ago struck me as being particularly suitable to Himalayan shooting. It was a single-

·375 Rifle. barrel ·375 Cordite rifle with Mannlicher action and magazine. Weighing no more than many a ·303 rifle, its trajectory, sighting, and striking velocity at 300 yards left nothing to be desired; and it is claimed that in killing power it equals the ordinary ·500 Express. This sounds perfection for mountain-stalking.

Much as I love the small bore-rifle in the Himalayas, or for any description of stalking, I admit that its advantages are thrown away when all that you expect is a pot shot in thick jungle, and I acknowledge to feeling much safer with a ·500 rifle and cordite cartridge when following up a wounded tiger or bison in the jungles of Central India.

In addition to the ·303 or ·375, I would recommend an ordinary shot-gun and a revolver. When following a wounded bear, as one so often has to, down-hill through scrub jungle, carry your rifle yourself, and your revolver in your pocket. Let your shikari follow with the shot-gun. The latter is a far more formidable **Shot-gun.** and reliable weapon for any shooting at close range in jungle than is generally recognised. You should mould your own bullets to ensure having them of soft lead and the correct size to fit either barrel of your gun. Then get some of the ordinary shot cartridges which you use in **Cartridges.** your gun with the ordinary charge; cut off the top of the case and empty out the shot and drop in your soft lead ball. Then pour in some melted bees-wax so as just to cover the ball, and do not turn over the edges of the cartridge case. If you have, as will generally be necessary, differently moulded bullets (say twelve and thirteen bore) for your right and left barrels you must of course have different coloured cartridge-cases, say red for the right barrel and grey for the left. The ordinary shot-gun with a ball-cartridge is very accurate up to 50 or 60 yards and a very useful weapon for a snap shot at any animal moving through jungle. With regard to ·303 ammunition, there is generally some delay in buying any now, owing to the restrictions imposed to prevent any finding its way over to the frontier tribes. A permit to buy 100 rounds has to be obtained from a deputy commissioner before any dealer will sell.

Having now dealt with tents, kit and arms, we must hurry on to Dalhousie. It is best to take with you a khitmatghar who can cook decently, but a bearer is unnecessary. The Punjab mail train viâ Amritsar, an old Sikh stronghold, famous for its golden temple, brings you to Pathankot about midnight. This is as near to the mountains as you can get by rail, and the train leaves you 52 miles short of Dalhousie. Tongas, which rattle you along at from 6-8 miles an hour, run as far as Dunera (about 28 miles), and from there on you can either ride, or go in a country "eckka," or be carried up in a dhoolie. At Dunera there is a prettily situated "Dâk bungalow"; and the most comfortable way to travel is to breakfast at Pathankot, reach Dunera by tonga in time for lunch, and be carried up to Dalhousie, sleeping in the dhoolie, during the night.

Dalhousie is a typical little Anglo-Indian hill station, the refuge during the summer of many ladies and a few unfortunate men.

It has several hotels, generally nearly full in the summer. The Springfield, the Strawberry Bank, and Balun hotels are the best.

Arrived in Dalhousie, there are several things to be seen to without further delay:—(1) get a good shikari; (2) write for a shooting pass; (3) buy stores.

Shikari. If possible, of course, you should write for a shikari a month before reaching Dalhousie and make him meet you there with a few coolies and a second shikari or lunch-coolie. If you have not done this you must either take your pick of the men who are sure to besiege you, judging by their "Chits" and, what is still more important, by the extent to which they know the country in which you mean to shoot; or else write to the Rajah of Chamba to engage a man for you in Chamba. I give the names in order of the three shikaris I can most thoroughly recommend in those parts: (1) Dhassa, (2) Mullah, (3) Bhagia; the last-named is the most experienced shikari, but is getting a trifle old and lazy now. The first, Dhassa, is I think about the best I have come across anywhere in Chamba, Kashmir or Central India, and in addition quite a young fellow and a fine specimen of one of nature's gentlemen; Mullah, Dhassa's uncle, is also excellent. A letter addressed to any of these c/o Postmaster, Tissa, Chamba State, will find them. It is often difficult to persuade a shikari to come to a place he does not know well, and he will always prefer to take you to the places he knows best, which, obviously are not the nullahs least shot in. Even the best of the shikaris, unless they see that they cannot deceive you, will endeavour to confine you to shooting black bears in the immediate vicinity of their own homes.

Shooting Pass.

Permission to shoot in Chamba has to be obtained from the Rajah, so that, on arrival in Dalhousie you should write to his brother and private secretary, "Mian Sahib, Bhurie Singh," to ask for permission to shoot and for a licence (costing five rupees) for your shikari. If, as I would advise, you only intend spending two or three days in Dalhousie, the licence and permit can be sent to meet you at Chamba Dâk Bungalow.

Stores. Very good stores of every description can be obtained from Saligram, a merchant near the church. For the benefit of anyone whose mind is a blank as to his requirements in this respect, the following may be of some help as a guide to, roughly, two months' supply :—

Butter	12 tins (½ lb.).
Jam	12 ,, (1 lb.).
Cocoa	4 ,,
Tea	4 lbs.
Baking powder .	6 tins
Curry	2 ,,
Corn-flour . .	2 ,,
Sago	2 ,,
Salt	4 lbs.
Pepper . . .	1 bottle
Chutney . . .	,,
Milk	3 tins
Bovril . . .	4-6 bottles
Worcester sauce .	2 ,,
Sugar	10 lbs. (more can be bought in some villages).
Biscuits . . .	
Candles . . .	8-10 packets
Oil	½ tin.

In addition to these, take five pounds alum for

rough-curing skins, some arsenical soap, and some brandy, as a medicine at any rate. The water everywhere in the mountains is perfection. The country flour is bad, except in one or two large villages. It is best to get a supply of flour, rice, sugar, potatoes and onions in Chamba town, in addition to the stores already mentioned.

Climbing requisites and boots.

A species of Alpenstock, or Khudstick, as it is called, is invaluable, and should be at least 6 feet long, of strong, light bamboo, and with a blunt iron point. When stalking, it must be used upside down, to avoid the clatter of the point against the rocks. Leather socks and sandals (called chaplies) should be bought in Chamba; they are very light and comfortable for marching. For climbing grassy slopes after red bear, or going down-hill after black bear under the pine-trees, or, above all, when crossing snow passes and glaciers, nothing can beat a stout pair of shooting boots with *big* nails. After ibex, markhor, thar, etc., where all the shooting has to be done over rocks and precipices, it is scarcely possible to move a yard in anything but the native grass shoes, which are made for you, as you travel, by your shikari. These shoes are not made so well in Chamba as in Kashmir; they should be worn over a very thick pair, or two pairs, of woollen socks. The Kashmiris make them of strands of plaited grass, and the most secure arrangement is the following:—first, put on a pair of thick woollen socks with a compartment for the big toe; over these a sort of

Grass shoes.

woollen cloth boot, lacing in front with similar big toe accommodation; then get your shikari to bind on and lace up the grass sandals as tightly as possible. The grass sole clings to rocks and slippery places better than anything else, and the absence of any restraint to the ankles enables one to cross with confidence over rocky slopes and inclines on which it would be impossible to stand still in any other boot.

An ice axe or two will be a necessity if you are to cross any unused pass, as you frequently have to cut steps for a considerable way. These can be obtained from the village nearest the foot of the pass.

Having now bought stores, engaged a shikari and written for a shooting pass to Chamba, the sooner you get on the march the better. If your shikari has not got good coolies for you, you had better take ponies or mules as far as possible from Dalhousie, until you can get some permanent coolies. Four or five permanent coolies, at any rate, are a necessity, and the remainder, from 3 to 6 or even 8, according to your luggage, can be hired stage by stage, at the rate of 4 annas per march of 12 miles. These Chamba coolies are generally excellent men and willingly carry loads up to 60 lbs.; the permanent coolies after a long march turn out to collect firewood, fetch water and watch the hill-sides for game as cheerfully as if they had done nothing. Their wages are Rs.8 a month.

If you are pressed for time, the march to

Chamba can easily be done in a day, as it is only 19 miles. Chamba is too hot to be pleasant, so in spite of the doubtful attractions of the last Dâk bungalow which you will see for some considerable time, it is as well to hurry on to a better climate. You should call on His Highness the Rajah of Chamba, and on his brother and private secretary, the Mian Sahib, Bhurie Singh. The latter will give you any information you may require about nullahs that are closed, and others that are already occupied by other sportsmen. Bhurie Singh talks the most perfect English and, being a genuine sportsman himself, is always ready to help others; though of course it stands to reason that everyone who calls on him cannot expect to be sent direct to the very best nullahs. Each of the three years in which I travelled through Chamba to shoot, I personally found Bhurie Singh most willing to help me in every way. A month's supply of potatoes, flour, **Provisions.** rice, etc. should be bought in Chamba, and some basket-work "Kiltas," in which to carry it. After leaving Chamba the only provisions obtainable in any of the small villages are sheep, or chickens, eggs (and these not everywhere), milk, and coarse flour and rice here and there only.

Next we must consider the most important question of all, and that is which route to take **Routes.** on leaving Chamba. It is quite impossible for me to recommend any particular route or nullah, though I may have no doubt in my own mind where I should go if I were marching out of

Chamba to-morrow. A place that was full of game two years ago may be closed by the rajah next year; or it may suddenly become a popular grazing ground for the large herds of sheep, goats and buffaloes taken up from the villages as soon as the snow permits. So the most that can usefully be done is to mention one or two routes, on which I know good shooting can be obtained, provided they are still open and have not been unduly worried by either sheep or doubtful sportsmen. I would not advise anyone to spend too much time in Chamba State itself, as the outlying country round the borders provides much better shooting.

Route No. 1.—From Chamba town strike east through Barmaor about five marches over the Kukti Pass into Lahoul. This is a good line for black bear, and there are several places where good thar can be shot early in the year, shooting commencing about the third march. From Lahoul a road runs north-west through Triloknath into Pangi, where good ibex ground can be reached. A good local shikari lives in a village near the Chamba border and will probably present himself to anyone marching by this road. There are a good many snow-leopards in Lahoul and to the more ambitious, with from three to four months to spare, a large and but little explored field is open by this route. Bearing north-east from the Kukti Pass, a road runs through Kulang, Darcha, over the Bara Lacha Pass (16,000 feet) to Kailang in Rupshu. Thence crossing the Lachalang Pass you reach Rukchen in eight marches from the Kukti. South-east lies the Tso Morari Lake, a good ground for Thibetan gazelle. North a road runs to Leh (six marches) over the Tagalang Pass, through Gya and Upshi, on the Indus. This road takes you through excellent burhel and good ovis ammon ground. Practically no supplies can be bought, and there is but little grass or fuel between Kulang and Gya.

Route No. II.—Over the Padri Pass into Badrawar.

Four marches, averaging 14 miles, to the Padri Pass, about 11,000 feet. This is an easy pass to cross and a very good locality for red bear. In October barasingh, or Kashmir stag, are to be found about the neighbourhood; after crossing the pass into Thanala turn to the right, or north, to get to the ground frequented by the stag. Signs of red bear will probably be found after leaving Langera, the fourth march from Chamba; there are some preserved nullahs about Langera, in which you should endeavour to get leave to shoot if you select this route.

As there are several interesting marches in continuation of the route over the Padri Pass, including a pretty, though somewhat hot, road to Islamabad and Kashmir, I will give a list of the stages:—

Dalhousie—

1. to Kajiar	.	12 miles
2. Chamba	.	7 ,,

3.	Manjira .	14 miles.	
4.	Bhandal .	14 ,,	
5.	Langera .	14 ,,	(forest bungalow)
6.	Thanala .	17 ,,	(red bear)
7.	Badrawar .	8 ,,	(over Padri Pass 11,000 ft.: hard march)
8.	Jaora .	17 ,,	
9.	Jangaiwar .	14 ,,	
10.	Kanani .	15 ,,	
11.	Kishtwar .	10 ,,	(a large village, capital of Kishtwar Province).

From Kishtwar there are routes branching off in several directions, and in many parts of the province good red bear shooting can be obtained, but a Kashmir licence is required :—

Kishtwar to Islamabad, five marches; thence by boat to Srinagar two days.

Kishtwar to Jammu, ten marches.

,, ,, Dalhousie direct, without entering Chamba, nine marches.

Kishtwar to Padar—

(1) Kishtwar to Bugna, 14 miles.

(2) to Pias, 10 miles.

(3) Seri, 14 miles.

(4) Gulabgarh, 14 miles. (Large village: flour, rice and chickens obtainable.)

Thence two marches up the Bhutna Nullah take you to the head of the valley, beyond Machail, about 24 miles to the last solitary hut.

Above you is the Umasi La Pass 17,500 feet, and beyond that the bare inhospitable heights of Zaskar. You should camp about 5 miles beyond the village of Machail (18 miles from Gulabgarh) and you will find yourself approaching some grand ibex country. At the head of this Bhutna Nullah the ibex are plentiful and very little shot, and they run to well over 40-inch horns, *if you reach Machail before the end of May.* The Padri Pass should be passable in March, while the Sach Pass is sometimes closed till late in May.

There is a shorter route to Gulabgarh, which will be given later, over the Sach Pass in Chamba, but early in the year this route is impassable. After the middle of June you will have to go very high for your ibex in the Bhutna Valley. In April they come quite close to Machail, and all round the single hut, about 11,000 feet above sea-level.

Having now finished with the Padri Pass, we will make Tissa, one of the largest villages in Chamba, our headquarters and consider the various routes which start from there.

Chamba to—

Musroond, 12 miles. The distance seems very much greater, and coolies take nine hours. There is a small forest bungalow, and the water is indifferent.

Sharoand, 10 miles. You camp on the roof of a disused hut, about 2 miles beyond the forest bungalow. Immediately below this hut there are thar and goural.

Tissa, 9 miles. Here are a post-office and forest bungalow with supplies.

Before discussing Tissa, I must mention a branch route from Sharoand eastwards to Tikri. From the Tikri Nullah several good nullahs branch off. Bagai and Barara and others are all good for thar and goural, and, if you pass over the head of the Tikri Nullah, you can reach good red bear and fair ibex ground. The thar and goural in Tikri are plentiful but do not run very large. The ibex run to 36 in. or 38 in. horns, but I think that a head over 30 in. is good in Chamba and would probably be as old as a 40 in. ibex head in Baltistan.

It is worth while to stop a few days in Tissa to find out what nullahs are occupied, and moreover you are certain to hear of a black bear somewhere down the deep gorge below the village. I shot two there the last time I passed through. The following are the principal shooting routes from Tissa:—

(1). *North*, through Alwas, over Sach Pass into Pangi.

(2). *North*, leave Alwas road and turn north-west, through Suela, over pass to Mahad in Balesh.

(3). *East*, up small nullah good for black bear; otherwise not recommended, as it leads nowhere.

(4). *West*, up Makhan Nullah and over into Balesh.

As No. 1 route is the one with most difficulties

and also most possibilities, I will leave that till last.

No. 4 *Route,* from Tissa to the Makhan Nullah.

Three or four marches from Tissa bring you to the foot of the Makhan Nullah, and you will probably hear of black bears all the way. When the Indian corn is ripe, all the villages on this track are surrounded by black bears, but they seldom appear, except at night. There is generally "Khubbar" (news) of a bear at Sai, five miles out of Tissa, and also at Kail, above Tanail, also in the forests above Jajja.

Makhan Nullah is a good place if you go high enough. There are several rocky, precipitous places where thar feel thoroughly at home, and the grassy slopes at the head of the main nullah must always attract red bear, as may be seen from the marks all over the hill where for years past they have been grubbing up roots. It was here that I saw and lost my first red bear.

Needless to say, it was the biggest that I have ever seen! The ground was covered with great holes, freshly dug, and it was not long before I saw a red monster grubbing away, about 600 yards off. My shikari, Dhassa, and I crawled and crept from one bit of rising ground to another, sometimes having to wriggle through the grass on our stomachs, till at last, when I put my head round a rock, I saw my bear, looking bigger than ever, barely 100 yards off. I watched him for half a minute, trying to recover my breath and steady my hand and then brought up my ·500 Express; I would have done better to have waited five minutes. As I fired behind his near shoulder, he rolled over, and I nearly yelled with delight and rushed after what I thought was his corpse. He rolled about 20 yards down hill, then stopped, got up on his hind legs and stared at me, and was off into the jungle before my shikari could bring me my rifle. Then we had a rare chase through thick scrub jungle, close on the bear's track all the way, till it was dark. All the bushes touched by his *off* shoulder were soaked in blood, so I knew that my bullet must have made a bad hole on the exit side. My shikari and I followed that bear for three days, and then I had to give him up, because I could not track him any further myself, and the shikari refused to proceed. We had put up the bear several times, and he had once or twice growled, and given a short rush at us in the jungle, and then gone off again. Once, on the third day, my shikari was helping me through some thick bushes below some rocks, when suddenly we heard a roar, and were both knocked flat to the ground. The bushes we were struggling through on the tracks of the old bear, hid the entrance to one of his caves. Fortunately he was content with jumping on the top of us and went on without coming back to see how we were. His skin was found by some cattlemen some days after, and was too far gone to cure. I had hit him only three inches too far from the shoulder, and the bullet had made a huge hole on the other side. However, that bear taught me a lot, so I must bear him no grudge.

No. 3 Route from Tissa, due east.—The ground east of Tissa always holds black bear, and occasionally a red bear high up. The shikaris like it, as they are always close to their homes. If your shooting is confined to ten days or a fortnight from Tissa, it is not a bad line to take, as also if you are waiting for the Sach Pass to be open in the spring. I spent a week there and saw several black bears. There are numerous caves in the neighbourhood, so you must kill your bear dead if you want to collect him. I have often tried smoking a bear out of his cave while I sat over it with a rifle and revolver, but never yet succeeded in making one bolt. A friend of mine, who went to Chamba to shoot on my recommendation in 1903, had a shot at a tiger in one of the small nullahs east of Tissa. Unfortunately, he missed. I could scarcely believe him when I heard of it, but have since heard the possibility confirmed by several men. There are supposed to be a few tigers in Jammu (a dependency of Kashmir) also, but they are extremely rare.

Second Route from Tissa, north.—Start on the Sach Pass or Pangi road, looking out for black bear and their marks during the first 4 miles. Some shikaris can track a bear in the fir forests, and the route passes through to the small ravine where he is probably sleeping after his morning meal. "Mullah" is particularly good at tracking. Camp at Baira at the junction of two streams 9 miles from Tissa. There are generally some goural in the vicinity.

Next day leave the Pangi road, about 4 miles from Baira, and climb the mountain ridge on your left for about 3 miles to the village of Suela. This is a stiff climb, and about as much as your coolies can do. In Suela buy as many chickens and eggs as you can, and get a few extra coolies to lighten your loads.

Next day, your third march from Tissa brings you over the Chamba border into Balesh, a part of Badrawar. A camping place will be found about 500 feet below the pass on the Balesh side, where there is a shepherd's hut. The march is a stiff one, 15 miles of climbing over a 12,000 feet pass. It is almost free from snow during June, July and August, but always very cold. Thus, my tent was pitched on edelweiss in July 1899.

Below (after a precipitous descent of 1500 feet), lies the village of Mahad, and beyond that Manoo. Black bear are very numerous down this valley. On your left and westwards across another ridge lies Brabonti, at the head of the Kalgooni Nullah, an excellent place for red bear. I should recommend a descent to Mahad or Manoo after black bear; then a 15-mile march to Brabonti and a halt for red bear. From Brabonti you can work south-west to the Makhan Nullah, and thence back into Chamba, passing through very good thar and red bear country. I saw more of the handsome Manaul and Argus pheasant in this part of the Himalayas than anywhere else.

A large portion of the inhabitants of these parts of Badrawar and Kishtwar are Hindus, who do not keep chickens, so that it is very hard to obtain any eggs. A sheep can be bought for about Rs.3, and it is as well to be on the safe side as regards age, and to buy one with a couple of milk-teeth still showing. When I was in Balesh, in 1899, the shooting was in no way preserved, and there were a good many native shikaris with guns about; but they did very little harm, and seldom bagged more than a small thar, or a black bear in the crops.

Referring to my shooting diary of 1899, I find an account of a good day's sport after red bear from my camp at Brabonti. Although I am trying to confine myself to useful information, and to avoid narrative, I think an account of this day may not be out of place, as it serves to show that stalking and shooting red bear are frequently attended by exciting incidents, and the account may also be of use to the novice in helping him to avoid the mistakes which I made. An extract from my diary will perhaps be the best way of describing the day's work.

August 9th, 1899.—"Long march to Brabonti, about 15 miles. First down to torrent below village of Manoo; then a long stiff climb. Fine day, and very refreshing to get up high again; camp on grassy down, about 12,000 feet. Started at 7.15 A.M. Coolies arrived at 5 P.M. All the black bear are down below round the villages, where the high corn and jungle make it very difficult to get a shot; any amount of them there, though. Here I hope to see a red bear, and have already seen marks of them in the grass.

"Mullah (my shikari) also says this is a good place for thar. Some of the rocky precipices I passed en route certainly look like their favourite ground." . . .

August 12th.—"At last some luck, and a really good day's work. Spent the morning in a world of clouds and could see nothing. Took up position in the afternoon on a rocky spur commanding the grassy slopes where I had seen the bears yesterday. Clouds clear off about 3 o'clock, and soon after two good-sized red bears make their appearance, emerging from a deep narrow ravine. A short and comparatively easy stalk brings us within 150 yards of them, grubbing, nearly hidden, in a patch of their favourite long weeds and grass. Presently I catch sight of the head of one of them, facing me, barely 100 yards off, I fire, and he collapses without a sound, shot straight between the eyes. Up jumps the second and bigger bear on his hind legs to see what has happened, and a too hurried shot, unfortunately through the stomach, drops him. He is up again at once, however, and crashing down the hill with Mullah and me in pursuit. No blood for the first 100 yards, then a few drops, and after a quarter of a mile a great deal. We are soon rushing through very thick jungle of rhododendrons, shrubs, thorns, and thick weeds and grass. After following the blood-stained tracks for half a mile, I now and then catch a glimpse of something moving in the bushes or grass close below me, and I blaze away several times, but my rifle is an encumbrance in such thick undergrowth.

"Once the bear turned on us in some long grass, and was within 5 yards of me before I could see anything to fire at, and then my rifle misfired! (I must own to a suspicion that I fired with my rifle at safety.) The ground was too steep for him to bring home his charge, however, and he turned off down hill again.

"Giving Mullah my rifle, I hurried after him, feeling safer

at such close quarters with my six-chambered revolver. On we went, tearing through the bushes, leaving many bits of hands, face, and clothing behind. Several more snap-shots at moving grass; then a check. As we are searching for the trail again, a bush close below me moves, and, with a roar, out comes the wounded bear, straight for me. There is just time to cock my revolver and fire a couple of shots straight between his eyes at barely 3 yards range. Nothing happens. Stepping quickly to one side as the bear is rising on his hind legs, I kick out as hard as I can with a new pair of heavily nailed shooting boots, and catch him just on the side of the ear. The bear is not very well (we had found a considerable portion of his interior economy a few hundred yards back), and the yells of Mullah, the steepness of the hill, and the unexpected kick on the ear combine to send him down again. On level ground the consequences would doubtless have been different.

"Examining my revolver as soon as I have recovered my wits, the reason of its failure is obvious and most annoying in its simplicity: I had previously fired two shots, and four times, expecting to get a shot, must have cocked it and let the hammer down again when I could not get a fair view of the bear. Each time I did this of course the chamber revolved, and when the bear came for me in earnest, I had come round again to the two used cartridges.

"Still dreading that my quarry will escape me, I continue the exciting chase, plunging through the dense undergrowth, with Mullah following, protesting at a respectful distance, more inclined to thanksgiving for our safety than eager to pursue. It is getting dark now, and the bear, poor beast, is on his last legs and frequently lying down, as is evident from the tracks he leaves. Soon another check, and as I listen, I can hear him breathing heavily in some bushes a few yards off. In the dim light I can just distinguish a brownish lump, but it is useless to fire into that, so I creep round to try to get a shot at some fatal spot. Game to the last, the old bear will stand no liberties, and, as he struggles stiffly to his feet, five yards below me, I send two revolver bullets into him just behind the shoulder."

Thus ended one of the most exciting chases in which I have ever taken part. Full 2 miles we raced down-hill after that bear, close behind him all the way and expecting to be charged from nearly every bush we passed. Had we over-shot the trail, and been charged from above, it would have been long odds on the bear.

These two bears, by the way, were sheep-eaters, and the "gujarlogue," or shepherds, looking after a large flock of sheep not far from my camp, assured me the bears had followed them from one grazing ground to another and were responsible for the loss of at least twenty of their sheep.

The best time of year for this route is either April, May and June, or else September and October. I personally went at the worst time, when there was a deal of rain and mist.

Route No. 1 from Tissa.

Now we come to what I call "No. 1 route from Tissa," that is north, over the Sach Pass into Pangi, and this offers the choice of several good shooting grounds, according to the amount of time available.

In Kilar (four rather long marches from Tissa) the first village reached in Pangi after crossing the Sach Pass (14,000 feet) and Chandra Bagh river, you can get flour, rice, chickens, etc. West lies Kishtwar; north-west, Padar; north, Zaskar, and beyond, Ladakh; north-east, Pangi, generally closed for shooting unless you can get leave from the Rajah of Chamba; south-east, Lahoul.

Route "A" from Kilar.

Time required from Kilar back to Chamba, one month.

Game: red bear, small ibex (up to 35 inches), thar, black bear and goural.

Follow the Chandra Bagh river down stream to Ashdari and cross it there by a rope-bridge into the Dunaitru Nullah. At the mouth of this nullah black bear are to be found in the pine forest, and thar above it. Four miles up the nullah you get clear of the forest and are on excellent red bear ground during May and June, or September and October.

Six miles up the nullah, close below the glacier at the head, there are nearly always ibex; the east side is the better. Crossing the pass at the head of Dunaitru Nullah, turn right-handed, or about north-west, into Gwentred Nullah in Kishtwar. This again is a most excellent nullah for red bear before the cattle are driven into it. The pass is a difficult one, in fact there is no real pass, but it is quite feasible in June or at the latter end of May, and in some years, even earlier. From Gwentred cross an easy pass into Narangwari Nullah, and thence back into Chamba by Suela, or by the Mangli Nullah to Alwas, or by the Makhan Pass.

In Narangwari there are generally red bear, but the cattle get into this nullah rather early. There is plenty of thar ground all along this route, and if you search with your glasses the wildest, rockiest cliffs you pass, you are fairly certain to see some good heads, over 12 inches.

Mangli Nullah is generally closed by the Rajah; but if you can get permission to shoot there, you are sure to find a red bear and some thar. There are a good many musk-deer about but shooting them is prohibited in Chamba, nominally from motives of sport, as they are becoming rather rare. However, I fear there are other motives too, for in the forests about Mangli and other nullahs I have seen that a good deal of systematic trapping goes on, and it is probable that these pretty little deer are a source of revenue either to the State or to some private individual. They have curious tushes from the upper jaw, about 2½ inches long, and I was told that their musk-bags were worth about Rs.25.

Route "B" from Kilar.

Time required from Kilar to Chamba, two months.

Game: ibex; red bear on return through Kishtwar or Chamba State.

From Kilar, march through Darwas and camp at Batwas, beyond the small stream that divides Pangi from Padar. This is a double march, about 16 miles. Gondari Nullah on your right, running north-east, is worth spending a few days in, *early* in the year. One march takes you to the head beyond the village of Sutal. Here the river divides, and the rocky spur in the angle between the two branches is good ground for ibex. During April and May, fairly big ibex come down into the small valley, and their tracks can be seen at any time. The village temple holds some horns over forty that have been shot or picked up by the natives. It was the 10th June when I reached Gondari Nullah, and, though I saw ibex every day on which I went out, the bigger animals had all gone off over the pass towards Zaskar. This pass is open during July, August and September, but nothing would persuade my coolies to cross in June. There are no red bears here.

From Batwas, two marches through Ashdari and Sola will take you to Gulabgarh or Attoli. Thence turn up the Bhutna Nullah, two marches through Machail to a small hut below the Umasi La Pass. Here there are undoubtedly big ibex to be shot, but the sportsman must get at them early in the year and must not be disconcerted by the herds of small ibex and females. A good local shikari lives in Machail. This country is very little shot over, and I am sure that it will repay a visit, especially if there is time to cross the Umasi La (17,300 feet) into Zaskar. Red bears, I fancy, do not remain in this nullah at all, but I was told a very curious tale by Colonel Sullivan, who has travelled and shot through pretty nearly every part of the Himalayas. He was camped above Machail in the Bhutna nullah some years ago, and late one evening he saw a red bear crossing the head of the nullah. It was too late to go after it, so next morning he went to follow the trail in the snow and see where the animal had gone. He soon came across the trail and after a short time found himself on the track, not of one bear, but on a regular beaten road along which any number of bears had been. He followed till dark, without seeing a sign of any animal, and next day sent his shikari to follow the track. The shikari followed for many miles and still the beaten road went on, running nearly due east, but he could see no sign of a bear or any objective. Those bears must have been making for some favourite nullah in Zaskar, probably in the ridge of mountains somewhere due south of Padam, where perhaps they have never yet been disturbed.

The nullah running south-east from Machail contains both ibex and amethysts, and should be worth exploring for either.

Should time permit, a visit into Zaskar should well repay the trouble of crossing the Umasi La Pass. Three marches will carry you over the pass and down to Ating. Thence you can reach Suru: Suru used, fifteen years ago, to be one of the best nullahs in Kashmir for ibex, but now a 40-inch head is exceptional, well known for ibex, in five marches, crossing the Pense La Pass and halting your third day at Ringdum, famous for its monastery. Colonel Ward, in his excellent "Sportsman's Guide to Kashmir," recommends the ground in the neighbourhood of the Pense

CHAMBA, ZANSKAR & RUPSHU ROUTE MAP.

La Pass as likely to hold big ibex. From Suru you can reach Srinagar either by the Wardwan, or by Dras over the Zoji La Pass and down the Scinde Valley.

From Ating a road runs through Padam into Ladakh, cutting the Leh road and passes good ibex and burhel ground. Another road runs south-east from Padam into Rupshu and Lahoul, meeting the road from the Kukti Pass (in Barmoar) to Leh.

Rupshu is the highest inhabited country in the world, and villages of sorts are found at an elevation of 15,000 feet.

I have mentioned the different routes through Zaskar and Rupshu because I am convinced that the sportsman of adventurous disposition, who does not mind "roughing it," will, with four months' leave, or even less, obtain better and more interesting sport in that direction than by keeping to the beaten track through Srinagar and Kashmir. I would, however, hesitate to recommend anyone to make, as his first attempt at a Himalayan expedition, a march through Chamba, Barmoar, Lahoul, Rupshu and into Thibet.

Route "C" from Kilar.

The third route from Kilar in Pangi runs south-south-east, up the Chandra Bagh river into Lahoul (Kulang). I have not been this way, but the mountains on the south bank of the river are sure to hold fair-sized ibex and red bear. Above Triloknath, five marches from Kilar and one from the Kukti Pass, was recommended to me as good ground by Bhurie Singh the brother of the Rajah of Chamba. Snow-leopards are supposed to be fairly numerous about there. This country can also be reached by the Tikri Nullah (on the Chamba-Tissa road), and a track leads up the Tikri Nullah to Tindi on the Pangi-Lahoul road. There are still numbers of both thar and goural in the Tikri Nullah, but good heads are scarce, and the nullah is rather shot out. I have seen a 38-inch single-horned ibex that was shot up above the nullah on the east side, I fancy, while working towards Triloknath.

Before closing my hints on shooting in and beyond Chamba, I will give a few extracts from my shooting diary of 1900, in which year I made my shortest; and perhaps most enjoyable, trip into the Himalayas. These notes may be useful and possibly of interest to the many sportsmen in India who cannot get more than two months' leave and who wish in that short time to get off the beaten track, without incurring any appreciable increase on their ordinary monthly expenses in the plains of India.

I left the Punjab for Dalhousie on April 14th, 1900, intending to march through Barmoar, over the Kukti Pass into Lahoul and on to the Tso Morari Lake and the Thibetan border about Lanak and Hanle. I calculated that I could reach the Tso Morari salt lake in twenty marches and that with three months' leave, I should get at any rate a month's shooting. However, I had to give up the project as I was laid up in Dalhousie for five weeks with water on the knee, a polo ball, driven hard between my knee and the saddle, being the cause of the mischief. Only seven weeks of my leave remained, so I mapped out my tour as follows, working on information picked up during two previous expeditions in and about Chamba :—

(1) March from Dalhousie through Chamba, Tissa and Alwas, over the Sach Pass seven marches, and try for an ibex or a bear in Danai Nullah across pass.

(2) March through Kilar, capital of Pangi, into Padar and try to get over the head of the Gondari Nullah into Zaskar, three marches to Batwas.

(3) Should that pass be impracticable, return and cross Chandra Bagh river at Ashdari and work up Dunaitru Nullah, three marches to the head.

(4) Return to Chamba viâ the Gwentred, Narangwari, and Mangli Nullas, ten marches to Chamba town.

I contrived to adhere to this programme, nor had I any cause to be disappointed. I stopped three days in Tissa, as I heard pretty reliable "Khubbar" of black bears in the nullah, and I was rewarded with two. The first fell to a single shot from my ·303 at 250 yards, rolled down 300 feet into the river, and was picked up with skin undamaged nearly a mile below. After having shot her, I was sorry to see two small cubs, barely a fortnight old, appear. However, I managed to catch them in a blanket, and one of them, after killing his brother, became quite tame and a most amusing pet.

On the 31st I made as early a start as possible and reached the summit of the pass about 10 A.M. after a climb of nearly 4000 feet over 6 miles of hard frozen snow. It was a trying climb, as there was no track to follow, and the most bitter wind blew in my face nearly all the time, carrying with it the cold of all the glaciers above. In spite of the freezing wind which cut through any description of clothes, I had to wear a big hat before reaching the top, such was the power of the sun. My shikari and servant were both incapacitated by mountain sickness on reaching the pass, and several coolies were much affected by the rarefied air. Personally I have never suffered from either up to 18,000 feet, so long as I have refrained from smoking.

Nine miles down a gorge blocked with snow, sometimes hundreds of feet deep, brought me to a ledge of rock wide enough on which to pitch a tent, and a rough stone hovel for my coolies. There I lay down and slept till the coolies arrived after twelve hours' marching.

In this nullah, called Danai, I shot a good ibex and a red bear leaving two three-year-old cubs behind. The ibex was a very old fellow, nearly white. His horns measured 35 inches and were 12 inches in circumference. That is about the maximum for these Chamba ibex, but their horns are massive and make better trophies than their length would lead one to expect. I saw five red bears altogether in this nullah, in addition to the two cubs. The climbing is very difficult everywhere, far worse indeed than any in Kashmir.

On June 9th I crossed the Chandra Bagh river at the foot of the nullah and marched through Kilar to the small village of Gistrie. Next day on to Batwas at the foot of the Gondari Nullah. After failing to get over the pass beyond Butal, at the head of the valley, and seeing nothing but small ibex, I marched down to Ashdari on the 13th June. Shot some excellent snow-pigeon en route, which were very acceptable, as chickens are rare about Padar. They can, however, be got from Kilar and Gulabgarh.

Diary, June 14th, 1900. *Ashdari Camp.*—"Fresh snow all round on hills, and very cold. March down through Tiari across river Chandra Bagh, and climb up part of the way into Dunaitru Nullah. A very hard march; coolies have all got light loads, but I don't know how they managed it. Crossed the Chandra Bagh by a swinging rope-bridge of twisted birch, about 80 yards wide; very seldom used and consequently the side ropes were nearly level with one's feet in the centre. Then we crawled along the side of a precipice for some miles, sometimes along a ledge on the side of a rock not 3 inches wide. Then across a miniature Niagara by a rotten greasy tree, blinded, as we went, by spray. Lastly, a stiff climb through pine trees till a level spot could be found. Pitched my tent at 7.15 P.M., and got an excellent dinner about eight o'clock, of roasted snow-pigeons and stewed wild rhubarb.

"*15th June.*—March up nullah about 6 miles and crossed a lot of marks of thar; saw one quite close, but not more than 7-inch horns, so I spare him, as my larder is well stocked. Villagers at Tiari say no white man has been in this nullah for five years and that natives never come.

"*16th June.*—Very cold night, and fresh snow all round above me. Am woke in the morning with the glad news that a huge red bear is close to my tent! Looking out I see him, digging up roots among some small bushes on the opposite side of the nullah, barely 600 yards off. With Bhagia, my shikari, I soon slipped down the side of the hill to the hard, frozen snow in the bed of the nullah and tried to stalk round and above the bear. Can see no sign of him, however, and my Tiffin coolie, whom we had left to watch near my tent, signals that he has gone into some bushes in a small rocky ravine, having evidently finished his morning meal. Return to tent and have the place watched. At 2 P.M. I cross the nullah again and take up a position to wait for him, hoping he will emerge for his evening feed. It is nearly 5 P.M. before I hear or see anything. Then I distinctly hear something moving in the bushes below me. I creep slowly down to a better position, and sit with my rifle ready on my knees. It was then that I discovered that I had none of my "bear bullets" with me and my cartridge bag only contained the flat-headed split bullets which I used for thar and goural.

Presently the bear emerges, and a magnificent fellow he is. As he unconcernedly walks straight towards me, barely 60 yards off, his huge head presents a good mark, and I take a careful aim between his eyes. He collapses at once with his head on his paws. As I stand up to empty my rifle and admire his corpse, however, he comes to life again and proceeds to walk away, somewhat bewildered. I get a nice broadside shot at his shoulder, the effect of which is instantaneous. It brings him to his senses at once, and seeing me for the first time and realising the cause of his annoyance, he turns and comes for me. My third shot hits him in the head again at barely 20 yards, and, as he tracks to gain cover from a bush, a fourth shot sends him crashing down the hill. Two more shots as I follow him through the bushes; and a final one from my revolver before he is dead. He is a very fine specimen of a red bear, his skin measuring 6 feet 10 inches from nose to tail and over 5 feet in width; and he had two bullet-holes close to his eye, one below the ear and three through the body. My first shot would have settled him, I am sure, had I been using my solid lead bullets."

I shot another good red bear and two ibex with poor horns in Dunaitru Nullah, leaving behind at any rate two small red bear, besides the thar and black bear lower down the nullah, and a good many ibex near the head.

On June 25th I crossed over the head close under the western peak of the Sach Pass, then bore half-right, or about west, down into Gwentred Nullah. Started at 5.30 A.M. and reached camping ground at 7 P.M. This march was one of the hardest I have done. As a matter of fact, I don't believe Bhagia took the right way, if there was a right way. The expanse of snow at the head of the nullah was tremendous. All the ravines and gorges between the peaks of the mountains were here levelled up to rolling downs or plateaux of snow and ice. My way of descent into Gwentred was distinctly dangerous and nearly cost the lives of Bhagia and myself, and still nearer the life of one of the coolies; the latter slipped down a frozen "shute," which we had to descend, and was brought to a stand-still only by a ledge of soft snow at the foot, overhanging a precipice of 500 feet. We had to be continually cutting steps, easy work going uphill, but disagreeable when going down an almost perpendicular "shute." Had we worked rather more north of west when we reached the snow plateau, I am sure we should have found a better way down the main line of Gwentred Nullah on our right. Without my heavy nailed shooting boots, I don't think I could have made the descent; the heels gave one a good grip where the ice axe had broken the frozen surface of the snow.

On my first morning in Gwentred Nullah I saw a sight worth going many hundred miles to see. After a long and well-earned sleep, I strolled at about 8 A.M. out of my tent to some rising ground on my right. Looking down the nullah and searching the series of grassy ridges below me with my field-glasses, I made out no less than five red bears! My stalk failed that day, as the bears winded me before I was within a mile of them; but in the next three days I shot the two best of them, could not find the third, and spared the other two as they were not full-grown. Anyone who can get into Gwentred Nullah before the cattle are driven high up, will, I am convinced, always find red bears there. It ought also to be a good place in the autumn, as soon as the sheep and buffaloes have left. Looking at my diary again, I find a curious instance of a bear coming very near to charging without any apparent reason. I was wearing a reddish-brown thick Norfolk jacket, and my belief is that the bear must have mistaken me for another of his own species perhaps trespassing on his preserves. When he discovered his mistake, his look of astonishment was almost amusing.

Diary, June 28th. Gwentred.—"Started at 5 A.M. to look for the bear I had marked down feeding about 4 miles off last night. When crossing a steep slope, covered with fir trees and jungle about 1½ miles from my tent, I suddenly heard a noise above me, and saw a good red bear crashing down full tilt at me; my rifle was in its case and before I could get it out the bear came to a stop 5 yards above me; a coolie was behind me and at this moment gave such a piercing shriek that the bear turned aside and rushed down into the jungle below me. It was useless to follow him, so I hurried on at top speed. It was 7.45 A.M. before I managed to climb above the place where I had seen the bear feeding last night, but he was there again, still grubbing up great patches in the grass. The ground was very open, but after a long crawl I gained a dip in the side of the hill and, following that, I crept up the far side and found myself level with the bear and about a hundred yards off. In the course of his digging he soon turned about three-quarters broadside on, tail nearest to me; I could not have posed him better for a fatal shot behind the shoulder. He rolled down 100 yards and was dead when I reached him. He was a very old bear with a dark coat, not "café au lait" like the Dunaitru bears, and measured 6 feet."

From Gwentred I crossed into Narangwari, an easy pass, and spent a few days there, but I was too late, and the place was full of "Gujar logue" and their sheep and cattle. From Narangwari I marched over the pass into Chamba above Mangli Nullah, but I had not got permission to shoot in it. Camped at Mansu, below Alwas. Spent a few days at Sai, and then near Tissa after black bear and reached Chamba village on July 9th, exactly seven weeks after leaving it.

Several of the instances here quoted may lead the reader to think that red bear will always charge. This is not by any means the case, and a charge is distinctly the exception; but it is advisable to be very careful when following a wounded bear, black or red, that you have the hill in your favour. With all dangerous animals the second shot is the one to beware of. It is the second shot that rouses the latent fury of the wounded tiger, that puts method and object into the madness of the charging bison, and that awakes the sleepy bear. It is the second spear in the wounded boar that means a certain charge to be held off; death to the bravest of animals if the spear be held true and the steed be staunch; otherwise, a bad look-out for horse and man, and victory to the mighty boar.

To return to the Himalayas, I will conclude my notes on Chamba shooting with a list of animals obtainable, a few routes by which they are to be found, and the time required to reach them.

Game to be found within the limits of Chamba State: thar, goural, serow, khakur, musk deer, bara singh (October to March), red and black bear.

Ibex, on the north-eastern borders, generally over the border.

Ovis ammon, sharpu, burhel, Thibetan gazelle and kiang, will be found in Rupshu.

Black Bear.—These are very common throughout Chamba, and are always to be found in the pine forests and rocky ravines within easy reach of a village. When the crops, or the walnuts, apples or apricots are ripe, the black bear will come down to them every night, in spite of all the villagers can do to frighten them away. A few outlying walnut or apricot trees, or an Indian cornfield a short distance from the village, will generally attract a black bear just before dusk; or they can be stalked by moonlight in the crops. Perhaps the best localities are north, north-west, east of Tissa, and on the Barmoar road. They afford the best sport in early spring when they may be stalked in the open. In Kashmir they are generally driven, which is not good sport. Large bags of black bears are sometimes made in Chamba, Poonch and other native states by driving the poor beasts backwards and forwards under machans. They occasionally kill cows and natives, generally, I fancy, when they happen to find them in their path when approaching their feeding-ground in the evening, or leaving it in the early morning. I shot a very old black bear on the Tissa-Makhan road one year, as he was approaching the remains of a cow he had killed when leaving the crops early that morning. The villagers were very delighted at his death, as they declared that he had killed a man about the same place a fortnight before and had been responsible for a good many deaths during the last three years.

Red Bear.—There are perhaps more red bear in the neighbourhood of Chamba State than in any other part of the Himalayas, within shooting limits. They offer, in my opinion, very enjoyable shooting. Though somewhat blind and deaf, they have wonderful noses and, as they are to be found right out in the open, they nearly always require careful stalking from a considerable distance; they offer a big target, it is true, but require very straight shooting, for, no matter what your rifle may be, your red bear must be hit in the right place, or you will lose him. Their pursuit combines most of the essential characteristics of sport: good stalking, straight and careful shooting, an element of danger, and a perfect climate, just below the snow-line. Like many other animals, the red bear cannot resist grubbing in the young grass in the early spring, soon after the snow has left the downs free. You must look for him close below the snow-line till July. Then, anywhere high up, where he will not be worried by sheep and goats; unless you hear of a "sheep-eater," who will follow the flocks from one grazing ground to another. As soon as the sheep begin to graze lower down nearer the villages in October and November, the downs that they have left will again attract the red bears till they retire for a three months' sleep during December, January and February.

The best places that I know for red bear are the nullahs across the north-western border of Chamba, between Sach Pass and Padri Pass. In particular, the Sach Nullah, Dunaitru in Padar, and Gwentred, Narangwari and Brabonti in Balesh. Also over the Padri Pass and in Kishtwar. A trip lasting from six weeks to two months should suffice to obtain good sport. When over the Padri Pass, a Kashmir license is required.

Bara Singh.—The red deer of the Himalayas is gradually working further east, and may perhaps soon penetrate well into Chamba territory. At present, he is only to be found from October to March on the borders of Chamba and Kishtwar. Reaching the Padri Pass, or the head of the Makhan Nullah, towards the end of September, you are sure to see some bara singh, but cannot be certain of a good head unless you are prepared to shoot over the Kashmir border. September 20th to October 20th would generally bc the best time, for in the Himalayas you shoot them when they are roaring.

Thar and *goural* are very plentiful throughout Chamba. A good thar stands about 9 hands, and a good head measures from 12 to 14½ inches, and 8 to 10 inches in circumference at the base. When well set up, with the neck skin cut off long, he makes, with his massive horns and long shaggy beard or mane, a handsome trophy.

The Tikri and Makhan Nullahs, all the precipices between Chamba and Balesh, and several nullahs on the Barmoar road are the best I know. Thar-stalking is no child's play, and, for difficult and dangerous climbing, compares very favourably with the pursuit of ibex and markhor, though carried on at lower elevations. The Chamba shikaris, however, are wonderfully good at helping you over bad ground, infinitely better than any I have met or heard of in Kashmir. I have frequently had to walk along the side of a precipice with nothing to step on but my shikari's hands and head. How he was supported I do not know; probably he had a toe stuck in some crevice in the rock. Dhassa, shikari of Tissa, is the best climber and the best help I know. Goural afford pretty shooting. Sharoand, between Chamba and Tissa, is a certain find; above Tissa there are always goural; also in the Tikri Nullah and Baira Nullah, east of the Alwas road. A good head is only from 6 to 7½ inches. A fortnight or a month is sufficient to secure some heads.

Ibex.—Chamba is not the country for really big ibex, over 40 inches. Some fair heads, however, may be got round about the borders, and the sport can be combined with other shooting. I should recommend the mountains north-west of the Kukti Pass. I believe there is a road and a pass leading from Barmoar to Triloknath. The Mian Sahib, Bhurie Singh, who, as I have said before, is always ready to help sportsmen, would give information on this point. The ridge running north-east and south-west between the Sach Nullah and Dunaitru Nullah always holds ibex up to 35 inches. Two months should be ample for either of these trips. With three months to spare you should be able to get some really good heads by going up the Bhutna Nullah in Padar. Cross the Umasi La and turn north-west from Ating over the Pense La Pass to Ringdum Monastery in Suru, about eight marches from Gulabgarh. This route takes you through some very little exploited country, and there is shooting of sorts most of the way from Tissa.

In March and April the ibex come low down the mountains after the young grass, but after that the big heads will keep by themselves as high up as they can. Because you only see herds of small males and females low down, you must not presume that there are no big heads, but must climb up till you can climb no higher.

There are ibex in Pangi, but it has always been closed for shooting when I have been through it.

Ovis ammon, burhel and Thibetan gazelle.— Ovis ammon are not inhabitants of Chamba or its immediate neighbourhood, but they can be reached almost as easily from Chamba as from Srinagar, by a far less exploited route. Through Barmoar and Lahoul into Rupshu, Rukchen can be reached in fifteen marches, and from Rukchen to Leh (six marches) you pass through good Ovis ammon country about Gya, also good country for burhel. The only advantage of the Kashmir route is that supplies are plentiful and you can make long marches.

With three and a half to four months available, a very interesting trip could be made by working east from the Kukti Pass to the Tso Morari Lake, twelve marches; then north through Rukchen to Leh, twelve marches; Leh through Zaskar viâ Wanla and Padam to Gulabgarh, twenty marches; and thence to Srinagar, thirteen marches, or Chamba, ten marches. From the time of leaving the Kukti Pass to the time of arrival at the Umasi La Pass, you would be travelling through country well stocked with game, and rarely disturbed by Europeans. Your bag should, with luck, include thar, black bear, ibex, Thibetan gazelle, *ovis ammon*, burhel, kiang (wild ass), *ovis vignei*, or sharpu, and red bear, the game being here enumerated in the order in which it would be encountered.

List of a few Routes from Chamba.

ROUTE NO. I.

Chamba to Leh, viâ Barmoar, Lahoul and Rupshu.

1-5. Chamba to *Barmoar*, five marches. Villages all the way; sheep, chickens and eggs, rice and atta. Black bear, goural and thar after third march.

6-8. Over Kukti Pass to *Kailang*, three marches. Pass is generally open in May. Beyond this, supplies very uncertain up to Gya. Advisable to take food for servants, also your own rice, flour, eggs, chickens and sheep.

9. *Kailang*.

10. *Darcha*. Small village, a few supplies.

11. *Zingzingbir.* Camp at foot of Baralacha Pass.

12. *Surchu.* Cross Baralacha Pass, 16,000 feet.

13. *Camp.* At foot of Lachalang Pass.

14. *Camp.* On far side of pass, 16,300 feet.

15. *Rukchen.* Tartar village.

16. *Debring.* Camp at foot of Tagalang Pass.

17. *Gya.* Cross Tagalang Pass, 17,000 feet. Supplies and sometimes yak transport can be got here. Good ovis ammon and burhel country.

18. *Upshi.*

19. *Marshalong.*

20. *Shushoti.*

21. *Leh.* Supplies and stores; capital of Ladah. Dâk bungalow.

NOTE.—There are cross routes from Surchu and Darcha through Serle and Reroo to Padam, all six marches. Leh to Srinagar is eighteen marches.

ROUTE NO. II.

Kailang to Kilar.

Chamba to Kailang, eight marches. From Kailang a track runs north-west down the river Chandra Bagh through Triloknath, Tindi and Sanch to Kilar in Pangi, six marches.

Supplies *en route,* and nullahs on left bank hold ibex and snow-leopard.

ROUTE NO. III.

Chamba to Tso Morari Lake and Hanle.

1-8. Chamba to Kailang, eight marches.

9. Kailang to *Gandla.*

10. *Sisu.*

11. *Koksen.* Here the main track leads to Sultanpur in Kulu; leave this and turn south east to Shigri, then north over Kulzum Pass to Losar; the track then runs east for two marches, then north-east over the Parangla Pass 18,000. Thence two marches take you to the south of the Tso Morari Lake and two more on to Hanle, over the Lanak Pass. In all, about fourteen marches from Kailang. From Hanle a track runs to Rukchen eight marches.

ROUTE NO. IV.

Chamba to Padam in Zaskar.

1. *Chamba* to *Musroond,* 12 miles, bad road. Rice, flour and potatoes should be taken from Chamba as elsewhere they are indifferent. Eggs and chickens can be obtained as far as Kilar. There is a forest hut at Musroond, but a tent is preferable. Water indifferent.

2. *Sharoand,* 10 miles. There is a fair Forest Department hut 2 miles short of this, but if you camp on the roof of a disused hut at Sharoand, you will find thar and goural immediately below you.

3. *Tissa,* 9 miles. Large village; supplies; clean bungalow; good coolies.

4. *Baira,* 6 miles. Goural plentiful; ponies cannot go beyond this.

5. *Alwas,* 6 miles. Forest bungalow. Take eggs, chickens, etc., to last till Kilar.

6. *Camp*, 7 miles. To foot of Sach Pass.

7. *Camp*, 15 miles. To Dunai; a Dâk-runner's shelter. Nearly all over snow in May. Cross Sach Pass 14,000 into good ground for ibex, and lower down for red bear.

8. *Kilar*, 12 miles. Chief village of Pangi; supplies and post-office.

9. *Darwas*, 6 miles. Small village.

10. *Batwas*, 8 miles. Cross boundary into Pader; small village at mouth of Gondari Nullah (ibex).

11. *Ashdari*, 6 miles.

12. *Ghulabgarh*, 12 miles. Post-office and supplies. There is a route to Kishtwar, four long marches.

13. *Chishoti*, 12 miles. Turn north-east up Bhutna river.

14. *Machail*, 6 miles. Small village.

15. *Camp*, 6 miles. To a single hut. Ibex ground.

16. *Camp*, 10 miles. To foot of Umasi La Pass.

17. *Camp*, 14 miles. Over pass, 17,400, nearly all snow and ice.

18. *Ating*, 10 miles. Small village.

19. *Padam*, 12 miles. Chief village of Zaskar.

Padam to Lamayuru, on Kashmir-Leh road, ten marches. Ating to Suru six marches, over Pense La Pass 14,000. Good ibex ground. Umasi La should be open by end of May or early in June.

ROUTE NO. V.

Chamba to Srinagar, Kashmir.

1. Chamba to *Manjira*, 14 miles. Hard march.
2. *Bhandal*, 14 miles.
3. *Langera*, 14 miles. Foot of Padri Pass.
4. *Thanala*, 17 miles. Over the pass, hard march.
5. *Badrawar*, 8 miles. Large village.
6. *Jaora*, 17 miles.
7. *Jangaiwar*, 14 miles.
8. *Kanani*, 15 miles.
9. *Kishtwar*, 10 miles. Supplies and post-office, etc.

A route runs to Ghulabgarh from Kishtwar (see Route IV.). By this route over the Padri Pass Gulabgarh may be reached early in the year when the Sach Pass is blocked.

10. *Mughal Maidan*, 10 miles.
11. *Chingham*, 12 miles.
12. *Sintham*, 7 miles. Over pass, 12,000 feet.
13. *Nowboog*, 12 miles.
14. *Islamabad*, 15 miles.
15. *Srinagar*, two days by boat.

There is a shorter route from Badrawar to Islamabad through Batoti, but it is not so good for red bear.

Supplies may be had everywhere, and ponies can be taken all the way.

KASHMIR SHOOTING

I.—ROUTES, SERVANTS AND OUTFIT

SHOOTING in Kashmir, with Srinagar as a starting point, differs in many details from the sport above described in Chamba. The lovely valley of Kashmir attracts every year a large number of visitors and "globe-trotters," who live either in one of the two hotels at Srinagar, and during the hotter months at Gulmarg in house-boats, or in tents in some of the beautiful nullahs and valleys that run from the main valley into the encircling chain of mountains. Sportsmen from India, and a considerable number from England, America, and even Germany, France and Russia, are to be met throughout the summer months, going to and returning from Kashmir by the Rawal Pindi-Srinagar road. All this, as may be expected, adds considerably to the expenses of a Kashmir shooting trip, and also means that the game, at any rate with trophies worth having, is being driven further and further away. The thanks of every sportsman are due to Colonel Ward, by whose endeavours game laws were introduced not long ago in time to preserve sport in Kashmir for many years to come.

There are three principal routes into Kashmir: viâ., Rawal Pindi and Murree, by tonga all the way; viâ Hussan Abdal (a few stations beyond Rawal Pindi on the North-Western Railway) and Abbotabad to Mansera, by tonga and thence by road, marching or riding, to Domel on the Murree-Srinagar road; lastly, from Gujerat station to Bhimber by "Gharry," thence marching over the Pir Panjal, twelve marches through fine scenery, to Srinagar. Should the Pir Panjal Pass be closed by snow, which is generally the case from October 15th to May 15th, a track turns off westward from Thanna Mandi (five marches from Bhimber) and takes you to Uri on the Srinagar-Murree road, in seven marches. There is also a fourth route through Jammu, but it is private, and permission is not often given by the Maharajah.

For shooting purposes in Kashmir the Murree route is the best, as, by tonga from Rawal Pindi, you can reach Srinagar in two days. I should only recommend the Abbotabad route to those who have travelled in the Himalayas before and wish to go direct to Chilas for markhor.

If travelling by the Murree route, my advice is to take as little luggage as possible. The quickest and least expensive way to reach Srinagar is to take a seat in the mail tonga and send your servant (if you are bringing one) with the remainder of your luggage in an eckka. A seat in the mail tonga takes you to Srinagar in thirty-six hours for Rs.43, and you can generally take with you a bedding valise, kit-bag, lunch basket, and gun and rifle. An eckka costs about Rs.25, including tolls, and can do the journey, 196 miles, in four and a half days easily. The only other luggage I should recommend is your own camp-bed and chair, cooking pots and plates, etc. Another kit-bag holds your shooting kit, warm Norfolk jacket and waistcoat, putties and nailed shooting boots. A cook can be obtained in Srinagar, but the best plan is to take your own kitmatghar (having tested his cooking beforehand), sending him three days ahead with your luggage.

The Punjaub mail train lands you at Rawal Pindi at 8 P.M., and after having dinner at the station, you must prepare for a cold night journey to Murree in the mail tonga. A more comfortable way is to travel early next morning to Murree only, in the Murree mail tonga, and go on by the Srinagar tonga about 5 A.M. the next day. The journey is pretty, and, if not pressed for time, it is well worth while to take three or four days over it and enjoy the lovely scenery. The road first climbs up to Murree, a distance of 36 miles, nearly 7000 ft. above the sea. The Chambers Hotel is the nearest to the tonga terminus.

From Murree the stages are as follows :—

1. *Murree to Kohala*, 29 miles. A drop of 4000 feet; Dâk bungalow with no particular recommendations.

2. *Kohala to Dulai*, 10 miles. From Kohala the road keeps fairly level all the way to Srinagar. At Dulai there is a pretty little bungalow.

3. *Dulai to Domel,* 10 miles. A good bungalow. The river Jhelum bends to the right, nearly due east and the Kishengunga joins it from the north. The road from Abbotabad joins the Murree road here.

4. *Domel to Garhi,* 13 miles. Another good bungalow but not so well situated as Domel. The scenery is very beautiful all along this part of the road.

5. *Garhi to Chakoti,* 20 miles. A most wretched bungalow, to be avoided if possible.

6. *Chakoti to Uri,* 14 miles. Perhaps the best bungalow on the road. Scenery lovely and bold. The Kajinag range of mountains can be reached from Uri, and holds plenty of markhor. The shooting was closed for several years, but was re-opened in 1903, and several good heads were shot during that year. The road to Poonch and the Pir Panjal runs eastwards close to Uri.

7. *Uri to Rampur,* 13 miles.

8. *Rampur to Baramulla,* 15 miles. Baramulla is a large native village in the valley of Kashmir. The Dâk bungalow is a large one and, with the exception of that at Chakoti, the worst on the road.

9. *Baramulla to Srinagar,* 30 miles. The journey may be done by boat in two days, or by road in four hours. There is a good hotel at Srinagar, with plenty of accommodation, open throughout the year. The mail tonga from Rawal Pindi, if you do not halt *en route* and wait for the next tonga to pass, will land you

at Baramulla at about twelve midnight, or twenty-five hours after leaving Pindi. There you will get about six hours' rest and reach Srinagar about eleven the next morning. The tonga can be stopped at any of the stages *en route* where you wish to have a meal.

Arrived at Srinagar, you must immediately procure your license and shikari, camp kit, and stores. A license may be obtained either from Major Wigram, Secretary of the Kashmir Game Preservation Department, or from Cockburn's Kashmir Agency. A summer license is valid from March 15th to November 15th and costs Rs.60. It permits you to shoot the following:—

Markhor . .	2	Thibetan gazelle	1	**License No. I.**
Ibex . . .	6	Kashmir stag .	2	
Ovis hodgsoni (ammon) . .	1	Serow . .	1	
Ovis vignei (sharpu)	2	Red bear . .	4	
Ovis nahura (burhel)	6	Thar . . .	6	
Thibetan antelope	6	Goural . .	6	

Black bears, leopards and pigs without limit; chikor, partridges, pheasants and wild fowl between September 15th and November 15th.

A certain number of nullahs are closed from year to year and are mentioned on the license.

A license value Rs.20 permits the holder **No. II.** to shoot black bears, leopards and pig from March 15th to November 15th.

A winter license, for which Rs.30 will be **No. III.**

charged, in force from November 15th to March 15th, will permit the holder to shoot—

Markhor . .	2	Kashmir stag .	1
Ibex . . .	3	Serow . .	1
Ovis vignei (sharpu)	2	Thar . . .	3
Ovis nahura (burhel)	3	Red bear . .	2
Thibetan antelope	3	Goural . .	3
Thibetan gazelle	1		

as well as pig, black bear and leopards without limit.

A small game license, for which Rs.20 will be charged, permits the holder to kill pheasants, partridges and chikor from September 16th to the last day of February, and also geese, duck and teal from September 16th to April 14th, snipe from September 1st to April 14th.

Rule No. 5 prohibits the shooting or killing of yak and musk deer in Kashmir territory.

For any further information application should be made to the Secretary of the Kashmir Game Preservation Department, Srinagar. At present Major Wigram is the Secretary (1904).

No shikari may take employment without a license from the secretary. Unless you can engage a good man on the recommendation of a friend before arriving at Srinagar, it is best to apply to the secretary, or to get one through Cockburn's Agency, mentioning the part of Kashmir you wish to shoot in. It is always an advantage to have a man who knows the country well. The wages of a good shikari range from Rs.25 to Rs.30 a month, in addition to which they demand, and get, Rs.5 to Rs.6 a month for "Rassad," or food money. A "second shikari" is quite unnecessary and perfectly useless; a local man at eight annas a day can always be engaged from the village nearest to your shooting-ground. He is supposed to possess the latest information regarding the game, and to know all the tracks by which it can be approached. A "tiffin coolie," with wages of Rs.10 a month, is a useful person; he carries your lunch basket on the march and out shooting, and makes himself useful in camp and in your tent. It is as well to have three or four permanent coolies also, at Rs.6 a month and Rs.2/8 Rassad. They will carry loads when on the march, and in camp you require one to help in the kitchen, one to fetch wood and water, one to bring eggs, chickens, and milk from neighbouring villages, and one to send occasionally to the nearest post-office. Your shikari will get all these for you.

When going any distance, it is advisable to give all your permanent employés a pair of "chaplies" or sandals and a warm blanket or coat to your cook, shikari, and tiffin coolie. These are not necessaries, but it is as well to give in so far to their demands and no further. I do not propose to give a list of shikaris. A good deal may be gathered from their "chits," or recommendations, especially as to what line of country they may be trusted to know; but a shikari, who will serve one master well, will take but little trouble with another. The best are always keen on getting a good bag and thereby adding to their prestige; the men I have usually employed, Azizza and Akloo, two brothers who live near Bandipur, have a large pile of excellent recommendations, and I do not consider that these do either of them more than justice. The majority, however, are getting very much spoilt and require to be held firmly in hand; they are apt to look on the "Sahib" as a means of making money for themselves and their hangers-on, and the instrument by which a shot has to be fired when the moment is considered propitious by the shikari. The Chamba shikari, at half the wages, is a better man. The coolies are fine men, but terribly lazy and not to be compared with the Chamba men.

Everything required in the way of provisions, such as butter, jam, tea, cocoa, soup, biscuits and salt, candles, oil, and matches can be obtained at Pestonjee's shop or from several other merchants. Two or three leather kiltas or a couple of yakdans will hold two months' supplies. In most villages you can obtain eggs, chickens, milk, and sometimes rice, flour and oil. It is as well to carry a "reserve ration" of flour, milk and meat, to be returned to the shop if not required. It is generally necessary to carry rice for your servants, as large quantities can be obtained only here and there. This is the case in Ladakh, Baltistan and Chilas.

A Typical Kashmir Camp: in the Scinde Valley

All camp kit, including your own tent, two servants' tents, furniture and cooking-pots, can be hired from Cockburn's Agency. Tent hire costs from Rs. 3 to Rs. 10 a month. My advice, however, is to bring your own camp-bed and chair, if they be of a strong and serviceable pattern, and also a set of aluminium cooking-pots.

A couple of pairs of leather chaplies, or sandals, with leather socks, will be found very light and comfortable for marching. They are, however, useless in the wet or over rocks. The Kashmir grass shoes are the only safe means of climbing in the rocky country frequented by ibex and markhor. They are made up by your coolies as wanted, but a supply of the special grass required for them must be carried with you. One pony load should be sufficient for three months. As a strand of the twisted grass has to pass between your big and second toes, you must have about six pairs of woollen grass shoe socks, and three pair of quilted cloth boots. These socks and boots are made with big toe compartments, and the grass sandal is bound on tightly over the quilted puttoo boot. They can be obtained from any of the Srinagar merchants. The result may be clumsy to look at, but they afford such a firm foothold on slippery, sloping rocks, that you feel you could climb the side of a house in them. Another pattern[1] consists of a canvas boot with

[1] Major Wigram's invention, I believe.

holes round the projecting edge of the sole; the grass sandal is fastened to the sole and the necessity for special socks is done away with. They are less clumsy, but not quite so secure as the ordinary kind.

For going up into the snow early in the year, you will require several pairs of warm gloves, and a "poshteen," or long coat lined with sheep-skin, is a great comfort. A Srinagar "dersi," or tailor, will make you, from a pattern, a suit of warm puttoo (Norfolk jacket and breeches) for about Rs.7. A couple of pairs of putties, a pair of strong, nailed shooting boots, and a khud stick will complete your kit. All except the boots can be obtained in Srinagar at two or three days' notice.

II.—SHOOTING ROUTES AND VARIOUS GAME

THE various shooting routes in Kashmir are nearly all well known and much travelled, and shooting of every description lies in far more beaten tracks than in other parts of the Himalayas, thereby being made much easier for the stranger, but at the same time losing much of its interest and charm. In Chamba and elsewhere it is best to fix your line of country first, and pursue whatever animals you may find in the neighbourhood of that line. In Kashmir you must first determine what particular animal you wish to shoot and then settle

A Kashmir Shikari en route to the Wardwan Range
(Above Wardwan Village)

the route by which you will reach his habitat, giving due consideration to the time available and the state of the snow passes which you will have to cross.

Roughly speaking, you have your choice of four different tracts of country. First, in the immediate vicinity of the valley of Kashmir, there are the Wardwan nullahs, east of Islamabad; the Scinde valley from which the Wangat, Chittingul and Tilel nullahs can be reached; and there is the Wular lake country including the Rampore, Bo, Pulwar, Trisingham and Erin nullahs (travelling round the lake from west to east), all of which still hold game. As may be imagined, the vicinity of the valley has been much harried and shot over; there still remain, however, plenty of black bears; a few decent ibex in the Wardwan nullahs, and in the Wangat, Tilel and Pulwar nullahs, 40-inch horns would be exceptional now. Red bear, I am sorry to say, are getting very scarce in Kashmir. There are generally some in Tilel, but Kishtwar is the best place for them. In all probability the limit of four will soon have to be reduced to two in Kashmir proper. Kashmir stag, or bara singh, still continue year after year to march from west to east during September and October, and their line runs within a few marches of Srinagar all the way, from the Tragbal Pass on the Gilgit road, up the Scinde valley and across to the Wardwan. A very pleasant time can be spent in these pretty nullahs bordering on the valley, but those who mean shooting in earnest would be well advised in going further afield.

The second line of march lies east up the Scinde valley into Ladakh, eighteen marches to Leh. Here the game would probably be ovis ammon and Thibetan antelope, with a chance of sharpu, burhel, and, if time permits, ibex, *en route.*

The third tract lies north, to Baltistan, with ibex as the object of pursuit, or to Astore and Gilgit after markhor.

Fourthly, with markhor again as the chief attraction, lies the difficult country of Chilas on the west of the Gilgit road.

Having now roughly mapped out the lie of the land, we will turn to the animals themselves, which must be the determining feature in the choice of direction. It must be borne in mind, however, that the nullahs which may afford the best sport one year, may be shot out or preserved a few years later, especially those near Srinagar. Of the game mentioned in the license, the following are the most important animals, any one of which may be the object of a shooting expedition :—

1. Red and black bears (*Ursus arctos* and *U. torquatus*).
2. Ovis ammon.
3. Markhor (*Capra falconeri*).
4. Ibex (*C. sibirica*).
5. Kashmir stag, or bara singh (*Cervus duvauceli*).

1. *Red and Black Bears.*

It will be unnecessary to describe the haunts of these animals at any length. As I have already stated, Kashmir is not the best country for red bears. Black bears abound everywhere in all the nullahs running up into the mountains from the valley, from Baramulla to Islamabad. While there are crops, walnuts or apricots near the villages, almost every small ravine will hold one or more bears. If they will not appear by daylight, you must beat for them, or wait about in the crops by moonlight. Early or late in the year they may be stalked on the hillside, grubbing under small rocks and stones, and eating berries among the bushes. Their coats are poor during July, August and September. It is scarcely necessary to mention the best places, because the most recent local information is the best to work on. Going by river from Baramulla to Srinagar (viâ the Wular lake), nearly all the villages and nullahs on your left hand will be worth exploring for black bear. Or if you start in the Lolab valley, or somewhere north of Bandipur, you will be able to get "khubbar" from all the neighbouring villages. The nullah, or valley, running nearly north from Bandipur, and ending in the Trisingham nullah, and another branch turning north-west from the village of Atroto, is well known for black bears at all times of the year. There is generally a cheetah to be heard of too. Following the north-west branch of the nullah from Atroto village, you reach a favourite haunt of serow, and during the winter, of bara singh.

Red bear in Kashmir are generally met with accidentally, when in pursuit of ibex or bara singh on the march. Their characteristics I have mentioned already. The best localities I know of are outside Kashmir proper, but there are plenty of nullahs not far from the valley where a few are to be found. With a month to devote to them, I should recommend going by river to Islamabad and thence over the Sinthan Pass into Kishtwar, there picking up the most recent information from the "Gujars," natives who take the sheep, goats and buffaloes up to the high grassy slopes to graze. During the months of June and July, the Deosai Plateau, on the way to Baltistan, is a sure find. The young grass and weeds spring up along the banks of the streams as soon as the snow has left the plateau, and this is an attraction which the red bear cannot resist. The ground first on the left of the track and then on the right, between Chanderkut and Ali-Malik Mar, is the best. Tilel is another good nullah for red bear and also holds fair ibex. Also try Gagai, west of Kanzalwan, on the Gilgit road, and the Pulwar nullah, due east of Tragbal Choki. In 1901 I shot an exceptionally good red bear and also a 40-inch ibex in the Pulwar nullah, about 6 miles east of the hut at the top of the Tragbal Pass. As I write this (December 1903), camped low down below the Pulwar nullah, I am told that a crafty old red bear which I missed two years ago, together with a particularly cunning stag, said to be a 14-pointer and to have fooled innumerable sportsmen, and the same herd of ibex, are still in the nullah.

When you have succeeded in shooting a red or black bear, the first thing to think of is his skin. Your shikari can generally be trusted to skin the animal, and the sooner he does it the easier it will be to avoid cuts. Have the skin pegged out at once and as much flesh as possible scraped off; then have a couple of men, in reliefs, rubbing in *cold* wood ashes with a round stone for five or six hours, till the skin is like parchment, all the flesh and blood having peeled off. While this is being done, another experienced man should be removing every bit of flesh from the lips, nose, ears and claws. To do this thoroughly, the ears must be gradually turned inside out as the flesh is cut away. Then rub in powdered alum. The skin should be pegged out in the shade until it is absolutely dry; it will do no harm to sponge the claws, lips and ears with carbolic lotion on the second day, and then rub in more alum. When thoroughly dry, the skin may be carried about without suffering, but during rainy or damp weather it should be sent to be tanned as quickly as possible. In Srinagar there are several natives who cure and clean skins apparently very well; none of them can set up heads, however, and they cannot be trusted with skins. A bearskin, which I had cured two years ago by the best of the Srinagar natives, seemed to me at the time wonderfully well done, better than any I had seen before, and the head very carefully stuffed too. The hair is coming out now, and the skin is worthless. The skin-curers in Chamba are infinitely worse, however, and it is fatal to send anything to them. Having experienced this, the second year I went to Chamba I sent my bearskins to the sappers' and miners' workshops at Rurkee, where they were excellently cured at Rs. 5 or Rs. 6 apiece and have not lost a hair in four years.

The best time of year for red bears is in March, April and May, when they have still got long winter coats and when (where they exist at all) they are to be found on any grassy slopes below the snow. I have, however, frequently found their coats very matted and woolly at this time of the year, and not nearly so good as in October and November, when they are both long and clean. They begin to hibernate about the beginning of December, whether there is a heavy fall of snow or not. Black bears, on the contrary, take shelter from the snow alone, and may be found throughout the winter where left free by the snow.

2. *Ovis Ammon.*

The pursuit of the great wild sheep on the far borders of Ladakh and Thibet is a far more serious undertaking than shooting the nullahs within

Photo] Ovis ammon (Altai Mountains) [*P. S. Van der Byl*

easy hail of the civilised valley of Kashmir. The sport, however, most undoubtedly improves in every direction out of all proportion to the increase of difficulties, wildness of the country, and greater keenness required of the sportsman.

The Kashmir license only allows one ovis ammon to be shot, but by crossing the border into Thibetan country you will be able to obtain more, and probably better, heads. Also if time permits, you should make certain of a few specimens of the other two wild sheep, sharpu and burhel, and some Thibetan antelope and yak. From three to four months are required for the expedition, and the best time to start is the middle or end of April, if you are prepared to withstand the cold. Later on in the summer you will have to climb higher and go further afield, but the game are to be found just the same. If you reach Srinagar early in April, it will probably be worth while to spend a week after bara singh and red bear on your way up the Scinde valley.

To reach ovis ammon ground, you must march up the Scinde valley, over the Zogi La Pass into Ladakh and on to Leh. Get pony transport at Dras, and if you are pressed for time and wish to do some double marches, mount your shikari and servants. Take a fortnight's supply of rice for your servants; if you have a good shikari it is sufficient to give him "rassad" at Rs.2 or Rs.2/8 per man per month, and he will buy the amount required. The route is as follows :—

Leave Srinagar in the afternoon, and march to *Ganderbal* at the entrance of the Scinde valley, about 5 miles.

(1) *Ganderbal to Kangam*, 11 miles.—On the right bank of the river lie the Chittingul and Wangat nullahs, containing small ibex, and bara singh in early spring and autumn.

(2) *Kangam to Goond*, 12 miles.

(3) *Goond to Gagangir*, 8 miles.

(4) *Gagangir to Sonamarg*, 7 miles.—Goond to Sonamarg might be done in one march, though the last part entails a steady climb. Sonamarg is one of the prettiest spots in Kashmir, and there are generally several encampments there. Milk, eggs and chickens can be obtained, and rice and atta in small quantities. Chickens can be made to travel very comfortably on a pony's load, and a supply should be taken.

(5) *Sonamarg to Baltal*, 9 miles.—An easy and very pretty march. There is a bungalow, but no supplies; 9000 ft.

(6) *Baltal to Matayan*, 15 miles.—A hard march over snow nearly all the way. First a steady climb on the snow which fills the bed of the ravine to the summit of the Zogi La Pass, 11,300 ft., then a descent on snow for 8 or 9 miles to Matayan, where there is a bungalow. The Zogi La is generally open in March, and can be crossed by ponies from May to December. No supplies.

(7) *Matayan to Dras*, 12 miles.—An easy

Ovis ammon

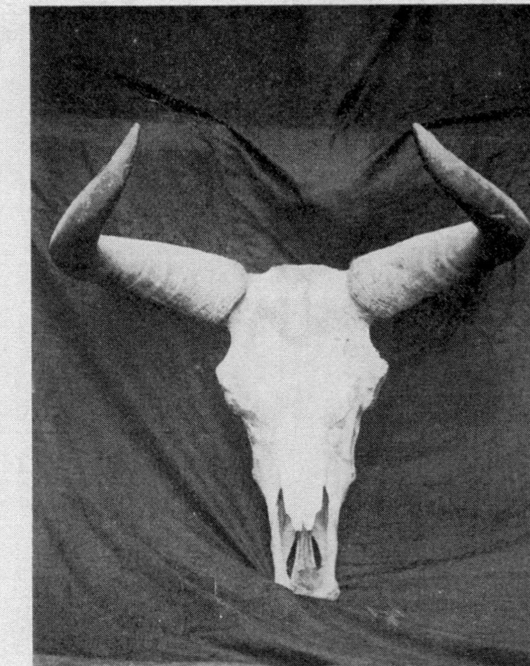

Yak, Thibet

march through typical Ladakh barren scenery into the valley of Dras. Post and telegraph office, and supplies and ponies.

(8) *Dras to Tashgam*, 16 miles.—Eggs, chickens and milk can be obtained from most of the villages between Dras and Leh.

(9) *Tashgam to Chanegand*, 16 miles.—A good road through Kharbu and past Karkitchu. From the latter place a road leads north-west to Skardu eight marches, and forms the ordinary long route to Baltistan when the Deosai Plateau is snowed up. The Shingo nullah, north-west from Kharbu, holds many of the red bears which find their way to the Deosai during June and July.

(10) *Chanegand to Pashkim*, 15 miles.—After 7 miles Kargil is reached, a well cultivated district with supplies, post and telegraph office. South lies Suru, where there are still plenty of ibex, but not nearly such good heads as there used to be. You would be lucky to shoot one with more than 40-inch horns. Pashkim is a large village with supplies.

(11) *Pashkim to Maula Chamba*, 16 miles.—This is a good road; scenery improving. Above the village is a Buddhist Lamasery.

(12) *Maula Chamba to Kharbu*, 15 miles.—Cross the Namika La Pass, 13,000 ft.

(13) *Kharbu to Lamayuru*, 15 miles.—Cross the Fottu La Pass, 13,400 ft., and descend to Lamayuru, about 11,500 ft. A route runs south from Lamayuru through Wanla and over the Singa La Pass (16,000 ft.) into Zaskar, about

eight marches to Padam. This would be worth exploring for ibex and burhel.

(14) *Lamayuru to Snurla*, 20 miles.—A hard march. Cross the Indus at Khulsi, 12 miles, and follow right bank to Snurla. Rest house. There are ibex near Khulsi.

(15) *Snurla to Saspul*, 15 miles.—Bad road. Rest house.

(16) *Saspul to Nimmoo*, 12 miles.—Past through Bashgo after 7 miles. In the Bashgo nullah there are big ibex, and, if the nullah is not preserved, it is worth spending a week in, as they run well over 40 inches there. This year (1903 and 1904) it is closed, but will probably soon be opened.

(17) *Nimmoo to Leh*, 18 miles.—Pass through Phyang at 10 miles and Spitak at 13 miles, into the Leh valley. Stores and all supplies; Dâk bungalow, post-office and hospital.

From Leh there are three routes by which good sport should be obtained, and a fairly mixed bag. There are—

(1) The Changchenmo valley.

(2) The Pangong lake country and beyond.

(3) The country south of the Indus.

The first is the most frequented, and to get a good bag in the Changchenmo country it is advisable to reach Leh early in May. In Leh you must replenish your stores, and your shikari should be able to tell you what rice or atta you will require for your servants. Warm sheepskin "poshteens" (species of long coat) can be bought

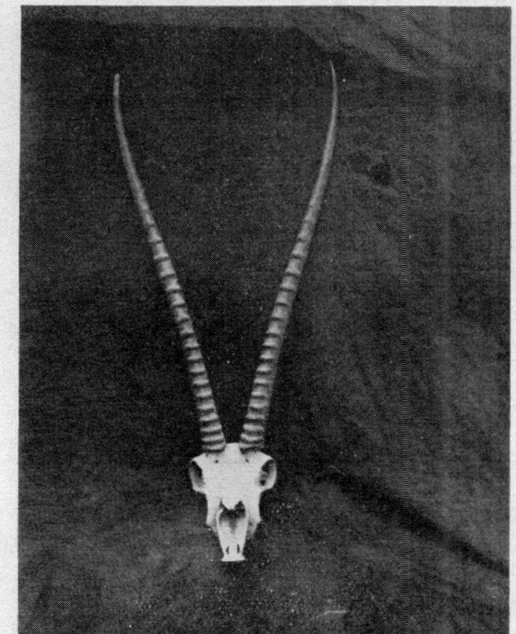

THIBETAN ANTELOPE

KASHMIR STAG, OR BARA SINGH

in Leh for Rs.5 or Rs.6, and your shikari and personal servant or cook will probably want them. Take pony transport from Leh over the Changla Pass, 18,000, to Tankse, five marches, and there get yak transport. From Tankse march to Chukkur Talao, 14 miles; thence to Lukang 6 miles, and try the country at the head of the Pangong lake for burhel. There are plenty there but the heads are not as good as they used to be. From Lukang march north to Pobrang and then north-east to the foot of the Marsemik Pass, 18,500 ft. One march from the pass takes you to the Changchenmo river, through ovis ammon ground, but you must go further to get good heads. Work up the Changchenmo river towards the pass at the head. The nullahs on both sides hold ovis ammon and burhel. The Ning Rhi nullah leads you towards the Demjor La Pass on the Rudok road, and is recommended by Colonel Ward. There is no doubt that ovis ammon are to be found wherever the characteristics of the country are suited to them, but they have been much worried by sportsmen, and to get good heads the further afield you go the better. The Changchenmo country holds plenty of Thibetan antelope and burhel. The right bank of the river in Thassa territory is perhaps the best for them. I should recommend working up one of the nullahs on the left bank first, after ovis ammon, shooting burhel when you come across them on the way from Lukang. Then strike up one of the nullahs on the right bank running north, and spend a few days after Thibetan antelope and perhaps yak.

The second route from Leh is the one I should recommend to anyone wanting several really good ovis ammon heads, because it is very little shot in. If you wish to get the best ovis heads, you must try to find comparatively new country, and there is plenty to be found still.

From Leh proceed as before to Tankse, and thence take yak transport to Chukkur Talao. From Chukkur Talao, which is near the north-west end of the Pangong lake, strike south-east between the ridge of mountains and the lake. There are burhel and generally ovis ammon in the nullahs running up to the ridge on your right, but the further south-east you go the better heads you will get. The best trophies in 1903 came from the south of the Pangong lake, and this tract of country has been seldom visited. About four or five marches from Tankse takes you to good ground. The Rudok natives across the border may be objectionable, but you are not likely to come across any, and, at the worst, they will only insist on your turning back. From the south of the Pangong lake a track runs to Rudok and another runs south-west over one pass to Chumathung on the Indus, five marches from Hanle.

The third route from Leh leads south of the Indus towards the Rupshu country, which I have already dealt with from the Chamba direction.

From Leh go up the Indus three marches to Upshi. Thence due south to Gya 15½ miles. The nullahs above, that is south-west and south-east of Gya, hold ovis ammon and burhel, but I fear from the latest accounts that there is not much chance of a good head of either, and it is best to hire yaks, cross the Tagalang Pass, 17,500 ft., and explore the Rupshu country. The tracks through Rupshu are given among the Chamba routes.

With ovis ammon I have also associated burhel, Thibetan antelope and, to some extent, sharpu. Neither of these three animals are likely to be the main object of a Kashmir expedition, but it will be seen that wherever you go after ovis ammon you will find burhel, and by the Changchenmo route you reach the best antelope country. Sharpu exist in several of the nullahs south of the Indus and up the Zaskar river, but they are also to be found on the borders of Chilas and Baltistan. A month's shooting in the country north of Mussoorie would probably give you better burhel heads than you will find in Ladakh, but not much else.

The ovis ammon requires most careful stalking, as he is gifted with a wonderful nose, though he does not possess the eyesight of the ibex. Grass shoes are not required; chaplies, or rope-soled sambhur skin boots, or ordinary shooting boots are sufficient for such climbing as will be necessary. When compelled to crawl, in order to get nearer to antelope or ovis ammon, I can recommend the reverse of the usual procedure. By travelling feet first with your back on the ground, you offer a smaller object, you can come to a sitting position to shoot over your knees in a second, and will find your hands and knees benefit considerably. Many nullahs that a few years ago held big rams are now only populated by herds of females during the summer, to avoid these, as much use as possible must be made of recent local information.

3. *Ibex.*

Baltistan is at the present time undoubtedly the best place for ibex within reach of ordinary leave. If you are prepared to face the difficulties of the Pamirs, and can get permission and assistance from Gilgit, that is the place to go to. There you will find the ovis poli, and ibex measuring 50 inches. Other places near Kashmir valley such as the Wardwan, Tilel and Suru, have had 50-inch heads shot in them, but that was many years ago. Nowadays I should call 37 inches or 38 inches very good in the Wardwan and Tilel, and 40 inches Suru exceptional. In Baltistan you should not shoot anything under 40 inches if you are particular, and if you arrive early in the spring, your six heads should lie between 40 inches and 45 inches. In several of the nullahs there will be heads running very close to 50 inches.

There are two routes to Baltistan, by the

Ibex

Bara Singh

Scinde valley and by the Gilgit road and Deosai Plateau. The former is seventeen marches but can be done in less, and the latter is eight or nine marches; unfortunately the Deosai Plateau cannot be crossed with any certainty except between June 20th and September 20th.

By the long route you must start from Ganderbal, at the mouth of the Scinde valley, with, in addition to your own stores, a fortnight's supply of rice or atta for your permanent servants and coolies, and about a maund of grass for grass shoes. The latter are an absolute necessity in Baltistan. From Ganderbal march up the valley on the Ladakh road till within about 3 miles of Chanegand, your ninth march. At this point cross the river to Karkitchu and camp at Har Dras, about 3 miles further. Thence to Skardu, the capital of Baltistan. The stages are as follows:—

10. *Har Dras to Olthing Thang*, 18 miles. A hard march along the Dras and Suru rivers.

11. *Olthing Thang to Tarkuti*, 14 miles. After a short climb descend to the sandy bed of the Indus. The track is a trying one, sometimes in the bed of the river, sometimes high up the mountains that rise precipitously on either side.

12. *Tarkuti to Karmang*, 17 miles. Cross Indus by rope bridge to Karmang on right bank. Eggs, chickens and milk can be obtained at all the villages on the banks of the Indus.

13. *Karmang to Tolti*, 12 miles. When the river is high the upper path must be taken

and the march considerably lengthened. Rope bridge at Tolti.

14. *Tolti to Parkuta*, 14 miles.

15. *Parkuta to Gol*, 12 miles. The Shayok river joins Indus near Gol.

16. *Gol to Skardu*, 20 miles. Fairly level, but the sand and, during the last 8 miles, the stones are trying. Can be made two marches by halting at Tergas, 7 miles short of Skardu.

Deosai Plateau route to Skardu. Send your shikari ahead to Bandipur to get baggage ponies, and grass for shoes, and ten days' supply of rice. If he has any doubts about being able to get ponies, write to the commissariat officer at Bandipur. The Deosai route is nearly always open soon after the middle of June; this year (1903) it remained open till the middle of October; in 1901 I crossed in the closing snow-storm on September 18th.

Engage a "Dunga" boat at Srinagar. This is a kind of barge with matting roof and walls. It can be made very comfortable, but if you mean to remain more than one or two nights in it, it is best to have a second small boat for cooking purposes. A dunga with crew of four men, women and children can be hired at Rs.20 a month. Leaving Srinagar at 2 P.M., with two extra boatmen (at 5½ annas a day), you should reach Bandipur at 5 A.M. next morning. The mosquitoes on the Wular lake and its vicinity are terrible. You should at any rate have some mosquito netting to tie round your head for the boat journey, and you will want it again on the Deosai. If your shikari meets your boat at Bandipur with your baggage ponies, and three or four permanent coolies, you should get started by 8 A.M. The route is as follows :—

1. *Wular Lake* (*Bandipur*) *to Tragbal* (9000 ft.), 12 miles. A level road for 3 miles, then an ascent of 4000 ft., the last 5 miles very trying. Road zigzags up steep mountains. There is a prettily situated bungalow at Tragbal, and the views are lovely, especially over the Erin nullah towards Mount Haramouk.

2. *Tragbal to Camp near Malik Kadal*, 21 miles. As time is an object to most sportsmen using the Deosai route, I give the route I took myself, doing long but quite feasible marches. From the previous camp a climb of 2000 ft. brings you to the top of the Tragbal Pass, where there is a small hut. East lies the Pulwar nullah, and west the Bo nullah, both good for stag in late September and October. The road is the best in Kashmir, being the main Gilgit road as far as Burzil. A march of 12½ miles takes you to a small bungalow at Gorai. Thence the road descends through lovely scenery to Kanzalwan, 17½ miles, where there is another bungalow. Below Kanzalwan lies the Kishengunga river, and a road to Chilas. Close by is the Gagai nullah, holding ibex, red bear and stag. Three and a half miles beyond Kanzalwan

a good camping ground is reached near the Malik Kadal bridge.

3. *Malik Kadal to Peshwari*, 21 miles. The pretty valley of Gurais is reached in 7 miles. Here there are a bungalow and post and telegraph offices, generally several encampments in the valley, and the pine-clad nullahs on the left bank of the river. There is a road to the Tilel nullah (red bear and ibex) and a difficult track leads to the east of the Pulwar nullah. Get a sheep or half a dozen chickens as you pass through Gurais. Peshwari bungalow is 14 miles further on.

4. *Peshwari to Camp Wambi beyond Burzil*, 13 miles. Minimarg, another spot that makes one loth to leave this pretty valley, is 4½ miles from Peshwari. Thence the road bends westwards and ascends to the Burzil rest house, about 11,000 feet. It is best to push on about 1½ miles up the Deosai track, which branches off to the right from the rest house on the Gilgit road to the highest point at which wood can be found. The scenery is quite changed now, and bare rocks and boulders take the place of pine forests and green valleys. From this camp you must carry sufficient wood to last out the two nights you will have to pass on the cold Deosai Plateau.

5. *Camp Wambi (Burzil) to Kala Pani*, 21 miles. A climb of a little over 1000 feet brings you to the top of the Burzil Pass, 12,800 feet. Then a slight descent to the valley called the Chota Deosai, whence a track leads to the

Shingo nullah. This is good red bear ground in June and July. From the Chota Deosai a stiff climb to the top of the Sari Sangor Pass, 14,200 feet, rewards your efforts with a grand view. The track is here very stony and rough, and descends past two small blue lakes at the foot of the snow-clad ridge to the Deosai Plateau, level about 13,000 feet. Eleven miles on is a stone hovel called Chanderkut, and 3 miles further a good camping ground at Kala Pani. There are valleys running to the left and the right of the track which hold red bears, and any grassy slopes that can be seen are worth examining with glasses. Marmots abound, and you are certain to get several shots without leaving the track, especially near Chanderkut. They are hard to kill, however, and a shot gun only sends them down their holes, over which they are generally sitting. The Deosai is indeed a weird and bleak region. It consists of a series of rolling downs, strewn with rock and stones; not a tree nor a bush for 40 miles; a little grass near the streams, and here and there patches of onions. The only living animals are red bear, marmots, and millions of mosquitoes. The mosquitoes only come to life between 11 A.M. and 3 P.M., while the heat of the sun makes itself felt.

6. *Kala Pani to Camp below Burgi La Pass*, 16 miles. A slight rise to about 13,600 feet gives a view of the wall of snow peaks which for three-quarters of a circle surround the cold

desert plateau. Some hills on the right generally hold red bear and sometimes sharpu. The nights and early mornings on the Deosai are most bitterly cold, and the only thing to do is to march nearly all day, as when it becomes warm the mosquitoes make it almost impossible to halt. They leave but little impression, however. The shelter called Ali Malik Mar may be recognised by a few crumbling stone walls, but it is better to camp about 4 miles further on at a level of 14,500 feet.

7. *Camp to Skardu*, 9 hours. An hour and a half of steady climbing with a very stiff rise of 500 feet at the finish, brings you to the summit of the Burgi La Pass, 16,000 feet. It is well to breakfast here under the shelter of some rocks and admire the desolate grandeur of the view. South lies the still freezing Deosai Plateau, with all the rugged solitude of Dartmoor magnified ten-fold. North-east lies a world of huge bleak mountains, culminating in the snow peaks of the gigantic Mustagh range, which forms the impassible northern barrier of India. Mount Godwin Austin is there, the highest mountain but one in the world, but his summit of 28,278 feet by no means dwarfs the rest of the range.

Then commences a terrible descent of 8000 feet to Skardu on the banks of the Indus. At first leading over snow and rather steep, then over a track of rough loose boulders and stones. After two hours you reach Pindobal, where the first trees are welcomed in the shape of a few

BURHEL

IBEX

cedar bushes. Five hours more bring you to Skardu, a large village surrounded by apricot trees. Below is the mighty Indus in its broad, sandy bed, from which on either side the mountains rise almost perpendicularly to 16,000 feet.

At Skardu there are a post and telegraph office and a polo ground! Rice, atta, sugar, and fruit can be obtained in Skardu, and eggs, chickens and sheep in most of the Baltistan villages. The Balti natives are weird-looking creatures, with Mongolian features. They are hard workers and cheerful, and wonderful climbers, as indeed they are bound to be if they move about at all. From Skardu a trying march of 14 miles brings you to Shigar, a village at the mouth of the Shigar valley, where the best ibex ground is to be found.

The nullahs on the left bank of the river are the best, and, taking them in order as you go up-stream from Shigar, they are—Shigar nullah, Askora, Hushu, Alchori, Kushumel, Braldhoo. The Shigar nullah is close to the village and holds red bear, but not as a rule any very good ibex. The Askora is a fair nullah, and there are always a few good heads there, but very high up. The Hushu and Alchori nullahs are both excellent. The best ground is up the left fork of the Hushu nullah, as high up as you can get. In the lower parts of all the nullahs you will find large herds of ibex, but no good heads. In Alchori there was a 50-inch ibex in 1901 and he may be still alive. Braldhoo nullah is the furthest north and the biggest and probably contains most ibex. When not pressed for time, it would be the best place to go to. Two marches from Shigar will take you to the shooting ground in the Hushu nullah, and you may see Sharpu *en route.* Four or five marches take you to the best ground in the Braldhoo. On the right bank there is a good nullah called Neali, opposite Hushu. There is an old markhor there who has defied many sportsmen. Opposite Braldhoo are the Basha river, and another very big nullah.

The strategy of ibex shooting consists in locating the portion of the nullah favoured by the wary old ibex; and they are there in every one of the nullahs that I have mentioned, as well as in several others. Then, by observation from a long distance, find out the patches of grass to which they come down to graze. The tactics consist in making a flank march with a favourable wind, getting round and above those feeding grounds, and taking up a commanding position before the ibex have come down from their rocks in the snow. This often entails a night march, it is true; but if the position occupied by the ibex commands all approaches, as is often the case, you must either sleep out under a rock or make a moonlight march. The sight and nose of the ibex are marvellous. When stalking, you must carry some dust or sand in your pocket and be continually testing the wind, as it varies frequently. The big ibex are scarcely ever to be found with the herds of small ones. They keep by themselves, sometimes six or a dozen together, all over 40 inches. At night and during most of the day they lie on carefully selected rocks as high up as they can, often in the snow within reach of a patch of grass to come and feed on morning and evening. From their rocks they can generally see everything that is to be seen, and it is perfectly useless to try to approach them by a road whence you can see them above you; but they seldom look up hill, and if you can get above them, and the wind keeps the right way, you will be rewarded with a shot.

A wounded ibex will invariably make for the most inaccessible part of the mountains, and the local Balti shikari can often tell you where that is. He may be tracked by the excellent Balti dogs, or, if he is mortally wounded, you will soon see the kites circling round the spot where he has fallen. A second shot at an ibex can nearly always be obtained if you do not disclose your position after your first shot. I must again impress on the reader that the most important point in ibex shooting is to get above the highest point where good feeding ground is to be seen. Do not be misled by seeing females and small heads lower down. Do not hurry over your shot when you have reached a suitable spot. Before showing your head or your rifle over the rocks that hide you, rest, recover your breath, and steady your hand and eye; also keep your shikari behind you.

A few extracts from my shooting Diary of 1901 may be more useful than any further hints.

EXTRACTS FROM SHOOTING DIARY, 1901.

Baltistan, August 29th, 1901. *Camp at Shigar.*—"Leave Skardu and cross the Indus in curious old ferry boat. March for several miles over the soft sandy bed of the river. Painfully hot; no shade and no water; all bare rocks and sand. Climb a rocky ridge and get a view of Shigar below; a genuine oasis the only green spot visible in the sandy plain shut in by bare precipitous mountains. I decide to go to the Braldhu nullah."

August 30th.—"My knee has not recovered from the disagreeable descent into Skardu, but I manage to get one of the Shigar polo ponies and start along a level shady avenue of willows and apricot trees covered with fruit. It is three marches into the Braldhu nullah, but I break down when close to the mouth of the Hushu nullah so have to pitch my tent there, 6 miles from Shigar. A man I met on the Deosai told me he had been three weeks in Hushu nullah and had only seen female ibex and heads under 35 inches, but I can get no further at present."

August 31st, and 1st September.—"Rest and have knee massaged. Am camped near some marble rocks. Excellent melons and apricots in Hushu village."

September 2nd.—"Climb successfully up to head of nullah and camp at about 14,500 ft. near the fork of the nullah. See ibex up right branch in the evening. Saw some sharpu while marching up from Hushu village, but no heads worth shooting."

September 3rd.—"Get up at 3 A.M. and climb by moonlight till 5 A.M. above the grass where those ibex were. Can see no sign of them, however, though I climb about in the snow till 8.30 A.M. Fear they must have winded me, as puffs of wind seem to come from every direction this morning. Find a very nice pure crystal in a half frozen torrent. Return to tent and start up the left, or northern branch of the nullah at 3 P.M. About 4.30 P.M. I see about six ibex very high up, and through my telescope they appear to be all good heads. Soon after, two more lots of does and small buck come into view lower down. It is too late to get near the big ones."

September 4th.—"Hardest day I have ever had. Get up at 2.30 A.M. and climb hard till 7.30 A.M. before I reach the head of the ridge between Hushu and Alchori. The patch of grass where I saw the ibex feeding yesterday is just below me, but alas! no ibex. They have finished their morning meal, and with my glasses I can make them out lying on the rocks half way up a perfectly unapproachable precipice. Have some breakfast, and, completely tired out, go to sleep in a cave while a snowstorm comes on. At 1 P.M. Azizza (my shikari) wakes me and says some big ibex have crossed over the crest from Alchori nullah. They could scarcely have come to a better place, and I watch them with delight, as they come slowly down the rocks and snow. When they have settled, we make our way round the bit of glacier at the head of the nullah, and the battle is won, for we have the ibex, eight of them, all with heads over 40 inches below us. I can get no nearer than 150 yards, however, and then, as I slide my rifle over a rock with my hat as a rest, they are up and on the move, suspicious of something. I fire carefully at the one that offers the best target, as there is no time to lose, and down he comes. The rest travel quickly up the side of the mountain, and I get three more shots at two of them, one with a very fine pair of horns. They are both hit, the big one badly, but are soon over the crest and lost to sight. We follow as far as we can and find blood on the snow, but can get no higher. Returning to the first ibex, to my joy I find that he is a beauty with a massive pair of wide-spread horns, measuring 43 inches. Reach my tent again at 6.30 P.M., after a grand but trying day of sixteen hours."

September 5th.—"Snow and clouds all day; can do nothing."

September 6th.—"Heavy snow in night, and hills are covered all round. Clear morning, so I send some Balti coolies to look for the wounded ibex. They say they know the point which they will make for, and sure enough there are the kites circling round, visible from my tent as I start out at 6 A.M. Going up the left branch again, I see some ibex just below the fresh snow, lower down than usual. The wind is light and shifting, and stalking very difficult, but I manage to reach a ravine that should lead me above them without being seen or winded. After three hours' climbing I get within range of the biggest, and a shot behind the shoulder brings him down. He is up again at once, however, and is lost among the rocks. I get several more wild shots at him as he comes into sight for a moment or two, but apparently with no effect. Just as I have put down my rifle in despair, he stands broadside on with a background of snow at over 400 yards. Taking very careful aim, I fire, and he scrambles forward 10 yards and drops dead. By an extraordinary bit of luck my shot went through his head! He is as good a specimen as I thought, and his horns measure 41½ inches."

September 7th.—"See two large herds of ibex up the right branch of the nullah, but no heads over about 34 inches. There must have been about thirty in one herd, and sixty in the other. The Balti coolies have not yet returned with news of my wounded ibex."

September 8th.—"Determine to work over the crest of the right branch of the nullah, towards the head of Askora nullah. Take my servant's tent and a Wolseley valise, and two days' food. Camp at about 16,000 feet in the shelter of some rocks, and in the evening see a herd of about thirty ibex. Whilst stalking them to see whether one of the heads was shootable, I come across the tracks of a snow-leopard in the snow; they are quite fresh and he is evidently stalking the same herd of ibex! Unfortunately he has crossed the snow and got among the rocks and shale, where he is invisible. I make out that there is no ibex in the herd worth shooting, the biggest being about 35 inches, so I wait for the snow-leopard to try his luck. However, he does not succeed while there is light, and I return to my small tent just as the snow comes on again. My tent, which only just holds my valise, is soon covered with snow about 6 inches deep all round; then the night clears and it freezes hard."

September 9th.—"Bitterly cold morning, freezing very hard indeed. Thanks to the sheet of ice and snow which covers my tent and all crevices round it, I had a very good night's sleep and did not feel the cold. Work to the head of Askora nullah in the morning, and find on the way that the leopard has killed a young ibex. See two big ibex and have a long and dangerous stalk after them across several "shutes" of loose, slatey shale and rocks. If one goes too fast, it means a fall; and if one dwells or hesitates too long on his steps, the side of the hill begins to crumble and slide away. When at last I creep over the ridge that has been hiding me, and expect to find the ibex not far below, I have the pleasure of seeing them steadily climbing over the next ridge nearly a mile away! The early morning variable wind must have played me false again. Return to my own big tent down below in the afternoon, and to my joy I find the Balti coolies have recovered the bigger of the two ibex that got away wounded five days ago. In trying to reach a difficult peak, he must have succumbed to his wound and fallen down a precipice, below which the Baltis found his remains with the help of the kites. In falling, he unfortunately broke one horn, but the remaining horn was very massive and measured 44 inches with a girth of 11 inches at the base. There was sufficient flesh left on the head to prove he was my ibex, and not one imported from a village below!"

Having got three ibex measuring 41½, 43 and 44 in a week's shooting, I returned over the Deosai Plateau to the Tragbal, and went into the Pulwar nullah. There I shot a 40-inch ibex (about as common as a 48-inch in Baltistan), a ten-pointed stag, and a red bear. Two black bears above Bandipur completed my bag, which was all that I could wish for in two and a half months' leave from Jhansi, in Central India, at a bad time of the year. I forgot to mention that the skins of the marmots shot in the Deosai are worthless in August because they are then "moulting." In June, early July and September they are all right.

A few routes from Baltistan may be useful. When the Deosai is not open as early as may have been expected, Skardu can sometimes be reached as follows:—Keep to the Gilgit road from Burzil for two marches, to *Gadhai* (one march short of Astore).

Gadhai to Alampi La Pass, two marches.

Alampi La to Khatsura, a large village on the Indus, two marches.

Khatsura to Skardu, one march.

From Skardu there is a route to Astore, six marches through Shigathang.

From Shigar to the Basha nullah, at the head of the left branch of the Shigar valley, is four marches. A man should be sent ahead to get ready the skin rafts by which the Braldhu and Basha rivers have to be crossed. On the Braldhu river is Askole, above which is a world of glaciers,[1] the largest known out of the Arctic regions.

To Leh there is a route by the Shayok river as follows:—

Shigar to Khapaloo, four marches.

Khapaloo to Khalse, seven marches.

Khalse to Leh, four marches.

A very good way of spending four months'

[1] Mr and Mrs Bullock-Workman spent many months in 1903 trying to find a pass over these gigantic glaciers into Hunza Nagar, but could find nothing worthy of the name.

ROUTE MAP. SRINAGAR TO LEH & BALTISTAN.

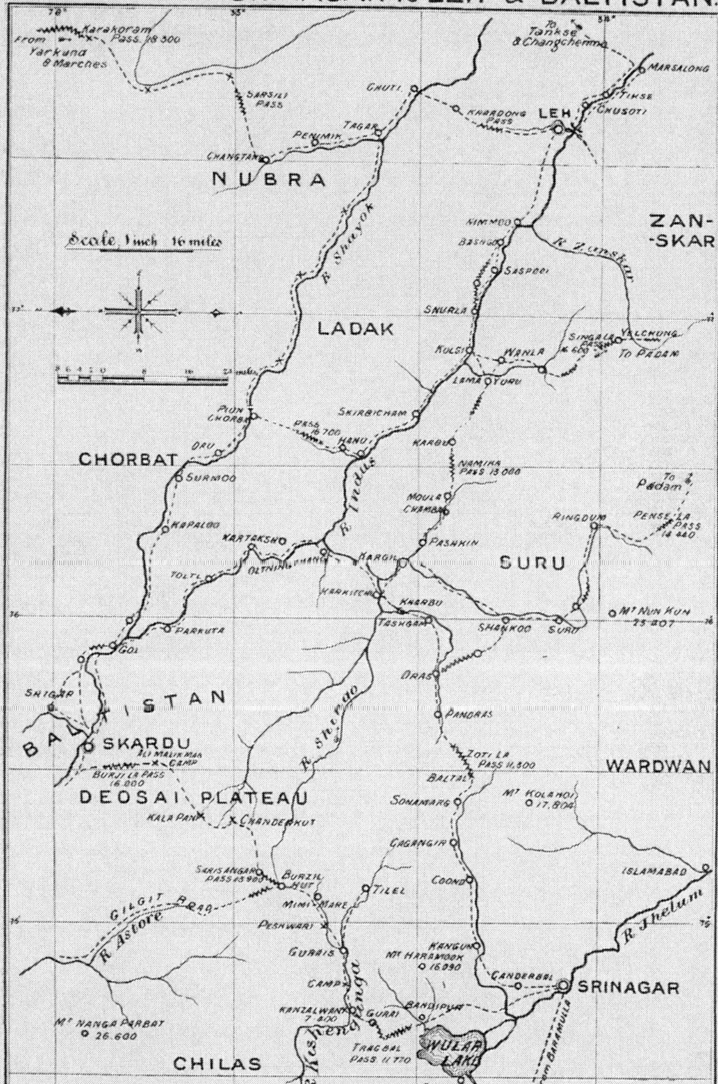

leave is to take Baltistan first, early in the year, and when you have shot some good ibex, march into Ladakh by the Shayok route from Shigar and try the Changchenmo valley for ovis ammon and antelope. Or, with longer leave, go to Ladakh first in April; return by the Shayok river to Baltistan in early July and spend two or three weeks after ibex, thence go to Astore and try for a markhor. This would give you a chance of shooting all the game worth shooting in the Himalayas.

4. *Markhor.*

Markhor divide with ibex the stalking honours of the shooting world.[1] Much that has been said about ibex shooting applies also to markhor, so I will confine myself principally to information regarding the best places in which to find them. A well-set-up markhor head, with 45 to 50-inch horns and a long white beard, is perhaps one of the finest trophies to be had. There are two varieties of markhor in the Himalayas, one the inhabitant of the mountains round Gilgit, Astore, and Mount Nanga Parbat (26,000 ft.) in Chilas; and the other the Pir Panjal markhor, to be found in the Pir Panjal mountains, south of Kashmir valley, and in the Kajinag and Shimshiberi range above Baramulla. The Gilgit species carries handsomer and more

[1] Markhor perhaps win the tie. At any rate they are much scarcer, and it is harder to get a moderate head.

massive horns, with a more pronounced spiral and wider spread.

To shoot in Gilgit and Chilas special permission has to be obtained from the Gilgit Political Agent. Supplies are a difficulty, and sufficient for yourself and servants must be taken with you. If marching by the Gilgit road, get the help of the commissariat officer at Bandipur. To shoot in Astore, Boonjie and Haramoush, a special permission must be obtained from the Secretary, Game Preservation, Srinagar. Of the Gilgit nullahs I fear I can give but little information, as I have never been there. With a good shikari who has been there before, and by making the most of local information, the reader should be able to get a couple of good heads. The nullahs west of Gilgit, I have heard, always hold big markhor and ibex. Colonel Ward recommends the Shingye nullah. The most recent information I can obtain, however, is to the effect that Shingye nullah is rather shot out, and the best markhor and ibex are to be obtained by working up the Kirgar nullah into Darel. There are several good nullahs between Astore and Boonjie, and a local shikari can always be obtained. The nullahs on both banks of the Astore river still hold plenty of markhor, but it must not be expected that a good head will be easily obtained. Having once sighted an old veteran, you must go very warily to work to get a fair shot at him. There is generally a kind of plateau on the top of the Astore ridges, and by sleeping out under the rocks you will be able to stalk your quarry from above, the only safe procedure with markhor, as with ibex.

The best markhor nullahs I know of when marching from Astore to the Indus along the Gilgit road, are the following on the right bank: the Ditchell nullah, one march beyond Astore, and better than that, the high ground drained by the Shelter and Duchkoot nullahs, two marches from Astore. On the left bank of the Astore river, a few miles before it flows into the Indus, turn south-west through Dooni and work up the Buldar river.

If the nullahs on the Astore river are occupied, or the information you gather as you pass them is bad, march on to the Indus and try the Boonjie nullah; or cross the Indus higher up by the Partab Singh bridge and try the country west of the river, provided you have permission from Gilgit. The Dumoot and Chukkurkoot nullahs should repay a visit. Wherever you go for markhor in this part of the country, you will probably find good ibex as well.

The Rondu and Haramoush country lies north of the Indus between the river and the Hunza Nagar glaciers. It can be reached from Astore and from Boonjie, or from Baltistan.

Astore to Rondu, four marches.

Shigar to Rondu, five or six marches, viâ Basha river, and over pass down to Indus. This route is difficult, but generally open in June. From Rondu march down the right bank of the

Indus, and you will have good markhor and ibex ground on your right hand all the way, beginning with the Askora nullah and ending with the Haramoush nullah, the entrance to which is one or two marches from Boonjie. The best nullahs about Haramoush are the Baloochi and Shunguhir.

The stages along the Gilgit road have been given as far as Burzil, but I will repeat the whole route from Bandipur to Gilgit to save reference to the chapter on ibex.

1. Bandipur to Tragbal, 12 miles.
2. Tragbal to Camp, 21 miles.
3. Camp to Peshwari, 21 miles.
4. Peshwari to Burzil, 12 miles. (Deosai route to Skardu.)
5. Burzil to Chillam, 16 miles.
6. Chillam to Gadhai, 16 miles. (Alampi La route to Skardu.)
7. Gadhai to Astore, 17 miles.
8. Astore to Dushkin, 15 miles.
9. Dushkin to Doyan, 11 miles. (Road to Chilas, and to Buldar nullah.)
10. Doyan to Boonjie, 18 miles.
11. Boonjie to Chilas, 5 marches. To Haramoush, 2 marches up Indus.
12. Boonjie to Gilgit, 36 miles, 2 marches.

Chilas.—The best way to Chilas early in the year is by the Gilgit road as far as Doyan and then turn south along the left bank of the Indus. If you can make arrangements for shikari, stores, permit and kit, without going to Srinagar, by far

MAP OF ASTORE & BOONJIE. MARKHOR GROUND

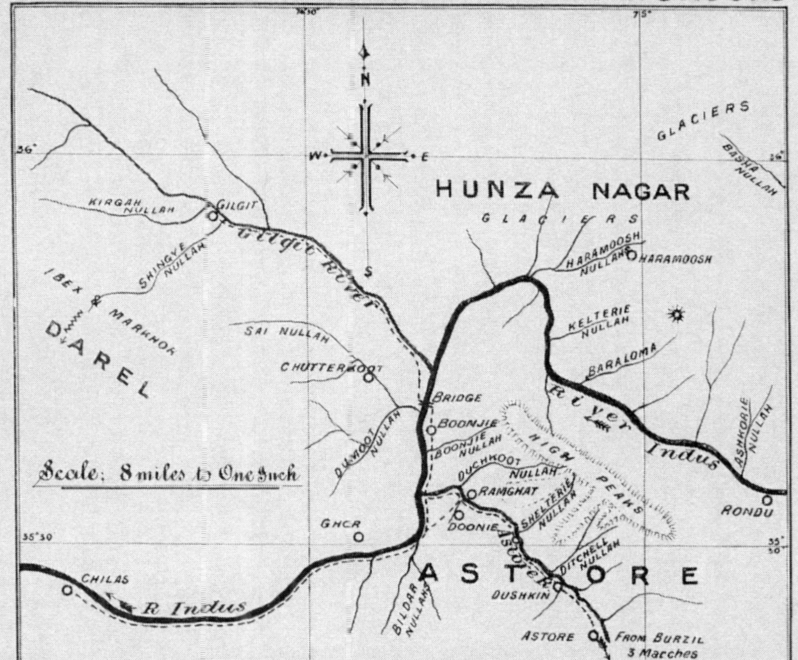

the best way will be to go to Hassan Abdal by train and through Abbottabad, Mansera and Babusar. The road is a good one, open to pony and mule transport, and the stages, by Dr Neve's excellent tourist's guide, are as follows :—

Hassan Abdal to Abbottabad by tonga about 35 miles.

1. Abbottabad to Mansera, 16 miles.
2. Mansera to Balakot, 20 miles.
3. Balakot to Kawaie, 12 miles.
4. Kawaie to Jared, 14 miles.
5. Jared to Kaghan, 16 miles.
6. Kaghan to Narang, 15 miles.
7. Narang to Waitar, 23 miles.
8. Waitar to Basul, 9 miles.
9. Basul to Babusar, 20 miles, over pass.
10. Babusar, to Chilas Fort, 20 miles.

(*Note.*—One march from Waitar will probably take you to shooting ground; it is unnecessary to go to Chilas Fort.)

There is a short road to Chilas from the Wular lake, generally open from June 15th to the end of September, and that is the route I should recommend to the majority of sportsmen. It must be remembered that a Gilgit permit is required for Chilas shooting, and the natives must be carefully treated with; they are by no means too willing to help sportsmen. Coolies even are hard to get sometimes, and you cannot calculate on obtaining rice or atta for your servants anywhere after leaving the Lolab valley. Suppose that your permanent servants consist of a cook, shikari, Tiffin coolie, and five permanent Kashmir coolies; making them an allowance of one seer (2 lbs.) a day of rice or atta, for a six weeks' expedition to Chilas, you will have to carry with you eight maunds (640 lbs.) of provisions for them, or four pony loads. In addition you must take about 1½ maunds of grass for grass shoes. It is advisable also to take a supply of small knives, and other small presents for the head-men of the villages. If your shikari dispenses these, and a few promises as well, judiciously, you will have no trouble in getting coolies, information, eggs, milk and chickens, etc., for which you are bound to be dependent on the goodwill of the villagers. The following is the route from Alsoa, near Bandipur, on the Wular lake :—

1. Alsoa to Lalpura.
2. Lalpura to Butnar.
3. Butnar to Mutchsil.
4. Mutchsil to Khel (long march).
5. Khel to Muri.
6. Muri to Paloi (cross pass into Chilas, long march).
7. Paloi to Managuch. Managuch is a small village below Mount Nanga Parbat (26,600 ft.). Coolies and provisions can be obtained from Bundar.
8. Managuch to Dembra, beyond Nanga Parbat.

There is sharpu ground near Gulli between Muri and Paloi. A good local shikari lives at Bundar village below Managuch, and the head

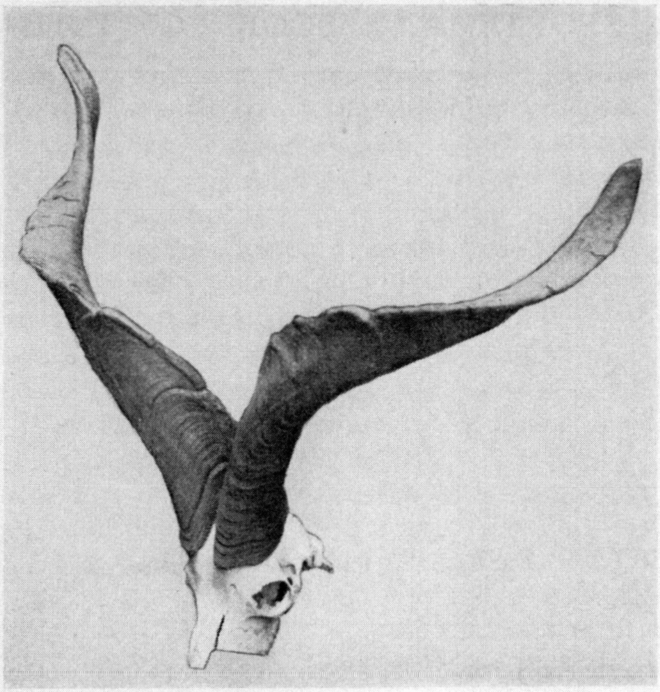

MARKHOR

SHARPOO (OVIS VIGNEI)

lumbadar or his son can help you as regards coolies and provisions. There are a few huts at Dembra, but no provisions; you must send to Bundar for whatever you want.

Dembra is within reach of good markhor ground, and you will probably see some decent ibex and a red bear or so. You must be prepared to leave your big tent at Dembra, and spend several nights with nothing but a bed-valise and possibly a servants' "tente d'abris." There is a very large herd of markhor near Dembra, over 100 strong, and there are several big heads among them, between 45 inches and 50 inches. Their usual ground is a large open "maidan" on the side of the mountain, and when seen there, it is practically impossible to approach them. There appears to be no track by which you can outflank them and get to the top of the ridge; the only way to defeat them is to watch from a safe distance, morning and evening, till you have sighted the track by which they usually travel up the mountain side after feeding. Then sleep out as near as you can to their feeding-ground, and get on their track before the sun rises in the morning. The biggest markhor will probably be a little separated from the main herd, and are generally the last to come down the hill and the first to go up again. In September 1903, a 45-inch markhor, a good ibex, and a red bear were shot in one morning in Dembra nullah.

The best time of year for markhor, as for ibex,

is in April, May and June; after that you must climb higher for them, and generally sleep out a few nights. I should recommend the Astore nullahs to sportsmen with from two to three months' leave commencing in April; and Chilas to those who want to get a markhor in August or September and a bara singh near the Wular lake on their way back, in, say, the Bo or Rampura nullahs. To combine a good ibex and markhor shoot, starting in the middle of June, cross the Deosai to Baltistan; go up the Shigar river, and get your ibex in the Braldhoo nullah. Then go up the Basha nullah, with a chance of more ibex, over the pass and down into Rondu. Then try the Askora or Haramoush nullahs for markhor, and return through Boonjie by the Gilgit road, and if you have not shot your two markhor, try the Duchkoot, the best of the Astore nullahs. A 52-inch markhor was shot there in 1903. Four months would be required for this expedition. If you can reach Kashmir in the spring, reverse the march and take the markhor ground first.

Pir Panjal markhor.—A month or six weeks' leave, the earlier after April 1st the better, should be sufficient to get a couple of Pir Panjal markhor, and perhaps a red bear and a couple of black bear. If you can avoid Srinagar and make your arrangements at Baramulla, so much the better. The Kajinag range was closed for a good many years, but was opened in 1903, and several good heads were shot during that year; but a good many sportsmen spent three or four weeks there without any success.

The best and biggest nullah in the Kajinag is the Katai. It can be reached from Uri, Rampur, or Baramulla. The Malangan nullah above the village of Luchipura, is closed at present, but the nullahs on either side are good. The Limbar nullahs are opposite Rampur, and are worth trying if they have not been much shot in. North of the Kajinag range lie the Shimshiberi mountains, which also hold markhor and red bear. There is room for eight or ten rifles in the Kajinag range, but very few of the nullahs stand much shooting. The autumn months are not likely to afford any sport, as by then the dryness of the grass makes stalking, or even walking, almost impossible, and the markhor has attained the summit of his cunning. When some fresh snow has fallen in December, and the rutting season has commenced, an old markhor may be more easily approached.

There are plenty of black bears within easy reach of Baramulla, Rampur, and Sopor, and a few days might be spent after them when accounts have been settled with the markhor.

Route to the Kājināg from Baramulla.—Cross the Jhelum at Baramulla and march down right bank 9 miles to the mouth of the three Limbar nullahs, 5 miles further down stream brings you to the entrance of the Luchipura valley, and 4 miles up the valley is the village of Luchipura, where supplies and shikaris can be found. The road is fit for pony transport, and Luchipura can be reached in one day. Just below the village the valley divides. The right branch takes you to Malangan and Puch nullahs, and the left to Gorital and Maidan nullahs, one march each. Three marches up the left branch will bring you to the shooting ground of Katai nullah.

5. *Kashmir Stag, or Bara Singh.*

The best month for shooting the Kashmir stag is October. It is then that they are "calling" or "roaring," and it is the only opportunity the ordinary soldier or civilian from the plains of India has of seeing them. Towards the end of September they begin to work their way eastwards, when their horns are set and the weather is getting cold. They appear to have a regular line of march from the country west of Kanzalwan on the Gilgit road, past Gurai and the Tragbal Pass, over the Erin and Scinde nullahs to the Wardwan. Thence into Kishtwar and Badrawar, to the borders of Chamba. They shed their horns and travel west again about the end of March or beginning of April. It is said that the old stags return to their favourite nullah year by year.

Working along their route from west to east, Gagai, one march from Kanzalwan, on the Kishengunga river, is perhaps the first and most westerly point where they are to be found from September 15th with their horns set. Most of

Photo] BARA SINGH (KASHMIR) [*P. S. Van der Byl*

the nullahs round the Wular lake attract some old stags and many does every year. The best are the Bo and the Pulwar on either side of the Trabal Pass; Rampura and Nagmarg on the west and Erin nullah on the east of the lake. The Wangat and Chittingul nullahs in the Scinde valley are good, and then we reach the Wardwan, which is now the best country for them since the Gilgit road has disturbed their more western haunts.

The best system to adopt in order to get a good stag at the end of September, or early in October, is to camp in a nullah which is on their line of march and wait for them. In the afternoon climb up high, above the pine trees, and you may see some travelling along near the crest. A fall of snow will bring them along for certain, if you are on the right line; you can soon tell by their tracks in the snow, or by marks in the ground where they have been rubbing their horns. In the early morning, either look for tracks in the snow to see where they may have passed into your nullah during the night, or follow a "call" if you hear one below among the pines. After a fall of snow, you must not let an hour escape you, for if there is a stag in your nullah it will make him call, and if there is not it will bring some in or through it.

The old stag is very wary, and it is no easy matter to get a shot at him, however much he may call. I spent nearly three weeks in Pulwar nullah one year after a 14-pointer, but never got a shot at him, and had to be content with a 10-pointer. After they have stopped calling, you must find their feeding grounds and wait for them to come out of the forests. Some years they call very little, but generally from September 25th to October 20th is the best time. After the middle of November the ground gets too slippery and noisy to admit of much stalking until more snow falls. The does and small stag may be seen quite low down near the villages, and in the fields where there are roots, but the old stags remain up above, even in the December snow.

Colonel Ward declares that from February 20th to March 25th is the only time that it is worth while to shoot stag. Unfortunately there are but few visitors who can reach Kashmir before the end of March. A good many very handsome heads, however, are shot every year in October. A 10-pointer, measuring 40 inches, with a girth of 6 inches, is a very fine trophy, and by no means uncommon. An exceptionally good head would be a 12-pointer, length 45 inches, and girth 7 inches.

The only other Kashmir game that I have not yet dealt with are serow, and the two species of leopard. Burhel and sharpu have received sufficient mention wherever the route after other more important game has crossed their ground. Nearly all the nullahs south of the Indus between Lamayuru and Leh hold both these species of sheep, and sharpu are also to be found in Western

After Bara Singh in the Pulwar Nullah in October

Kashmir. Neither is likely to form the primary object of a shooting trip in Kashmir, although from Mussoorie a very nice six weeks might be spent after burhel, and probably better heads secured than in Ladakh.

Serow.—The serow is but seldom seen or shot in Kashmir, and his head is a very poor trophy when secured. If you come across one, it will probably be by chance, when looking for bear or stag. A German sportsman, who went as far as Askole in Baltistan this year after ibex, but only secured some photographs, returned to the Pulwar nullah for stag. There by pure chance his shikari twice pointed out a good serow, with from 10-inch to 12-inch horns, but could not persuade him to shoot, because the horns were not as big as a stag's. Serow are to be found in the preserved "rukhs" between the Scinde and Liddar valleys, and in the Trisingham and Atroto (or Atawat) nullahs at the head of the Bandipur valley, as well as in the forests below the Pulwar nullah. In Sikkim and the eastern Himalayas they are more common.

Leopard.—In the Himalayas there are two species of leopard, the *Felis pardus* or ordinary leopard, and the *Felis uncia* or snow leopard. The former is generally called a cheetah in the hills, and the latter "safed cheetah." The leopard does an immense amount of harm in the Himalayas, destroying a lot of game and occasionally becoming, like his brother in the plains, a veritable curse to the locality he favours, by killing cattle wholesale, though he does not often turn his attention to man-eating.

He may sometimes be met when after game, but more often haunts the hillside near a village, or follows herds of goats and sheep to their grazing grounds. It is difficult to get a shot at him, as he cannot even be relied on to return to a partly eaten "kill," knowing that the birds, foxes and dogs will have left but little by the next evening. Tying up a goat and sitting over it may sometimes be successful, but it is weary work and poor sport. Your sitting-place, whether in a tree, or on rocks, or in bushes, must be very carefully concealed from all sides, and must above all be comfortable, for the slightest movement or rustle will spoil your chance of a shot. The leopard will generally circle round the "kill" or the goat before advancing on it, to satisfy himself that the coast is clear.

The snow leopard is generally to be found in ibex and markhor ground. He does not come below a line that seems to run from Gagai nullah, through Gurais and Tilel along the heights above the Wangat nullah and northern portion of the Scinde valley. In Baltistan there are many snow leopards, and they levy a heavy tax on the herds of small ibex. In Astore they are plentiful, but very seldom seen. It is useless to spend time in trying to get a shot at one, but you are sure to come across them sooner or later when after ibex. They are, as a rule, smaller than the ordinary yellow leopard,

CAMP IN DECEMBER: AFTER MARKHOR

LEOPARD SHOT BY CAPT. ARBUTHNOT, NEAR BANDIPUR

Measurements, unskinned, 8 feet $5\frac{1}{2}$ inches; skinned, 10 feet 1 inch; cured and dressed, 9 feet 6 inches

(Believed to be the Record)

but carry lovely coats, with very long fur. They are plentiful also in Ladakh, Zaskar and the northern borders of Lahoul and Chamba.

Small game.—The small game shooting of Kashmir comprises pheasants, chakor and partridges, duck, geese, teal and snipe. The season commences on September 16th, and a license of Rs.20 is required.

The low hills round the Wular lake hold plenty of chakor, which give the best sport, in particular the hills covered with small scrub jungle between Kunas and Alsoa on the west of the lake. The entrances to the Erin nullah and Scinde valley also have some likely hills.

The handsome manaul is to be found high up in the Kajinag range, and in the Scinde valley. I have seen more on the borders of Chamba and Badrawar than anywhere else.

The duck shooting is good, but the best of the jheels are preserved by the Kashmir State. On the Wular lake there are generally thousands of duck and many geese towards the end of November, but a punt-gun is required to reach them. Natives are continually shooting them with weird weapons, 10 feet long, made of wood with iron bands! There is a string of good jheels on the left bank of the Jhelum, as you go by boat from Srinagar to the Wular lake, and in the evening the duck flight well there, but rather high. The beginning of December is the best time.

APPENDIX I

A ROUGH estimate of the expenses of a shooting expedition of two or three months in the Himalayas may be useful. Excluding license, travelling expenses to Srinagar or whatever the starting-point may be, and stores, the following should be a fair estimate of the monthly expenses likely to be incurred :—

Shikari . . .	Rs. 35
Tiffin coolie . .	Rs. 12
Cook . . .	Rs. 12
4 permanent coolies .	Rs. 34
8 baggage coolies for 15 marching days .	Rs. 30
Local shikari for 16 shooting days .	Rs. 8
Food	Rs. 20
Tips to lumbadars and rewards for game .	Rs. 15
Miscellaneous cash .	Rs. 20
Total	Rs. 186 (£12, 8s.)

This estimate allows for twelve coolie loads of baggage. In places where much rice or atta has to be carried for your permanent servants, the expenses are slightly increased. Pony transport, where available, is quicker and, if anything, cheaper. After once leaving civilisation Rs.200 a month in Kashmir and Rs.160 in Chamba is a very fair allowance for expenses. Stores naturally vary according to individual tastes. Rs.25 to Rs.30 a month should cover the cost of necessaries.

When going far afield in Ladakh or Thibet, of course, the cost of transport is considerably increased.

The following average prices of articles of food vary considerably in different years and in different localities :—

Chickens, 4 to 5 annas each.	Potatoes, 10 to 20 seers a rupee.
Eggs, 2 annas a dozen.	Rice, 6 to 10 seers a rupee.
Sheep, Rs.3 to Rs.4 each.	Flour, 5 seers a rupee.
Milk, 16 seers (32 lbs.) a rupee.	

APPENDIX II

Local Names of various Game

Ovis ammon	Nyan (in Thibet).
Burhel .	Narpoo (in Ladakh).
Sharpu .	Same name. In Astore, Oorin.
Markhor .	Same name.
Ibex . .	Kāle. In Astore, Mayar.
Kashmir stag	Bara singh.
Thar . .	Same name.

Goural . . .	Same name.
Serow . . .	Same name.
Musk deer . .	Kustoorah.
Black bear . .	Kalē Bhalu.
Red bear . .	Lal Bhalu.
Leopard . .	Cheetah.
Snow leopard .	Safed Cheetah.
Wolf . . .	Shanko.
Fox . . .	Lumbri.
Tiger . . .	Sher.

APPENDIX III

Jammu and Kashmir State

Game Laws Notification—1903-04

1. The rules apply to all European and Native residents, and visitors, ladies as well as gentlemen, also to all State subjects and officials with the exception of those who have been especially exempted by order of His Highness the Maharaja in Council.

2. The rules are applicable to the Kashmir Province, and Astore District, Ladakh, including Zaskar, Baltistan including Kargil, Dras and Suru, and to the Kishtwar Tahsil of the Jammu Province as at present existing, and to Padar in the Udhampur Wazarat, with the following exceptions:—

(*a*) All Jagir lands belonging to General Raja Sir Amar Singh, K.C.S.I.

(*b*) The Ilaqa of the Raja of Poonch, and

(*c*) All State Game Reserves which now exist or may be hereafter framed. The existing Rakhs or State Game Reserves are: (1) Drogmula (Machwara) on the Pohru River, (2) Chashma Shahi and Dachigam,

(3) Khonmoo, (4) Khru, (5) Tral Cum-Kerrim, (6) Achabal with its extensions towards Kachewan, (7) Koolgam, (8) Hokra Jhil and the Kowsa Jhil near Amirgund, and Pushkar (near Gulmarg), Namla Nala including Kandi and Lajri, and Kanthua including Khoras and Phala in the Uri Tahsil.

In General Raja Sir Amar Singh's Jagir and in the Ilaqa of the Raja of Poonch, no one is allowed to shoot without the permission of the respective Rajas.

Shooting in any of the State Reserves is also strictly prohibited, unless the special permission of the Durbar is first obtained, nor can any one, without a special pass issued from the Durbar, shoot in any of the lands situated in the Jammu Province except in Kishtwar and in Wardwan and Dachan (which are part of the Kishtwar Tahsil), and in Padar and Zanskar, nor can any one shoot or wander within any of the Game Laws' sanctuaries mentioned hereafter.

A special permit is required for the Astore District, including Bunji, without which no one is permitted to travel or shoot; and all routes leading into Astore from Baltistan are closed except under special permission from the Resident in Kashmir, application for which should be made to the Secretary, Game Preservation Department, Srinagar.

3. The driving of Bears, Leopards and Pigs is permitted from May 15th to November 15th inclusive; and on the grounds open to sport in any of the hills between Vernag and Baramulla, and in the hills on the south side of the Vale of Kashmir, the driving of these animals is allowed from April 1st to November 15th inclusive. With the above exceptions driving game with men and dogs is prohibited wherever the Game Laws apply.

4. Except in the rare instances, where, owing to the excessive number, other arrangements become necessary, the destruction of females of Ovis Hodgsoni (the ammon of sportsmen), Sharpu, Burhel, Markhor, Ibex, Thibetan Antelope, Gazelle, Khakur (Barking Deer), Goral, Serow and Kashmir Deer is forbidden.

The Secretary, Kashmir State Game Preservation Department, is, however, authorized to give written permission for a fixed number of females of Sharpu, Burhel, Goral, Serow, Ibex, Markhor or Deer to be shot within a defined locality, when he is convinced that such action is necessitated in the interests of sport by the existence of an excessive number of females of these animals. Such permission, if given, is to be restricted to License-holders or to State servants detailed for this work.

5. Shooting, killing and catching, etc., of Yak are totally prohibited. No Musk Deer, either male or female, may be killed, taken or caught by any resident, visitor or State subject within the territories of His Highness the Maharaja, except under the authority of a written order obtained from the Durbar through the Secretary, Kashmir State Game Preservation Department, and such permission shall only be given in rare instances.

6. The possession of a net for the express purpose of taking birds or wild animals is illegal, except netting used in Kishtwar for the purpose of catching Hawks.

7. The sale or export for sale of horns or skins of the game animals mentioned in Rule 4, as well as of the skins of Brown Bears, is prohibited. The sale of the skins of Black Bears and Leopards is allowed.

8. The breeding season of Chakor, Partridges and Pheasants is considered to extend from March 1st to September 15th, both days inclusive, that of Geese, Ducks, and Teal from April 15th to September 15th, Snipe from April 15th to August 31st both days inclusive: and during the season thus defined no one shall destroy, net or capture in any fashion any of these birds, nor shall any of their eggs be taken. Neither shall any person sell any such birds after the breeding season commences.

9. The shooting season for Chakor, Partridges and Pheasants is considered to extend from September 16th to the last day of February, that for Wild Fowl, such as Geese, Ducks, and Teal from September 16th to April 14th inclusive, and Snipe from September 1st to April 14th. During this season, villagers may noose Wild Fowl in their fields which have been under cultivation during the previous harvest or which are still under crop, but no nets or lines with hooks may be set,

nor may any one capture with snares, nets or hooks any Wild Fowl on any Lake, Jhil, River or Stream.

10. The following Nullahs are closed until further orders, and no shooting is permitted therein, nor is any grazing allowed :—

I.—The Oor in the Liddar. This is on the right bank of the Liddar close to Dowhut.

II.—The *Zais Nai* in the Wardwan. This joins the Kreashnae above Furriabad, and the stream is the Western source of the Furriabad River.

III.—The *Gueo Nai* in the Wardwan. This is the Nullah which joins the left bank of the Wardwan River one march above Maru Wardwan.

IV.—The Phoo, or as it is sometimes called the Kurtsee Phoo. It joins the right bank of the Suru River above Kargil.

V.—The Basgo in Ladakh. This is above the village of Basgo on the Leh Road.

VI.—Melangan in the Kajinag.

VII.—Kachnambal and Chattergul in the Sind Valley.

11. Licenses to shoot large and small game, and without which no person is permitted to shoot, will be granted as follows :—

I.—A license, for which Rs.60 will be charged, in force from March 15th to November 15th, permits the holder to shoot, in the Nullahs and Districts which are open for sport, the following numbers of animals only :—

Markhor of any variety in all	2	Thibetan Gazelle	1
Ibex	6	Kashmir Stag	2
Ovis Hodgsoni (Ammon)	1	Serow	1
Ovis Vignei (Sharpu)	2	Brown Bear	4
Ovis Nahura (Burhel)	6	Tahr	6
Thibetan Antelope	6	Goral	6

Also subject to rules 8 and 9 above, small game up to

November 15th, and Pigs, Black Bears and Leopards no limit.

II.—A License of the value of Rs.20 will permit the holder to kill Black Bears and Leopards and Pigs, from March 15th to November 15th inclusive.

III.—A winter License, for which Rs.30 will be charged, in force from November 15th to March 14th, will permit the holder to kill:—

Markhor any variety	2	Kashmir Stag	1
Ibex	3	Serow	1
Ovis Vignei (Sharpu)	2	Tahr	3
Ovis Nahura	3	Brown Bear	2
Thibetan Antelope	3	Goral	3
Thibetan Gazelle	1		

Pigs, Black Bears and Leopards without limit.

IV.—To meet the special circumstances of Baltistan and Ladakh, a license of the value of Rs.10 will be issued by the Secretary, Kashmir State Game Preservation Department, on application being made through the Wazir-Wazarat of Ladakh, and this license will enable the holder to kill in Baltistan or Ladakh between November 16th and March 14th inclusive:—

IN BALTISTAN.		IN LADAKH.	
Ibex	6	Ovis Nahura	6
Ovis Vignei	2	Ovis Vignei	2

Chakor and Ram Chakor, Leopards (including the Ounce) no limit.

The holder of this license will not require any special permit to shoot wolves, lynxes, foxes or martens, and, if desired, the reward in force at the time can be recovered for the destruction of such vermin. No one individual can hold licenses III and IV at the same time.

V.—A small game license, for which Rs.20 will be charged, will enable the holder to kill Pheasants, Chakor and Partridges from September 16th to the last day of February inclusive, and also to kill Geese Ducks, and Teal from September 16th to April 14th inclusive. Snipe from September 1st to April 14th.

Sportsmen holding any of these licenses may kill Ram Chakor between the dates of September 16th and May 1st. Quail shooting is free.

12. All regular Kashmir Shikaris taking service with sportsmen will, in future, be registered and licensed annually under the Game Laws. Any Shikari, watcher, or State servant employed or registered under the Game Laws who wilfully commits or abets the commission of any infringement of the Game Laws, or fails to report any such infringement on its being brought to his notice, or who having been suspended for misconduct under rules 13 and 14 shall during such period take service with sportsmen, shall be liable to be proceeded against under Sections 13 and 14. Any sportsman wishing to employ a villager or local man is requested to communicate his name to the Secretary when he will become liable to the above penalties.

13. Whoever intentionally commits a breach of Rules I, II, III, IV, VI, VII, X, XI, (I) (II) (III) (IV) and XII shall be punished, on first conviction, with a fine not exceeding Rs. 25 or with imprisonment for a term not exceeding one month, or both, and on second conviction with a fine not exceeding Rs.100 or with imprisonment not exceeding four months or both, together with forfeiture of the guns or other weapons and dogs of the offender to the State, and if the offender is a Shikari, with the forfeiture of license for one year, provided that, when the offender is a European or the servant, who is not a Kashmiri subject, of a European, in addition to the forfeiture of license the case shall be immediately reported to the Resident for disposal in such a manner as he may think fit.

14. Subject to the same proviso, any person convicted of a breach of Rules VIII, IX, XI (V) and XII shall be punished with a fine not exceeding in each case Rs.25, and, if convicted of a breach of Rule V, shall be punished, on first conviction, with a fine up to Rs.100, or with imprisonment not exceeding three months, or both. In case of second conviction, the

punishment shall be a fine not exceeding Rs.100 or imprisonment up to four months, or both, together with forfeiture to the State of the guns or other weapons and dogs, if any, accompanying the offender, and, if the offender is a Shikari, with forfeiture of the license for a period of one year.

15. *Rewards.* Any person or persons who shall give such *bona-fide* information, with proof, as shall lead to a conviction under the above sections of the Game Laws shall receive a reward not exceeding Rs.25, and further any person or persons who shall give similar information of a breach of Rule 5 shall receive a reward not exceeding Rs.40. Applications in all cases to be made to the Secretary, Game Preservation Department.

16. License-holders who, by the conditions of the license, are enjoined not to kill more than a specified number of animals, are requested on the expiry of the period of the license, to return the same to the Secretary, Kashmir State Game Preservation Department, with a statement showing the number of animals killed by them.

17. Sportsmen are particularly requested not to give presents to the Game Preservation Department servants, and to report any irregularities on their part to the Secretary, Game Preservation Department. Game Preservation Department servants receiving presents from sportsmen will be dismissed.

18. His Highness the Maharaja may, in writing, relax any or all of the Rules I-IX inclusive in favour of any individual.

(Sd.) E. G. COLVIN,
Resident in Kashmir.

(„) AMAR SINGH,
GENERAL, RAJA,
Vice-President of Council, Jammu and Kashmir State.

21st January 1903.

NOTE.—Applications for Licenses may be made to Cockburn's Agency, Kashmir General Agency, Motmid Durbar (Officer in Charge European Visitors) or in person to the Secretary, to whom all other communications should be addressed either personally or by letter to care of Post-master, Srinagar.

(Sd.) H. R. WIGRAM, MAJOR,
Secretary Kashmir State, Game Preservation Department, Srinagar.

Books and Maps

The Ordnance Survey Maps of the country surrounding Kashmir will be found very useful. They can be obtained in four sheets in Bombay or Calcutta, or may be seen at Cockburn's Agency, Srinagar, and tracings of the parts required made.

Dr Neve's "Tourists' Guide to Kashmir, Ladakh and Skardu" will be found very useful, as it contains much information regarding routes. It can be bought in Srinagar.

Colonel Ward's "Sportsman's Guide to Kashmir" is an excellent book, but the nullahs which were recommended in 1886 cannot be relied on to hold good heads now.

THE DEER AND ANTELOPE OF THE INDIAN PLAINS

The former of these two distinct classes is particularly well represented in India, especially if we include the mountains; the latter only sparingly so as to variety, though in actual numbers they probably exceed the deer. The essential difference between the two is sufficiently well known; the deer shed their horns, and the antelope do not. This difference is very important to the sportsman, as he shoots for a trophy, and, in the case of the deer tribe, the horn-bearing period is necessarily a restricted one. This period, moreover, being, roughly, from October to April, occurs just at the season when leave is seldom obtainable, and so the chances of a shot at any but those which may be within very easy reach are, for the military officer at least, much reduced in consequence. Again, all the deer inhabit forest tracts, more or less dense, and this also naturally increases the difficulty of obtaining a shot. With the antelope it is different. They, with the exception of the Nilgai and four-horned antelope, which are not of much account, prefer the more open plains, and, as they also have their horns all the year round, the sport is more easily obtainable, and specimens are far more common.

Like most other countries, there is no doubt that India in the matter of sport is not what it was a hundred years ago, but in comparison with many other regions, where the white man's ruthless hand has not been restrained, the change has not been nearly so great, and what is left is by no means to be despised. Some writers and many sportsmen are inclined to attribute the diminution of game animals chiefly, if not entirely, to natives. In this I cannot agree. It seems to me, on the contrary, quite apparent that it is to the white sportsman and his deadly weapons that by far the greater part of the decrease is due, to say nothing of the indirect responsibility for much destruction by natives incurred by those non-sportsmen, who are always ready to purchase horn or skin trophies. Look at the Ibex and half a dozen other grand animals of Kashmir, now not a tenth in number of what they were, or at the sadly diminished numbers of black-buck, ravine deer, sambur and cheetal of the plains. Why were there so many of all these when the white man arrived in the country, if the native is responsible? No doubt, the continual improvement of weapons has had a great deal to do with the increase in destruction, but are not these chiefly in the hands of the white man? It is all inevitable, I suppose, and it certainly does not become me to cavil at the sporting instinct which has helped on the destruction. But there is reasonable sport, and there is useless and unconsidered slaughter, and protest cannot be too strong against the latter, especially the killing of females and under-sized males. As to the native question, again, if it is beyond dispute that there are many meat-eating and hunting tribes scattered over the country, whose methods are undiscriminating and ruthless, it should also be remembered that it is to the natives after all, that is, to the religious scruples and general gentle character of a vast proportion of the population, that we *owe* the survival of so many of the animals, especially the antelope. Some protective legislation has no doubt become very desirable at the present day, but the process of annihilation will not be greatly stayed unless it restrains the white man as well as the brown.

The Indian Antelope, or Black-buck.
Vernacular, Hiran

He deserves the premier place both from his numbers and his ubiquity, and we might add, his beauty. With exception of the north-western portion of the Punjab, and the denser jungle tracts, he may be said to be all over the country —*i.e.* the plains of India proper, for he does not extend to the hills.

Travelling through almost any district, you will come across them, sometimes in large herds, and herd after herd ; you see them from the train window, a regiment on the march is always after buck, and notwithstanding their general sad diminution in numbers, there are still localities where hundreds are to be seen in a single herd, and you may get three or four good heads in a day. This antelope is a never ending source of interest and excitement to the subaltern, and the pursuit of him supplies a perenniel and perfectly excellent school for exercise of his ingenuity, patience and marksmanship.

His habitat is simply the natural country, the cultivated fields interspersed here and there with light jungle or bare plain. He feeds from the same lands as the cattle and goats of the villagers and takes heavy toll from their fields. Though essentially an animal of the open plain, he, how-

Photo] BLACK BUCK (N.W. INDIA) [*P. S. Van der Byl*

ever, accommodates himself to fairly thick forest country in the Central Provinces, and here some very fine heads are to be got. But the best localities for big heads are Bikanir, and the country towards Ferozepore from there, and Gujerat and Katiawar in Bombay. In Madras they run much smaller, seldom up to 17 ins., wheras in the north, nothing less than 20 ins. is a good head, and they run up to 25 ins., and even to 28 ins. Though for the most part dwelling actually in the midst of men, the getting of a shot is not such an easy matter, and, fine target though an old buck presents, a beginner, or anyone who is not careful, will find it the simplest thing in the world to miss when he does get the chance. In stalking, you must just use the best common-sense you can muster. Endeavour, first, to see your game before he sees you, to which end it is well to keep the sun at your back. Take advantage of all cover; don't wear conspicuous clothes. If you think you are discovered, keep stock-still till the suspicion is past, etc., etc., and so gradually work your way nearer. Then for the shot. What I would say to a beginner is, don't waste time, but whatever you do *remember the bend* as you pull the trigger. A rifle is not like a shot gun, with which you may hit if the aim is there or thereabouts. If the aim is not quite true at the moment of discharge, you *must* miss, get that into your head and always bear it in mind. Some will use a bullock cart, and even dress like a native to get a shot, but this I always thought just bordering on the illegitimate. You may, however, make good use of your horse in various ways: hide behind him, dismount and get to cover while he is sent on, etc. A horse is sometimes useful to overtake a wounded buck, or, as a variety, you may try what I have occasionally practised with success. Gallop hard, so as to cut in on the line of retreat of a herd on the move, dismount, and have a shot or two as they go by. Aim a yard in front of the chest at a hundred yards, and you should bag your animal. I have also sometimes kicked them up, lying in long grass in the middle of the day, and shot them like rabbits. When shooting among crops, be careful to see there are no natives in the line of fire.

The Indian Gazelle, or Ravine Deer.
Vernacular, Chikara

This is a much smaller animal, and his horns, as compared with those of the black buck, insignificant. But in shape he is a truly graceful little creature, and his head a beautiful and much desired trophy. His distribution, though not nearly so general as that of the black buck, is wider, extending from the extreme south to the extreme north-west, and continuing into the plains among the Baluchistan mountains. He may be found on the same ground as antelope, but prefers more secluded spots, and more broken ground. He is not difficult to approach, but is restless, and a shot must be taken quickly. For him, as also for black buck, it is most useful to know how to shoot from the shoulder. Being small and coloured like the ground, he is not easy to see. A good horn measures from 13 to 14 inches.

The Four-Horned Antelope

This is even smaller than the *Chikara*, being only about 2 feet high. He inhabits thick jungle; and, as it is usually when after more important game that one comes across him, and that not often, specimens are comparatively rare. His distribution is wide, from south to north. The posterior horns are from 4 to 5 inches, anterior 1 to 1½ inches.

The Nilgai

This, a very different animal from all the above and by far the largest of the antelopes, stands from 13 to 14 hands, and is somewhat heavily built. The name means blue bull, which shows that the natives believed him to be bovine. And indeed, except for his head, which is fine and game-looking, he bears little resemblance to the antelope type. It is only the male which is of a bluish colour, the females being, like those of all the other antelopes and deer, light brown. His horns are from 8 to 10 inches only, and he is not otherwise much worth shooting. He is sometimes speared from horseback, but oftener has the best of the run. His distribution is pretty general, but he is not found in Mysore or south of that, though occurring in most forest land farther north.

The antelope family are still further represented in the Himalayas by the Thibetan antelope and ravine deer, quite distinct from their prototypes of India and by the Takin, a very curious variety inhabiting the mountains to the north of Assam, a region not yet freely open to the sportsman. But a description of these is outside the scope of this section.

The Sambur

We now come to the deer tribe, of which the sambur, or sambhur, may be reckoned the finest representative in the plains. Standing as he does from 13 to 14 hands, having a great shaggy neck, and horns that may run to 40 and even up to 46 inches, particularly conspicuous in thickness and generally with a fine wide spread, he is altogether a grand animal and few are more worthy to be bagged. He has a wider distribution, too, than all other deer, extending from the southern Indian hills up to 8000 feet of elevation in the Himalayas. Plain and hill seem to suit him equally well, but he must have more or less thick forest, and broken ground. The Siwaliks, and Terai in the north, Central India and Central Provinces, Eastern and Western Ghauts of Bombay and the Neilgherrys in Madras are all well-known localities. The only place in which he actually occurs in the Himalayas is, as far as I am aware, a tract to the north and west of the hill station of Mussoorie. Here he is mis-called Bara Singh. In Madras the heads are not nearly so fine as farther north, 35 inches being considered a good specimen. The horns are shed in April, and are not again free from velvet till about October. Besides the brow antler there are only two points, and these are not fully developed till the animal is four years old. Sambur may be obtained by stalking in the more open forests, by still hunting, or by beating. The stalker is, however, much hampered by the dead leaves which in the dry cold weather are in a perfect condition for outrageous crackling, and the same drawback is, of course, equally in evidence in still hunting. For this reason, therefore, and also owing to the unbroken continuity of many of the forests, beating has to be resorted to. This, to my mind, is not nearly so fascinating, and when it is remembered that even in fairly good localities it often takes about fifty drives to bag one good sambur, the sportsman will be excused if he sometimes complains of monotony in this form of sport. Yet there is fascination in it too, and there is the chance of seeing many kinds of animals—a pig or a panther, a peacock or a troop of monkeys, or even a tiger. There is the need for absolute stillness, and the anxiety to see what is coming when a distant rustle is heard. Of all the deer, the sambur is the most timid and cunning in refusing to be driven: at the last moment he will suddenly break back, charging right through the beaters, or over any man who bars his way, and so many drives are in vain. Adequate concealment, and perfect silence and stillness are therefore necessary.

The Spotted Deer—Cheetal (Chital)

If the sambur is best described as a grand animal, the most appropriate adjective for the cheetal is beautiful. The lightness and symmetry of his form, the graceful proportions of his long horns, and his bright white-spotted skin all warrant this. He is considerably smaller and lighter than the sambur, his usual height measuring about the same as a good pair of horns—36 inches or thereabouts. His general habitat is much the same, but he does not reach such high elevations, and when found in proximity to the sambur he will be in the lower valley bottoms between the spurs, while the sambur will be near the crests of these. The period of shedding the horns is very irregular, and he may be found in hard horn in the hot weather almost as frequently as in the cold—a point to be remembered. His horns have the same number of points as those of the sambur, but are proportionally thinner and more graceful. He is sought for and shot by the same methods. One other method which may be tried for both is that of sitting by moonlight over water where they come to drink.

Swamp Deer

This is a fine deer, standing 11½ hands; horns from 30 to 40 inches. The points are not so regular in numbers as in most of the other deer, generally twelve, and hence called by the natives Bara Singha, but often more and sometimes as many as twenty. He is found in considerable numbers generally along the foot of the outer Himalayas—Dehra Doon, Nepal, Assam—and also in parts of Central India and the Central Provinces. The horns are shed in spring.

The Hog Deer—Para

This is a smaller animal than the spotted deer, the horns similar in shape and points but measuring only 15 inches or so. He is essentially a jungle animal, not gregarious and not stalkable. He is not found in the south, but plenty in the Terai jungles, where he may be shot from an elephant when beating for a general bag. He sheds his horns in spring.

The Muntjac or Barking Deer—Kakar

He has a very wide distribution, being found in all forests from south to north, where he reaches an elevation of 7000 feet. He is a small animal, horns from 5 to 7 inches with only the beam and one tine. He has canine teeth projecting downwards from upper jaw, and can use them when attacked. His call is often heard, and he may frequently be seen when beating or walking through jungle, but it is seldom one gets a satisfactory shot.

The Mouse Deer—Pisuri

A pretty little animal, only 12 inches high: to be found in jungle all over the country, but seldom seen, and still more seldom shot.

Eld's Deer—Thamin

This deer does not belong to India proper, but as his range extends from Burmah up to the eastern borders, and as he is essentially an animal of the plains, a short notice here may not be out of place. He has a fairly wide distribution, from the Chindwin Valley south-eastwards to Tennasserim, Siam and the Malay Peninsula, and on the north-west is said to extend to Manipur and Assam. He is most accessible to the British sportsman in Lower Burmah, where he is to be found in many parts of the vast plains between the mountains and the sea. He is described as frequenting high elephant grass, and may be stalked in the open patches, shot from an elephant or driven. A head is specially worth procuring, not only on account of its comparative rarity, but from the unique peculiarity of the horns. The brow antler is not only of phenomenal length, but there being no burr at the base, it has the appearance of being a prolongation of the beam. Ten points is the usual number, and a good horn measures 40 inches exclusive of brow antler. The horns are not out of velvet till February, consequently the shooting season cannot begin till March, and may go on till May. This is a very hot time in Burmah, but the nights are described as cool.

[The Bara Singh of Kashmir and the Sikhim stag complete the list of the Indian deer family. They are perhaps finer and more desirable than any of the foregoing, but these belonging as they do exclusively to the mountains, do not come within the present category (see page 178).]

Two other animals, not deer or antelope, but belonging to India proper, may, however, be noted here, as, being somewhat isolated specimens, they might not find a place elsewhere.

The Neilgherry Ibex

This animal is of the goat tribe, and being found nowhere else but in the hills of Southern India—Neilgherry, Pulneys, Western Ghauts, etc.—is a somewhat peculiar example of isolation. He has no resemblance to any of the ibex family but appears to be closely allied to the tehr, another goat of the Himalayas, and frequents the same kind of ground, steep, rocky, but jungle-clad cliffs. To bag a good specimen nowadays, requires all that patience and toil which a good hill shikari should appreciate. His horns measure from 14 to 17 inches.

The Oorial

Here we have a sheep. He is best known as belonging to the Salt Range in the Punjab, but extends to the Baluchistan and Afghan mountains. He has also pushed his way all up the valley of the Indus, and figures as the Oorin in far-off Gilgit, Astore, Baltistan and as the Sharpoo in Ladakh. Heads of 30 inches and over were not uncommon in the Salt Range thirty years ago, but now 24 inches is, I believe, considered well worth shooting. Like all the sheep he is very wary, and gives ample scope for all usual stalking precautions. A herd when disturbed will go a long way, and at a great pace. His flesh is excellent camp fare.

Rifles

As regards rifles, I have no very positive or peculiar fancies; my experience has rather lain the other way. The ·450 and ·500 Express I have, like others, found quite good and reliable, but at the same time all those on the market are not to be trusted. Again, the necessity of the high velocity and hollow bullet principle seemed contradicted by the excellent work I have seen done with the American Maynard ·400 bore, with which a very small powder charge and solid bullet are used. Then, personally, I have done a great part of my shooting with the ordinary (now ancient) Government Martini-Henry, both rifle and carbine, which for deadliness I found quite equal to anything else. I had on one occasion eleven kills for the same number of shots, the animals accounted for being bears, tehr and ibex, all recognised as tough. I substituted a hollow for the solid bullet, but made no increase in the powder charge. My last rifle was a sporting ·303 Lee-Metford carbine, and I found it very excellent, good enough for anything except the most dangerous animals.

SMALL GAME SHOOTING

SURELY no country is more favoured than India in quantity or variety of sport for the shot gun. If you are not in a region for snipe and duck, then you will probably be within easy reach of partridge and hares, or quail country, and if not these, then there may be pea-fowl or sand grouse, koolen, or *houbara,* or even the great bustard. These are in the plains.

If you are stationed in the hills or submontane country, you may have one or more of the numerous pheasants, jungle-fowl, pea-fowl again, wood-cock, or that grand sporting bird, the chikore. And again, failing all these, or in addition, you will find the common blue rock scattered over all the land, plain and hill, or you may often have plenty of fun with green pigeon among the pipul trees around your own station, nay, in your own compound.

With exception of the Government reserved forest lands, and some native states, all shooting in India is perfectly free, and trespass on fields, even standing crops, is little regarded either by the shooter or the cultivator. All this is no doubt a matter for congratulation, but at the same time it would be well if there were more protection. For many parts of the country, formerly alive with game, have been sadly denuded, some famed spots being indeed now not worth trying. The migratory birds—snipe, duck, geese, koolen, quail, wood-cock, etc.—seem to be least affected, and there is little diminution in their numbers, but the various partridges and the hares, have suffered much from over-shooting. If you have not, then, to pay for your sport, you must be prepared to take trouble, and to do some work for it, and if you would avoid disappointments, you must be careful to get good local information.

Shooting is practically confined to the cold weather, that unbroken succession of bright days with delicious cool air, but no wind, which is such a revelation and delight to the storm-inured Englishman. Yet the sun can be hot even at this season, and you may expect many a sweltering day after snipe in a sticky jheel in September or March, when you will come to know how to enjoy a drink.

THE SNIPE. *Vernacular*, CHAHA

I begin with the snipe because he may be said to be not only the most widely distributed, but also the most numerous, and perhaps affords the best sport. Wherever, all over the land, there is marshy ground of the right sort, there he will be found in September or October, as regularly as the months themselves come round, and he does not take flight again until March. There are two varieties of the common, or "full" snipe as he is called, but the difference is not easily distinguishable. The jack snipe is quite another species, much smaller, and though quite worth shooting if nothing else to be had, he is not much attended to if plenty of the others are about. The so-called "painted" snipe is not, I believe, a snipe at all. He frequents the same ground however, and although his flight is much slower and more "floppy," he is generally shot, by mistake or otherwise, if he has the bad luck to get up when a snipe is expected. He is not common. The solitary snipe and the wood snipe are two other varieties, still more uncommon. It would be hopeless to attempt an enumeration of good localities for snipe. The biggest bags are perhaps made in Burmah and Bengal, but I have a notion that the birds are not so strong of flight there as in the colder Punjab and United Provinces. Snipe certainly vary much in this respect: in rice land, or other good cover, in the heat of the day they will rise close and fly somewhat lazily, whereas on some of the barer Punjab jheels, and with a cool breeze, you will have a 40 to 50 yards rise, and a succession of lightning twists, sufficient to test any man's quickness. At this kind of game you will find (and I am assuming that you are a *good* shot, but not shooting for an *average*) that you will not do much better than hit and miss during a season. The usual method of shooting is in line with beaters, two coolies per gun. In some parts you may shoot from an elephant, and in Kashmir a boat is often used, the snipe sitting among the floating water plants.

DUCK AND TEAL. *Vernacular*, BATAK, MURGHABI

Like the snipe, and at the same season, duck in vast flocks and great variety come down from their northern homes, and take up their abode for the cold weather in India. And as snipe are found wherever there is suitable marshy ground, so every bit of still water, when there is the necessary food, will, as a rule, have its duck, more or less, according to capacity. Mallard, pintail, gadwell, spoon-bill, shoveller, pochard, not to mention the handsome and ubiquitous ruddy sheldrake (the familiar "Brahmini"), are the commoner sorts, while there are the common, the cotton and the whistling teal. All, except perhaps the last, give fine sport, and all require some hitting and killing. But of the lot my favourites were the lusty mallard, the "breedy" pintail, and the beautiful common teal. It is by no means easy to make a good bag of duck. You must suit your methods to the nature of each place. You will often commence the campaign with a cautious stalk for a pot shot, thereafter concealing yourself and waiting for the return of the duck, or following them on to some other bit of water. In other places boats are the only means of approach, and in others again you will take to the water and do a deal of deep wading among reeds and weeds. When there are plenty of reeds, or other cover, and plenty of duck, several guns posted at points of vantage around or in the sanctuary is the best method of all, and in such conditions you may come in for a real hot corner. When this comes off no shooting is more satisfactory.

GEESE. *Vernacular*, HANS, RAJ-HANS

There is always great satisfaction in circumventing a goose. He is not the best of eating, and he is easy to hit when you get a fair chance. But there it is, he is so big, and tempting and tantalising, with his leisurely flight, coming *almost* over you, but not quite, and his aggressive, truculent cry, that you long to get at him. But he is a wary fellow, none more so, and he will give you many of the proverbial chases before you have the laugh on your side. There are two kinds in India, the grey and the bur-headed—crowds of them too—and they come in with the ducks.

THE KOOLEN. *Vernacular*, KOONJ

This is a large crane of bluish-grey colour. His habits are much the same as those of geese, coming in large flocks from rivers or other waters to feed in the fields, very wary, and thus very satisfactory to bag. He is better eating than a goose. Learn early to distinguish him from the sarus, and spare the latter. He also is a crane of much the same colour, but larger. A fine, handsome bird, harmless, and affording no sport.

PARTRIDGES. *Vernacular,* TEETUR

The grey is most numerous, and the most widely distributed; he is all over the country, very plentiful in places, and affords quite good sport, being not too easy to hit. He knows how to use his legs, but is not over-hard to flush. He is apt to be a foul feeder, and it is only when killed at some distance from villages that one cares to eat him. He frequents jungly tracts, and some standing crops. His cheery call soon becomes familiar to the sportsman.

The black partridge is a fine, handsome bird, but his distribution is much less general. He is not, I think, found in Madras, and only sparingly in Bombay, but in many places to the north of these, extending, in fact, right up to the outer spurs of the Himalayas. He frequents jungly tracts, and often feeds among crops, but his favourite cover is long elephant, or other reedy, grass. He is not so hard to kill as the grey, but, being inclined to rocket, the shots are more sporting. Altogether a satisfactory bird, being both handsome and good for the table.

The painted partridge is another variety, but not common anywhere.

The Sisi is a small species, found in the hilly country of the north-west frontier, and, I believe, in the Salt Range. He is a great runner, and, affecting bare, stony ground, cannot be flushed satisfactorily.

But the finest of all the partridges is the chikore, a very handsome bird, somewhat larger than a grouse. He is not found in the plains proper, but all along the northern sub-montane country, and over all the mountains to the west, north and east of India, from Baluchistan to Thibet, his habitat extending from 2000 to 13,000 feet of elevation. In the higher ranges he frequents steep mountain sides bare of everything but grass, and being a great runner, here nothing but a pot shot, or an occasional right and left can be hoped for. He never goes into really thick cover, but in the lower hills—from 4000 to 8000 feet—he will be found on rocky hillsides with occasional patches of low scrub interspersed with open, grassy slopes. This is the sort of place where a bag may be made. But it requires a "bundobust" (*i.e.* careful arrangement). Trustworthy men must be sent out very early to locate the coveys, the birds revealing their whereabouts by their cackling cry. The subsequent duty of these men is to mark where the birds alight after being flushed, taking up successive points of vantage for the purpose. One or two coolies work along the hillside above the sportsman, as the birds never fly uphill. And what a pace they go! It is no uncommon thing to have to aim 4 or 5 yards in front, and the bird, though killed, may be picked up a quarter of a mile away. For the rest, the ground is as steep as you may care to walk on, and you may be sure you will not ask for more exercise after a day with the chikore. He is an excellent table bird, none better.

QUAIL. *Vernacular*, BATĔR

There are several varieties, but the common quail is the only one which receives much attention from the sportsman. He is migratory, arrives in India in the autumn, and departs in April. He distributes himself generally over the whole country at first, and fair bags may be made in many parts. But towards the end of his stay he seems to work up to, and concentrate in the north, preparatory to again taking flight. So it is here that the best sport is obtained. The shooting is done among standing crops, wheat, cotton, or millet, and from fifty to one hundred couple of a morning is in some places no uncommon bag. But I have not seen such bags without the use of call-birds. This is the common device of the natives to collect the birds for netting and the same answers equally well for shooting. A few live quail in cages are set down in some central field. These are covered with a cloth, and this causes the birds to keep up a continual twittering, which attracts others from far and near, and a real hot corner in quail is the result. The shooting is fairly easy, but the birds get up with such a lively whirr that it is, to my mind, very attractive. You must be up very early for this sport. You meet with the other varieties—rain, bush, bustard and button—frequently when beating for partridge or hares in jungle or field, but they are not specially sought for, and they generally give you such a start when they get up just under your feet that you most likely miss.

SAND GROUSE. *Vernacular*, BAT-TEETUR

There are two or three varieties of these. They all frequent open, dry, uncultivated tracts, more or less stony, and with or without patches of scrub jungle. They go in flocks, and are fond of taking long flights, high up, and their peculiar cry can be heard from afar. On the bare ground they sit very close, and are so protectively coloured that even when marked down one often fails to see them, though within a few yards. I, however, once shot one thus squatted with a pea-rifle at 70 yards—a shot to brag about! When for the first time you see a sand grouse rise you would back yourself to hit him every time, but if you live long enough, you will alter that view. The common sand grouse is not of very much account, but the imperial is really a fine bird. His distribution is, however, circumscribed, and I only know of him in some parts of the Punjab and in Baluchistan. Pretty shooting and good bags can be got by watching over water where they come to drink of an evening.

THE BUSTARDS

The great bustard is the king of this tribe—a fellow as big as a turkey and with much the same general look. His distribution is extensive, but scattered, and he is nowhere found in great numbers. He is very wide-awake, and it is not easy to get within effective range of a shot gun, but it is satisfactory to bowl one over with a rifle. He is met with in extensive jungly tracts in Mysore, the Deccan, parts of Bombay, Central India, Rajputana and Punjab.

The next in size, but far smaller, is the houbara, inhabiting open jungle or grassy tracts of the Punjab, Baluchistan, Rajputana, Gujerat and Katiawar, but not farther south. In some parts considerable bags may be made with the gun, sometimes from camel back. But it is with hawks that the best sport is to be had. He is an ideal bird for this purpose, and this is well recognised by natives of the Punjab and border-land; but owing, I suppose, to his scarcity near cantonments, the sport is not much practised by Europeans. Two other varieties, the Bengal and the Lesser Florican, complete the list. The former is found in Bengal and north-east India, and the latter in Madras. Being excellent eating, a shot at any of these is welcome, but they have a weak, owl-like flight, and are easily killed.

PEA-FOWL. *Vernacular*, MŌR

These may be said to be all over India. In many parts of the plains they are too tame to be worth shooting, and in others, being held sacred, interference with them is prohibited. But when met with in the more jungly tracts away from villages in the plains, or better still, among the low sub-montane hills, he is a very different bird, and may afford quite good sport. I can testify that it is not at all impossible to miss one: indeed, when rocketing like a pheasant from one side of a nullah to another, it is astonishing how many may get off, not only unkilled, but untouched.

Wood-cock

Although wood-cock are known to frequent many parts of the outer Himalayas and offshoots of these, and are also found in the hills of Madras, the places are few where they are in sufficient numbers to make the sport a recognised one. The only places I know of where it is so are the Neilgherrys, the Kulu valley to the north of Simla, and in some hilly country near Kohat on the north-west frontier. I have often seen and heard them flitting over my tent of an evening in Kashmir, but always in vast forest tracts where it would be impossible to find them when wanted.

Pheasants. *Vernacular (general)*, Jungli Murghi

The Himalaya is the home of the pheasant, and here they are perhaps found in greater variety than elsewhere in the world, but as far as I know, nowhere else in India proper. But though in great numbers, the shooting is not often a conspicuous success. The forests are so vast and continuous that one's ingenuity is taxed, generally in vain, to find a suitable spot where they may be flushed, the shooting at birds darting down hill with lightning speed is desperately hard, and birds are often lost when killed. Still it is sometimes to be done. The best success is obtained with the kalej and koklas, the latter a lovely game bird. The argus and chir are runners, and difficult to flush, and the grand monul, though very numerous, and quite well behaved in the matter of rising, is so wary and so powerful that big bags are a thing only to be dreamt of. Of the grey peacock pheasant and crimson tragopan of the eastern Himalayas I know nothing. The snow pheasant, or ram chikore, is met with only at great heights, far above the forests. You hear his weird whistle on the tops of passes, and he seldom allows you a shot. For all, except the latter, if you cannot organize a beat, the best plan is to send one or two coolies to walk along the hillside above you, or with a dog you may cause the birds to take to trees.

JUNGLE FOWL. *Vernacular*, JUNGLI MURGHI

There are two kinds, the red and the grey. The former is found all over the lower Himalayan spurs up to 5000 feet or so, and the latter in Madras. Sometimes fair shooting may be had, beating in suitable places, but no very big bags need be expected. The red variety is just like a bantam.

Green Pigeon—Hariāl

These are by no means to be despised. They are to be found all over the plains of India, and also in the lower hills, frequenting peepul and other berry-bearing trees. You flush them off the trees and shoot them, if you can, as they dart out, then follow on to the next tree or wait till they return. A lovely bird and most succulent eating.

Blue Rocks. *Vernacular*, Kabutar

These also are found all over the country, and extend up to any height in the Himalayas, becoming almost snow-white at the higher elevations. As everyone knows, they always require some hitting and killing. In the plains they are apt to be too tame, but I have found them very wary and swift of flight in the Himalayas.

Miscellaneous

Of birds there are few more worth mention. I have shot curlew in Kashmir, and have heard of a wood pigeon, to be met with sometimes in flocks, in some parts of the outer Himalayas. Plovers are not well represented. The goggle-eyed is worth shooting for the pot if you come across him in jungle, but there is no representative of the sporting golden plover, nor, I believe, any lap-wings, though the closely allied Did-ye-do-it is ubiquitous. For the rest you may get an occasional shot at a flying squirrel in the Himalayas, worth bagging for his skin, and those who care for it may slaughter as many flying foxes as they like—no good for anything, except practice for the pea rifle.

HARES. *Vernacular*, KHARGOSH

This is the only ground game animal for the shot gun in India. He is much smaller than the English hare, and, both as to size and in regard to the character of shots he affords, is altogether more like a rabbit. Found in the same sort of jungly country as partridge, and sometimes fairly numerous. He is very generally distributed over the plains, and appears again beyond the main Himalayan range, in Baltistan and the Thibetan plateau. It is very good fun shooting him, and he is fairly good for the pot.

PART II

FISHING

CHIEFLY ABOUT THE MAHSEER
WHERE TO GO FOR FISHING IN INDIA
COMMUNICATIONS FROM CORRESPONDENTS
SEA FISHING

FISHING

I.—CHIEFLY ABOUT THE MAHSEER

INDIA has long been known as a land of sport, and deservedly so, for, I suppose, in no other one country will be found such abundance and variety of game for gun and rifle, to say nothing of the unusual facilities for sports and amusements on horse-back. And no doubt it is this which for long led to the comparative neglect of fishing. And yet there is, undoubtedly, excellent fishing, able to bear comparison with that of other lands, and surely only awaiting more general knowledge of its existence to receive far more appreciation than hitherto. It has, indeed, not been altogether neglected, and in more recent years its votaries have been rapidly increasing; but, in comparison with the great extent of fine fishing water, they are still few, some grand rivers being as yet little known, and others hardly touched.

The scope of this section of the book will not permit of more than a very general idea of the possibilities of sport with the rod in various parts of the country, with some remarks on the different fishes, the seasons, times of day, rods, tackle and general means of capture. It has not been found possible to obtain sufficient first-hand information for the compilation of any comprehensive list of localities over so vast an extent of country, and this, indeed, will not be attempted. At the same time, I shall be able to indicate a considerable number of the best-known waters, and also to append some useful notes received from obliging correspondents, which, if they reveal no absolutely unknown places, may at least be relied on as accurate, and, in most cases, up-to-date; and will also serve in some cases as interesting illustrations of certain recorded conclusions arrived at from personal experience and from the opinions and practice of others.

Although the sport seems so little known, Indian fishing has received some attention in literature. The works on the subject are not many, but they are quite excellent of their kind; and, indeed, Mr Thomas, the author of "The Rod in India," and "Tank Angling," must take high rank among living angling writers for his love of his subject and for his comprehensive and entertaining treatment of it. Every Indian fisherman should have "The Rod in India" at least, and "Tank Angling" will also be found indispensable if he should wish to take up this branch of the art. Then there is "The Angler's Hand-book," a much more modest publication in both size and price, but thoroughly sound and full of information, especially on localities in the Punjab and North India generally. "Fishing in the Kumaon Lakes," by Dr Walker—a delightful

A Typical Indian River

book to read—treats of the sport to be had in the lakes near the hill station of Naini Tal, and as this does not resemble the fishing to be had in any other part, the book would be most useful to those who desire to try their luck there. These, I believe, complete the list of available works, but, indeed, they supply quite sufficient information for most parts of the country; and if, in regard to some localities, there may be a lack of minute detail, a good sportsman will not be too captious, remembering that, after all, there is great fascination in exploration and discovery on one's own account. For those who may wish to take up the zoological side of the subject as a study, Day's "Indian Fishes" is the book.

I think it may be asserted without fear of contradiction that the great mahseer himself, in one of his two or three varieties, will be found in every perennial river of the country, his size only varying with the volume of water. And where he is not, as also where he is, there will be other fish too, some, as we shall see, well worth catching, and others at least far better than nothing. In short, although the fact is too little known, India is behind no country in its possibilities of sport for the angler, whether it be in variety of fish or their sporting character. With the fullest confidence we can for size, strength and gameness, pit the mahseer against the salmon. Trout and grayling are worthily represented by *Barilius bola*, the so-called "trout" of Central Indian rivers, and the Ganges and Jumna tributaries, to say nothing of the mahseer himself in his smaller sizes. Pike are quite out-classed by the great predatory goonches and saulis, mulleys and murrels, which give the same character of sport, but on a far grander scale, some goonches having been landed weighing nearly 150 lbs. Then the roaches, dace, chub, perch and such-like fishes must be counted the merest small fry when compared with the great Indian ground-feeders and dwellers in still waters, the labeos, rohu, catla, seetal, etc., which are very widely distributed, and run to 50 and 100 lbs. In addition to all these again we have the Carnatic carp, a fly-taker hailing from Madras, averaging 5 lbs., and running to 20 lbs. or so, and also a considerable number of small fly-takers—black spot, *bachwa*, *chilwa*, and several kinds of barils, which, if small, are at least plentiful in many places, and may often afford good fun of an evening when there is nothing better to do. And, to complete the list, there are on the west coast of Southern Madras a grand estuary fish, the bahmin, and more than one sea fish which, from all accounts, must be in all but size worthy rivals of the tarpon himself. These fish are dealt with by another writer with special knowledge of them.

India is, however, a large country, and it is not to be expected that all these varieties are to be found in all parts. Yet, as has been said, there are very few districts where a man may be stationed in which he will not be able to use his rod on one or more of them. And, most fortunately, it is the mahseer which is more widely distributed than any other. Then it has to be remembered that, whereas the sport for both gun and rifle has greatly deteriorated in many districts, this is not, with a few exceptional localities, the case with fishing. And so, again, I say to all who may be going out, whether for the first time or not, take a rod.

In all countries there must be rivers, and the size and character of them will naturally vary according to the rainfall, the height and breadth of the mountains among which they take their rise, and the extent of plain country over which they subsequently flow to the sea.

It may also go without saying that all rivers contain fish, but it does not necessarily follow that these fish will be of what is known as a sporting character, *i.e.* ready to take one or other of the recognised lures, and able to fight for life with strength and dash when hooked. This, however, is very distinctly the case in India. Now, all fishermen probably recognise the general fact that where the rivers run strong, there too the fish will be strong and active, whereas those found in sluggish waters, or in ponds, will as a rule have a character corresponding to their environment. There are no doubt exceptions to this rule, more indeed than we might expect from its reasonableness, but I think that on the whole it holds good as regards India.

A fisherman, then, in looking for likely

localities, will first locate the mountains of a country; and in India his attention will at once be arrested by the grand Himalayas. From these, the highest and vastest range of the world, issue many great rivers—the Ganges, Jumna, Brahmaputra, Indus, Chenab, Jhelum, Sutlej, Bias, Ravi—each with its complement of tributaries, and all holding mahseer. All this water is free as air, or practically so, to anyone. Lucky indeed are those anglers whose lot has been, or may be, cast within reach of this region! But it is a far cry from many other parts of the country to this paradise. What of the poor exiles in the more southern districts? If we look at the map again we shall find that there is no lack of other mountains, albeit not of the vastness of the Himalayas. The great plateau of Central India and the central provinces, rugged and forest-clad, holds many a bright stream well stocked with the Indian trout, the mahseer in his smaller sizes, and some of the other less important fly-takers. Then come in succession the Vindhya range, the Western Ghauts, the Neilgherrys and the Pulneys, which take us down with little break to the very south of the peninsula, thereafter to be continued in the lovely highlands of Ceylon. And from all these mountains issue rivers, every one of which with pretence to be called perennial holds mahseer. Some fine rivers there are—the Chambal, Godavery, Narbadda, Cavery, Bawanni and Kistna, among them—whose sporting praises have been so well extolled by Mr Thomas in his great book, in which he shows them to be almost the equal of the waters of the north, superior perhaps in the variety of their fish.

Thus, to complete the list, it will further be noticed how from the Himalayas at either extremity other ranges shoot out. From the one end, in the Peshawar direction, that great stretch of rugged hill country extending all along our north-west frontier to the sea near Karachi; and again from the south-eastern extremity a vast ramification of mountains running by the Khassia, Garo and Chin hills along the northern frontier of Burmah and well down into that province. All these mountains mean rivers, and the rivers breed fish, and the fish is the mahseer; an important point, for, when all is said, there is no doubt that the mahseer, as a sporting fish, surpasses all others of India as clearly as the salmon does all others at home. Before leaving this part of the subject, it may be well, to avoid misconception, to say, however, that in the case of the Himalayan rivers the fishing localities will not be found in their higher reaches. Actually within the mountains the cold appears to be too great and the flow of water is perhaps too uninterruptedly rapid. The best places for the best fish will always be found just where the rivers begin to leave the higher hills to flow through the lower outlying spurs.

It is sufficiently well known that the climate of India differs in many respects from that of the

British Isles. I refer here not so much to the notorious fact of greater heat as to the greater regularity, one may almost say monotony, of the weather and seasons. Instead of the four distinct seasons with which we are familiar in England, it seems more convenient to distinguish only three—the hot weather, rains, and cold weather—the duration of these being roughly as follows:—Hot weather from March in south, April in north, till June in south, July in north; rains from June or July to September; cold weather from October to March or April. In the hot weather we are pretty certain of plenty of heat and no rain; in the rains we shall, as a rule, have enough and to spare of water; while the cold weather, again, is a very certain and constant quantity, the temperature varying according to latitude or elevation, but not much year by year in each locality. A delightful time this—constant sunshine and bright, cool air, with only an occasional shower to lay the dust and freshen the greenery, the anticipation of which goes far to cheer one through the discomforts of the other seasons. So, with all this regularity, it will be understood that there is far more certainty as regards both seasons and days than we are accustomed to in the old country. The water will, as a rule, be found pretty much as we expect to find it at any given time; hence disappointments are to a great extent spared. Yet it is well to confess that such do occur, and often enough too, caused by rain in the hills from which the river comes, snow-water

A Good Mahseer

appearing before the usual time, or something mysterious in the air or water, which prevents the fish from taking—for these fish have their ways and ideas, even as trout or salmon—and many a time, from one or other of these causes, has my leave been in vain.

Fish are known to be "kittle cattle" all the world over, and it need not therefore cause surprise that there is little finality of either fact or opinion as to seasons, times of day, state of water, etc., which are best for the capture of the mahseer and other sporting fish of India, to say nothing of the difference of views and tastes in the matters of rods, tackle, and lures. It will therefore be best to touch on all these questions in a general way, endeavouring to present to the reader some conclusions more or less definite on which he may start work.

And first, as to seasons, with which is naturally connected the state of the water. There is one fact which appears to be so generally true, and which is yet so different from the conditions obtaining at home that it seems necessary to emphasise it from the outset, especially for the benefit of those who, from their experiences in the old country, may have preconceived ideas on the subject. This is that mahseer take best, as a rule, in very clear water, and, conversely, that if the water be much coloured there is very little hope. At home we have certainly to wait until the first spate has run off before commencing work with the salmon, and fish are taken thereafter in fairly clear water; but then the water soon runs too low if there is no fresh rain, and little or no more good can be done. So in India also we must wait for the subsiding of the rivers after the rains; but, after that, it is not too much to say that improvement goes on day by day—in fact, the clearer the water, and the weather too, the better. Some of the smaller rivers, especially those of the south country, will indeed run too low late in the season, the fish retiring to deep, still pools, where they cannot be tempted. But these exceptions only suffice to prove the general rule. Mr Thomas lays great stress on this point for Madras and Bombay, and I can thoroughly endorse his views from my experience of many rivers in Northern India.

Yet not only have I known men who have had success in dirty water, but, according to the experience of some, it is *only* in dirty water that the best fish are to be had. As far as my information goes, however, this condition appears to be especially characteristic of the Ganges and Jumna. There is also, however, an instance, mentioned in the "Angler's Handbook," of a man having had three days' excellent sport with spoon and fly in the Korang river, near Rawal Pindi, the water being described as "very *thick*." (And it is well to note here that it is of spinning or fly-fishing that I am at present writing. The taking of a stationary live-bait, or lump of dough, is an entirely different matter, depending as it does on the sense of smell, not of sight.) Perhaps, after all, thick water may not be so hopeless as is generally supposed, and he who may be unfortunately caught by such conditions may be at least encouraged by these examples not to give in too soon. Personally, after considerable experience, I had, like most others, given it up as, if not hopeless, at least not worth the trouble, and it always seemed to me only common sense to conclude that one very sufficient reason for fish not taking in dirty water was simply that they could not see the lure. There are, however, the exceptions to be got over. The fish in the Ganges and Jumna cannot be supposed to have better eyesight than those of other streams, and yet the evidence seems to show that it was good enough for them to see the spoon or natural bait of such fishermen as have recorded their successes. Perhaps the explanation is that the successes were obtained where clear and dirty water mingled, as, when a stream in spate flows into a clear river or *vice versa*, we then get a condition of things which will be recognised by many fishermen as eminently favourable. In such a place fish are often very numerous, and one might well stumble on, or even smell out, a natural bait, even in the actual dirty water; and, again, the bait, when taken, might appear to be in the dirty water, but in reality there might be an under-current of the clear, making the mixture sufficiently transparent to be seen through.

Concluding, however, that clear water on the whole is best, if not in some places a necessity, we have now to determine at what seasons we shall find this. From the foregoing general remarks on seasons and their regularity it will be seen that this condition should, and does with few interruptions, prevail from the falling of the rivers in September till the next rains in July, and, if clear water alone were necessary for success, the fishing season would last continuously for this period. There is, however, another factor which has to be taken into account. September, October, and November are in most districts to be fully relied on; in some they are the very best months.

Then comes the cold weather — December, January, and in the north, February—and during this time, for some obscure reason, it is generally agreed that, in the northern rivers at least, fish—*i.e.* mahseer and some others—simply will not take. The natives of some parts will tell you that their mouths are "sewed up" at this season, and we have the analogy of trout and other fish emerging in the spring very lean and lanky after a spare winter diet, to say nothing of the case of hibernating mammals. But the mahseer appears in as good condition as ever in the spring. In fact, owing, it is supposed, to some intermittent method of spawning, he is never out of condition. He must, therefore, eat. Yet he refuses all the angler's lures. Is it that he changes his diet at this time and becomes a real ground-feeder, retiring to the big pools and to the very bottom even of these? Likely enough, for small fish too no doubt also retire from the colder, shallow streams; and there is not so much other life—insects, larvæ, etc.—on the move at this time. Yet this phenomenon of the fish not taking is, again, only a general rule, for there are not wanting instances of quite fine hauls being made in the very height of the cold weather, while many fishermen know that some waters are well worth a trial after good rain at this time, not an uncommon condition. The rule, too, is naturally not so drastic in more southern districts, Assam and Madras for example, where the cold is not so severe.

As soon as the weather begins to warm up—*i.e.* from February or March, according to latitude—another fine fishing spell commences. It is a disputed point whether this or the autumn season is the better, and the answer is dependent to a great extent on locality. In some parts of Madras, Burmah and the Terai districts, the presence of malaria in autumn settles the matter, quite apart from the technicalities of the sport, in favour of spring, although, of course, this would not affect the actual "taking" of the fish. But all over the Punjab and the greater part of the United Provinces malaria is unknown, or at least need not be considered; and so here, if for no other reason than its longer duration, the autumn may be reckoned the better season, especially for a fishing trip of any length. The limitations of the spring season are two—heat, and in the north, also snow-water. On all southern rivers, and in the north on all tributary streams, the sources of which do not touch the higher snow-clad mountains, you may go on fishing as long as your constitution will allow you to enjoy it, but it will be found that these river valleys become powerfully hot after the middle of May, and the pleasure is apt to become somewhat of a toil. In the larger rivers, again, which have their sources away up in the high Himalaya, the season is limited by the down-coming of the snow-water. This usually happens towards the end of March or beginning of April, earlier or later according to season and locality; and most men will tell you that when you see the snow-broth you may as well pack up and go home.

This is, perhaps, the least controverted of any question where difference of opinion is possible; and it is interesting to note that the case of the salmon in Scotland is in some respects analogous.

The question of the best time of day for mahseer brings out much difference of experience and opinion. Locality, season and weather no doubt partly account for this, and everyone may be right for the time being. Still more, I think, does it result from the vagaries of the fish themselves in this respect, and these it would seem hopeless to understand. Fishermen all the world over have this complaint against fish: all conditions may seem favourable, and yet with no lack of perseverance, or, we may say, skill, the basket may remain empty. And no better answer to kind enquiries can be given than that the fish were not "taking." The man who knows everything will, of course, always have an excuse—weather too hot or too cold, water too thick or too clear, wind too light or too strong, or not blowing from the right quarter, yet he knows quite well that he has often been successful before under what seemed precisely similar conditions, and in his heart he confesses that he does not understand. The conditions of seasons and water, as set forth above, must certainly be considered general and necessary guides, and certain times of day and states of weather are no doubt generally more favourable than others. But distinct from all these are the "times of the take," which are established and controlled entirely by the fish themselves—at least apparently so, for no explanation or rule has ever been given to suit the experiences of all.

This I believe to be one great reason for the variety of opinion about the best time of day. One swears by early morning, and says that it is no use fishing while the sun is on the water. Another vows that the very middle of the day is best. A third may fish with no interest, and many rests, through all the first part of the day, waiting for evening for his main chance. Even Mr Thomas, notwithstanding his very wide experience, permits himself to dogmatise on this subject. He discusses the question with his usual fairness and fulness, and, while not denying that fish may be got all through the day, he comes to the general conclusion that from sunrise to 9 or 10 A.M. and from 3 P.M. till sunset are, on the whole, the best times. This entirely accords with my own experience. But when he goes on to say that it is hopeless to fish after sun-down, that this is indeed so certain, and proofs so numerous, that we must just take his word for the fact being incontrovertible, I am compelled to join issue. I have myself had experience of one glorious exception to this rule. Returning on one occasion, weary and disgusted, towards camp, on the evening of the last of three most unsuccessful days, I managed to muster sufficient energy to try one more pool. It was about an hour, or less, before sunset, and I found the pool full of fish, and ravenously on the take. I got fourteen fish, weighing over 50 lbs., in less than two hours; the last two or three being caught, not only after sunset, but when it was so dark that I could not at the last see where my spoon struck the water!

That is good enough for an exception, but I do not for a moment claim that it does more than prove the general rule, that it is not much good going on after sunset, and also that other rule, that the ways of fish are past finding out. I think, then, the general conclusion we must come to is that it is a mistake to permit ourselves any hard and fast ideas on this question at all. What may suit one locality, one season, or even one day may not apply to another, and the very fact of good fishermen holding these opposite opinions should at least give the necessary hope that if you keep at it, you may hit on the time of the take at any time. And here I would say, when you do hit upon it, make the most of it; don't waste more time than necessary in playing your fish, or changing your lure, and whatever you do, don't get "hung up."

It is useful to remember that fish are more *likely* to be on the move in the middle of the day when it is cold, and *vice versa.*

We now come to rods, tackle and lures, and, as said, we shall, as regards these also, have to take into account much difference of opinion. Mr Thomas is very strongly and uncompromisingly in favour of a very supple rod—the style best represented by those known as Castle Connell. He works out his theory so well, and has put it to such successful practice, that I do not hesitate to advise a beginner to be guided by him in his selection. At the same time I have just a word to say on this matter, which may at least give some comfort to those who may be in possession of something less supple. I only once used a Castle Connell, and having been accustomed to a different kind, I did not much care for it. It seemed so "wobbly" to carry, for one thing, and I did not understand, nor do I now, its wonderful advantages. So I went back to what Mr Thomas would, I suppose, call my "barge-pole" pattern. There was nothing peculiar about this — simply a very ordinary 16-foot salmon-rod for the larger rivers, and a 14-foot trout-rod to be used where smaller fish were expected—both perhaps being on the stiff side of what I call ordinary, which again does not, or did not in those days, come near the Castle Connell in pliability. To fix more exactly the amount of pliability I would describe, I may say that the rod I preferred above all others *for spinning* was a single bamboo, or Ringal, of 14 or 15 feet, and it was always with regret that I had to leave this behind, owing to the difficulty of packing. This sort of thing would, I suppose, give the Castle Connell advocates a fit. But all I can say is that I have had excellent sport with one of these rods, and have noticed neither the number of fish lost, nor the devastation of tackle, which from theory we are made to understand must be the inevitable consequence. Mr Thomas says that it was not himself, but his supple rod, which enabled him to land his fish so often under "even time," *i.e.* one minute allowed for each pound; and he gives several instances, one in particular, of the hooks dropping out of a fish's mouth when landed after a hard fight. This also, he says, was due entirely to his rod, and that it could not have happened with a stiffer one. Now, with regard to this last, I would remark first that it seems quite reasonable to suppose that with a stiffer rod that hook *would* have penetrated beyond the barb, and so given less chance of the fish being lost; and second, that I too when using my Ringal have known the hooks to drop out of the mouth as described.

I can also say that I have often been surprised, and even disappointed, to find how much under "even time" I have often landed my fish. And why should I not also attribute this as much to my rod as to myself? Again, lightness is claimed as a special recommendation of the Castle Connell: this, too, strange to say, was the chief quality for which I prized my Ringal! And I still stoutly maintain that in this regard nothing will beat it short of the American two ounce contrivances. So the result is that, while I very willingly defer to Mr Thomas's far greater experience, supported too, as he is, by so many other good fishermen, and accordingly recommend all beginners to go in for a Castle Connell, or some such rod, I still advise those who have rods of their own of a less "wobbly" pattern, to stick to them. The rods with which you have been able to land your salmon and trout will do equally for mahseer, or any other river fish; and if you take care to have your line clear and your reel in good order, you need have no fear even of the great first rush of the mighty one. Standing snake pattern rings are decidedly the best, though these need not be of such enormous size as sometimes seen, and some kind of revolving top ring may also be advised.

About the reel there is not much controversy. Any of the recognised good patterns serves the purpose, but if a new purchase is to be made specially for India, then no doubt one of the new pattern brake winches would be advisable.

You dare not put your finger on the line to check a big mahseer in his wild career, yet it is very important to have the means of doing so, and, judging from description, I should say nothing could be better than Mr Thomas's own invention in brake winches. As a substitute, I sometimes used a very simple device—a leather tube fastened to the butt of the rod where grasped by the left hand in playing a fish: the line passed through this, and pressure could so be put on it without cutting the finger. The idea of Malloch's patent reel for casting a long line may appeal to some, and it is quite sound, but somewhat expensive. A neat, and a very practical, arrangement of gathering the line in coils previous to a cast will be found described in one of the contributions from correspondents published on a later page, the exponent being, as I know, a fisherman of very great experience, and *practical* in all his ways.

As to lines, I strongly recommend those of the Manchester Spinning Company as better, even though cheaper, than all others I have tried. From 120 yards to 150 is quite sufficient. There may be some exceptional waters where more might be on occasion safer, but it is scarcely worth while cumbering one's self with an extra bulky reel for such rare chances. I have not had happy experience of the American waterproof lines; the waterproofing does not appear to prevent the water soaking through during a long day's trolling, and then the varnish, I think, actually retards the drying process, causing rot, and thus defeating its own end. For your light rod 30 to 50 yards of ordinary plaited silk line is usually considered sufficient, with reel to correspond, but if you should wish to use this rod in places where you have a chance of fairly big mahseer, you must, of course, have more line.

Strong tackle is required for mahseer, stronger, on the whole, than for salmon. Twisted wire traces are recommended and used by many for the larger waters, and the newer wire-gimp appears to be very excellent, while a single wire may also be used. Personally, I was more conservative in this respect, and have found gut—treble for large fish, and good single salmon gut for the smaller rivers—to be quite good enough. But you must not neglect to soak well before using, and to take all precautions against rotting. Hooks, like the tackle in general, must be specially strong, but for a different reason. The mahseer's jaws have quite phenomenal crushing power, and if you were to conduct a campaign against him with the class of hooks and mounting usual in England, you would have many disasters, and your tackle-box would soon contain nothing but a tangle of ruins. The hooks, therefore, and especially the trebles, must be made of special stout wire. There is no difference of opinion about this, and the fact is now well known to most good tackle makers. We shall again have to notice some matters of controversy when we describe the various lures and the methods of using them, but first a short notice of the mahseer himself (already perhaps too long delayed), his habits and tastes, will be appropriate.

Allusion in the first part of this article will have prepared the reader for something worth looking at and worth catching ; and, indeed, I have never yet met anyone who was disappointed by actual experience of a mahseer. His name is commonly supposed to be derived from the Hindi words maha sir, which means big head; but this, if taken as an obtrusive characteristic, is a pure slander. For, although his head is, in proportion, somewhat larger than the particularly dainty one of the salmon, still in a well-conditioned fish it has no appearance of being unduly big for the body. In general shape he is, indeed, very like a salmon, sometimes a little deeper in the shoulder, and with greater expanse of tail and fins. When fresh from the water he is surprisingly beautiful ; in place of the bright silver of the salmon, we have burnished bronze-gold on the sides and fins, the back a greenish-brown, and the under parts like those of all fish, pure white. The scales are very large and prominently marked, and as they are also thick and tough, the use of a gaff is uncommon, and not to be recommended. He has no teeth in his jaws, but, to make up for this, there are a very formidable set in the throat, with which he crunches his shell-fish and other hard food. The lips are very tough and strong, affording grand hook-hold ; and he has such power of compression with these, and he seizes his prey so fiercely, that a stout spoon is often found to be crumpled out of all shape when he has happened to catch it end on in his jaws, the hooks also being often bent and flattened in a marvellous manner. And here we may remark that this characteristic of his rushing at his prey is a very great factor in the fascination of fishing for him. There is no quiet sucking in of the lure with him, and no striking is required. He makes up his mind in a flash, and his method being to capture his prey with a sudden dash, kill or stun it with one deadly snap, and instantly make off with it to his den, small wonder that the fisherman is left in no doubt as to whether his fish is hooked or not, and that he has no time to strike before the fish has done it for him. This is the beginning of that great "first rush" which has been so often extolled, and which, if there should be any flaw in your tackle or check in your reel, will surely be all over as soon as begun. He does not, however, leap out of the water like the salmon. The mahseer is a ground-feeder, but by no means exclusively so, and perhaps, indeed, very sparingly so at the seasons in which we fish for him. At least, my idea is that he does most of his ground feeding during the cold weather, and when the rivers are running thick with the melting snows or during the rains. At other times he seems to prey upon small fish, frogs, fruits, insects, floating spawn and such like, and so is altogether more on the move and nearer the surface, and more ready to take our spoons or flies. He is a lover of rough, strong waters and rocky bottoms, and in such places he is found at his best, not only in appearance and strength, but also as to his readiness to "take." Yet he goes down, too, to the lower reaches of the big rivers, and here, as I know well, many fine fish are caught where there are no rocks, although, if I remember Mr Thomas aright, he appears to have had no experience of this down south. Although he does not visit the sea like a salmon, he is a migrant, moving up from the great rivers of the plains to the higher reaches to spawn; and it will be seen what stress one of my correspondents lays on the proper appreciation of this habit. Mahseer have been affirmed to run up to 100 or even 150 lbs. in weight, but such may be put out of reckoning for the ordinary angler. In any of the larger rivers, however, you are quite liable to get one of 50 or even 60 lbs.; 40-pounders are fairly common, and the lesser sizes, of course, still more so. All this will show how small is the resemblance of a mahseer to a carp, as we know the species in our English ponds. Yet he is a carp too—*Barbus tor* being his scientific designation—and this kinship only shows what difference of habitat can accomplish.

Having now got some general idea of the qualities and tastes of the mahseer, we can understand better what has been said about the necessity of strong tackle, and may turn with more appreciation to the consideration of the methods of his capture, and the lures best suited to circumvent him.

Photo] A NATIVE FISHING [*Laurie, Naini Tal*

By the native of the country, we may be sure, the mahseer is not neglected, but, as might be supposed, his methods are more of the practical, wholesale order than scientific, or sporting. We do not therefore find him interfering, or competing with us in what we are accustomed to consider the only legitimate ways of fishing; and indeed he does not with a rod trouble the mahseer so much as the other more pronounced ground-feeders. As all the world over, netting by various methods is his chief stand-by, but he also uses the rod and line in the still waters, and is fond of night-lines, a lump of dough, a frog or a small fish being the usual baits. One method of using the net, which I have seen, is particularly attractive to watch. A net is first stretched across one end of a pool, so fixed as to project two or three feet above the water. A crowd of men and boys then form line at the other end, and armed with sticks and stones, thoroughly beat the pool down towards the net. These are generally supplemented by several swimmers, who keep diving down to hunt the fish out from among rocks and other shelters, and some of these are wonderful performers under water. But it is at the end of the beat that the chief interest and excitement occur. The fish will then be seen rushing about, trying to escape the net in every possible way, many leaping clear over it in splendid style and at a great pace, while the crowd of beaters redouble their efforts and yells to prevent doubling back.

The circular cast-net is universally used all over the country, and this may be recommended as a most useful article to have in possession for procuring small fish for bait. Then fish, chiefly *maral*, are sometimes shot with gun or rifle; in some places they are snared by horse-hair nooses, in others speared; and in a certain outlandish district I once came across some natives shooting mahseer in shallow water with bow and arrow, a very singular survival of ancient practice, for I never saw or heard of this weapon being used for any other purpose at all in the whole country. All these methods may be said to partake somewhat of the nature of primitive sport, but not so dynamite, the use of which in some places has in late years become lamentably common.

The reader will already have gathered that the diet of a mahseer is not nearly so restricted as what we are taught to regard as that of a salmon. Besides what he finds on the bottom, he will eat frogs, worms, insects, and even young birds when he gets the chance, to say nothing of berries, grain and any kind of paste. But what he prefers is another fish, and, as long as it is somewhat smaller than himself, it is a matter of no concern whether it be a near relation or not. So that, besides fly, which he will on some rivers take as freely as a salmon, we have the choice of a variety of other lures, natural or imitative.

I believe there can be little doubt that natural bait, *i.e.* a small fish, is the most killing of all, and so we may take this first. I have read that among the ancient Egyptians one of their great "negations" in giving in their last account was that they had not "caught fish with the flesh of other fish," an ultra-honourable view of the question to which we ordinary moderns have not yet attained. We must at all events assume that good anglers have no such scruples, but apart from this, the use of natural bait has its disadvantages—difficulty of procuring and keeping alive or fresh, time lost and tediousness in adjusting on the hook, etc.; and so, although the most deadly, it is by no means the most common. For spinning with dead bait any of the well-known spinners may be used: Geen's Richmond Spinner, the Coxon Spinner, Dee Minnow Tackle, or Luscombe's Chilwa Tackle, all being good. Personally I always used, and preferred, the baiting needle process with single treble hook. It is, I think, quite unnecessary for the bait to spin; in fact, I believe a "wobbly" motion is more natural, more like a small fish in distress, and that is what we want. If you have an excess of hooks on your spinner, swift spinning is no doubt required to conceal these, but then you might just as well be using a phantom or other artificial minnow, and the idea of the *natural* bait seems to be gone.

There are occasions when live bait may be resorted to, but being a stationary process, it is, to my mind, tedious. Still, if you are caught by really dirty water, there is nothing else to be done, so it is as well to know how to use it. Perhaps the best method of hook attachment is that of Colonel Parsons, known by his name—a large single hook on a snood of stout gut, or other material, passed in a peculiar manner (which must be learnt) through the skin of bait near the tail, and a lip-hook, adjustible on the snood, so as to suit different sizes of small fish, passed through the lips. A sinker is attached some two or three feet from the bait, and the whole is thrown out to some likely spot, and you sit and smoke and watch for a bite. This is an outline of the usual practice, but in one of the communications from correspondents in Part II. of this article will be found another method of using natural bait, alive and dead, which is new to me, and which appears to be a most simple and valuable novelty.

Mahseer will take almost any kind of phantom or other imitation fish spun in the ordinary way, and it is well to have a few of such in the tackle-box, provided the mounting is not of a too flimsy description. The most deadly of this class of lure that I ever used was what was called a pearl minnow, used for sea-trout in the north of Scotland. It was simply a rough outline of a fish in mother of pearl, uncoloured. Such are apparently not common, and I simply give the hint for what it may be worth.

But by far the most useful and most generally used lure is the spoon. It is strong, clean, easily mounted with the hooks most preferred, and, above all, eminently acceptable to the mahseer and to many other fish as well. To look at, a mere man would hardly imagine it could represent anything living, but fortunately fish think otherwise, and the inventor, whoever he was, has certainly earned the gratitude of the angling fraternity. If you have nothing else in your tackle-box, indeed, you may do very well. As used for mahseer, spoons may vary in size from ¾ in. to 3 in. or even 4 in., the larger naturally being used in the heavier waters, where big fish may be expected and *vice versa*, strength of tackle also corresponding to the size of the spoon. Some men will get quite excited over the shape of their spoons, but it is really not worth while discussing this question, any shape that will spin being good enough, and all patterns in general use spin quite well. The colouring may be gold, silver, gold and silver, or the old copper and silver. My personal favourite was gold back and silver inside, but this may have been more my own fancy than that of the fish. For in cases of this sort, when a man has once established a predilection he of course uses it more, and other baits only get an off-chance. Spoons, except those meant to be cast as a fly, are generally made too light. A little more weight gives greater strength and may also allow one to dispense with lead in some kinds of water. If you use lead (and many will tell you that you *must* fish deep if you want big fish), it should either be attached to the line by thin, breakable thread, so that it may break away if you get hung up, or else it may be in the form of thick wire which you can coil neatly round the line. The mounting of spoons is a vexed question; this particularly with reference to the flying mount, and to the use of split rings.

Mr Thomas sounds a strong anathema against both of these, and demonstrates from both theory and experience that they are utterly wrong, and that to use them is to court pretty certain disaster. Yet many other men use them, and some are hardy enough to defend them in print too, also using both theory and experience as arguments. I think, on the whole, that the mounting of the hooks either with the usual permanent unsplit ring or by a neat wire fastening is the safest, and unless you adopt the flying mount, the best. Even for this it is probably the safest and best too, but it is a little more troublesome, and split rings are *so* convenient, if a little risky. Never have side hooks on your spoons; they are quite unnecessary and greatly retard the spinning.

Now we come to fly, undoubtedly the most fascinating of all methods of fishing. It must be recorded against the mahseer that he does not, as a rule, take fly so well as most of the other lures; at least this is true of the large fish and of most waters. But, even so, I am not sure that as good sport with fly alone is not obtainable on some waters as is to be had on many salmon rivers. Fish up to 10 lbs. will often take readily enough, while much larger ones are also caught, and, owing to greater certainty of water and weather, one is not nearly so liable to so many blank days, not to say weeks, as is too often the lot of the fisherman at home. It is simply because we can get more, and especially bigger, fish with spoon or natural bait that fly is not more used, and the idea therefore prevails that there is little to be done with it. I feel sure, moreover, that if a number of good fishermen were to bind themselves to use nothing else for a whole season the result might be surprising. The method of casting is exactly as for salmon, *i.e.* across and down stream, and striking is seldom necessary. A great variety of flies is not required; if you have two different sizes of the Blackamoor, Cock-o'-the-walk and Smoky Dun, as recommended by Mr Thomas, you will do very well, though some men prefer more colour —jungle-cock feathers with lots of red and yellow in body tinsel, etc.

Of catching mahseer with paste, parched gram, berries, etc., much need not be said. Still a man may be in a locality where nothing else is possible, and really good fun may sometimes be had if the necessary preliminaries are carefully attended to. The selected pools must be baited for several days beforehand, the fish being in this way educated up to the unusual diet.

But, of course, it is the labeos and other ground-feeders that are more usually fished for in this way, and before leaving this subject of rods and tackle, it should be mentioned that for this sport—*i.e.* tank and other still-water fishing—a rod of quite different pattern, shorter and stiffer, and a very fine, strong line with a "detective" float is recommended by Mr Thomas. But any who intend taking up this branch of fishing should at once get his book on "Tank Angling." This is quite necessary if you would learn the art quickly, and, as an incentive, I may remark that Mr Thomas gives it as his deliberate opinion that this tank angling is *superior* to any other! I have little experience of it myself, but can scarcely imagine this.

Some prefer taking their tackle out from home, but there are several firms in India where good material and a fair variety may be relied on: Rodda, Manton and Walter Locke in Calcutta; Oakes & Co. in Madras; Messrs Murray, Naini Tal, and Luscombe in Allahabad, the latter himself a practical fisherman. He can be specially recommended for spoons and flying mounts, and makes up excellent Ringal rods.

It is to be regretted that so little is done in the way of protection of fish and fishing waters in India. Attempts have certainly been made in some parts of the country, but the laws regarding ownership and riparian rights appear to be too complicated and uncertain for effective action, and the native is hard to circumvent. I understand that the Punjab Association, after many and prolonged efforts to evolve some scheme, have at last given it up, and their failure has probably deterred others from trying. On the other hand, there is welcome news that the Kashmir authorities, under British advice, are at last giving valuable assistance in the protection of their waters, and as these include the well-known and excellent rivers Jhelum and Poonch, at the junction of which is the far-famed Tangrot, the Mahl and the two rivers Tawi, this is a matter of much importance for anglers. At Dehra Doon there is an association, which manages to do something in the way of protection, and as a small charge (Rs. 10 per season) is made, this may have some effect in preventing over-fishing. At Calcutta there is also a club for the preservation of the tanks in the vicinity, and excellent bottom fishing is said to result. In the Neilgherrys and in Ceylon there are also associations, whose efforts have been chiefly directed to the acclimatisation of trout and other fish. The success hitherto achieved in the Neilgherrys has not been great, but the results in Ceylon are most satisfactory, especially in regard to the acclimatisation of the rainbow trout. This species has also, I understand, been introduced into Kashmir.

A few notes of advice before concluding this part may be useful to beginners or men new to the country. Those who are already fishermen will readily recognise where to fish after arrival at the river-side. Mahseer will be found in exactly the same sort of runs or pools in which you would look for a salmon or a trout. Beginners can only learn this by experience. As you will fish for the most part in very clear water, common sense will be sufficient to teach you that great care in the matter of concealment is necessary. Wear inconspicuous clothing, do not cast from a bank if you can get low down, flounder as little as possible when wading, stalk your pool for the first cast and don't forget to try first the part of it nearest to you, use as fine tackle as you dare and no more hooks than necessary, do not whip the water more than you can help, cast across and down stream, spin slow and put all thoughts of striking out of your head. I suppose I should also say avoid splashing when casting a spoon, but for one thing, you cannot avoid it, and besides, I am not sure that the splash does not actually attract the fish. I have seen a man with a cast-net throw in stones for this purpose just before making his cast. So I will say instead avoid a loose line, and try to have the spoon working as quickly as possible after touching the water. Play your fish as you would a salmon, avoid sudden checks, keep the line always taut but be always ready to yield to a rush, better not try to use a gaff, a net is useful, but big fish should be lifted out of the water by an attendant. It is convenient to have a man to carry a spare rod, you can then ring the changes between the large and small one, indulging in the luxury of a few casts with fly or fly-spoon where water is favourable—a great relief after the bigger spinning rod. Waders are not necessary, and are far too hot: wear breeches or knickerbockers with stockings or putties, or nothing at all below the knee; also stout boots with hob-nails—not too many—the new aluminium nails, if strong enough, would be an improvement. Look well after all tackle; dry your line immediately after a day's work, soak gut well and test everything before use; keep flies in a tin box with naphthaline, if you keep them in an ordinary book you may find nothing but dust when you want to use them. Look after your supplies, especially on going to a new place, and inquire about other sport, for gun or rifle. Treat natives as sympathetically as possible; you will certainly get more information and help by doing so, though no doubt you will be tried sometimes. Always have the Ordnance Survey map of whatever district you may be in; besides being almost a necessity it adds to the interest.

These hints are few, and most of them, perhaps, somewhat obvious. Still they are the outcome of practical experience, and the points referred to are certainly not always kept in mind. My hope is that, taken along with others in the foregoing part of this article, they may be of some help to aspirants, and lead to the landing of many a good fish.

MAHSEER FISHING IN INDIA.

Note by Sir Edward Buck.

The mahseer (big-head) is a carp which imitates the habits and ways of a salmon. Coming up from the giant rivers instead of the sea to spawn in the mountain streams, it affords in the latter excellent sport in spring and autumn. This is in Northern India, where the best weeks are from the end of March to the end of May, and again in October. In Assam the season is earlier and later. For South India, with which the writer is not acquainted, the fullest information will be found in the "Rod in India," by Thomas, a most interesting work. There, I think, the record fish is given at 120 lbs.

Thirty years ago a mahseer outfit consisted of what has been described as "a barge-pole, a rope, a tablespoon, and an anchor." *Nous avons changé tout cela.* A double-handed trout rod or light bamboo, a Manchester cotton line, a Malloch reel, and fly spoons on medium gut with light trebles suffice for general purposes. A friend, fishing with the writer on a river where the mahseer ran up to 20 lbs., used a single-handed trout rod, a light gut, and a spoon no bigger than a grilse fly, and was never once broken in ten days, though landing several fish of all sizes daily. One of the merits of mahseer fishing, by the way, is, that one never knows whether the next fish will weigh 3 lbs. or 30 lbs., and it *may* be 50 lbs. or 60 lbs.

But the mahseer is not always to be tempted by a fly spoon or fly. Broadly speaking, when the water is cold and heavy, the natural bait is best. When warmer, a spoon of the size of a dessert spoon will take fish. When warmer still, the fly spoon, and then the fly may be used. But, like all fish, the mahseer is a coquette, and there are variations. In Assam he seldom takes the natural bait.

A hooked mahseer by no means behaves altogether like a salmon. On feeling the prick he makes one furious swift rush, which, in the case of a big fish, may be from 100 to 120 yards. A minute or two later a second and shorter rush; and so on, each rush shorter than the last. Sometimes he will sulk for a considerable time between his rushes. But there is no leaping and struggling like that of the sea-trout and salmon. And his mouth is tough, not tender, so that if the angler is prepared for the rushes, light tackle with strong hooks suffices. The fish tires quickly after the first three or four rushes, and eventually comes in like a log. We never use gaff or landing-net. The native creeps behind the fish and hoists him by the gills.

In strong streams where there are miniature Niagaras, the best place to find a good fish is in the eye on each side of the waterfall, where he lies in wait for a tumbling fishlet. At a bait thrown with accuracy there he will spring like a flash of lightning, and then off with express train speed for his 100 yards or so. But he watches, too, for passing prey behind a well or stone in swift waters or in a still depth under a bank. As the weather and the water get warmer he may rise anywhere in pools big enough to hold him, and sometimes in shallows apparently not big enough.

For an angler who does not mind dry heat and wading in warm water, the most sporting fishing is in the mountain streams of North India. But for a cold weather visitor Assam is preferable. There excellent sport may be had in a pleasant climate from January to March, whether trolling or casting from a boat with spoon, or wading in the smaller and swifter hill streams. An account of an Assam trip, in which the writer accompanied "Rohilla," will be found in some of *The Fields* of 1897, signed by that well-known name. As he relates, angling may be sometimes varied by a shot at the wild buffaloes which come to drink on the river bank.

Those who visit Northern India should apply to the secretary of the Punjab Angling Club (Lahore) for the "Anglers' Guide," maintained up to date by the club.

One word more. A mahseer wants a good cook. But a 5 or 6-pounder will, if the cook *is* good, be found excellent eating.

II.—WHERE TO GO FOR FISHING IN INDIA

I PROPOSE to devote this section to a consideration of localities, but the greater portion will be taken up with the reproduction of communications from correspondents, whom I would desire here to thank for many most interesting and excellent contributions. The majority of these give more or less complete notes of localities, many of them specially valuable as being up to date, and some will, besides, be found interesting and useful as examples of varied experience in regard to some of the vexed questions alluded to in the foregoing pages. First, then, a short and very general review of the fishing possibilities of the various provinces may be helpful. These provinces or districts I name below, as nearly as possible in order of merit, as I personally have found them.

1. North-West Punjab, including Kashmir waters fishable from there. United Provinces. Assam and Sylhet. } About equal.
2. Madras.
3. Baluchistan and North-West Frontier.
4. Burmah.
5. Kashmir and Jammu.
6. Central India.
7. Bombay.
8. Central Provinces.
9. Bengal and Orissa.
10. Scinde and adjacent country.

Ceylon and the Kumaon Lakes I do not classify at all, the sport being of quite different character. For accounts of these I refer the reader to the appended communications.

I think it will be well to dispose first of the lowest in the foregoing scale.

Although I hold to the general statement that the districts are very few where some of the many fishes will not be obtainable, still it must be confessed that there are large tracts about which anglers hear very little, a sure sign that there is not much to tell. Others there are again, which, although well enough exploited, have yielded little sport.

The tract which includes Scinde, all the adjoining north-west portion of Rajputana, Gujerat, and, I may add, the stretch of country up by Multan to

Lahore, is not of much account, notwithstanding that we have here the lower reaches of the Indus, Sutlej, and Ravi. It may be that more might be done if properly worked, or it may be that my information is at fault, but this is certainly not well known as a fishing locality.

To Bengal and Orissa the same general remarks are applicable. Tank fishing is, however, no doubt to be had in many parts of this enormous tract, and in the vicinity of Calcutta, as has been said, this is of sufficient excellence to warrant the establishment of a club. No doubt, bottom-fishing is also available in the numerous rivers and streams, which must here of necessity be sluggish.

The Central Provinces hold, besides the Narbadda for a great part of its course, many streams which look very fishable; and there are, indeed, mahseer and other fish in all. But owing to some reason, known only to themselves, they do not take spoon, or other usual lures, at all readily. They are successfully circumvented with paste, and parched grain, especially the latter, but the process is, as has been said, a somewhat tedious one. Still, a real enthusiast may find plenty of interest, and here too fishing may well be combined with other sport, which in many parts is excellent, as the sportsman may shoot tiger, sambur, cheetal and other game.

Again, of Bombay but little is heard, although here we have the lower reaches of the Narbadda and Tapti, and the upper waters of the Godaveri and Beema and their tributaries, all flowing through hilly country, and all known to hold mahseer and many other fish. In the north Canara district, sport is reported good about the famous Gairsoppa falls, and there are one or two places fishable from Poonah, notably Karakwasla on the Muti Mula river, and the same river lower down near its junction with the Beema. Again, in the Jeypore hills, Vizagapatam district, good fishing has been had in Godaveri and Machkanda rivers, and the Kolub and Garepirs are also known to contain quite a variety of fish besides mahseer. I have also read that round Chitor good sport is to be had with trout, besides tank-fishing. But all this is a poor record for such a large province, the praise of even those mentioned being somewhat faint, and I cannot help thinking that some places may still await the right man.

I put Central India above all the foregoing districts, chiefly because of its trout, the *Barilius bola,* of which passing mention has already been made. This, though of course not in the running with mahseer in either size or strength, is such a handsome and lively fellow, and such a willing fly-taker that he affords most excellent sport. He is very generally distributed over all the rivers of the central part, the most important being the Chambal, Betwa, Banas, Sind and the tributaries of these. Mahseer are also plentiful, though only of moderate size, and here they too take fly particularly well at certain seasons.

Jhansi, Nowgong, Deoli and Lalitpur may be mentioned as good centres, and from and between these no water of any size should be tried in vain. Breaks in the rains for trout, and in the larger streams, just after the water has cleared after the rains, *i.e.* September and October for mahseer, are described as the proper seasons. In tanks, and still waters of rivers good bottom-fishing is also to be had—rohu, tengra and murrel.

The best waters of Kashmir—Poonch, Tawi and Mahl—I have, in my estimate of districts, included in the Punjab area, all being best reached and fished from there. In the valley itself, though large mahseer are occasionally taken from the Jhelum at Sopor, Ningal or Shadipur, the sport cannot be said to be particularly good. Live bait is the usual lure, and except to the enthusiast, this is apt to be a tedious process. The Chirroo, or Kashmir trout, as he is sometimes called, however, affords some amusement to anyone loafing by the river instead of ibex-shooting, as he should be. Though not hard fighters, they are free fly-takers, and there are plenty of them. All places on the route into Kashmir from Murree, where other streams join the Jhelum, are worth trying in spring or autumn. The best known are at Domel, Chathar and Hatti, and at all these very large mahseer are sometimes to be had.

Of Burmah I have no information which is quite up to date. It seems quite certain that there is no lack of fish, mahseer and others, but even in the northern hilly country the fishing does not appear to be so satisfactory as in the neighbouring region of Assam, while in the more southern parts we hear of both worm and paste being used, which is not a good sign. A correspondent makes note of a few localities in the north, and some others are mentioned in "The Rod in India." In the moat at Mandalay, and also in the ponds in the palace gardens, labeo, white carp and fresh water sharks are to be caught; and in the Bhamo district the Nampoung, Namsiri and Namli are mentioned as good rivers. Altogether I must class Burmah as doubtful, rather than certainly inferior.

The fishing in Baluchistan and N.W. Frontier districts is also an unknown quantity. There is not much information, and some of this is contradictory. We hear from one source of really excellent sport with small mahseer in streams near Quetta, while a correspondent asserts that sport is poor all over Baluchistan. I knew the Kuram to be a delightful fishing stream in 1879, but I hear nothing of the Gomal, Zhob and other affluents of the Indus flowing from the Suliman mountains. The chronic state of unrest of this region has no doubt prevented exploitation, and probably more will be heard of the fishing as time goes on.

This may be said to complete the category of second and third-class districts. Of the remainder, Assam is the only one which is not now well-known, and I regret that I have been unable to obtain fresh information. Still I feel sure that I am not misleading the reader when I say that from what has been revealed from time to time in letters, and from what I have myself heard from friends, the fishing there must be at least equal to that in any other district. The fishing there is, I understand, best in the cold weather; a great advantage, especially for a holiday trip. The fishing localities of the United Provinces, Punjab and Madras are, however, far better known to sportsmen, and so are more generally recognised as *the* fishing districts of India.

A fair amount of information and detail of localities in both Madras and the northern districts will be found in the appended communications.

I shall only here give a bare mention of the spots which are best known and generally recognised as the cream of all places, for the most part easily reached, and to which men resort from far and near. Hardwar and Raiwala on the Ganges may come first, as their reputation is undisputed, and here the railway takes you to the very gates of paradise. The spot where the Asan joins the Jumna is in the same general direction, and equally good: rail to Dehra Doon, then on by road to Rajghat or Dhalipur, 25 miles. Tangrot, at the junction of the Poonch with the Jhelum, cannot rank lower than third, and indeed has perhaps a better record than all for many and large captures: rail to Ratyal, beyond Jhelum on the North-Western railway, then by road. The Poonch, Tawi, and Mahl, being fishable en route to Kashmir, are favourite resorts. All are good, the former holding the best fish, but more uncertain. Torbela on the Indus used to be a grand place, but difficult to get at. Dadupur on the Jumna is another. The Giri, near Simla, has always had an excellent reputation, but is now under the control of a strictly limited club, while Okhla, near Delhi, is a wonderful place for variety of fish.

I have now only three pet places of my own to note, which have not, I think, been made sufficiently prominent. Sialkot, a civil and military station in the north Punjab, is not often mentioned in connection with fishing. Yet there is, in my experience, no better centre. It lies close to the Jammu frontier, and within 10 to 12 miles of the Chenab river. Two tributaries, both of the same name—Tawi—flowing respectively from the eastern and western sections of the Pir Panjal mountains, join the Chenab within a few miles of each other and just to the north of Sialkot. Of the Eastern or Jammu Tawi, I have little experience; access to it used to be somewhat restricted owing to exclusive State regulations with regard to the use of the route near which it has its course. But, leave being obtained, the fishing was excellent in some parts. The other—Western or Naoshera Tawi—however, I know to be an ideal water for moderate-sized mahseer. Its upper waters, *i.e.* from Naoshera upwards, are very well-known, and have been often described. But not so the section from its junction with the Chenab upwards to Naoshera. This was our fishing preserve from Sialkot, and I wish I had space to enlarge on the pleasures of a trip there. But I must restrict myself to meagre details, assuring the reader that it is well worth many visits. The lower part up from the junction is not good. Commence at a place called Chakla or at Chamb, fish all the way up to Asan or Jogwa, camp there in a lovely spot and fish in lovely water. Then make arrangements for a sarnai (skin-raft) to help you on to Machi Bawan, which can only be reached in this fashion. Catch 40 or 50 lbs. there, and after trying a few miles further up, work back again. This for short leave; with longer time at disposal you can continue on to Naoshera and as far as you like.

Then for big fish we had the Chenab itself, and the water we used to work was from Beni Singh, at the junction of the Jammu Tawi, down to some way below the junction of the other Tawi. Very unfortunately there were no pools at the junctions themselves, but many streams elsewhere well suited for trolling from a boat, which is both necessary and procurable. Beni Singh, Khoja Chak, near Foklyan bungalow, Gondal, and just below the junction of the Naoshera Tawi were the best spots, and many fish from 45 lbs. downwards were landed while we were there. Being so close, we could canter out for an evening's fishing after work. The other river I would mention is the Bias, well enough known to some, but not so notorious as the recognised crack places; yet I believe it is behind none of them. The stations nearest to it are Jallandhar, Amritsar and Dharmsala, a hill station, and you may either work up from Pathankot, reached by rail from Amritsar, or down from Gopipur Dera, just south of Fort Kangra. A boat or skin-raft (sarnai, or here, drey) is necessary, and the latter is easily obtained. It is not necessary to fish from the raft, but it is most useful in getting you to streams on either bank. Fish run to any size, and take fly better than in most rivers.

III.—COMMUNICATIONS FROM CORRESPONDENTS

FISHING NEAR BAREILLY, &c.—SOME USEFUL HINTS—SOME NATIVE METHODS

From a Correspondent

"The Sardah is one of the best fishing rivers in India, and I wonder that so very few have found it out. There is no club or association of any sort, nor are there any restrictions. The great beauty of the river consists, to me, in its not being well known; you never collide with anyone, and it is as wild as can be. It is a large stream, and a small portable boat, or, better still, an elephant is useful to enable one to cross when desired. The best parts of the river I have found from Banbassa, nine or ten miles up stream, to a point at which it leaves the hills. Between these two points it is more or less broken up, and the water is perfection. This was my particular spot, but I have always heard that there is first-class fishing about six miles off, in the hills at the junction of the Luddyar and Sardah, and also at Pachesar and Ramesar. The former is at the junction of the Kali and Surjoo, and the latter at that of the E. Ramgunga and Surjoo. Pachesar is perhaps the best place on the river, and March the best month. The fish obtainable are mahseer of any size, and occasionally a trout, called by natives 'gullara.' The biggest mahseer I have caught was 36 lbs., but there are plenty between that and 20 lbs.

"Another spot well-known to many is Bagesur, about thirty miles north of Almora, on the Surjoo. Here you must fish fine and with care, as fish are very shy. On one occasion I recollect that in five days I here got twenty-three fish, including one of 21 lbs. and another of 17 lbs. These were all caught with live bait, in the manner I shall describe below. The water is full of rocks and the fish give excellent sport. There is a dak bungalow and khansamah at Bagesar, and from here the fishing is good for 3½ miles up, and 2½ or 3 miles below. The route to the Sardah is as follows: Rail from Bareilly to Pilibhit, 28 miles; then by ekka, 21 miles to Katema, where there is a bungalow hut (no khansamah); from Katema to Mandi, 14 miles. At Mandi (real name Tanuchpur) there is a dak bungalow, and usually a khansamah; large bazaar and plenty of supplies, and the river is close by. The fishing is both above and below the bungalow, so that this is the best centre. But if you want to shoot as well, a tent should be taken.

"I usually fish with spoon or natural bait, but just before the snow-water comes down about the middle of March I have caught them with fly—any large fly with a good deal of yellow in it does. Personally I am an advocate for using the natural bait alive, *i.e.* as a 'live bait,' but not in the manner usually associated with this style of fishing. I fish at the head of the runs, or pools, and simply let the bait slip gradually down into the deeper water, keeping it out in the stream as much as possible (the bait will always swim to the side if it can), and then after it is dead, I spin with it, casting out and drawing in in the usual manner. It will be found that with the lip-hook put through the lips, as I shall describe, the bait will spin, or wobble, quite enough, nor is any firmer fastening with hooks or spinners required. In fact I hate all spinners, and prefer the wobbly motion, as being much more like a fish in distress, and so more natural. And I *know* it to be deadly. I use a small lead, usually about the size of a pea or larger in deeper or more rapid water, when fishing with live bait, and it is attached to the line by a thin thread; without the lead the bait is apt to stay too near the top of the water. The bait should last alive for about a quarter of an hour, if you just work him gently about, sometimes letting out and again drawing quietly in. I have found that this method of fishing somewhat resembles worm-fishing for trout. Sometimes the line will simply seem to stop, and when you then strike you find that you are in a fish. I fancy the line gets slack somehow—the bait perhaps swimming towards you after being let out—and this prevents you feeling the jerk when the fish seizes it. For the mahseer certainly does seize his prey with a rush, and this you will always know when spinning in the ordinary way, your line being then taut.

"My method of putting the live bait on the hook is very simple. The hook is a single large Limerick, with a small lip-hook whipped on to snood about 3½ in. or 4 in. from the bend of the big hook, and not moveable as in Parson's tackle. This will suit any small fish up to 4 in. in length: if you ever wish to use larger baits, you must simply make up another hook. I put the lip-hook through the lips of the bait—from *below*, as this keeps the mouth shut, and keeps the fish from drowning. The big hook lies loose at the side of the fish.

"I should recommend anyone who wishes to fish with natural bait to take a native fisherman with a cast net from Bareilly or Pilibhit: I use the net myself, and take a small zinc bucket with a piece of net over the top to keep the fish in. The water must be constantly changed if the bait is required alive.

"The best season for the Sardah is from 15th February to 15th March. I have, however, caught fish all through the cold weather. The autumn fishing is of no use, as the Terai is deadly at that time. I always find myself that the water cannot be too clear, and when the snow-water comes down, you may pack up and be off. I think, on the whole, the middle of the day is best, with a good sun out, especially for spoon-fishing. For fly, the evening.

"A word about my method of casting may interest you. I have found it a real good tip myself. Standing in any depth of water, even up to the middle, I take in the line in coils in my left hand, the first coils (nearest reel), say 1 ft. or more in diameter, the remainder gradually getting less towards the bait end down to about 6 in. diameter. After I have finished the coiling, and before casting, I transfer my rod into my left hand, where the coil is resting, and with the right hand pull out half a yard or so of extra line from the reel. This last is the important thing, for it prevents the line in the coils from turning over or kinking. I always vaseline about fifteen yards of my line; it runs easier so, and will float at first.

"After mahseer the most sporting fish I know is the rohu. He is a tank fish and a ground feeder, but I have also caught many in rivers, and many a hot day in the rains have I enjoyed fishing for them. They are very hard indeed to hook, as their bite is exceedingly gentle; very few anglers are skilful with rohu, and for ten strikes, you may very likely hook no more than one fish. When hooked, for a moment you might think you were into the bottom, but the next moment our friend is very often flying out of the water, sometimes doing three or four jumps in succession. You want 100 yards of good fine line; none better than the 'Tussar,' or rather 'Moonga' line, which you can get anywhere in Calcutta. But you must remember Tussar line requires dressing, and the only way I ever succeeded in doing this properly was by rubbing it with a berry off a tree called the 'Moomsurry.' This tree is to be found in almost any cantonment in Bengal; it should be unripe, and when broken a white sticky juice comes out of it; this rubbed in two or three times stiffens the line and makes it quite waterproof. The rohu runs large, and I have caught many over

20 lbs.; on one occasion in the Havildar's tank, outside the fort at Calcutta, I got two in one afternoon weighing together 58 lbs.

"When rohu fishing you may catch other varieties, such as mirgal, kalabans, etc., which also give good sport. But to practise this class of fishing successfully a good deal of previous preparation is quite necessary. A *trustworthy* man should be sent a week beforehand to bait the place three times a day with oil cake, and any old coarse flour, etc., and then for two days before you fish small lumps of paste, about the size of the pieces you would put on your hook, should be thrown in to accustom the fish to your bait. If this education is properly carried out you are sure to have sport. I always use good, stout single gut. The bait should just touch the bottom, and of course a float is used.

"Natives that I have seen fishing for mahseer with a rod generally use a short one, about 7 ft. with rings made of cane, the line being very simply wound on a rough board not attached to the rod. When the fish runs they drop the board, letting the line run, and wind up again when he stops. I have also seen them use the board alone with no rod. The bait they use is either a small fish, dead or alive, a sort of caddis cricket found under stones, or a dark coloured prawn, also found under stones with green weed on them. They are best found near the rapid water, but where it is shallow close to the bank. They make a first-class bait, but are not easy to obtain. A single hook is simply passed in at the mouth, and he is run on to it like a worm. I once saw a native kill a 32-pounder on a prawn with only the piece of board for his line, and I too have killed many large mahseer on prawns.

"The murrel or sowl is a fish to which natives devote much attention. He is found in weedy, still waters, runs to 15 lbs. or so, sometimes gives good sport, and is good eating. The natives generally fish for him with a frog, either alive or dead. I, too, have often caught them in tanks by making trimmers of empty bottles, and baiting with a frog or live fish. In some of the swamps in the Bareilly district, which are full of thick reeds, with open water here and there, they get long pieces of dry reed, about 8 or 10 feet long, which are made to fit into each other like a fishing rod, and with this they push the bait (a frog) out through the reeds into the open water. The foremost reed has a split in the end, and into this the line is loosely fitted close by the hook. When the bait is pushed far enough out, the reed is withdrawn with a jerk, which leaves the bait in the required position.[1]

"Another method of circumventing the murrel is to shoot him. A female murrel always keeps her young—several hundreds of them—with her until sufficiently grown to be able to shift for themselves, and the natives take advantage of this habit. Having often shot them myself, I can explain the process. You get up into a tree, or on to a high bank, from which you can get a good view of some likely spot, and when you see, as you shortly will, the crowds of young murrel come to the surface, wait for a minute or two, and you will *certainly* see the big fish come up in the centre of them to breathe. This is the time, and having already had your aim on the expected spot, you can let her have it at once. And if you don't actually strike the fish, it does not much matter, for you will surely go close enough for the shock to stun him, and your attendant fisherman will jump in and retrieve him."

SURJOO RIVER.

Note by Major B. Hobbs.

"Bagesur best place to fish from; six marches (66 miles), from railhead at Kathgodam, or five marches (61 miles), from Naini Tal. Best to engage coolies for whole trip. Bungalows at every stage; good one at Bagesur, but better to take tents, especially for Pagla, an excellent place, 4 miles down stream. Mahseer run to 40 lbs.; best lures, natural bait and spoon. Best seasons, last half of May and first half of June; also end of September and beginning of October."

[1] I should mention that the frog is first killed and blown out with a reed to make him float.

THE WESTERN DOON, GANGES AND JUMNA, AND TRIBUTARIES.

Note by Lieut.-Col. MACLAREN, M.D.

"My experience in mahseer fishing was limited—

"(1) To the Ganges at Raiwala, and its tributary the Suswa from Kansrao to its junction.

"(2) The Jumna at Rajghat, or Rampur Mundi, and its tributary the Asan.

"I have fished the Suswa and Asan in *clear water* from the end of the rains—middle of September—up to Christmas, and got good sport with fly, that is, with the usual Scotch salmon flies—Jock Scott, Durham Ranger, Black and Silver Doctor, and also with the gilt fly-spoon, as described in Dr Walker's book, "Angling in the Kumaon Lakes." I have frequently got baskets of 30 or 40 lbs. of fish from ½ lb. up to 6 or 7 lbs. mahseer, but occasionally a so-called trout. I began fishing at daybreak, and found the sport continued all day, but was best at early morn and dewy eve. The best basket I can recollect was once in September, when I got 90 lbs. of fish, and at the same time a friend got 40 lbs., the fish running from 10 lbs. downwards, all, or mostly, caught with fly-spoon. Next day our baskets were much lighter. My success in the Asan, though also good, never came up to that in the Suswa. I well remember one morning, at the mouth of the Suswa, 24th May, when, with the flies mentioned above, but mainly Jock Scott, I got over 80 lbs. of mahseer from 1 to 5 lbs. The water in the Suswa was then, of course, very clear and warm; that of the Ganges being fairly clear (snow-water), but cold. I began at daybreak and stopped at 10 A.M.

"On occasions I used to ride out of a morning during a break in the rains in August to the higher reaches of the Asan or Suswa, when the fish were running up. At these times I used to get fair sport when the water was not very clear, but with fly-spoon only.

"The above are samples of my experience with the smaller fish. Now for the big fish and big rivers.

"My usual and favourite practice was to visit Rampur Mundi *any time* during the winter months when there was a spate on; being stationed and stationary at Dehra Doon for so many years I was able to do this. On such an occasion the water of the Asan comes down muddy before that of the Jumna, and I used to get big fish at the junction, from 45 lbs. downwards for days in succession, *i.e.* as long as the water remained muddy in either of the rivers. When it became either muddy or clear in both there was no continuous sport, but the sport was always steady and good as long as the Asan was discoloured and Jumna clear, or *vice versa.* I well remember hooking a 46-lb. fish in muddy water in the Jumna, and landing him nearly a mile down, when the river was in high flood, carrying down trees, sleepers, roots, grass, etc.

"At Raiwala my practice was much the same and the sport similar. There the Suswa and Ganges were alternately muddy and clear, and when one hit off the lucky day—when the former was clear and the latter clearing, the sport was invariably something indescribable.

"I always fished the Ganges and Jumna from a sarnai (a raft on inflated skins) with a 17-foot rod, strong American silk line, 8-ply gut cast with steel swivels, a 6-inch phantom or half-pound natural bait being the lure, and in the former have frequently had bags of six or seven fish a day, running from 40 or 50 lbs. downwards. The largest I ever landed was 59 lbs., and the biggest I have seen was 63 lbs., caught by the late Fred Wilson ("Mountaineer"). In neither of these rivers did I ever do much in clear water and dry weather, and under such conditions I found the early morning, *before* sunrise, and after sunset the best or only times for big fish."

FISHING FROM RURKI.

"Hardwar and Raiwala are the two best places on the Ganges, both reached by rail; former twenty-seven miles, latter ten miles further up. At Hardwar is a dak bungalow, and at Raiwala a forest bungalow. No boats, but a 'sarnai' (raft) generally obtainable.

"Beyond Raiwala are two tributaries, the Soni and Suswa; in these there is excellent trout-fishing, fish running to 6 lbs. These streams are under the Dehra Doon Fishing Association.

"In the Ganges, mahseer run very large, the biggest I have heard of being 69½ lbs. Mahseer are also to be had at nearly all the falls in the Canal.

"February, March and April are best months for the river; excellent fly-fishing also in October and November, Bhimgoda, three miles up from Hardwar, being a specially good place. I prefer water when a little silt is coming down, or just after a spate begins. Fish will not take when the snow-water comes down.

"In the Canal I have found that a spoon, which does not revolve too rapidly, is best. Anglers must fish deep if they want big fish. It is no use fishing longer than five minutes in one place; it is best to go away and come back again."

FLY FISHING FOR LARGE MAHSEER NEAR MEERUT.

Notes by Capt. RIVETT CARNAC, R.E.

"Good sport can be had in the Ganges Canal near Meerut in February, March, April with spoon-fishing from the buttresses of bridges crossing the Canal. But this sport is uncertain, as water never clears properly, and snow-water comes down early in the hot weather. The best time of day varies with the temperature. In January I have caught fish at mid-day, in March best about 9.30 A.M., and in April 7.30 A.M. The Bola and Salawa Falls are best places.

"The best sport is to be had in the monsoon. As soon as crops require no more water, the Canal supply is cut off, and water then runs low and fairly clear with no perceptible current. The mahseer can be seen in numbers by anyone walking along the Canal bank, moving lazily about and coming up to the surface now and then. This is the time to catch them, using an 18-foot rod, single gut and No. 8 or 9

Limerick hook. When you have spotted your fish, swimming close to the surface, make your cast so as to drop the fly about 18 inches in front of and same distance *beyond* him; if you don't drop beyond him he will only follow up but won't touch it. The reason seems to be that the weight of the line in falling draws the fly sharply in front of his nose, and he seizes it before he has time to inspect. Again, you will often see a fish coasting along the edge in search of insects, etc.; get some 10 yards ahead of him and keep out of sight, then throw your fly 3 or 4 yards out, and as he comes opposite, draw your fly slowly till it passes just in front of his nose, and you have him to a certainty.

"The fishing is not easy owing to the long casts that have to be made, and also to the trees on the canal bank: this latter cause, as also the fact that the morning sun would be in your eyes, quite debars the right bank. Then the fish do not remain long near the surface, and are constantly on the move, which necessitates quickness. Wind, with the consequent ripple on the water, prevents you seeing the fish: the wind usually rises about 11 A.M., so you must begin early and stop then. I have found a claret body fly most effective, but have also used with success Jock Scott, Silver Doctor and Blackamoor. On eight *successive* days' fishing I have killed in this manner seventeen fish, averaging 12 lbs."

NOTE.—The above is a most fascinating style of fishing, involving, as it does, the preliminary excitement of first finding your fish and then stalking him. I have practised the same method with spoon as well as fly.—P. R. B.

The same correspondent sends the following notes on fishing in Coorg (Madras):—

"Hatti or Fish River: this is a tributary of the Cauvery rising in Mercara. It is fishable for mahseer only towards the end of the monsoon, October being perhaps the best month. Sport is uncertain, as one cannot depend on the weather. Heavy rain in Mercara will bring the river down in flood, but it clears again in a day or two. The fish run large, between 20 lbs. and 50 lbs.: largest I have heard of, 64½ lbs., after cleaning. Coracles, with experienced boatmen, are required, and have to be procured beforehand from Mettapollium. Natural bait, 5 to 6 inches long, is generally used. Near Holeri, some 5 miles from Mercara, is the first place worth fishing. Carnatic carp are plentiful, and can be caught whenever the river is not in flood.

"The Cauvery flows through Coorg from west to east, and holds some very large mahseer, which, however, very seldom take. Carp-fishing is good; fish run from ½ lb. to 6 lbs. or more. Coracles are necessary. The water is never really clear. The fisherman starts from Lidapur, 17 miles from Mercara, and fishes down-stream. There are travellers' bungalows at Lidapur and Fraserpet, forest bungalows at Dubarri and Ramasamy Kame.

"The Kuttum Hole, or Barepolay, rises in Coorg and flows west. Generally speaking, the rivers flowing west are far better for mahseer than those flowing east, being more rapid, more rocky and therefore clearer. Mahseer here take spoon and natural bait feeely; spoon perhaps best. Fish run from 1 lb. to 15 lbs. River usually in order about first week in November, but runs down very rapidly: as it clears, one should move down to deeper water below. It is useless trying higher up than Meengoondi. The upper reaches are fishable from the bank: lower down, a coracle is useful. Large murrel and also nair fish are sometimes caught while spinning for mahseer. Mahseer are mostly of the blue-backed variety, and have an objectionable habit of boring to the bottom, and smashing hooks against boulders. For this reason single hooks are preferable to trebles.

"There is no fishing association, but in 1903 a regulation for meshes of nets and a close season were established.

"A forest licence of Rs. 5 is necessary: this includes shooting."

From Another Correspondent.

[In the following the theory of the writer, that success depends on the study of migration, is expounded, and illustrated by phenomenal example. He says]:—

"Speaking generally, and with the possible exception of the Ravi, every river from the Ganges to the Kabul river will, if the migration of fish into, and out of, the hills be hit off, whilst the water is fairly clear, yield fine sport. But the migrations of mahseer, and the conditions of rivers, differ so widely from year to year that nothing but exploration on the spot can be relied on. That is my system; it takes time and trouble, and often ends in a sell; but when it comes off, I get such bags as I have never seen recorded—a ton and a third of fish in twenty-nine days being my record, and 440 lbs my best day. This same place might, however, utterly fail the next year on the same date, if the migrating fish were not there, and indeed this is exactly what happened to a veteran angler, who went to the spot by my advice.

"Torbela and the Sirin were utterly spoiled some years ago by natives using dynamite, etc., and I cannot say if they have since recovered."

[*Remark.*—The results being so extraordinary, the reader will share my great regret that the "system" is not more clearly explained. It does not appear indeed that the exponent did more than other fishermen usually do—viz., go to a place where they expect fish and do their best to catch them. But possibly he may mean to imply that, on reaching his ground, he refused to be seduced into wasting time over pools previously thought to be the best, *if the fish were not there*, but continued his search for the fish themselves, up or down stream.

Regarding the exception of the river Ravi, see note by another fisherman—Capt. Graham.—P. R. B.]

FISHING FOR "CHIRROO" IN KASHMIR.

Success on the Ravi.

Notes by Captain Graham, *Devonshire Regiment.*

"When I was in Kashmir in 1898, I had no end of fun with 'Chirroo' in the Jhelum at and about Shadipore. The biggest fish were got with live bait, but the best fun was with a fly manufactured by my boatman. This was meant to resemble small fry. Floating down in a boat this was cast into the middle of a shoal of feeding fish, when something was invariably hooked. The fish ran from ½ lb. to 2 lbs. as a rule; 4 lbs. was my biggest by this method, but with live bait I caught one of 10 and one of 17 lbs. I never had a blank day. I tried the Lidder Valley, but found the fish there small, and could only catch with worm. I was not very successful with mahseer; only got three all the time I was fishing at Shadipur during many days.

"In October 1898 I had five days' good sport on the Ravi. The spot was where another stream joins, near the Rope Bridge (Jhula), about 15 miles down from Dalhousie. I found the fish would only take paste, however. A lump about the size and shape of a hen's egg was put on a big treble hook, and I fished with this very much as one would use a spoon. I got fourteen fine fish, and lost many more. I fished up to 9.30 A.M., and for three hours before sunset."

[This is interesting, as one seldom hears any good word of the Ravi. The reason of the fish taking paste may probably be found to be that the Gurkhas from Bakloh fish this place, and have been in the habit of baiting it for their own benefit. —P. R. B.]

[A correspondent writes from Jhelum]:—

"Tangrot does keep up its reputation: plenty of boats always obtainable, charge Rs.1 per day.

"Close time for rods, 15th November to 15th February; for nets, 15th November to 15th July. Jungoo Pool, 15th October to 15th July.

"*Licences:*—Rod for season, Rs.5; rod and net combined, Rs.20.

"*Best seasons:*—March to end of May, limited by the heat, and in Jhelum by snow-water; then, again, September to 15th November.

"Very possible brand new place now being created—Rasul, the head works of new Jhelum Canal, but untried yet.

View in the Liddar Valley

"There are one or two good places within easy reach of Jhelum, but they are apt to be precarious, depending much on the conditions of water and weather being exactly right.

"I can get no information of the Punjab Fishing Club, though I have had enquiries made at Rawal Pindi, the headquarters. I fear it is defunct."

CENTRAL PROVINCES.

[The following is the merest "precis" of some voluminous notes supplied by an obliging correspondent, but as he himself condemns the fishing of the whole district with the faintest praise, he will not cavil at the curtailment.]

"There are plenty of fish in many of the C.P. rivers, but they do not take the usual sporting lures at all readily. The usual practice is to fish with paste or parched grain, and this entails careful baiting of the pools for days beforehand. You may then catch fish, but it is not fishing! The commonest fish obtainable are Maha-Sir, Rohoo, Murrul and Parhun. Maha-Sir do not run large, one of 10 or 12 lbs. being considered a good fish. I, however, caught one of 25 lbs. with small spoon in a small stream joining the Nerbudda near Naraingunge, on the Jubbulpore-Mandla road. I never repeated the performance, or anything like it, there or elsewhere.

"The months to fish are from end of September to middle of March. After that it is too hot, but after good rain in end of May or June is a good time, and the temperature is then quite bearable.

"The following is a list of fishing localities, which I know or have heard of:—

LOCALITIES.

District.	River.	Localities, etc.
Mandla	Nerbudda	Mandla, Ramnuggur, Suhej Dharra, Singhurpoor
Saugor	Beema Dussaun Sonar	Various

District.	River.	Localities, etc.
Damoh	Sonar	Hutta
Hoshungabad	Nerbudda	Bundarabun, up stream, also below the town
Nimur	Nerbudda	Kerryghat
Wardha	Wardha	Not known, but have heard of good sport in this river
Nagpore	Bora	Ab Boree, 18 miles by rail from Nagpore
Chindwara	Pench	Machigora
Seoni	Waingunga	Not known, but said to hold big fish; probably not mahseer, but another carp
Chanda	Waingunga Wardha Prankeeta	Not known, but all said to contain big fish

UPPER BURMAH, CHIN HILLS, ETC.

From a Correspondent who was there in 1890.

"I caught a lot of mahseer in the Myiltha (?) river, below Kalemgo, on the road to Fort White in the Chin Hills. I used a tiny fly-spoon. The water was rapid and clear. Fish were small; biggest 6 lbs., but I was afraid to try for bigger fish, having only the lightest of rods.

"Some men before me had been trying paste, but, meeting with no success, had taken to dynamite! The Manipur river which joins the Myiltha contains heaps of mahseer, but I fear that here too dynamite was playing havoc.

"I fancy that all rivers in this neighbourhood are full of fish, conditions being practically the same as in Upper Assam. But I understand the rivers in the Shan states are not nearly as good — probably, more exploited by natives. Above Bhamo a considerable deal of fishing is done, and I know there are plenty of mahseer in the Nampoung which runs into the Tæping. So too at Myitkyina on the Irrawaddy, but perhaps only taken with paste.

"From what I hear, the Kala Nadi near Bolgaum (Madras) is well worth trying, but is uncertain."

RIVERS KISTNA AND BEEMA IN COORG, MADRAS.

["R. M. B.," A correspondent of ten years' experience, writes from Raichore]:—

"The Beema is reached from Yadgiri station and the Kistna from Kistna station on the G.I.P. Railway—about ¼ mile in either case. Beema joins Kistna 3 miles above Kistna station. Both rivers clear, roughly, from end of November to middle of May. Mango showers improve fishing in April. Best time is while water is clearing and just after. After middle of February water runs too low. It is *no use whatever* to fish before 10 A.M. at any time of year; best time, 11 to 2, and 4 to dark. Boats are necessary, but none obtainable locally. I recommend a 7-ft. berthon.

"The fish are all mahseer, and run heavy—up to 36 lbs. at least. On the Beema I have seen 92 lbs. caught in a day; two rods fishing from boat and one from shore.

"The best lure is spoon; if not taking this well, try natural bait, which you can get by sending to nearest village for fisherman with a cast-net.

"The fly is no use. Owing to numerous rocks, I found it best to use wire traces. Hooks and tackle must be strong, the former not less than 16 standard gauge wire. Avoid split rings.

"At Yadgiri there is 2 miles of water; best place, opposite railway station, near a temple, where a nullah runs in.

"Near Kistna station the best water is under the railway bridge, and ½ mile above and below. Junction of Beema and Kistna no use; nor either river for some miles above the junction. Two miles down stream from Kistna station is a traveller's bungalow (no attendance): supplies for servants but not much for the angler. From the bungalow good fishing to ½ mile below an island with large tamarind trees: best water is opposite island and ½ mile below. Seven miles below the bungalow is a splendid pool, full of fish: pool about a mile long and from 100 to 200 yards in width, narrowing to a 40-ft. very deep channel in the middle.

Village of Koorthoocoondi here: no accommodation; tents necessary. Direct route from Kistna station is to Mundipla—12 miles—on opposite bank to Koorthoocoondi."

[My correspondent ends by saying that he had, when writing, just begun to fish the big pool, had landed one of 14 lbs., and had been broken by four big fish.—P. R. B.]

SOME RIVERS, MADRAS PRESIDENCY, AND NOTES ON TROUT ACCLIMATIZATION IN THE NEILGHERRY HILLS.

By Major BAGNELL, *E. Yorkshire Regiment.*

"The Bawani flows round north of the Neilgherry hills, meeting the Cauvery near Crode: it holds mahseer and Carnatic carp; the former above Manaar junction; below it, only the latter. Water difficult of access; pony transport; no bungalows; climate feverish. River rapid, and clear except in monsoon. Nearest centres Metapollium and Coonoor. Best lure for mahseer, natural chilwa, then spoon; for carp, fly or grasshopper. Best months, October; then December to April, and any interval between S.W. and N.E. monsoons. Best time of day, early morning. Coracles are quite necessary; can be had from Metapollium, charge Rs. 1 per day. Clear water universally best for mahseer. Neilgherry Preservation Society preserves in a sort of way, but no licence is required.

"Moyar flows north of the Neilgherrys, is full of a kind of carp up to about 6 lbs.; take fly or grasshopper freely. Water much poached and dynamite used. Can be reached easily and fished from many places: fishing times same as Bawani.

"The Cauvery contains mahseer, Carnatic carp and chilwas. Baits as for Bawani; coracles are required and available.

"Trout have been imported here (Neilgherrys) for some years, and have been put into most rivers and lakes. We only know of *Salmo fario*, and of these there are many survivors of large size—up to 7½ lbs. Female fish in spawn are often seen, but I have seen neither milting males nor small fry.

"*Salmo irridens* (the American rainbow trout) was imported in 1902, but the few hundreds hatched were all swept away by a flood: this was most unfortunate, as, from their success in Ceylon and Kashmir, they should do well here. The selection of other fish for acclimatization has been most injudicious. Tench and Russian carp are in swarms in Ootacamund, Burnfoot and Snowdon lakes: they give no sport and are useless for the table. More than one species of small barilius are plentiful at Ootacamund, Wellington and Billikal: these are sporting little fish, and take fly freely.

"The big trout I have caught have been sluggish, and gave little sport. I am convinced that the rainbow trout will yet succeed.

"The only really indigenous fish in these hills is a kind of minnow, almost identical with the English species.

"Of estuary fish we have in Southern Madras the bhamin (or bamin) and nair fish, both free fighters, giving excellent sport, and are good table fish.

"The sea fish on the same coast are the seer, the pulamin, pālamin, butter fish, dog fish and sharks. I will back the seer for ferocity and pluck against any fish that swims; it takes out 150 yards of line without stopping, and then throws marvellous leaps in the air.

"Natives fishing for bhamin show great skill in casting the line from coils on left wrist, the way in which the man in the stern of the boat just misses with the heavy weight the head of him in the bows being particularly fascinating."

Communication from Deesa, Bombay. Fishing near Ahmedabad.

"Although the Banas river contains innumerable small fry, they never seem to grow, and in a word 'nil' best expresses the fishing to be had at Deesa.

"I had, however, a good day near Ahmedabad on the march from Poonah to Deesa, which I will describe.

"You go from Ahmedabad, by camel or bullock cart, to

Rayasan, a village 14 miles up the Sabermati river. Here there is a sluggish pool, some 200 yards long, by 40 to 60 yards broad, and deep in the middle. Here one morning, fishing from 9 to 11 A.M., with a 1-inch spoon, I caught 28 lbs. of fish, twelve being mahseer, biggest 3 lbs. One murrel weighed 10 lbs., and a rohu 3½ lbs. This pool seemed to be full of fish, but in no other pool could I rise a fish at all."

[This was evidently a one-day visit, and the best time of day probably spent at the big pool. The river should be well worth trying.—P. R. B.]

Note by Capt. WAKE, *43rd Gurkhas.*

"The best fishing obtainable from here is in the Barak river, five marches from Manipur and six from Silchar. It is a large river, rapid and clear; the banks are steep and covered with jungle, so fishing is done by trolling from a boat. Boats are obtainable at Trang, and cost 8 annas per diem; good boatmen can be hired through the political agent. Only mahseer obtainable; these run up to 40 or 50 lbs. They take spoon and dead bait, the latter being easily obtainable. Best season—November to March. Best time of day—when the sun first strikes the water in the morning, and at sunset. The water cannot be too clear.

"There are two smaller rivers on the road between Manipur and Trang, both fishable with fly."

FISHING NEAR LORALAI, BALUCHISTAN.

"The only fishing obtainable near Loralai is that in the Nari river, alongside of the bed of which the Harnai section of the Sind-Peshin railway has been built. Distance from Loralai is by road to Harnai 56 miles, thence about 60 miles by rail to Babar Kach. The Nari is only fishable from Babar Kach to Tanduri (another station on the railway), about 30 miles distant. The Bheji river joins the Nari at Babar Kach, and is fishable for about 40 miles up. The only sporting fish obtainable is the mahseer, average weight about 6 lbs., greatest weight not over 16 lbs. Natural bait—chilwa—is the most killing. The fish will not take fly, and are shy of the spoon. They can be obtained in a small stream below Babar Kach station. The water is generally crystal clear, and light tackle—single gut traces—is necessary. The streams are not much fished. The best times are at the beginning of summer or winter. The heat is too great in June, July, August, and malaria is very prevalent. I have never met with much success in winter. Two or three 5 to 6 lbs. fish in a day is a good bag. Transport and supplies are very difficult to obtain, and can only be got through the political agent of the Thal Chotiali district. The fishing throughout Baluchistan is very poor."

THE KUMAON LAKES.

Notes by Capt. HICKLEY, *3rd Gurkhas.*

"The various lakes are Naukachia, Sath-Tal, Bhim-Tal, Malwa-Tal and Naini-Tal. The latter is not now worth mentioning from a fishing point of view, and Bhim-Tal also has been somewhat over fished, and fish are very shy.

"House accommodation is to be had at all the lakes, but for Naukachia and Sath-Tal this must be previously arranged for. One can camp at all of them if preferred. Malwa-Tal is the lowest, and is hot and feverish. Boats are obtainable at all, but for Naukachia and Sath-Tal it is better to have a boat taken over from Bhim-Tal for one's exclusive use. The hire is Rs. 1 per diem, with something extra to the boatman.

"My preference is for Naukachia in the early season and Sath-Tal in the autumn. The fish run much larger in the former, but are bolder risers in the latter.

"The best seasons are from 20th March to end of May, and again from middle of September to middle of October. In the spring the best times of day are from 6.30 to 11 A.M., and again from 4 P.M. till too dark to see. In autumn fish rise all day till sunset, but it is not much use fishing before 8 A.M.

"Fly is the usual and best lure, but the fish also take a small fly-spoon well. The claret, silver doctor, cinnamon and white moth are the best, the first distinctly the best of all. All these are procurable from Messrs Murray, Naini-Tal, or Luscombe, Allahabad. Tackle must be of the finest, and one fly only should be used. The flies used—about size of those for white trout—are too large for this fine gut, but this cannot be helped. A small trout rod, 9 to 12 feet, is the thing. The fish feed round the margin of the lake, and so the casting is done from a boat towards the shore; cast close up to the bank, or better still, on to it, and let the fly drop quietly in.

"The fish are mahseer. They run up to 5 lbs. or so, but 2½ lbs. is about the average. Fishing on a favourable morning in April, seven to eight fish weighing 22 lbs. would be a good take in four hours; but I once got in Bhim-Tal in this time twenty-seven fish weighing about 85 lbs. This was in 1891.

"Natives fish much with paste, but since 1903 a licence is required of them."

CEYLON.

Notes on Trout Acclimatisation, etc.

Notes by T. Farr, Esq.

"Brown trout were introduced in 1886, and again in 1893-94, when the Ceylon Fishing Club was formed, and protection secured by legislation. The trout did well and grew rapidly, even up to 10 lbs., and good fishing was obtained. But observation showed that they were not breeding. So in 1899-1900 rainbow trout were introduced, and these have proved in every way an eminent success. They grew to 3 lbs. weight in fifteen months, have bred abundantly in many streams (notably those of the Horton Plains, 7000 feet high), give excellent sport, and are the best of eating.

"No free fishing is allowed, and no lure but fly is permitted, Open season from March to September. Cost of licence is for members Rs.50 and Rs.10 annual, non-members double.

"Mahseer (Singalese 'lela') are caught up to 2 or 3 lbs. in up-country streams, and are plentiful, but not fished for, in low country.

"Sea fishing—dolphin, seer, mullet, etc.—is good at times."

IV.—SEA FISHING

THOSE whose fortune it is to be stationed up-country, near the larger rivers, soon find out the quality of the sport to be had with the river fish; but those whose luck it is to be kept on or near the coasts often remain for long periods in ignorance of the chances they are losing, and only find out, when perhaps too late, what excellent fishing may have been available, often without any expense or trouble, at their very doors. It will simplify matters if I give, first of all, a short list of some of the best of the sea and estuary fish commonly found, with their native names, and then deal shortly with each of them in detail. They are as follows:—

1. Bahmin or Raōs (*Polynemus tetradactylus*, *Polynemus indicus*).
2. Seer or Surmi (*Cybium guttatum*, *Cybium commersonii*).
3. Khokari (*Caranx carangus*, *Caranx malabaricus*).
4. Dangara or Begti (*Lates calcarifer*).
5. Skipjack or Parah (*Chorinemus toloo*).
6. Rock cod—gobra (*Serranus malabaricus*).
7. Mullet—Taru or Magi (*Mugil consula*).

The Bahmin or Raōs.—This excellent sporting fish is far and away the best of the estuary fish. It enjoys a wide range, and wherever there are broad estuaries into which fresh water streams run, wherever the tides are strong and the current rapid, there will it be found. The finest specimens appear to be caught at the mouths of the larger rivers. They take a bait freely. During the monsoon months they run into Bombay harbour, sometimes in incredible numbers, and large quantities are caught by the natives in nets. They are to be caught during those months at two or three places in the harbour, and notably up at the head near Hog Island, and lower down the harbour where the Sunk Rock Lighthouse has been built to mark the site of a dangerous rocky shoal. In fact, this last is probably the best place known for them, and by asking permission (which is always readily granted) from the port-office the base of the lighthouse itself may be used, and will be found a very good spot to fish from.

They are most numerous, run larger, and are in the best condition during the monsoon months, from say the end of May till the end of September; and, curiously enough, they can be caught here only on the ebb-tide. Spring-tides are the best, and it should be borne in mind that the worse the weather the better the day for fishing. The best bait is a large prawn, 5 to 6 inches long; but when these are scarce recourse should be had to small mullet or

BAHMIN

Caught in Bombay Harbour. Weight 10¼ lbs.

"bomalo" (Bombay duck, *Harpodon nehereus*), a semi-transparent, gelatinous fish, which somewhat resembles a young whiting. These latter are easily got, and can be purchased at any time in the local fish markets. They are not quite as good a bait as the prawn, but better than an artificial lure. At other times a large phantom minnow will be found useful, and when the water is more than usually clear (as it often is during neap tides) a spoon bait from 1½ inches to 3 inches should be tried.

The fish themselves ordinarily run from 4 lbs. to 15 lbs. in weight. A good average would be from 7 to 9 lbs. Much larger fish are caught in the nets further out at sea, but not often by line in the estuaries, even by the natives. They are very active and powerful, and run and fight well when hooked. Other very good places for these fish on the Malabar coast are the backwaters at Cannanore, Calicut, Mahé and Tellicherry, and the estuary at Cochin; and at times during the cold weather, from November to February, they are often very numerous in the Paumben Pass.

The run through the bridge over the backwater at Mahé is a very well-known place, and there are other runs near the bridges between Cannanore and Tellicherry. It is a curious fact, but it seems by now to have been established, that the best time to fish, on this coast at least, is on the ebb tide; and as long as the tide is falling, the fish should, when once found, be kept to.

On the east coast they are found in the creeks

at Masulipatam and Nizampatam, as well as in nearly all the Burmese estuaries and notably at Akyab, off the spot known as Scandal Point. On the Coromandel coast, my own experience has been that they should be looked for on the flood, and the reason for this, I think, is to be found in the different configurations of the estuary courses. At Masulipatam and Nizampatam, the creeks and backwaters are nearly dry at low water, so that, as a general rule, the fish retreat to the outer side of the bar, there wait for the rising tide, and then, as the water flows in, and the mud and rocky flats, which are their feeding grounds, become submerged, they enter the creeks and at once begin to feed. Here, at any rate, I have never done much good on the ebb, while on the flood, and generally on the first of it, I have on several occasions had notable baskets.

After a good many years' experience, I have come to the conclusion, that a good, strong split-cane rod, not exceeding 12 ft. 6 in. or 13 ft. in length, or a similar rod in green-heart, is the most useful size. I suggest split cane for choice, because it is lighter, but such rods are apt to fall to pieces, unless exceptionally well-made, from the effects of the climate. The reel should be not less than 4½ inches, and at least 150 yards of line will be required. Avoid oil-dressed lines, and give the preference to those of plain undressed tanned cotton, as they last much longer. The trace may be of good gimp, but a better plan is to buy fine softened brass wire (35 S.W.G.), and with it spin up traces as required. Five strands of this wire will be found sufficient, and the trace should be 5 ft. long. Swivels should be fitted at both ends and in the middle, and a lead may be used of from ½ to 1½ oz. weight, according to the strength of current. For the bait, ordinary prawn tackle is often used, but I prefer a single Limerick hook, 4/0 to 7/0, as it is more easily baited. Between the hook and the trace swivel about 8 inches of a stiffer wire (21 S.W.G.) should be used, and the bait tied down to this. This will keep the bait straighter and more natural-looking. The way to use either prawn or "bomalo" is the simple sink and draw. The bahmin, if cooked shortly after capture, will be found most excellent on the table, particularly if boiled in a solution of salt and water with the juice of two or three limes.

Seer or Surmi.—This is another very fine sporting fish, which occasionally runs up into the estuaries, but is more often to be found in the clearer salt-water and further out to sea, or in quiet land-locked bays. It is found close in shore when the small fry are about, and at such times it is easily induced to take a lure.

The entrance to Karachi harbour, in the neighbourhood of the breakwater, is a favourite spot, and from there they are found all down the coast, especially off Mangalore, and in the quiet bays and lagoons of the Laccadive Islands, and Minicoy, as well as off Colombo and Galle harbours, and in all the rocky entrances and shallows from Madras to Vizagapatam. They run up to 5 and 6 ft. in length and weigh 50 or 60 lbs., but the average would be from 9 to 28 lbs. They are long and rather narrow fish, like large mackerel, with a formidable set of teeth, and they are a perfect scourge on the coast at times when the so-called sardine are about. The best bait for them are some of the small sardines, but they will take phantoms and spoon baits freely. As they are generally to be found in clear water, the tackle to be used for them should be finer than what I have described as suitable for bahmin, but must be quite as strong. They appear on the coast towards the end of the monsoon, and are to be caught all through the cold weather. They are not so susceptible to the influence of tides, and will take often the bait all day long. The chief controlling element in their case is the presence of the shoals of sardines. These are at times difficult to locate. One very good guide is the presence of the sea gulls. If the shoals of sardines are about, the gulls will be busy. This fishing is invariably carried on from a boat, and the rod described for bahmin will answer very well. The line may be the same, but a longer single steel-wire trace is preferable. Swivels must be fitted, and the bait, if a sardine, should be threaded on a piece of stiff brass-wire. The hook should be a Limerick, 6/0 to 8/0. When struck, they go off with a terrific rush, and throw themselves out of the water repeatedly. Though

Seer or Surmi

Caught by C. J. J. Jones, Esq., R.I.M. (3 of 20 lbs. each; 1 of 18 lbs.)

they fight brilliantly, they seem to have no great staying power, and when once hooked they should seldom be lost, as they can be followed up by the boat. A good, sharp gaff should always be at hand, as from their length they are difficult to get into a net; and as they are a small-scaled, tender-skinned fish, they present no difficulties to the gaff. The smaller examples are excellent eating, but when they grow large the flesh gets coarse and oily in flavour.

Khokari.—This fish deserves to be very much better known than it is. It is a full, deep-bodied fish, something like a perch; the body is oblong and more or less compressed. It has resplendent scales, high shoulders, a small and shapely head, and very powerful tail and fins. In colour it ranges from a bluish silvery sheen on the back to a golden colour below, and in season the fins look as if they were of beaten gold. In size it ranges from 3 to 80 lbs., and very ordinary fish run from 15 to 35 lbs. Its distribution throughout Indian waters is very extensive, but it is never found up estuaries or elsewhere than in the cleanest and clearest salt water. I have seen it caught off Karachi, and have caught it further south, off Mangalore and the Travancore coast, and in the Paumben Pass; but to get the best and the finest it is necessary to go further south. On the southern and eastern coasts of India, all round Ceylon, near Madras, and again at Vizagapatam, they are numerous; but probably the two best places in the east for khokari are Aden and the Andaman Islands. They appear at certain seasons in Suez Roads, and the natives there look out for them at the time of the date harvest. In the Andaman Islands they run very large indeed. Like the seer, their appearance in the bays and close inshore is regulated by the appearance of the shoals of sardines, and they follow these shoals persistently. When the shoals are about, no other bait is of much use; but at other times they will take a spoon bait, towed behind a boat sailing, and yet again at times they will take pieces of dead fish off the bottom; and one bait greatly in vogue among the native crews of vessels is a piece of a half-boiled potato.

The khokari is a bold, game fish, and when struck fights magnificently. Its first rush is as dashing as that of the seer; it never shows above water when fighting, but, after two or three splendid runs, settles down to an absolutely dogged fight; and, weight for weight, it tries the tackle more perhaps than any fish, unless it be the "dangara."

A very powerful rod is required. One of 13 feet is long enough, as it is generally a case of boat work; 200 yards of line will not be too much, and the steel wire trace and swivels recommended for the seer are also the best in this case, as, in fact, they are in every case where the fishing is in clear water. Hooks 3/0 to 6/0 (Limerick); but if spoon bait is used, the triangles should be of extra stout make, as a khokari can, as a rule, chew up the ordinary English tackle without much effort.

The smaller and moderate-sized fish are good eating, but the larger ones are rank and coarse.

Dangara or Begti.—This is a very fine fish, and one that, from the angler's point of view, runs the bahmin close. He is purely an estuary fish, and is seldom found far away from the mouths of the larger rivers. He is very common all down the coast, from the mouth of the river Indus right round India and up the delta of the Ganges. In spite of this, however, there are not very many places where the ordinary angler can reach him, although the natives, of course, catch him in nets and by lines everywhere. Among the best places for this fish, where he can be got at easily, are the upper parts of the harbour at Karachi, where the creeks enter the harbour, and where there are long reaches of muddy flats with deep channels between. These flats become submerged every tide, and here, as the tide flows, these fish are often to be had quite easily. The upper parts of Bombay harbour, where the Panwell and Thanna rivers enter, are also good; and some backwaters connecting these creeks are simply full of them from May to October. All the backwaters mentioned before, near Cannanore, Calicut, Mahé and Tellicherry, are good places, until the waters begin to dry up and get stale after the end of the monsoon, when the fish retreat and find their way again to the larger rivers. The river at Cochin is a noted place, where one can most easily hire men and boats. The natives thereabout are born fishermen, always after begti, knowing exactly when and where to find him, and quite willing to help a stranger. That part of the country, too, below Calcutta, called the Soonderbuns, situated in the delta of the Ganges and intersected in all directions by tidal creeks, with long sloping muddy banks and flats, is the home of this fish. In Bengal he is known always as "begti"; in Scinde, and down as far as Bombay, he is called "dangara," while the Cochin people know him best as the "nair-min." Both Day and Thomas allude to him as known to Europeans as the "cock up."

Though essentially an estuary fish, and frequenting the same localities as the bahmin, they are seldom found together, the reason being that the dangara loves a quieter corner and a less rapid stream. He is a large and powerful perch, deep in the body, with large scales of a dark golden bronze colour, the personification of strength. He is generally found feeding on a flood tide. The dangara grows to a large size. I have seen two magnificent specimens. One was 84½ lbs., caught in Karachi harbour, and the other, 61 lbs., was caught in one of the dry docks in the Government dockyard, Bombay. These fish are taken ordinarily from 6 to 30 lbs., and, if cooked shortly after capture, are a most excellent fish to eat, as the flesh is white and flaky and resembles that of turbot. When well cooked, the bigger the fish the better it tastes. The best time to go out for dangara is when spring-tides and the first of the flood occur shortly after dark. In all these creeks on the muddy banks there are large numbers of a curious little mud-fish (Periophthalmus kolreuteri), an almost amphibious fish that spends its existence basking in the sun; and as soon as the tide makes, the dangara rush into the creeks and chase these little fish. At this time, if it be dark, it is quite possible to sit in a small canoe close into the bank and to watch the large fish foraging about in all directions. The bait, needless to say, should be one of these small fish. In any case, and wherever you may be, I consider this the best bait; but if it be not obtainable, a prawn, hermit crab, or small mullet should be tried. The time is at night, on a rising tide; but day tides are also good, especially spring-tides with the water thick. The tackle is the same as is used for bahmin, except that you ought to have more line, 200 to 250 yards being none too much where the fish run large. The twisted brass wire trace is best, mounted with three swivels and 6/0 to 8/0 hooks.

A dangara, once he begins to run, never knows when to stop, and it is simply impossible to hold a heavy fish. At times, all hurry and rush, he will dash up and take what you offer him with a splash; at other times he will take the bait in a very quiet manner, no rush, no fuss, but, at the same time, no nonsense. He just gulps it down and lies quiet. After a time he will begin to move quietly away, and often the larger the fish the quieter will be the whole proceeding until an attempt is made to stop him. Then he is really off, and, unless he is given his head freely, a smash up is inevitable.

Skip-jack or Parah.—Under ordinary circumstances one would hardly be inclined to include this fish with the others, but as he is so often met with when trailing or spinning for the seer, and as he is invariably to be found feeding on the shoals of sardines he will very often force himself upon the notice of the angler. Much smaller than the seer he is in no way to be compared to him. Skip-jacks run up to 6 or 8 lbs., but are most often caught from 2 lbs. to 3½ lbs. in weight. They are of a greenish tinge along the back, shot with blue, and silvery below the lateral line. They can be easily recognised at a distance from their habit of splashing and jumping about on the surface of the water, most commonly on a bright, calm day; and when hooked they fight and run well. They would undoubtedly give good sport if taken on light rods and tackle, but as they usually fasten on when heavier fish are being tried for, they gradually get to be looked upon as a nuisance, and they are useless for the table, as their flesh is dry and tasteless.

Rock Cod or Gobra.—Though not a very sporting fish to catch, it would be inexcusable

THREE FISH CAUGHT BY C. J. S. JONES, ESQ., R.I.M., OUTSIDE PORT BLAIR HARBOUR FROM A SAILING BOAT

Bait, small Garfish about 7 ins. long, mounted on an ordinary flight with 3 triangles. Left-hand fish, *Sphyræna acutipinnis*, 11 lbs.; centre fish, *Cybium commersonii*, 48 lbs.; right-hand fish, *Caranx*, 33 lbs.

to pass over this fish, for two reasons, firstly, because he is to be found almost everywhere; and, secondly, because he will be found, in spite of his repulsive appearance, one of the very best Indian fish for the table. Essentially marine fishes, the rock cod enter the estuaries to prey on other fishes. They are found all round the coasts and grow to an enormous size. I have seen them over 150 lbs. in weight, being brought ashore by natives, having been caught by hook and line; but for the angler they average between 8 and 50 lbs. Very large specimens are taken off the coasts, between Negapatam and Madras. The best bait is a small, dead fish, put on whole (the small, highly-coloured rock fish for choice), or a small mullet, or a green or hermit crab. It is almost better, when fishing solely for "gobra" to put the rod aside. Playing a fish is infinitely preferable to hand-lining, but in most cases it becomes not a case of playing him, but of pulling him up by sheer force from the nook or cranny in the rocks, to which he has rushed for shelter on feeling himself hooked. They would appear at times to be able to cling to the rocks, and on these occasions it will be found necessary to use such a strain as no rod could possibly survive. If, however, they are hooked in comparatively open ground they will make one or two very short, sharp rushes, then give in and come up to the boat like a log. If hand-lining, a moderately thick cotton line dressed with fish oil, such as is made by the natives, is much the best. It is flexible and does not cut one's hand as readily as hemp. A twisted wire trace and a large swivel, with just sufficient lead on it to ensure its touching bottom, and a hook from 6/0 to 8/0, will be all that is required. These fish take most freely about nightfall and after dark, and thus give the best sport.

Mullet, Taru or Magi.—This fish is too well-known to need much comment. At times, when the weather is rough and it is not feasible to go far afield, it may be convenient to try for mullet. They are very numerous in all estuaries and backwaters, and find their way into docks and harbours among the shipping. They are continually being fished for from the wharves and piers in Karachi, from the quays inside the Bombay docks, and from the breakwaters at Colombo and Madras. The natives are fond of them, and fish for them with a sort of paste made from "attar," a coarse flour and fish flesh bruised up together.[1] Another good bait for them is the plain brown crust of a loaf of bread. They run up sometimes to 7 or 8 lbs., but that is exceptional, and I should put the average at between 1 and 2½ lbs. Tackle for them should be much the same as that used in England for roach-fishing, and the finer the hook and gut used the better the chances as they are very shy and timid.

[1] This is not unlike one of the favourite Italian baits for mullet in the Mediterranean, a compound of bruised anchovies and arrowroot biscuits made into a stiff paste.—ED.

The above notes do not pretend to include all the good sea and estuary fish that may fall to the angler, but only bring to his notice some of the better known and more prominent. There are a large number of species of perch- and bream-like fishes, which the fisherman will often come across, and which give very fair sport, run fairly large at times, and are good for the table. Again, fishing farther out than usual from the land, he may, when trailing, hook barracuda, tunny, bonito, and even shark, and with them he may have magnificent sport. Sport varies with every locality, but everywhere there is sport to be had by the keen angler.

ADDITIONAL NOTE ON ESTUARY AND SEA FISHING IN SOUTH MADRAS.

By Capt. Gibson, *Durham Light Infantry.*

"Station: *Cannanore*—Hotel Choyis, which will make all arrangements for boats (jutkas), etc.

"*Fish to be caught*—

1.	Bahmin	up to 12 lbs.
2.	Seer (vernacular, *Icurra*)	" 100 "
3.	Pallamin (*tunny*)	" 25 "
4.	Moimin (*butter-fish*)	" 70 "

"*Tackle and Bait*—

1*st for Bahmin*—200 yds. salmon line, brass-wire trace (single wire), any flight mounted on brass wire to take a 5 or 6-in. fish. I have found that the salt-water rusts everything except brass wire.

Bait: a mullet or small sardine, one or other of which is always obtainable fresh from local fishermen.

"*Where to fish—*

(*a*) Bellapatam river (at mouth of bar), five miles from Cannanore by pony jutka, fishing from a boat by spinning. Calm weather necessary, as a rough sea makes the bar dirty and then fishing useless.

(*b*) Mahé river, in town of Mahé (1½ hours by train). Hotel beside river. Fishing near bridge about half-a-mile from the bar. Tie boat to bridge, and as soon as fish hooked take him away from the bridge, or he will either tear his jaw on the hook or cut the line on the piers. If the fish happen to be in, this is a first-class place, but it is hardly worth going on chance unless one hears the fish are moving.

"Best time for bahmin — October to June. My best days have been in November. The bahmin is the most sporting fish for its size I have ever killed. He has tremendous fin power, makes real good runs, and fights right up to the gaff. He is generally caught at Bellapatam when the tide is running in or out, which it does at about 8 miles an hour. At Mahé, the best time is at high-tide.

"*Other Fishing—*

Seer.
Pallamin.
Moimin.

"For those who don't mind a choppy sea in a small boat, with a very hot sun, there is no better sea-fishing than for the above.

"If one can borrow a small sailing boat, so much the better; but, if not, a fishing-canoe with a sail is a fair substitute, but neither so comfortable nor so safe. The fishing is done from 4 to 12 miles out to sea, according to the varying distance from land of the clear water.

"*Tackle*—An 8-foot very strong rod with 300 yds. stout salmon line, brass-wire trace with 4 or 5 double swivels, and a flight to take an 8 to 10-in. bait.

"The only baits I have found of any use on the Malabar coast are mackerel (Malay or Javanese 'iley') or a large sardine, the former being much the best.

"Seer and pallamin will take a bait from a boat sailing at anything from 1 to 6 miles an hour, and will run out 100 yds. to 200 yds. before one can get the boat's head round, so that everything must be clear. I have twice had the handle torn off my reel by it catching against something.

"Two or three runs generally finish them, and they become fairly amenable, but not so the moimin, or butter-fish, which fights like a bull-dog. It hardly ever makes a run of more than 20 yds., but will keep it up for hours.

"I saw a well-known colonel spend two hours with a 36-pounder, and the fish was the less tired of the two at the finish.

"The best season for seer, pallamin and moimin is from November to February.

"*Notes on Tackle.*—I have obtained my tackle. *i.e.* triangles and swivels, etc., from Manton & Co., Calcutta, though I always make up my own traces. Size of triangle for bahmin, No. 4; for seer, pallamin and moimin, No. 5/0.

"The above sea-fishing applies to the whole of Malabar coast, and every backwater or river contains bahmin, provided the water is fairly clear."

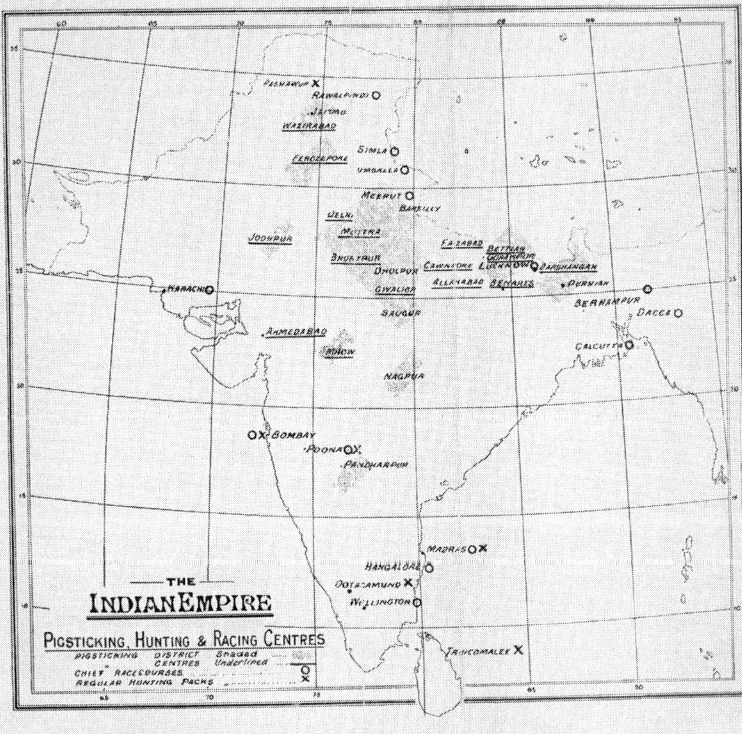
THE
INDIAN EMPIRE
PIGSTICKING, HUNTING & RACING CENTRES
PIGSTICKING DISTRICT Shaded
" CENTRES Underlined
CHIEF RACECOURSES
REGULAR HUNTING PACKS
PESHAWUR
RAWALPINDI
JAMMU
WAZIRABAD
SIMLA
FEROZEPORE
UMBALLA
MEERUT
BAREILLY
MUTTRA
JODHPUR
FAIZABAD
BETTIAH
GORAKHPUR
BHURTPUR
DHOLPUR
CAWNPORE
LUCKNOW
DARBHANGAH
ALLAHABAD
BENARES
PURNIAH
KARACHI
GWALIOR
BERHAMPUR
DACCA
SAUGOR
AHMEDABAD
MHOW
CALCUTTA
NAGPUR
BOMBAY
POONA
PANDHARPUR
MADRAS
BANGALORE
OOTACAMUND
WELLINGTON
TRINCOMALEE

PART III

SPORTS AND GAMES WITH HORSES

PIG-STICKING
POLO
HUNTING
RACING AND STEEPLE-CHASING
PAPER-CHASING

PIG-STICKING

I.—GENERAL AND GEOGRAPHICAL

THE form of sport known as pig-sticking is essentially an Indian sport, being confined almost, if not quite, to that large peninsula: moreover, it is very local, even in that land of the wild boar. The whole of the Punjaub, with a few notable exceptions, is either devoid of pig, or else the homes in which they live are large Government grass lands, from which all but officials are excluded. In a general way, there is no pig-sticking in the Bombay or Madras Presidencies, although there are a few famous places in each. Bengal is the headquarters of the sport. Central India abounds in pig, but the country there is very rough and stony, and the going very bad in consequence, while the yearly bag is small; hence, although the soldiers and civilians quartered in Central India have the finest sport in its true sense, yet no one would select it as the place for a first pig-sticking experience. To the old hand, who delights more in defeating the cunning of a fine old boar than in the fierce dash for "first spear," this class of country presents many charms; but the trouble is great, and the bag small. The "stations" in that part of the country are mostly small, so that the places which show great sport one year or series of years, fail entirely or in part at other times, on account of the paucity or inexperience of the "spears." This, it is true, also applies to any place where the community is small, only in a lesser degree, inasmuch as the easier the country the less is the experience required. The class of horse required, as well as their number, and the consequent expenses entailed, differ with the country and the amount of actual "riding" after pig. For instance, in most parts of Central India, where the going is over hills, stones and ravines, more importance attaches to a hard-footed hardy horse than to the very fast one. The hunter who would shine in such country, might very easily be only second-class in the galloping country of parts of Bengal, just as a hunter from Devon would be out of place in Leicestershire. In the same way, also, the mount for Central India is cheaper than that for Bengal. One good boar a day, obtained after hard and scientific hunting, would be as much as would be generally expected in the former country, but would be deemed a very poor bag in the latter, where three or four pig are an ordinary number, and ten or twelve a not improbable bag. Hence it may readily be seen that not only is the horse himself cheaper, but the number required is less in one country than in the other.

Before deciding on our hunting centre, it is necessary, therefore, to consider carefully how much money we propose to devote to our hunting. It is also necessary to remember that there are other restrictions to a free selection. Most of the well-known districts are under the very jealous rule of pig-sticking clubs, called "Tent Clubs," who, by precedent, hold the exclusive right to kill pig in their neighbourhood. The limits of the districts are clearly defined, as they are often bounded by others under a similar rule. All active votaries of the sport, and many who are so in mind only, join the club, which is put under the charge of an honorary secretary, who is responsible for the preservation of the pig, the arrangements of the meets themselves, the commissariat and the direction of the actual hunt. That is to say, supposing a meet is advertised, all that a member has to do, is to take himself and his horses out, and all the rest is done for him. The honorary secretary has, to assist him, his head shikari and perhaps his two assistants, and with their aid every inch of the ground and every pig in the country should be known. If this staff is a good one, it will be friends with all the villagers, who will readily give the most detailed information, and the most will be made out of the available information. Hence it will be seen that the most convenient way to see pig-sticking is to join a "tent club," which, as a rule, is easily done. There are, it is true, a few well-known clubs who suffer from having too many hunting members; but, on the other hand, there are many that cannot raise more than three or four good spears towards the end of the season, by which time accidents and illness have thinned the stables, so that any man with an introduction may reckon to receive a warm welcome from most of them. The objection to this method of seeing sport is that the number of days hunting per month is fixed by the time and inclination of the club and not by that of the visitors; the other members have their duties to do besides local amusements and sports, so that a man who comes to a station for pig-sticking alone would hardly view a ten days' break in the hunting with the same complaisance as he who, besides his work, could have his three days' polo a week. On the other hand, in a keen club, every available opportunity for hunting is taken, and a "thrusting" visitor would be likely to get as much hunting as his stud and he cared for. In the selection of your club you must be guided by your own inclination and by your purse. It is impossible to give any certain information as to the vitality of any particular club at any given moment, but anyone in India can readily find it out: it depends entirely on the garrison at the time. In some regiments every man hunts; in others, literally not one. If, however, a man prefers being independent of a tent club, he can combine with friends and hunt some district which for some reason is not being worked at the

A 34-INCH BOAR

time, or one which is not under a tent club. To do this, the party must contain some organiser, who will have previously arranged for a shikari and his assistants, and who knows the country to be a good one. Then, indeed, he can hunt seven days a week as long as the party and horses hold out. I once joined a party of this sort, intending to hunt for sixty consecutive days. This party was never at any one time more than five strong, and we never had less than 100 horses in camp. Owing to accidents and the consequent changes of "spears," we had eventually had eight men through our camp, and we had to return home at the end of thirty days, because we had not a single man capable of getting on a horse, and hardly a horsc capable of being hunted without a few days' rest. We had, however, a bag of 100 real good boar. Moreover, although enthusiasts to a man, we had all had too much of it. The point that I wish to make is, that I think fifteen days' hunting a month is ample for the veriest glutton, while the number of horses required rises, after a certain point, out of all proportion to the amount of hunting. It is quite possible to find a tent club that hunts fifteen days a month.

II.—THE VARIOUS HORSE MARKETS

THE next point to consider is the question of what description of stud to get and how to get it together. In the matter of the style and breed of horse everyone has his own opinion, likes and dislikes; so I propose to take each class and show how and where they can be bought; going into their points as pig-stickers afterwards. Two points must always be kept in sight:—

1. We are only considering the class of horse capable of carrying his rider well up in the hunt.

2. The hot weather is the season for pig-sticking, which extends from 15th March to 30th June.

The Australian may be bought direct from the importer at Madras, Calcutta and Bombay. The largest selection is available between 1st October and 1st April, November and December being the best months, as by that time all the horse ships are in, and not many of the horses sold; the horses themselves also are in better condition than when just landed in October and November. To be able to select a really good one out of a large number of very thin, rough horses, taxes the judgment of even the best judges. When bought direct from the "shippers" in this way, the absolute raw, unbroken article is generally to be had very cheap, unless the shipper fancies any particular horse on account of his breeding. For Rs.500 a very useful horse should be got by a knowledgeable man. Fifteen rupees go to £1, so that £33 may be said to be the price to pay for a horse likely to make a good pig-sticker. Of course much depends on the man who is buying. The

Australian is a dealer born and bred, and, moreover, is a very independent class of man. He requires to be taken quite as an equal, and he very soon finds out how much you know. To buy really cheaply it is necessary to know the shipper, to examine the horse yourself, instead of sending him to a veterinary surgeon for examination; to be able to judge whether a technically unsound horse will do your work; to be willing to take a thin horse or one with a bad knock; to buy quick, and in short to be a good judge of the raw horse. If you happen to be able to do all these things you should be able to buy a horse thoroughly suitable for pig-sticking for Rs.350, or say £25. It must be noted that we are now talking about the raw, unbroken article, and before leaving the subject it is just as well to note the points that should be borne in mind when buying this class of animal.

Government give £45 or Rs.650 for their remounts, and, therefore, any horse which looks good enough for Government should be viewed with suspicion if he is offered to you for half that price. On the other hand, if the buyer knows his market, this need not disturb him. He can easily find out the points for which Government disqualify a horse. Say over height or over age. The Government limit of height used to be 16 hands, and that of age seven years. A horse 16 hands 1 in., or one eight years old might, however, suit you. Again, Government only require a certain number of horses of each class, and if there is an excess of horses of that class they cannot take them. Then the Government veterinary surgeon, like all men, may have a tendency to attach too much importance to some points which do not really matter. I once had the whole of my pig-sticking stud examined for sale purposes by a veterinary surgeon. None of them had ever been lame, and they were all in the hardest of work, and yet they all, thirteen in number, were found to have spavins. They were examined later by different veterinary surgeons at different times, and all passed sound. What I mean is this: Supposing you are trying to buy a hunter for £30, and you are shown a very likely looking horse, which, if perfectly sound, you could not have imagined that Government would have refused. If, on examination, you find that he is over Government height, or over Government age, or has a tendency towards the weak point that the Government veterinary surgeon dislikes, be it spavin, insufficiency of bone, or what not, or that he belongs to the class which have been imported in excess of Government requirements, then there is no reason why you should not trust your own opinion with a clear conscience, provided you have a right to have confidence in it.

Again, there are certain technical unsoundnesses which, in some cases, may be disregarded, and certain formations which, though not unsoundnesses, should be avoided. As an example. A spavin in a horse seven years or over hardly

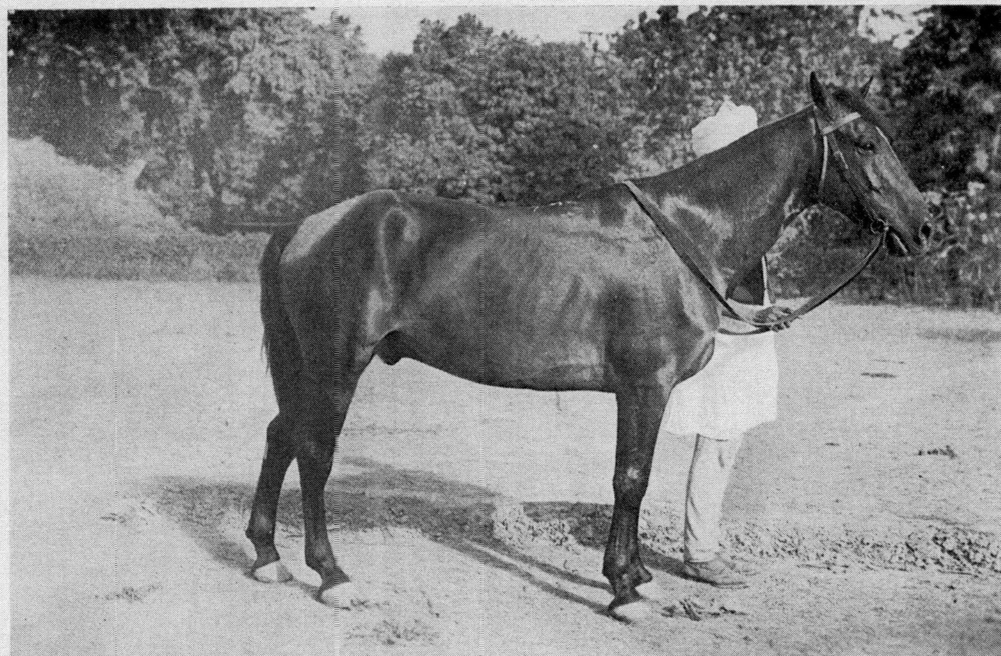

Australian Horse

Heavy-looking, but a fine hunter

ever affects him for pig-sticking work, provided his hock action is good, and curb may be almost disregarded; whilst straight pasterns, though not unsoundnesses, should be looked upon as fatal to the usefulness of a pig-sticker.

There are one or two other points to be remembered by a man who has never before bought raw Australians. It must be borne in mind that many thin horses never recover; that a horse who has been known to have had a bad attack of fever after landing remains subject to it and is especially liable to go wrong in the wind during his first hot weather; that big horses over 15.3 are more liable to become roarers than are smaller ones; that few Australians are wrong in the wind when landed; and that blacks and browns are the most liable to skin disease, which renders the best horse a trouble and an eye-sore during the hot weather, putting him out of condition at the very time when he has all his powers taxed to the utmost. It must also be remembered that it takes a year to train a raw Australian horse, so that he cannot be counted on as a hunter, even if the climate does not affect him sufficiently to incapacitate him during his first hot season.

Besides the raw unbroken horse a certain number of horses trained to saddle are always to be found. Some of these are merely horses which have been used by the drovers as riding horses while bringing the "mob" down country to the ship or to market. The education these horses have received is merely that they have been caught, had a saddle put on their backs, and ridden in a snaffle by a man whom they could not throw. Hard work and short commons soon made them fairly quiet; but they are, as a rule, in no sense broken horses, as will readily be seen if they have not been ridden since they landed, for not even an Australian roughrider will then venture on their backs unless they have been lunged for a short time with the saddle on. A few worthless broken "station" horses may be found among them, but the whole of this class of cheap "broken" horse has nothing to recommend it in particular, and because to the inexperienced rider the real unbroken nag is a nightmare, the broken article has a market value out of all proportion to its real worth.

The next kind of "broken" horse is the one that the shippers' "hands" break in themselves in their spare time after landing them in India. These horses command a slightly higher price—about £5 or Rs.75 extra—than the quite raw one, and they are worth it just to the extent that it is easier to judge a horse that can be ridden, even if you can do no more than merely sit on his back. The roughriders themselves can, and will, gallop him about, but, unless you are a good rider, and understand the art of riding a newly broken Australian, it is just as well to content yourself with "getting the feel of him." The reverse of the medal is that the shipper may find he has a nice horse, where he thought he had an ordinary one; and your mob of unbroken ones thereby loses one of its best horses.

The cheap horses, then, which may be looked at with a view to getting a pig-sticker are to be found mostly among the horses which Government do not care to buy as remounts for the various reasons above enumerated. At about Rs. 500 there is an ordinary class of horse brought over for private sale, on which Government have no claim; and from among this class a useful hunter may often be got, but the pick of these generally find their way into the stables of the many big dealers, where they are broken and conditioned and sold at from Rs. 700 to Rs. 1000 during the next hot weather. Another chance lies before the would-be purchaser of hunters. There are shippers who do a special trade in the smaller horses brought over, especially for native cavalry remounts. Rs. 500 will generally buy their best if taken immediately they are landed, since the average price of a lot for the native cavalry is generally Rs. 350. It must be done, however, before the native cavalry buyers arrive, as a shipper would lose his connection if it were found that he had been selling his best beforehand. Such horses would not be over 15.1.

If the buyer does not mind riding what are practically ponies, that is to say horses about 14.2 or 14.3, he can very often get a superior class of animal, brought over especially for racing or polo, but which has "failed to measure." On account of the "odd height," he should be able to get a good one for 500s. to 600s., and it would be probably a thoroughly broken animal and well bred.

Then there is the stock horse proper, which can only be got with great trouble and to special order. Stock horses—so called—can be got in any number, but not the real thing. These horses are the real good hard, honest, handy horses, used in Australia on cattle stations, for drafting cattle out of a mob. Very few horses make stock horses, and when proved as such they are valued very highly in the colony, and can only be got by accident by a friendly shipper. With a standing order for several years, I have only managed to get two—and good ones they have proved themselves. As a rule they are rather small—about 15 hands, with no particular looks. They are certain to be at least eight or nine years old, hardly ever technically sound, and generally scarred and blemished, but they make the very best of pig-stickers on account of their brave disposition, their extreme handiness and their practical soundness. Not only are they very difficult to buy, but in the open market in India they do not fetch a good price, as no one who does not thoroughly know his shipper would pay say Rs.700 for the ordinary looking knocked-about veteran, who makes a poor show beside the handsome and spirited youngster that can be got for the same price. Hence no dealer will bring a stock horse over except to a definite order, and even then he often fails to get him.

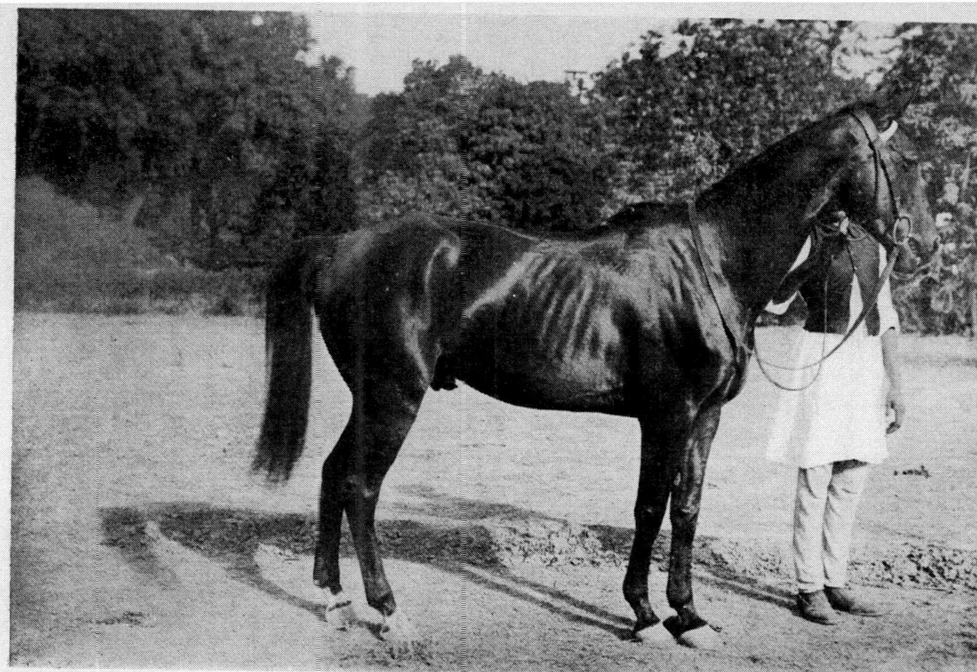

A GOOD AUSTRALIAN HUNTER

(Carried 14 stone for [illegible] Seasons, and still full of work)

Finally, to the rich man there is the open market of the big commission stables, where can be bought almost anything, and at any price from Rs.800 to Rs.20,000; but this I do not consider to be the market for pig-stickers, for if a man can afford these prices for the raw one, he would do much better to pay his money and buy the "proved" one.

Before buying the unseasoned Australian, it would be well to consider of how much use he is likely to be to you, and what he will really have cost you, before he can really be called a useful hunter.

Let us begin with the perfectly made horse in good condition, landed in October. What with the delays of buying and railing to your head-quarters, you will not have him in your stable until the beginning of November, which gives you four months in which to get him fit for hard work, since hunting begins in the early days of March. This is not a day too much either. The horse has just gone through a six weeks' journey, during which he has never lain down, and never had any exercise, and he has, consequently, for some weeks had hardly any circulation in his feet. If taken into work at once he will contract diseases of the feet, from which he may never permanently recover; and therefore, for at least a month, he should get no work beyond walking exercise, and that only on the soft, and without shoes. Shaving the coronet and painting it with iodine to the extent of keeping up a mild inflammation, will help the vitality of the hoof immensely. There are now only three months left. Henceforward he may be taken into constantly increasing exercise, and, if all goes well, he should be as fit as is necessary by March. But then there are so many "ifs." He has to get used to standing in head and heel ropes. In one moment a rope gall can occur which will put him out of work for three weeks. Next he has to adapt himself to the alteration of food. This is a very drastic change, for, as a rule, he gets nothing in India that he has ever eaten before, except, indeed, the grass, and even that is the same in name only, and totally different in its properties. The common dogfly drives some Australian horses nearly mad, and annoys all extremely until they get used to it, which takes generally a year, and not only does it affect their condition markedly, but it makes it almost impossible to avoid rope gall, that bugbear of the owners of unseasoned Australian horses. Finally, and most important of all, comes the fact that the new horse has to adjust himself to the opposition of the seasons in India and Australia. The Indian summer is the Australian winter, and *vice versâ*. He lands in October with his heavy winter coat just coming off, shedding it during the cold weather in India. Just as it begins to get hot in March and April, Nature—as was her wont heretofore, proceeds to provide him with a heavy winter coat, finds out her mistake towards the end of April, and adapts herself slowly and unwillingly to the new conditions of life. It is while this war is being carried on that the new horse is expected to work his hardest, and it is small wonder that he "feels the weather." It takes the whole hot weather before Nature completely adapts herself to her new surroundings. Hence it is that an Australian cannot be said to be acclimatised till he has gone through a hot weather in India. The best method of helping the newly landed horse is to clothe him warmly in the cold weather when he has his summer coat, and to clip him as soon as he begins to grow his ill-timed winter one, keeping it as short as is possible until Nature falls in with the new conditions. Unless this is done, the new horse will be living in a coat constantly wet with his own sweat, and a chill, followed by fever, will be the inevitable result. A severe attack of fever in an unseasoned Australian means that he is useless for anything till the rains at earliest, by which time the hunting season is over, and it generally means, what is more, that he is a roarer for ever. Certainly not more than 10 per cent. of the perfectly made, newly-landed Australians can be expected to be useful pig-stickers during their first season, and even then they are a constant source of anxiety.

There is, however, to the above, one exception, if so it may be called, where the conditions are not similar, and this exception I will explain.

There is always a small shipment of horses landed every year in the beginning of the "rains," *i.e.* about the last week in July. A "made" horse bought then has time to get three parts acclimatised by the following March, and he should have a very good chance of doing well. This shipment, however, rarely includes any cheap horses, owing to the slackness of the market in India at that time of the year, when all who can manage it are away in the hills, and also to the fact that "Government" horses are only bought between October and March. The only horses brought over at that time, are race horses, polo ponies, and carriage horses, which are wanted for work at the beginning of the cold weather.

There is practically no special market for pig-stickers. The reason that the shippers select the beginning of the rains is because the extreme heat of the hot weather is then over.

If there is such a serious doubt as to whether the perfectly trained horse is likely to be of any practical use for hunting during his first season, the case of the raw horse would appear hopeless; and this is exactly the right name for it. There is no chance whatever of buying a raw horse in October and converting him into a handy pig-sticker by March, even if there were more than an off chance of his standing the climate.

It may be fairly asked why this is ever done, and the answer is, that it is not everyone who has grasped the fact; but I am sure that everyone who has given the question a fair practical trial will agree that it is true. There is of course a very strong temptation to buy a fine young horse cheap, thus providing yourself, if not for this season, at least for next, with a class of horse which you could not otherwise afford, or for less than a made one would cost you. This is in itself found to be a fallacy, if a cold-blooded, commercial calculation be entered on, for by the time his original price, railway fare, keep for eighteen months, and risks are added up, the total mounts up to a surprisingly large figure.

The only reasonable excuse which any man has, from a business point of view, for buying raw Australians for pig-sticking purposes, is that he cannot buy real trained pig-stickers in the open market at any but a prohibitive price, and in this answer he would be going closer to the mark than one would be inclined to believe at first sight.

Hereafter it will be necessary to compare the relative costs of the different classes of horses suitable for pig-sticking, so it will be as well to see now what the Australian horse, bought direct from the shipper, costs us before he is fit to be taken out hunting. The likelihood of his being a safe mount, and of his probable staunchness, as well as his manners, soundness, capacity of standing heat and the like, will be gone into on a later page. What we want to see now is how much the horse will cost us before he is fit to be taken out hunting at all. This stage of the pig-stickers' education is common to all classes, save only the proved hunter, and consequently is the most convenient one at which to compare their relative "cost price."

1. The unmade, unseasoned Australian horse.

Original cost	Rs.500
Keep for eighteen months at Rs.20 per month . . .	360
Climatic risks — deterioration from sickness . . .	150
Training risks (risk of not breaking well, bad temper, pulling and unsoundness) . .	100
Yielding a practically sound nice six-year-old for . .	Rs.1110

2. The thoroughly made but unseasoned Australian.

Original cost	Rs.700
Keep for eighteen months at Rs.20 = 360, but as this horse will probably do half of the first season—say keep . .	180
Climatic risks	100
Yielding a practically sound eight-year-old horse for .	Rs.980

3. The horse landed in July—thoroughly made.

Original cost	Rs.700
Keep for nine months at Rs.20	180
Climatic risks	100
Yielding a practically sound seven-year-old for . .	Rs.980

I am presupposing that the raw horse is aged five and the made horse a full six when bought.

There are many other points in the actual cost of the horse to the owner, which have been left out purposely, as they are in common with the above three cases. The same considerations affect the price of Arabs bought from dealers, and also made horses, if the owner wishes to see or try them before purchase. Such questions as expenses of selector to and from the port of disembarkation, and the hotel bill while there; cost of railing the horse to his headquarters and the like—these are common-sense points, the cost of which must be considered by each individual when purchasing.

If the above figures are at all accurate, it will be seen that the raw horse is much the most expensive, though his original purchasing price was less, but that he begins his pig-sticking career as a six-year-old instead of as a seven-year or eight-year-old. This I consider to be a very doubtful gain, but still it should be noted. Further, it must be borne in mind that these figures are only intended as a guide to men buying horses for pig-sticking. If a man is forced to keep three horses for district work, he may fairly strike off the keep of these three horses from the calculation. The same holds good for the man who has to keep chargers, ladies' hacks, trappers or what not. These details each can adjust to suit his own case.

The next class, from which we may hope to be able to draw our hunter, is the trained, seasoned Australian horse, other than the proved pig-sticker. A few last year's horses are to be found in the big stables at Calcutta, Bombay and Madras. All civilian officials have to keep horses for their work, many for their pleasure as well; every officer in a cavalry regiment has to keep two or three chargers; there are a large number among the planters of Behar, Mysore and elsewhere, and when they wish to go home they all generally try to sell them. From among these a certain number may be got, but they have either to be taken without being seen or tried, or else a lot of time and money may have to be spent before success attends our endeavours. When found the article will probably, exclusive of expenses, not cost more than Rs. 1000.

There is one more source which is not generally known and which requires explanation. The native cavalry in India are under a contract to provide their own horses. Many of them have found that they can no longer get suitable country-bred horses, and have consequently taken to mounting their regiments on Australians.

A Good Australian Pony Hunter

Now, the lowest price of any kind of Australian horse is considerably beyond their contract price, with the result that they are driven to sell some of their best horses every year to keep the head of their remount fund above water. There is no actual big sale, but at the same time they are always willing to sell a well-made horse at a profit. This they are enabled to realise, since the whole question of "keep" is struck out from their expenses. The price at which the best horse in a native cavalry regiment can be bought has fixed itself at about Rs.800, which price, if we compare it with our estimate of what the same raw article costs us to produce acclimatised and trained, is distinctly cheap. As I said before, most native cavalry regiments are ready to sell, but the only one I know of which openly states that they are prepared to sell any of their horses at Rs.800 is the 14th Bengal Lancers. These regiments are 613 strong, and it should not be difficult to select a dozen useful horses from among that number, thus reducing to a minimum the expenses entailed in going about the country in answer to advertisements.

To summarise, then, the cost of the different kinds of Australian trained, seasoned horses, which are not pig-stickers, we find that, exclusive of railing and other expenses entailed in selecting, we have the prices roughly as follows :—

If bought as unmade, unseasoned horses Rs.1110

If bought as thoroughly made, landed in October . .	Rs.980
If bought as thoroughly made, landed in July . . .	980
If bought as made in the private market	1000
If bought as made from native cavalry regiments . .	800

The entailed expenses are much the same in the first four cases, and markedly less in the last. The final, and best, method of buying pig-stickers, if the occasion offers, is to buy the proved article. Pig-sticking is rough work, and horses get blemished and knocked about, and, perhaps because of their looks, they do not fetch high prices. If they are for sale at all, they are sold cheap: in fact Rs.1000 will buy most of them. There is, however, as a rule only one way to buy, and that is to wait till an opportunity offers. While the season is in full swing, hardly any price will buy a good one, but at the beginning of the cold weather, when everybody's mind is turned to polo and manœuvres, and when the next day's hunting is six months off, poor men get tired of feeding animals from which they get no value, and probably would be glad to sell the horse and buy one more pony for their impending polo tournament. Then, if you know the horse to be a good one, buy and keep your treasure against the day when you could not buy him for love or money. Looks! what do they matter?

It is true, at the first meet, your veteran will not look so clean in the legs as that splendid young bay with a pedigree as long as your arm, nor will he fly along the first open field with that grand sweep; but wait a bit, there is a nasty rough bit of grass in front, and when you are sailing over it like over a lake, yonder bay novice is going like a ship in an Atlantic gale, lucky if he does not founder. At the last meet of the season, the bay, if there at all, has learnt his manners, lost that sweeping stride, and probably shows "gummier" legs than your veteran; and which of the two riders, think you, has had the nicer rides during the season, and which the more falls?

Before leaving the subject of Australian horses, I should like to say that the risks connected with the acclimatisation of raw Australian horses and the cost of keep have, if anything, been under-estimated, and in support of this I would point out how it strikes the advisers of Government. The Government Australian horses, bought at Calcutta, after having been bought by a selected officer, and passed by a selected Government veterinary officer, are transferred by train to a Government horse run. They are there summered, get the most elementary of training—*i.e.* they can most of them be ridden by a fair rider, but are in no sense trained—and when in this state, as a great favour, and to a very limited extent, officers in the mounted branches are allowed to select any horse, paying Rs. 1050 for what Government gave 650, and there is very little doubt that, considered in a business light, Government loses money over the transaction.

The country-bred is much the most difficult animal to come by, if required, as we do, for immediate work. Owing to the system by which Government buys its country-bred remounts as youngsters, and to the drain on the country-bred market by the demands from native cavalry and Imperial service troops, it has come about that in a modern fair one hardly sees even a four-year-old, so that we may consider the question of buying at fairs as closed.

The private market holds a fair number, especially in the Punjaub. The Government allows officers entitled to chargers to buy an occasional one from their country-bred depôts, while officers commanding native cavalry will doubtless sell a few of their troop-horses.

On the whole, a good class of country-bred is very difficult to get. In a general way, he is a cheap horse and can be generally got for from Rs.300 to 600.

The little Arab can only be bought direct from the importer in Bombay. None are landed in Calcutta or Madras, though a few come to Karachi. The high-caste Arab is a grand little workman, and the coarse one a real bad riding-horse. The Arab dealer asks huge prices for the high-caste ones and generally gets them, and I think one cannot expect to buy a good six-year-old for less than Rs.1100, unless satisfied with a very light one. In the private market, which is a limited one, 1000 rupees will buy most Arab horses. As the ordinary height of an Arab horse is 14.2, and the polo ponies are very big 14.1's, there is not much room for an odd-sized one, hence this hope may be given up.

A miscellaneous lot of coarse-bred horses exist, such as the Gulf Arab, Cabulis and the like, which occasionally give a good horse, but which are not worth serious consideration as a source of supply.

Finally there are the rare horses, such as Argentines, Cape, Americans, Irish and English, which, on account of their scarcity, may be disregarded. The first two make excellent hunters, as the hard ground and climate do not affect them; the last three are, for the opposite reason, not suitable.

III.—THE POINTS OF A PIG-STICKER

Having before us the markets in which we can buy the various kinds of horses, as well as their relative prices, we may now go into the points to be remembered when buying either the raw or the trained unacclimatised horse of all the various classes or even the trained hunter, concerning whom we have not absolutely reliable information. The record of the proved pig-sticker, if quite trustworthy, speaks for itself and provides all the information required.

In selecting a pig-sticker, no matter of what breed, the purchaser, unless he be buying him with other objects in view as well, such as using him as a charger, for instance, can afford to disregard many points for which he would "cast" an ordinary horse; but, on the other hand, there are some points so essential that, if they be forgotten, he simply courts failure. If we think carefully what we want of the horse, these points become evident. To begin with, the season in which the horse has to work, is the hottest of the whole year and the work itself is of the roughest type, entailing very long hours. To be standing about in the sun, even without a run, from 6 A.M. till 2 P.M. is a strain on the constitution of any horse, and to work hard in the fiercest heat is excessively trying. Hence it is evident that our selection should be of the sort that does not easily get put off his feed. The formation for this, we have been taught by experience, is a good round barrel, with the back ribs well arched and leaving the spine as far back as possible, in fact what is generally known as " well ribbed up," combined with a short back, while it is only commonsense to say that the hardiest horses for this work are likely to be those who have been born and reared in the hottest climate under the most trying circumstances and have come through the trial satisfactorily. In this respect the horses from the wilds of Queensland have the call over those from the more civilised New South Wales, while the

Arab and country-bred are more used to Eastern heat. Next, your selection will have to endure many hits and knocks and have to travel at speed over rough and generally absolutely blind going. Here again, the bush horse has the advantage over the paddock-bred one in that he has had the experience of the whole of his life to make him clever; and if hits and knocks are likely to make him throw out splints, he will probably already have them. The country-bred and Arab have not had the advantage of this experience. It is impossible for any horse to prevent making mistakes in rough blind going, and the clever hunter is not the horse who makes the least mistakes, but he who saves himself best. The life of any good pig-sticker is made up of mistakes rectified. It is quite wonderful to see a horse going full speed over ground really difficult to cross at a walk; yet I myself have a horse who has carried me through two seasons and never yet given me a fall, a horse, moreover, who is fast and apparently reckless in his style of going. To attain this capacity of "saving," it is absolutely necessary that the hunter should have the very best of shoulders. Mark this with red ink; write it up on your wall; gum a slip on your looking-glass; do what you will; but let nothing in the world induce you to buy in the rough for pig-sticking purposes anything that has not got not only a good shoulder, but a *very* good shoulder; and try and get a *magnificent* shoulder. To any but a very first-class judge, it is most difficult to say what is and what is not a good shoulder. Everyone knows that it should not be heavy and that it should be sloping; but the eye gets deceived, and mistakes are readily made. A high wither gives the horse the look of having a sloping shoulder and a low one the reverse; therefore never be sure that the high withered horse you like the look of has a good shoulder, unless it looks surprisingly sloping, but a low withered horse with a shoulder that looks sloping probably has that all-desirable commodity. To the ordinary man, the only way to settle this question is to have a saddle put on the horse's back and to mount him, if only to ride him at a walk for a few yards. Then if your saddle sits well back and you have a good length from the front of your saddle to the spring of the neck, you may be sure you have a horse with a good shoulder. But, alas, this is one of the difficulties in dealing with raw Australians. With all other breeds it can be done; but it is not possible with him. Remember, then, about the wither, and watch carefully how he moves at the walk and trot—the gallop is hardly possible. If he brings his fore-legs well to the front with a nice clean swing, the shoulder is probably all right.

For handiness, it is essential that your choice should have a fairly long neck, put well on to his shoulders, and a naturally high carriage. Give even the nicest horse in every other way a badly set-on head and neck, and he will hardly ever be a handy pig-sticker. Handiness is all-important, for without it it is impossible to follow a jinking pig through cover, in which he is lost to sight if he gets more than a few yards away from you. With a safe, handy horse alone does one get the real joy of pig-hunting, provided the horse is staunch. And this brave spirit which enables you to take your horse up to the very intimidating spectacle of a grunting, charging pig, how is that to be judged? Just in the same way as you judge a man—by the general look of his face and expression, by the shape of his head, and, above all, by his eye. The eye in all classes is the same. The eye we want is full, steady, mild, and brave. The head we like is what is known as a "sensible, well-bred" one, and not the "flashy," taking sort. The head of the Australian is a study in itself; very often the most highly bred horses have hideous heads. Very notably the progeny of the famous horse Panic almost always have Roman noses.

Having got the desired shoulder, neck, and head, we may rest satisfied that the horse is well bred. Good breeding is essential, as a common bred horse is always disappointing; and we should also have the right temperament. His legs should be strong, showing good muscular fore-arm development, short from knee to fetlock, with the very best of sound, round feet. Anything approaching an upright pastern is to be avoided, and the error, if any, should be in the direction of too much obliquity, for the upright formation jars the legs on the hard going. Then, again, strong loins and a short back are important to give him capacity. In bad, blind going a good hunter travels with almost all his weight on his hind-quarters, hence he must have the best of hocks. Now, as you will very rightly object, we have described very nearly a perfect horse; and how is that to be bought for a low figure? This is quite true. The pig-sticking horse is the very best all-round type that can be found; but, though the perfect horse is the best, yet a horse with many imperfections may yet be a thoroughly good hunter. We have laid down as essentials a good shoulder, neck, carriage, legs, feet, and hocks, combined with a short back, good barrel, and good breeding. Let us see what fault the hunter is permitted.

He may be as "plain" as you can find him. He may have a hideous head, of the most pronounced "ugly, well-bred head" style. He may have a "goose rump," which would disqualify him for anything in which looks are a consideration; in fact, that ugly formation which gives the appearance of having been "chopped off behind" is a very safe and handy one and not much against his pace. Then, again, scars do not matter, nor does colour, and there are the whole set of technical unsoundnesses which still leave the horse practically sound.

So much for the general description of the hunter, and now we must notice how the points are modified and altered in the cases of the three main breeds, namely, the Australian, the Arab, and the country-bred. To begin with the shoulder. The Arab horse without a good shoulder is invariably a stumbling brute. Nevertheless, the buyer cannot expect the same good sloping shoulder in an Arab as he would in the other two, because it is not the natural formation of the breed. The Australian and country-bred *must* have it. The Arab is generally a stallion, which gives him a "heavy"-looking shoulder, and this must be allowed for, and much of it would disappear if, as should always be done, he is "altered." The head in an Arab must be a good-looking one; it is one of the points of the breed, and without a real nice head the Arab can hardly be well-bred. The best Australian head is generally on the plain side, and the country-bred with a little breedy head is liable to extreme excitability, and therefore it is not an advantage to him. The eye, which is passable in an Arab, being a little wild-looking, would be very undesirable in an Australian and fatal in a country-bred, because it is counteracted by the sensibility of the Arab disposition, may be due to terror in a raw Australian, but means madness in a country-bred. This wildness would vanish in most cases with the Australian if he were gently and sensibly trained, and might get worse if he were roughly handled; but with the country-bred he is either wild or not, according to his nature, and with a country-bred a wild eye generally means a wild disposition. The feet are different in all three breeds. The Australian has a somewhat large, open, sound foot, and this is what should be required of him. A flat foot or a wired-in heel should disqualify him as a raw horse, because, as he has always lived a natural life, the malformation is probably due to some constitutional disease. With an Arab this is modified by his life having been artificial, and he is liable to have wired-in heels and thrushy frogs through bad management and not unsoundness. These may be altered and rectified by stable management. A somewhat flat foot is rather a typical Arab shape, especially with a horse with sloping pasterns. The country-bred, on the other hand, never has a flat foot, unless the foot is diseased; but he very often has contracted heels and sometimes "donkey feet," and yet he will work hard and well, so that the foot which is most natural to the different breeds, and consequently the one we prefer, is different in all three cases.

Then as to backs. A long-backed Arab is never a good one; he must be "jumped up." The best of Australians, especially mares, have a tendency to be long in the back, while a country-bred with a long back is invariably of the "washy" sort, which gets tucked up and is unable to work hard.

Again, as to colour. Chestnut is a "hot" colour, which does not matter at all with the quiet Arab, and not much with the Australian, but is very likely to indicate a wild horse in the case of a country-bred. Bay is about the best all-round colour for horses. Blacks and browns are the most liable to skin disease, which, however, need hardly be considered, except in the case of Australians, when it becomes a very important point. Grey is about the best possible colour for both Arabs and country-breds, and is a rare colour for the Australians. Roans and duns are generally good horses in any breed.

Among country-breds we find an extraordinary variety of duns, roans and "splashed" animals, all of which are good enough colours, though ugly. They indicate the indigenous country-bred without much of the English blood in him; hence all the pure country-bred faults of formation and temperament must be expected in him, as well as his virtues of constitution.

We now know where our horses are to be bought, and how much to pay for them. We know the points to look for, in a general way, modified to suit each of the various breeds; and now we want to be able to apply all this information to suit our own particular cases. We will, therefore, take each of the three classes in turn.

The Australian and New Zealander—they are practically identical—have the advantage over the other breeds in that there is a much greater variety of style among them than among any of the other available breeds; and, consequently, a man has more chance of buying his own stamp. In fact, every stamp is represented:

the pony, the cob, the thoroughbred, weed, hunter, charger, race-horse, ladies' hack, horses of all sorts and sizes up to from ten to twenty stone, so that the light and the heavy weight can alike suit themselves, the latter being the class of man to whom the Australian especially appeals. In selecting the stamp of horse required, it must be remembered that the pig-sticker cannot help "making mistakes," and to enable him to "save" himself, he ought to be well up to the weight he has to carry; and by "up to weight" I do not mean that he should have merely legs which measure big below the knee, or that he should have big quarters or a big body. What would carry fourteen stone in India would be a light-weight horse in England. There are no deep ploughed fields to be crossed, and no big fences to be jumped out of deep-holding ground. In dealing with the hard ground of India, where a horse is always "on the top of the ground," one should go by shape rather than substance; and in the matter of legs, quality rather than quantity should be looked for. Everybody has his own idea as to the best size. A powerful man and a strong rider can ride a big horse and have him handy, where a weaker rider would find him unhandy, while the big horse should have the advantage in being stronger. The big horse has the disadvantage of having a tendency towards a long stride, and this is a distinct fault in rough going, as a long-striding animal is not so "collected." For choice, a short, quick-striding mount is far preferable, emphasising the advantage of a short horse, of whatever size he may be. A heavy-looking horse, who moves in an active manner, must not be disregarded. We should go rather by signs of activity when moving than by appearance of clumsiness when standing still, when judging a heavy-looking horse. Most men prefer a horse 15 hands to 15.2 hands, while there are many first-class pig-stickers as big as 16.2. Many, again, prefer ponies. Of one thing, however, there is no doubt, that a powerful horse, whatever his size, goes through thick cover more quickly and easily than a light one; so that it may be laid down as an axiom that, provided the pig-sticker is a collected goer, and handy, the bigger the animal the better, if the rider is strong enough to manage him. In the matter of the controversy of the preferability of ponies to horses in some countries, I can only say that, with a very varied experience of pig-sticking country, I have never yet seen one in which a horse was not better than a pony.

The New Zealander is a more easily broken animal than the Australian, and many prefer him in consequence. Owing to the better pasturage of New Zealand, he has much bigger bone. There is a grave doubt, however, whether his bone is of the same good quality; while the very luxury in which he has been bred militates against his usefulness as a hunter. The Australian horse is almost always clever over bad ground; stands the heat; is more powerful than any other class. There are more to select from, and in a general way he is stauncher than either of his other two competitors. Provided he is shown a pig properly for the first two or three times—of which more anon—and provided also that he is of the proper temperament, he is quite certain not only to become staunch, but to continue staunch. The only Australians I have ever seen which never became staunch to pig, were those who were injudiciously treated with their first two or three pigs, or were of one peculiar character.

This character requires studying and almost always goes with a small eye, the odd thing being that the eye may not be small naturally, but becomes so if the horse gets spoilt in training. The disposition I allude to is the one which induces a horse to "have ideas": the sort of horse to avoid is the one who wants to go one way when you want to go another, who goes home nicely enough, but is always stopping and semi-rearing when going away from home or from other horses. The buck-jumping horse probably is staunch enough, as is he with almost any kind of temper; but the small-minded nuisance, who probably has no other form of vice but the sort just described, is mean and is the one who is most likely to go up well when the pig is running in the open, but will not do so in cover, or when he is charging.

The Arab, when bought, is almost invariably a stallion, and, being a quiet, gentlemanly fellow,

A Good Arab Hunter

(Up to 14 Stone)

is generally left so. As far as staunchness goes, he is invariably staunch at first, but gets "cunning" as he goes on, and generally ends by being so clever that a pig can hardly be killed off him. This is due not to his being in any way frightened, but to his having ideas of his own and not trusting implicitly to his rider. At first he does not understand what the object is, and does not know how formidable an enemy is the pig. After a little he learns this; and the fighting instinct of the stallion being roused, he has his own opinion when to close and when not to, and even when he does close with the foe, he does so with the view of attacking him himself, and not so as to enable the rider to get a good spear. In thick cover, or when he does not see the pig himself, but knows he is close, he probably will not advance at all, generally with the result that while the horse and rider are settling their difference of opinion, the pig charges, and the horse gets cut and is worse than ever next time. Every Arab, if for this reason only, ought to be gelt. There are the further advantages, that his forehand loses much of the tissue which loads a stallion's neck, giving his legs less to carry, that in camp he can be led with other horses by one man, and that if he breaks loose he is easily caught again, instead of being a nuisance to the whole camp. A good Arab gelding has very many points to recommend him. He is very hardy, a good doer, up to a lot of work, and does not feel the heat. He is very clever and almost invariably staunch. He can be hunted the first season after he lands, provided he is bought early enough in the year to enable the owner to make him handy and have him cut. He can be ridden before he is bought, and hence one should have a good idea of what he is before he comes into the stable. His main fault is that he is small. A good, compact Arab seldom stands over 14.2. In examining him for soundness, you may take his "wind" for granted, unless he makes a very marked noise; and you must be very particular as to his eyes, which are very liable to cataract. Otherwise, he is an exceptionally sound breed of horse, and is longer lived than either the Australian or country-bred. He is at his prime at ten and twelve years, but will work hard even at twenty. The country-bred is the most peculiar of all horses, and it is very hard to give any guiding rules. He is an animal apart from all others, and, if really good, is a treasure to any one. Anything except a good one is useless. Country-breds are generally undersized, crooked-legged, misshapen horses about 15 hands high, up to very little weight, excitable, non-stayers, "run up" like a greyhound when worked, and quite likely to become unmanageable in cover. Every now and again you find a well-grown horse with a quiet disposition and a good body. Then indeed you have a nice horse, for his legs and feet are as hard as iron, he will eat anything, cares little or nothing for privations, rarely gets skin-disease or fever, does not feel the climate, and is as active as a cat. As regards staunchness, he will be always the same as he is the first day; he is either staunch, or he is not, according as he treats his first pig. If he goes up boldly at first, so he will afterwards; and if he is shy at first, he will never be really bold. I have only owned three country-breds, and they were all first-class, and carried 14 stone regularly; but, as they were all bought out of my own regiment, I had the advantage of knowing their characters, and, although they had never been shown a pig, there was no doubt that they would be thoroughly staunch.

Country-breds are hardly ever affected in the wind or eyes and have a way of working well, in spite of all sorts of technical unsoundnesses.

All these three classes of horses are capable of carrying a man well up with the hunt after a pig in any going, and unless a man can ride well to the front he loses the cream of the fun after a pig. If, however, a man cannot afford to mount himself well, he can still have an outing, learn the principles on which the hunt is worked, and have a great deal of fun, on a well-selected, cheap mount. Men generally buy horses for pig-sticking on the same principles as rule their price in Spain for bull-fights, that principle being that when the horse is badly hurt or killed it does not much matter, and the most ordinary way to come by a pig-sticker is to buy a caster from a regiment for about Rs. 150. Considering what the horse has to do, what chance has a man of seeing much fun on a £10 horse? Moreover, men thus mounted, if left to themselves, will only kill an occasional pig under very favourable circumstances; and unless the party have one or two well-mounted men to do all the work, the bag in most countries will be small indeed. Better than riding decrepit or worn-out horses is to get some cheap and second-class form of horse or pony who, though not first-class, can still be very useful if he is made the most of by training and care. A slow, strong pony or horse, safe on his legs and thoroughly handy, will show his owner much sport. In this class I include such animals as the Cabuli and Gulf Arab; and there are many horses and ponies of the kind to be bought in the open market. For instance, ponies which have failed to measure as polo ponies, and which are not steady enough to be sold as trappers, or are too plain for hacks, vicious horses, racing failures, etc., all this class have the advantage over the caster, that they are at anyrate fit to do their best, and also that they are likely to last for several seasons. Moreover, there is no reason why they should not be safe, even if somewhat slow, mounts, which can hardly be expected of an animal which, when cast by knowledgeable men as being incapable of even light work, is put to the most trying work it is possible to ask a horse to do. If circumstances force a man to hunt "on the cheap," he will get much more real fun out of one good second-class horse than out of a number of cripples or worn-out ones, while there will be fewer mouths to feed.

To sum up the general subject of which is the best horse to buy, the best policy is undoubtedly to buy the proved, made pig-sticker, of the style to suit the country in which you propose to hunt. The price you pay may sound high, but it will be your cheapest deal in the long run, and better value than any other. If this article is not available, and if time be no object, you can buy, train and season any of the three types of unmade horses, reckoning out their "cost price" to suit your own case; or else any of the various kinds of horses which, though broken, are not proved hunters. In the matter of class, size, and weight-carrying capacity, each man must judge for himself.

To a man coming out from England I would advise that he should put the matter entirely into the hands of some friend who is an expert at the game. To a novice I would say, "On no account ride anything but the proved hunter, as you will surely spoil an untrained horse."

The size of your stud depends on how much hunting you propose to do, on what luck you have in not getting horses laid up, and on the goodness of your stud and its management. You should be always able to have two horses at least fit and well to hunt any day. If you only do four days a month, two or three will do. For ten days a month four should be sufficient;

for fifteen days a month, five; for more than that, six to eight; always supposing that they begin with being proved sound horses of the working sort. To enable you to hack out to the meet, to and from hunting and explore the country, it is a great comfort to have a "galloping hack." This should be any cheap animal, who will always go at an easy canter with a loose rein. He must be clever and comfortable. The work required of him is not hard, and, when found, he should be cheap, say Rs. 200. If one of the hunters has the requisite paces and manners, and wants a comparative rest, he may be utilised for this work. It is first-class training for a young unmade horse, especially if he be of the fractious sort, as it has a most steadying effect. The ideal animal for the work, however, is a cheap country-bred, as you feel no consideration for him, and he does not mind the heat. The best "galloping hacks" are usually the "mad" country-bred that every Bengal cavalry regiment likes to get rid of. Although they run away from excitement in a cavalry charge and fret themselves to "fiddle strings" in the ranks, they generally are comfortable, hardy, light-mouthed, and clever and temperate at this work.

IV.—SPECIAL TRAINING OF THE PIG-STICKER

Having in your possession a horse broken to saddle in the ordinary way, the next thing to consider is what sort of special training he should undergo to fit him to take his place in the field with the best prospect of being a nice mount. A regular course of training in a cavalry or artillery riding-school is useful, provided always that the soldier who is to teach him has good hands. In this respect, the native is, as a rule, preferable to the Englishman. Having done this, your hunter should be further trained on exactly the same principles as the polo pony, and the object should be to make him as handy as if he were expected to play in a tournament. Any practice which tends in that direction is useful, but I suggest two important exercises. He must be taught to turn on his haunches, and not on any account on the forehand. To do this, he should be stopped at first at a corner in an enclosed school and turned outwards—that is, towards the side wall. The wall in front encourages him to stop, and the wall at the side prevents him from turning on his forehand. This should be done from the walk, trot, canter, and finally from the gallop, it being always borne in mind that the strain thrown on the hocks is great, and consequently only a little should be done at a time until the limbs get used to the strain. Gradually the same practice may be carried out, only not at the corner, though still close to the side wall; finally, the horse should turn on the haunch at a gallop in the open, without the check afforded by either the front or the side walls. Galloping him in a figure of 8 teaches the hunter to "change his legs." These two practices should make him handy. If the horse tries to avoid the bit by putting his head up, have no scruple in using a standing martingale during his training; and it must be even used in hunting if the hunter is not handy without it. It is not pleasant to ride over bad ground in a tight standing martingale, but it is better than riding a horse which, whenever you want him to turn, puts his head up and does not look where he is going.

For the rest, the best finish to the pig-hunter's education is to hack him about as much as possible. Nothing makes a horse quieter and more tractable. A steady canter across country with a loose rein teaches him to look out for himself and to adjust himself to the various obstacles he meets. Following a clever horse over bad ground gives him confidence and shows him how obstacles should be negotiated, besides teaching him the trick of "following" the pig.

Now, having got your horse actually out hunting for the first time, you will in all probability have a very fairly comfortable ride. He may get a bit excited and may make some bad bungles, and perhaps give you a fall, but remember that every mistake makes him more clever, and that a good fall, though unpleasant, is an invaluable education. If you can do so, keep right on the tail of the pig, and the education you have given him in following your clever horse and copying him, will have taught him to watch how the pig negotiates obstacles and to imitate him. When you get your chance of spearing, on no account hurry in the hopes of first spear. What does a "spear" matter, compared with spoiling your horse. Do not try to spear till you get into open ground; then go up gradually on the left of the pig. If the new horse is nervous, do not press him, but wait and try again. After a little, if nothing happens, he will not object, especially if taken up a couple of horses' lengths on the flank and edged in towards the boar. Do not forget to be at least level with the pig, never behind that, when you begin to close. The pig will now probably charge, and you will spear him well forward and stop him, enough to make him pass behind you; even if you miss, he will merely pass under your horse's stomach without doing any harm. If, on the other hand, you have not been as far forward as I have said, when the pig suddenly turns half left and charges, he will either be stuck and cross in front of your horse, causing the latter to stumble about over your spear or the pig, or, being missed, he will run into your horse's fore-legs, possibly cutting him or knocking him right over.

In cover, the new horse cannot see the pig well, and does not always like to close or to stand a charge; but he very seldom minds in the open, while the pig is running. He may be nervous of a charging pig in open ground even, and he will surely dislike going up to the animal when lying dead. Remember these points, avoiding what he dislikes as far as possible. Every possible precaution should be taken against any accident, or even a bungle, occurring the first two or three times. After this, the horse gets keen himself, and understanding that, when the pig charges, he will be saved by your spear, he becomes quite confident, and hence staunch.

There are many horses which will follow the pig keenly and also stand a charge well, but which, when close behind a running pig, decline to approach near enough to allow you to "get a spear." This is a somewhat common and very annoying fault. It generally comes from the horse's natural aversion to treading on a live animal. In this case, if the horse be brought up alongside of the pig, a length or two on a flank, he will almost always then close.

If, after the new horse has had a fair chance at a few pig, he is still nervous, he should be ridden after a very small pig, or squeaker as he is technically called, and galloped right over him several times. When he has ceased to be afraid of him, the practice may with advantage be repeated with a small, and finally with a big sow, none of which can "cut" him, having no tushes. Finding that he does not get hurt, unless an arrant coward, your horse will then probably face a boar. The more pig you can encounter with him without an accident, the stauncher will he become. Once staunch, a pig cut does not affect a plucky horse.

V.—PIG-STICKING GEAR

Every horse should have his own saddle especially fitted to him, and any saddle which begins to spread in the front arch should be ruthlessly discarded. In a hot climate, the slightest error is liable to give a sore back. The saddle therefore should be a real good one, Souter's 10-lb. one being about the best that can be got. For Australians and country-breds the front arch should be rather narrow and high, and this Souter has hit off exactly. For Arabs it can be somewhat wider. The saddle itself should be lined with leather instead of serge, as this prevents the stuffing from getting wet with sweat. Munnahs should be used only when the object is to "save" some particular spot, a hole of the requisite size and shape being cut in it opposite that spot. A saddle used with a thick munnah never sits really close, and consequently rolls, which, besides being uncomfortable, tends towards sore backs.

Souter's saddles wear well and are well worth the money, but, landed in India, they will have cost at least Rs.120 each. The North-West Tannery, Cawnpore, makes a saddle covered with kangaroo hide — the toughest hide that can be got—and Australian trees, which are sound and serviceable, and it costs complete only Rs.50. This company understands the shape most suitable to the different animals used in India.

The best pattern is the Fitzwigram, made of gut, raw hide, whipcord or string. The last two are the best, as they do not get hard from sweat and want of care. A very useful form for horses that "girth gall," is that made of muslin, or "mul-mul" as it is called in India. The girth should be made of this cloth, folded twelve times, stitched through lengthways, and about 3½ inches wide. Mul-mul can be bought anywhere in India.

The ordinary double bridle is the best all-round bit, but a "Liverpool driving-bit" is often very useful. You see horses ridden in all sorts of fancy bits, but, as far as my experience goes, any horse ought to go in one or other of these two, failing which, if a "Segundo" won't hold him, nothing will. A tight nose-band is very effective. With a judicious use of this and the above three bits, any horse should be fitted out. English bits are all too wide in the mouthpiece, A 5½-inch bit will fit the largest Australian, while 4¾ inches is wide enough for Arabs and country-breds. This is, of course, the width of the mouthpiece, inside to inside.

It is undoubtedly much more pleasant to hunt a horse without a martingale, but it cannot always be done. The only inoffensive form is the "Irish martingale." The worst is the ordinary "running" one, because, when your horse comes down, if you hold on the reins, as you should do, you are landed close to his head instead of well clear, and probably get trodden on, if indeed the horse does not roll on you. The standing martingale, unless very tight, does not interfere with the horse's safety, and it does enable the rider to fall clear. In a fall the reins should never be let go, as, apart from the nuisance of losing the horse, holding the reins turns the rider over and he falls on his back instead of on his head.

On the Bombay side men generally use the long spear, about 8 feet long or more, and it is generally known as the under-hand spear. In all other parts, the short spear or over-hand is used. I know of no advantage to be got out of the former whilst those of the latter are manifest. In riding through cover which is at all high, the great length of the long spear projecting behind the hand is very troublesome, and the spear itself more unhandy and cumbersome, while there seems little or no object in the greater length of reach, and it cannot be used over-hand. The unhandiness due to length is such a disadvantage that most men use very short spears, and in my opinion the best length is only 6 feet. With a spear of this length, heavily weighted at the base, the rider has a weapon which, balancing 1 foot 4 inches from the base, gives a reach of 5 feet 3 inches when in actual use and is as handy as a foil. It can be used "under-hand" as in tent-pegging or else "over-hand," the difference being that in the former the spear is held with the knuckles down, and in the latter with the knuckles up.

When "sticking" a boar in thick cover, it is impossible to use the spear under-hand, because at the moment when the boar, who has been galloping alongside you, turns into you in his charge, which may happen at any moment, it is more than likely that the point of the spear will be carried back by the cover, leaving you at the mercy of the pig.

Some men prefer using the spear over-hand always, but, although very deadly when skilfully used, there is a much greater chance of the horse getting "cut."

The ordinary spear used is a very clumsy affair, because few men take the trouble to weight it enough at the butt. Also the wrong class of bamboo is almost invariably supplied. The shaft universally used is cut from the top of the bamboo spray, and only tapers very slightly. Of much stronger texture than this is the part near the root. A shaft should be cut from a young spray, as close as possible to its root. You then have one with a sharp taper, most of the weight being in the butt-end. If this be heavily weighted, and a light head selected, the spear will be heavy, but perfectly balanced and very strong. The bamboo, thus cut, is used by every villager as a staff or "lathi," and, as such, can be bought in most places in the bazaar. These "lathis" are seldom longer than 6 feet and are mostly too thick and heavy, hence there are not many that will be suitable for spears. Those best applicable to the purpose will be 5 inches in circumference at the butt, and 2¾ inches at a point 5 feet 6 inches up, this being about the base of the spear head. The balance of the spear is the important point. The weight due to the lead, while not tiring the hand, gives more power to the blow. Eroom & Co., Calcutta, have the above pattern spear and provide it at Rs. 10. A spear should be a powerful weapon for offence and defence, and not a toy with which to get "first spear."

As far as the spear heads themselves go, there is a great diversity of opinion. There are all sorts of shapes, such as the "bay leaf," "the bayonet," "the diamond," and lastly a very complicated one, made by the famous maker "Bodraj" of Aurungabad and others. In my opinion those made up by the ordinary good armourer of a native regiment are better than any, because they can then be made of the exact size and weight desired, and the steel is not so highly tempered and therefore less brittle, though a little soft. The edges can be sharpened easily with a file, daily, if necessary, provided the pattern is not complicated. The widest point of the head should be sharp and rounded, not having an angle, like the diamond pattern, as the spear should withdraw as easily as possible. The best all round head is the bay leaf, shaft 5½ inches, blade 3½ inches, 1½ inches maximum width, ⅜ inch thick in the middle, with only two cutting edges. This fulfils all the necessary conditions.

The Bodraj head is of very hard steel, seldom

requires sharpening, and is too complicated to admit of it. The diamond has the objectionable "corner." The "bayonet" is not so easy to sharpen and does not stop a charge, as it enters too easily.

Efficient protection for the head is very essential, both as a precaution against the sun and to save the head in a "fall." Many a man owes his life to a good hat, which may be seen by the appearance of it after a good fast fall. It is then generally a pulp. The hat must be light and have good ventilation. To obtain the latter there is a space between the band which fits the head and the hat itself. The attachment of this band to the hat should be strong, but very seldom is so. The fit of the band to the head is always the difficulty, as, if too tight, it becomes uncomfortable, and, if too loose, the hat "sits down" too much on the head. The best way is to have the fit loose, and to adjust two strong tapes at right angles to each other which will rest on the top of the head when the hat is in use. To prevent the hat coming off, a strong chin-strap is indispensable. Neither the tapes nor the chin-strap should be attached to the band, which is the weakest point and is always selected by hatters for attachments of all sorts. The tapes must be fixed firmly to the body of the hat, as should also the chin-strap, unless we resort to the best method of putting the latter over the top of the hat and letting it pass through a slit in the rim. Murray & Co., Lucknow, provide the best hat on this system at Rs.6, but any thick pith hat with a karki cover will do perfectly, provided the band is fixed on firmly and the tapes and chin-strap are properly attached.

The coat should be made of hard, thin, tough material, with a thick pad attached to keep the sun off the back, with pockets, and on the Norfolk jacket system, with a waist belt. This belt allows the rider to leave all the buttons undone when the weather is hot, and so long as the belt is buttoned, the coat does not fly about. A waistcoat is unnecessary. A fairly thick flannel shirt prevents chills and is the most comfortable and healthy, far preferable to the thin cotton shirt, which is responsible for much sickness. The breeches should be of fairly stout cord ; if thin, the legs will rub. If they rub even in thick breeches, drawers will generally save even the most tender skin ; but if they do not, then a very certain method is to rub over with nearly dry soap the parts that chafe, before putting on the drawers.

Boots are better than gaiters or Jodpore breeches, as they save the legs from blows. They should be easy to pull on and off. Greased boots are much hotter than those that have not been greased, though this is apparently not generally known. In selecting material for clothing it must be remembered that no one attaches any importance to appearance. Comfort and efficiency are the main objects; and the clothes are subjected to the severest treatment. They must keep out thorns and not tear, and invisibility is the point to aim at in the choice of colour. Rough clothes of this sort are made very cheaply in India, and the class of cloth for the purpose can be obtained there with ease.

If used, spurs should be either blunt, or else, if sharp, they should be made just long enough in the neck to take the rowel and no more. When crashing through cover, it is not possible to avoid spurring your horse if the ordinary long-necked spur be used, as the legs get dragged back. With the proper pattern, the horse can only be reached with the spur by turning the toe out. Many riders do this habitually and should not on any account ride in sharp spurs. In the excitement of a run, most men use their spurs more than they intend to. A cane carried in the left hand with a loop over the wrist is more effective, and has the advantage of being only used when required. A cutting whip is just as good, but no better, and, since the implement, whatever it is, is getting constantly lost, it is more economical to buy the ordinary cheap cane, which can be got in Bombay at the rate of ten for the rupee. For use in camp, and for riding out to the meet, a pair of thick flannel trousers will be found cool and comfortable, while for dinner a loose flannel suit is all that is wanted.

Your horses always require head and heel ropes, and blankets according to the weather. As it is always in the hot weather that the bulk of pig-sticking is done, blankets are usually not required at all, except towards the end of the season, when the rains are approaching, for they are as a rule heralded by heavy showers and a sudden, though temporary, fall in temperature. A blanket should then be put on, or fever will be the invariable result. During the day, throughout the hot weather, a light cotton sheet should be used to keep off both flies and the sun. Eye-fringes preserve the eyes from flies and are a necessary. A bucket apiece for each horse, as well as a curry-comb and brush, and a set of flannel leg bandages or putties, an empty kerosene oil tin or two for cooking "boiled food," and a good stable lantern complete the essentials.

In poor tent clubs, tents as a rule are not used. Every soldier and civilian in India has his own small tent, which he can take out if he wishes to do so, but a small tent has only the advantage of affording shade and the disadvantage of keeping out the little breeze there is. Moreover, there is the trouble and expense of taking it out. If big tents be left out of the question, the best form of shelter, which is as follows, can be owned by each man, and can be made up economically in any bazaar. Get any ordinary canvas and make of it a sheet 8 feet long by 4 feet wide. Make this two or three folds thick and line one side of it with yellow cloth of any kind. Into each short end of it sew a light bamboo. Support each end on a bamboo 4 feet 6 inches long. Make a ridge pole of another light bamboo in two pieces, stand the whole up, supported by guy ropes, and put your bed under it. If care be taken to place it under a shady tree, with the long side pointing north and south, the bed will always be in the shade, because, by tightening the guy ropes on one side and slackening them on the other, to suit the angle of the sun, perfect shade is always obtainable. When you are sleeping in the shade of a tree by day, the sun is very clever at peeping through the gaps between boughs, and unless some other steps, such as the above, be taken, a good day-sleep is impossible. This mid-day rest is necessary to men who have been up since 4 A.M., and have worked hard and are very tired. It will be noticed that the longest bamboo measures only 4½ feet. This shelter is very portable, as it is merely rolled up with the bamboos inside, making a small roll 4½ feet long; it weighs little, will keep off a shower of rain, as well as the insects which fall out of trees, and allows the sleeper every breath of air which blows. When sleeping by day, your sun-hat should be put over the face, as it keeps off the flies, hides the glare from the eyes and saves sunstroke.

In the extreme heat, from the middle of June, a good tent is a necessary, and at all times it is a luxury, in the middle of the day, provided it is big enough. It is cooler by night outside a tent than in it, so that any tent is useless, unless by day you can make it cooler inside than out. A punkah may be used as a substitute for a breeze, but to enable a punkah to be rigged up at all the tent must be of a certain size. The temperature inside can be generally lowered to 90° or less by using "tatties," and letting the hot, dry wind which generally prevails blow through them into the tent. If these tatties are kept constantly wet, the drier and stronger the wind is, the cooler the tent. Tatties can easily be made at any camp by a few coolies out of bamboos; these furnish the frame, and are filled in with grass. The best are those made from "Jawasa," or camel thorn, a plant which generally grows wherever pig live. The bigger the tent, the more comfortable, but the smallest, which will at a pinch accommodate four men, is the double-poled Swiss cottage, and that costs Rs.500. Tents of any size and of all sorts can be got from the Elgin Mills, Cawnpore, at the shortest notice, but they are costly to buy, take a lot of carriage, and require a specially trained staff to pitch and pack them.

Any simple form of camp-bed will do. The points to look to are (1) that the bed really is simple—any complicated form is a nuisance; (2) that it is strong (3) and long enough, (4) and has some sort of rail at the end to prevent your pillow falling off during a restless night. The bed should be at least 18 inches longer than the sleeper, unless he sleeps curled up. The bed supported on trestles is to be avoided studiously, as the canvas soon stretches, the owner's body sinks on to the trestles, and sleep becomes impossible.

A basin and tooth-mug must be taken by everyone. The enamel basin with a leather cover, which makes it a covered receptacle for the washing gear, is the best. A light stand for the basin is also convenient.

A rubber bath is very convenient, but a waterproof sheet, put into a hole dug in the ground, gives a far more luxurious bath and is more portable.

A portable, comfortable camp-chair is invaluable; the best form is that sold by Luscombe & Co., Allahabad, of wood and canvas with leather arms. The legs, however, should be shorter, the seat being within 1 foot of the ground.

Everyone requires a light of some sort to enable him to undress in comfort at night. The best form for this is any sort of candlestick with a glass protector to keep the light night airs from guttering the candle. Candles are more portable than oil, and give quite sufficient light.

A couple of rugs, a pair of sheets, and a pillow is all that is required.

These are always provided by the tent club, but in the case of private expeditions they must be either bought or hired privately. Some good servant of experience will be necessary in such cases to "run" the food arrangements, and he will know exactly what is required.

In the matter of expenses, everything depends

on the style in which things are done. With a tent club, in which rich men predominate and matters are not gone into carefully, the general expenses may amount to Rs.20 per hunting day, but in a poor club, carefully managed and only essentials provided, Rs.5 a day should cover everything, including drinks, coolies, rewards, and carriage The usual rates, which, however, differ in places, are as follows. (*N.B.*—These are annas, 16 to the rupee.)

Bullock carts,	per march,	As.14 ;	per halt,	As.8
Ekkas,	,,	Rs.1 ;	,,	As.8
Coolies,	per day,	As.2		

Rs.1 per pig killed is paid by the man who gets first spear. It is also wise to be liberal with the men who are supposed to look after the covers. One rupee per pig killed should encourage their preservation and ensure good information as to their whereabouts. Of the pig killed, one is sufficient for the servants. The rest should go to the coolies.

Servants' wages differ slightly, but the following staff should be sufficient. The wages are for a month:—Bearer and khitmatgar combined, Rs.15; one syce per horse, Rs.7; one grass-cutter per horse, Rs.4 As.8; one bheastie or water-carrier, Rs.7.

Horses' expenses, including all servants connected with the stable, food, and upkeep of live gear, at least Rs.20 the month.

VI.—STABLE MANAGEMENT

On the management of the stable depends the number of horses required, and there are a few points which should be carefully observed.

First of all, never rail your horses if it can be avoided. The hot train journey is very trying, and accidents occur in entraining and detraining; moreover, there are always long delays in shunting, and the horses can only go when the train does. As there are generally very few trains a day, there is not much selection, and the horses may have to travel in the heat of the day. If the train goes at night, the horses have to be entrained by daylight and wait for hours in a stuffy horse-box before starting. Often, too, horse-boxes are not available when wanted. Unless the distance to be travelled is very long—say, over fifty miles—it is much better policy to march the stud. The best plan is to have a saddle for every horse and make all the syces ride; to have an arrangement by which all their gear and their food for the journey travels with them, and then to march them at a trot and walk averaging five miles an hour, including short halts. The syces must walk when the horses walk and ride when they trot. In this way a march of thirty miles will occupy six hours. For instance, if the hunt is fixed for Sunday and is thirty miles off, the stud can start on Friday afternoon in the cool and march ten miles in two hours. They camp at a convenient spot for the night, leave again at 4 A.M., arrive in camp by 8 A.M. on Saturday morning, and will be ready to hunt on Sunday. Horses will always let their own syce ride them, and, however bad a rider he be, they go quietly enough. There may be a little trouble the first day or two, but, if this be done systematically, the horses know that a march is impending and go quietly and steadily. Given a convenient train leaving in the evening for the same place, and given a meet at the railway station itself, the horses going by train would leave their stables about the same time as those marching to enable them to be entrained by daylight. They would have to wait for daylight at the other end, and would be in camp about the same time as those who marched. The marching does the horses good, and the train does them harm.

Rope galls are responsible for keeping more horses out of work than anything else. They are due to sheer carelessness on the part of the syce, and it should be thoroughly impressed upon the syces that a fine of Rs. 1 will be inflicted in every case of a rope gall, and this fine should be rigorously inflicted. Next in order of avoidable damage comes "sore back." Given a perfectly fitting saddle, a swollen wither can be easily caused by removing the saddle while the horse is still hot. It should be a standing rule that every horse is watered immediately he comes into camp, the girths being previously slackened. After drinking the horse will break out in a sweat again, and he should be led about for half an hour to enable his back to cool quietly under the saddle. On the first sign of a "back" the horse must be laid up and treated, unless all chance of pressure or rub can be avoided by means of wearing a folded blanket under the saddle or a nummah with a hole cut in it. The body-roller, carelessly put on, often gives a "back." A handful of grass put under the roller on either side of the spine is a useful precaution, and the owner would be wise to examine the back of every horse before he starts for the day's work, as all syces will hide a "roller back."

After the horse comes in from a hunt put a bandage soaked in hot water on each of his legs, with a dry bandage over it, and leave these on for several hours. This relieves the soreness due to hits and thorns. Do not neglect to search the hoof very carefully for any signs of a "stub," which is a very common accident, especially with horses with thrushy frogs. In any case a foot poultice is a good precaution. Thrush is very common in most stables, and is very difficult to cure. It is important, as thrushy feet get so easily stubbed. The cure is, firstly, good shoeing; after that run the edge of a rag through the cleft of the frog saw-ways, and insert "burnt alum." A horse with thrushy feet is, in his pig-sticking capacity, a broken reed for the time being.

Horse feed should be looked into very carefully, and it is generally best to take the grain with you from home, as carriage is cheap. Good crushed oats is the best food. For economy it may be mixed with grain. Bran also must not be omitted. A good all-round mixture is 50 per cent. crushed oats, 25 per cent. bran, 25 per cent. grain or crushed barley. Each horse, however, has to be studied. With horses in hard pig-sticking work the main points to watch are that they digest what they eat and that their coats do not get "dry." Every horse should therefore get boiled food after a day's hunting—say, boiled barley or boiled gram mixed with bran and linseed. Some require the whole of their food to be boiled. After an outing they want a little rest, and this change from hard work often upsets them. Six ounces of Epsom salts daily for two or three days and light feed does them good. With an Australian a liberal supply of good grass is more important than grain. With an Arab or country-bred it is not so important.

For the "stable" the cart which marches with the horses must be able to travel five miles an hour on ordinary roads, with capacity sufficient to carry the stable necessities for the journey, a grass-cutter or two, and a little grass. A good form of cart for this is the ordinary "ekka" well horsed. The best animal to pull it is a mule, because he is stronger for his size and more tractable than a pony. The ekka of the North-West Provinces is small and takes a 12-hand animal. A new one costs Rs.70, and a suitable pony Rs.60. A good mule would cost Rs.150 and is more difficult to acquire. Care must be taken that the "wheel track" is of the same width as that of the cart of your district. If not, a new axle is all that is required, and that can be substituted for Rs.10. This "track" is very important. On all metalled roads not well kept up, and on all unmetalled roads the wheel tracks are better "going" for the wheels than the rest of the road, and this makes a vast difference to the draught animal. This is especially the case in low-lying, or irrigated, countries, where the ruts may be two feet deep. To carts or ekkas with a different wheel track from that of the carts that made the ruts, such roads are well-nigh impassable. Perhaps the best form of "stable cart" is a light bullock cart with a good pair of trotting bullocks. The advantages of this over the ekka are that it carries twice as much, and is cheaper, the whole turn-out costing only Rs.150. On roads with deep ruts it is altogether better than the ekka, for the reason that the bullocks walk in the ruts, followed by the wheels, whereas the pony pulling the ekka walks on the high ground in between the ruts, and consequently is not on the same level as the load he pulls. Often, too, the space between the tracks is very irregular and difficult to walk on. The disadvantage of the bullock cart is that it is slower on good roads than the ekka.

The personal baggage, main grain supply and grass-cutters can precede the horses in an

An Ekka drawn by a good Mule

A Trotting Bullock Car

ordinary bullock cart, while your own personal bedding and body-servant and such things as are wanted at home as long as possible will arrive quicker by ekka, provided the load is light, the wheel track correct, and the ekka well horsed.

VII.—VETERINARY

THE following instruments and medicines should be taken :—

Instruments.—Procurable from any surgical instrument maker. "Smith Stannisstreet" in Calcutta, and Maw & Sons, Strand, being well-known firms.

1. Drawing knife.
2. Scissors curved on flat and probe pointed.
3. Dissecting forceps.
4. Small pair sequestrum forceps.
5. Scalpel.
6. 2 pairs fenestrated artery forceps.
7. 2 pairs Spencer Wells artery forceps.
8. 6 half curved needles.
9. 1 large brass syringe.

Medicines.—From Smith Stannisstreet & Co., Calcutta.

1. Tabloids of perchloride of mercury. One tabloid to 4 pints water makes a good disinfectant and antiseptic.
2. Lint—1 pound.
3. 6 bandages—calico.

4. 6 yards calico.
5. Cotton wadding.
6. Iodoform.
7. Boracic acid.

{ A useful powder for dressing wounds can be made of $\frac{1}{3}$ iodoform, $\frac{2}{3}$ boracic acid.

8. Sugar. A handful pushed down the throat has a marvellous effect in cases of choking.
9. 1 reel thick silk ligature.
10. 1 reel medium silk ligature.
11. 2 hanks of horse hair.
12. 4 ozs. compound tincture of benzoin. 1 drachm iodoform to 1 oz. of this tincture makes a very useful dressing for big raws, which you are unable to cover with a bandage.
13. 1 oz. carbolic acid pure. 1 in 40 makes a good antiseptic lotion.
14. 1 quart olive oil.
15. 10 ozs. turpentine.

{ A dose for colic from chill, 1 pint oil with 1 oz. turps.

16. 1 oz. phenacetin.
17. 2 ozs. quinine sulphate.

Pig Cuts.—The ordinary cut is an incised wound of varying depth. The following is a simple and safe treatment. Carefully syringe out wound with perchloride lotion; then, if the wound is deep, take a strip of lint, dip into the lotion, wring it out, dust it with iodoform and boracic powder, and pack the wound. Do not stitch it up. Send the animal home to hospital. If the wound is superficial and clean cut, carefully cut away all the surrounding hair, thoroughly cleanse with the lotion, and close the wound with the necessary number of sutures. Keep the horse in camp, as he will probably be fit for work shortly.

(Roughly speaking — fluid measure. 1 teaspoonful equals 1 drachm, 2 tablespoonfuls equal 1 oz.)

Fever.—Give 30 grains phenacetin, and, when the temperature has come down, 1 drachm quinine sulphate.

VIII.—HINTS

Hints to Beginners.—As at everything else, it takes the beginner a little time before he is of much help, but a few hints may help him not to spoil sport. It is all merely common sense, but at the same time it is wonderful how often so-called "men of experience" spoil sport by disregarding evident facts.

The hunt is conducted on different principles, according to the country. If the cover is a sea of grass, the spears mostly go with the line of coolies, a few being sent on to the end of the cover in case the pig run on. When in the line, keep at least two horses' lengths behind it, and do not wander in front of it. The coolies cannot always see far to their right and left. Endeavour, therefore, to see what the honorary secretary wants, and try to assist him to keep the line in order. When a pig jumps up near you, close with him as fast as you possibly can, and endeavour to ascertain if it is a good boar, or only an "unrideable" one, or a sow, and signal accordingly. This is to save unnecessary riding. If a rideable boar, scream as loud as possible, and keep screaming as long as you are on him, and shout "lost" continually if you lose him. When another man comes to your help, let him know what the pig is doing by shouting "right," "left," "back," or "here he goes," according to the beast's movements. When the pig "squats" suddenly, stand still, commanding some clear place if possible; keep yourself in the grass, and look to see him stealing on. If you find the pig is not "rideable," pull up at once and hold up your spear horizontally to indicate the fact. If sent on to the end of a cover, keep hidden as far as possible, look at the "ground," and make up your mind what the boar's objective will be, and what route he will take A good pig always takes advantage of any "run" of the ground or cover which will lead him towards his point as nearly unseen as circumstances permit. Keep out of sight yourself and command this route. If you see the pig coming, do not move a limb till he is fairly "committed." If he sees you he will not "break" at all; and if you ride him too soon he will go back into the cover, and you will have lost your chance. When you have posted yourself, if you see that the jackals and foxes run by another route, which you do not command, you have probably made an error in selecting your place, and had better rectify it at once; but, whatever you do, make up your mind finally, and do not wander about. When in position keep every faculty on the alert. The beat may take two or three hours coming, and at any moment a pig may break. If you begin playing with ants, or drawing pictures in the sand, you will probably not see the very wily pig sneaking away, and his tracks will give you away and make you, temporarily at least, unpopular. It is not very uncommon for a whole party to be found actually asleep by the "line" on its arrival at the end of the beat.

When you are close on a boar, remember that, with open ground in front, he will "squat" if you press him, so go as slowly as you can, consistent with keeping him in sight, and allow him to break. Also keep in mind that a run pig generally keeps going, so, if you should lose sight of him, press on towards his objective, calling out "lost" for the information of your party. If you see him, scream again, and keep on at it as long as you are on him. A wounded or tired pig, if lost, always makes for water; try and remember that, and you will pick up many a lost one.

The second style of cover usually met with is that in which the cover is so thick that a man cannot "ride" in it. Thorn jungle is of this kind. The beaters go into this, and the spears are posted at different points commanding "runs." If you have a syce with you, see that he keeps under cover, and impress on him that he is to stay there and not move. A syce delights in jumping up and pointing just as the pig is trying to "break." He also loves being dressed in glaring white clothes and hunting flies off the horse with a very white kerchief. See to this point, and do not wear a white hat, coat, or breeches yourself, and keep your attention strictly to watching your own bit of ground. When a pig breaks, let him get well away. If the ground is open and the pig is going unwillingly, he should be given as much law as you think you can afford. Make up your mind definitely whether the pig breaking is rideable or not, and do not change your mind when he looks huge in the distance. A really big pig is unmistakable in the open, and, unless the sight of him makes you catch your breath, he is not worth riding. A good boar is higher, shorter, and lower behind than a very big sow, and he has a shorter head. A small boar or an ordinary sow has an active stride, quite different from the lumbering gait of a fine boar. Every time you go after an "unrideable" pig you spoil your chance of fun. The pig knows all about it in the cover, and will not come your way at anyrate. There is one thing more that no novice and few "experienced" men will ever believe: when the beat is at the other end of the cover, and all is quiet, then is the best chance of a good pig breaking at your end. It seldom happens, because by then the party in rear has given up hope, and are discussing the last dance or some other topic of interest; but it is *the* chance of the day after all for getting a head to put up in your home. In the actual ride bear in mind that the closer you are to the pig the better ground you get, because he knows it and selects it; that your horse is responsible for where he puts his feet and not you; and that the faster you are going, the "clearer" you fall. All *you* have to do is to lean well back, ride with your reins very long, follow the pig like a terrier, sit tight, avoid interfering with the horse, and trust to his honour to do the rest. As for "first spear," do not think about it, unless the pig cannot escape. The first consideration is the death of the pig. Ride in the public interest and you will achieve more honour than can be got by any number of "first spears."

Hints to men coming from England to hunt.—In these days of easy access to India from England, it is quite possible that some sportsmen may wish to come to India for three months of sport, in which pig-sticking should take a prominent place. These will find it very difficult to arrange matters, unless they have someone in the country to help them. India is a most hospitable place, and, once there, no sportsman will find anything other than a warm welcome; but he must make up his mind how much money he is prepared to spend, and what sort of sport he wants. Having done that, he must find someone in India to arrange matters for him. If the sportsman wishes to "pig-stick," pure and simple, and can afford the necessary stud, he will join some private hunting party, if he can find one, which will hunt seven days a week. Failing this, he will join the best tent club he can hear of. In both cases, he will have to authorise someone to get his stud together, and also to engage servants for him. This cannot be done in a day, so he must allow ample time. In the second case, he will require some occupation for the days when he is not hunting. He may wish to play polo, shoot blackbuck, or do something else. All these things will have to be arranged for. Moreover, his choice of "district" will depend on his inclinations. The country which will supply fifteen days a month pig-sticking may also give first-class polo, beginners' polo, blackbuck, or anything else, but it does not necessarily do so. Furthermore, as previously pointed out, few places in India can be pointed to and described as a place in which you will get good pig-sticking to a certainty. That depends on the garrison. This is also the case with polo or any other form of collective sport; whereas, there is always shooting to be had in a shooting district, or fishing, where there are good rivers, in their own season.

What I wish to make clear is, that every place has its own special advantages and drawbacks, which, in general, vary. A visitor, therefore, must obtain local information and help; in the first instance, to find where he can get the sport he requires, and in the second, to assist him in matters which take time to adjust. It takes months to collect a stud of pig-stickers and polo ponies and a staff of good servants.

Almost everything for sporting purposes can be got better and cheaper in India than in England. Therefore, do not bring anything, except, perhaps, riding boots, saddles, rifle, gun and bedding, and one pair of breeches as a pattern. Sporting clothes, tents, beds, chairs, spears, bits, blankets, etc., are understood in India. English horse gear is all too big and heavy; clothes too thick or too thin; and, in fact, little that is brought out ever suits the country.

It may be that a man touring in India, though not wishing to hunt regularly, would like to have a few runs after pig, just to see what the sport is like. He may have some devoted friend, who will permit him to ride one of his good horses, but it is very improbable, as few men would trust a novice to this extent. Among the hospitable native chiefs of India there are, however, a few who would do so, if the introduction was sufficiently good; and among these are those of Rajputana, Gwalior and Kapurthala.

POLO

POLO, perhaps the king of all games, is, in most countries, so expensive as to be beyond the purse of all save the favoured few. In England, for instance, both the pony and its keep are very expensive. In India, the pony used to cost very little, and his keep was cheap, at least compared with England. This is one reason why in India the game became almost universal. Matters, however, have undergone a great alteration during the past few years.

Fifteen years ago a first-class tournament polo pony could be bought for Rs.500, but now three times that amount is necessary if a real good one is required. Hence it would be expected that a great number would be forced to give up so expensive a luxury as polo. To a certain extent many have done so, but there is, from the poor man's point of view, another side to the question.

In the days of the very cheap ponies, say thirty years ago, there were really no such things as tournaments, and every man rode at polo any sort of pony he happened to own, using the same for a tournament, if such a thing chanced to come his way. The ordinary country-bred pony, so played, cost about Rs.100, and had no especial value as a tournament pony; in fact, Rs.150 would be the value of a good polo pony. Such ponies as they were, too, little fellows of thirteen hands or so, they did their best, and that is all that can be said for them. About the year 1885 further tournaments were instituted; the height rose to 13.3; and the class of pony improved, till the best pony might be sold for as much as Rs.500, costing in the fair about Rs.180. Then, about 1890, a few venturesome people gave Arabs a trial, and found them successful; ever since then the run on Arabs has continued; a better class has been imported; and the price has been raised. In 1901, the height of ponies was raised to a nominal 14.1. I say "nominal," because, as will be shown hereafter, the real limit height is now about 14.2. The quality of the ponies went up with their height, until now the country-bred is, in a general way, not good enough for tournaments. The Australian pony has also got a fair footing in the country; and, in fact, the Arab and he almost have the monopoly of tournaments. These animals "in the raw" cost Rs.500 or Rs.600 apiece; but when made, they may fetch double and treble that sum, or even more. Although the prices of the ponies themselves have gone up so tremendously, the cost of keeping them has remained practically the same; so that a poor man who buys his ponies in the raw, and occasionally sells a good one for a high price, gets a very much larger sum towards the "keep" of his stable than he could have done formerly. This it is that in a great measure enables the majority to continue playing a game, which at first sight would appear to be growing beyond their purse.

Take, for instance, the comparison between a man who sold a first-class tournament pony in the eighties, and one who does the same now. The former bought it for Rs.180 and sold it at Rs.500, having made Rs.320 to help expenses. The latter buys at Rs.600 and sells at Rs.1500, and clears Rs.900 as against the old Rs.320, the keep of the pony being practically the same in both cases.

Whatever the reason may be, there is no doubt that the quantity of polo is as much, if not more, than ever it was, and that the quality has improved out of all recognition. The number of small tournaments now held everywhere, tends to encourage regiments, batteries and stations to get their teams some practice together, and a station game is now a series of small matches in which all can see that what wins is combination and not individual brilliancy, resulting in a corresponding improvement in the game. The amount and quality of polo played at any station depend entirely on the keenness of the garrison at the time. In most stations there is a polo ground capable of being kept in good order, provided there are a sufficient number of people in the place interested in the game; but in small stations, unless more than the average amount of interest is maintained, the ground and the game must be of poor quality. To anyone, therefore, who is keen on having good polo, and is in a position to be able to select his station, it is necessary to have information as to the quality of the game in any particular place at any particular time. There are a few big stations in which the garrison is so large that a good game is a certainty always; and again there are a few, which, though they have a large garrison, have not the facility of a good ground. Typical in the former category are Meerut and Umballa, and in the latter Rawal Pindi. It may be taken as a general rule, that wherever troops are stationed there will be polo, and that the quality and quantity of it depend entirely on the garrison. Even in places where there is a large civil population, much depends on the regiments quartered there. In a regiment there is always a certain number of good players, who are in a position to coach the men in their own regiment. This team will surely have a match with the civilian team, and the advantage of a team which plays together on a system over that which does not, will soon become evident. The civilians will probably select their captain, and try to wipe out their defeat by combined play, and the game soon becomes a good one. Given a place where there are no troops, or only a regiment that has no team, no man, however good and experienced a player he may be, feels himself justified in criticising the play of individuals who have not asked him to do it; hence, under such unfavourable conditions the noble game of polo degenerates into a number of men hitting the ball about. To take the instances of our two largest towns, Bombay and Calcutta. In the former, there has been practically no polo for years, while in the latter there has, of late years at all events, been plenty of polo, but of very poor class. If we look for the reason it is not difficult to find. The regiments quartered there have no teams and merely provide a few individual players. The manner of making up sides is as follows. There is a black board on the ground, and as each man arrives he writes down his name and the number of "chukkers" he requires. The four men with the first claim play the four men with the second call. No one cares for the result, or attempts to play together, as is only natural, seeing that none of them know what to expect the others to do with the ball. In short, they cannot and do not know one another's play. If selecting a place, therefore, in which good polo is to be obtained, do not jump to the conclusion that, because it is a place holding a large number of monied men, and the place of all others with facilities for buying ponies, the polo must therefore be good.

Again, it may be that money is an object to you; and, if it is, you must select your station accordingly. If you go to a place where those playing at the time are very wealthy as well as good players, you may find yourself so outclassed in play or ponies, or both, that it will not be amusing. It is possible to get first-class polo among men who are not extraordinarily well mounted.

But before being able to play polo at all, it is of course necessary to have the ponies, and it is as well thoroughly to sift the question as to the best way to get them, and the best sort to get. The price of a likely raw, unacclimatised pony, likely to make a first-class tournament polo pony, bought direct from the dealer, should be no more than Rs.600 for an Australian and Rs.700 for an

Arab. Good-looking country-breds can be bought in fairs for Rs.400, but they are very uncertain animals, and it is hard to say how they will turn out. They are seldom to be bought older than five years, and, with the good food they get in your stable, they may grow a great deal between the ages of five and six. Since the "height certificate" cannot be obtained till a pony is six, there is always a very grave risk of the young country-bred growing over height, and, as he is a lighter animal than the Arab or Australian, he is useless unless he is as near the limit of height as possible, so that the buyer of raw country-breds runs the double risk of finding his pony is a failure on account of being either too small or else too big. A 14-hand Arab or Australian may be first-class, but not a 14-hand country-bred. In looks they are often very taking, but in reality they are not nearly as strong as the other two classes, and are non-stayers. By good feeding for two years most of them attain sufficient staying power to be good ponies, but the keep for this long period makes the eventual cost price of the made country-bred polo pony high. The distinctive points in their tempers are trickiness and excitability, with a small heart. In the days when almost all ponies were country-breds, hardly any of them would go on the ground without the aid of a "hunting-crop behind," and a large proportion had to be blindfolded before they would allow themselves to be ridden. Some of the very finest tournament ponies have been country-breds. A likely looking raw pony of this class might repay a light or medium weight, though not a heavy man. The polo pony is in all essentials of the same stamp as the pig-sticker, and the same points should be observed when selecting him: it is therefore unnecessary to go into this question, it having been dealt with in every detail under the head of "Pig-sticking." Handiness, activity and strength are as essential in the one as in the other. The staunchness required to face a pig is necessary in the polo pony, else he will not "ride off" well and will be unsteady when his rider is striking the ball, or when meeting other ponies. The good hock is, if possible, more important in the polo pony than in the pig-sticker, as nothing but the best of hocks will stand the severe strain which a handy pony throws on it.

With regard to the eventual cost of a tournament polo pony something more must be said. The Australian, if bought "raw and unseasoned," on account of the elementary training which he needs, will not be fit to be taken into the game at all till the following cold weather, and he cannot be expected to become a tournament pony for a year after that. In fact, two years must be calculated on as the probable time required to produce a tournament polo pony from the Australian, if bought quite raw. If he be bought as thoroughly handy and broken, in all probability he will have had all the necessary special polo education during the first nine months, and should be a tournament pony at the end of his first year.

The Arab may be considered as on the same footing as the thoroughly broken Australian and will take about the same length of time to train for a tournament. One thing should be remembered with regard to the Arab. On no account keep a stallion. It is the most common mistake, made by almost everyone. The Arab, when bought, is generally in good condition and fit to go into polo training; in a few days he will be fairly handy and not be afraid of the stick and ball. The owner will probably then take him into a slow game, and the pony will "frame" well, and give him a fairly pleasant game. The temptation to go on playing him is, of course, very great, but it is the worst of policy. The probable result will be that the pony will be very satisfactory for months, and the owner will flatter himself that he has done very well. In the cold weather the game will get faster, and he will begin to feed the pony highly, and it is now that the mistake in keeping a stallion pony for polo will begin to show itself. Your promising pony will begin to "feel himself," and, his fighting instincts being roused, he will show signs of wishing to bite the pony he is "riding off." The more and the harder he is played, the more will this tendency be evident, until one day he will actually seize with his teeth the rider or pony of one of the opponents. The pony will then have to be taken off the ground, and you will have to do what you should have done at the beginning. Having done this, you have not necessarily cured your mount. Tricks once learnt are not easily forgotten, and, though your pony will probably come all right in the end, it does not absolutely follow that he will do so. In any case, he is not available for the best season of the year, or for your tournament. The stallion has other tricks which militate against his play. He learns to refuse to gallop, to shy off the ball, to be "sticky," and generally unreliable.

By having him gelt immediately you get him into your stable, you reduce to a minimum the chances of failure due to these common polo faults, and in addition you have a much more pleasant animal to deal with in every way. The operation is a simple one, with little risk attached to it, throwing your new pony out of work for a month only. During his enforced idleness you can be utilising the time by getting his feet in order, and his preliminary education can be better carried out while he is somewhat low in condition. His strength and capacity for work increase at just about the same rate as his training, so that no time is really lost.

The gelding has the same advantage over the stallion at polo as he has at pig-sticking, in respect that his forehand becomes lighter, to the manifest advantage of his legs.

With regard to the superiority of the trained Arab gelding and the trained Australian polo pony, there is some doubt. Both are strong and fast, but for a heavy man the Australian has the advantage in so far as there are greater weight-carrying possibilities in his class than in the other. I do not think there is much, however, to choose between them in other ways. When we try to compare the probabilities of the two classes ever becoming tournament ponies, there is little doubt that the Arab has the pull. Most Arab geldings make tournament form ponies, provided they are sound enough, fast enough, and of the right make and shape; and if they fail in any of the last three points they are, in any case, sure still to be good station game ponies and general utility animals. Australians, under the same conditions, take longer to make, have not so good a probability of ever making tournament polo ponies, and, failing this, not being so tractable, they are less likely to be so generally useful. In soundness, the Arab, though not sounder in limb, is very markedly so in "wind," and is more free from fever and skin disease.

If we take a glance through the various points of comparison, we find that, if bought as a raw article from the importer, the Arab in every way has the advantage, except perhaps for an extraordinarily heavy man. If the Australian be bought thoroughly made, even then the advantage lies with the Arab, in that he is less likely to "go wrong" during his first hot weather.

In my opinion, given similar opportunities for buying Australians and Arabs direct from the port of disembarkation, the advantage of the Arab over the Australian is very marked, except in the matter of original price, when I should say that the pony who would carry a similar weight with similar effect, would in an Arab cost Rs.100 more than in an Australian.

To get at the cost of producing a tournament polo pony from the three kinds, bought direct from the shippers and the fair respectively, we may make then the following rough calculation :—

The pony bought broken but not acclimatised from the Australian shipper—

Original cost	Rs.700
Keep for 12 months at Rs.20 per month	240
Climatic risks	100
Training "	100
Total .	Rs.1140

The pony bought unbroken—

Original cost	Rs.600
Keep for 24 months at Rs.20 per month	480
Climatic risks	100
Training "	150
Total .	Rs.1330

The Country-bred from the fair—

Original cost	Rs.400
Keep for 2 years . . .	240
Climatic risks	nil
Training „	300
Total .	Rs.940

The Arab bought direct from the dealer in Bombay—

Original cost	Rs.700
Keep for 12 months . . .	240
Climatic risks	nil
Training „	100
Total .	Rs.1040

All of these should be tournament form polo ponies. It is to be noted that, as in the case of pig-stickers, these prices are exclusive of all the extra expenses necessarily entailed in the selection of the ponies, and of their transport to the purchaser's stable. This is done intentionally, because this item would vary according to individual circumstances. A—— may have in Calcutta a kind friend who will select and despatch his one pony for him, thus saving him his ticket to and from Calcutta, and he may be lucky enough to live fairly close to the capital. B—— may have to go in person from a station situated two days' rail from the horse market to buy perhaps only a couple of ponies. C—— is selected by his brother officers to buy twenty Arabs from Bombay, and in consequence he has twenty people to share his expenses, besides being able to bring the lot up together, which materially lightens the bill for transport. In working out the eventual cost price of a polo pony, this item for extras must be worked out by each man for himself, according to his circumstances, and added to the figure above arrived at. As already shown, in the case of the pig-sticker, this question affects the trained animal in the private market also.

Before putting any pony through a special course of polo training he must be taught the elementary points that any nice riding horse must know; that is, he must understand what are technically called the "aids." In other words, he must have no doubt as to what his rider wishes him to do when he signals to him by means of his reins and legs. This is done by an ordinary course of cavalry riding school. The unmade Australian should have learnt this by the end of his first hot weather; the made Australian has learnt it already. The Arab and country-bred take only a few months; nevertheless, it must never be left out of the calculation that with Australians climatic troubles have to be dealt with; with Arabs they have to be "altered"; and with country-breds, anything is possible. The latter are shifty, fickle animals, who require as a teacher a man with a long and active experience of the class, or failure is nearly a certainty. The length of this ordinary course is also dependent on the age of the pony ; Arabs and Australians can be bought at a suitable age, and are fit enough for work fairly soon ; but the country-bred is generally bought younger, and takes longer to get strong and set enough to begin the special course, which is of a somewhat severe character, throwing extra work on special parts, notably on the hocks. The objects of this special education is to fit the pony to take his place on the polo-ground, with nothing to learn, save only that which cannot be learnt anywhere else except in the actual game. By hitting the ball about in all directions he will be taught not to be afraid of the stick and ball ; by the two school practices described for the pig-stickers, and by the use of "long reins," he will become handy and know how to turn correctly on his haunches ; and for the rest, exercises may be invented by which to rectify any peculiar fault. He may be shy of closing with a pony in riding off, in which case assist him by forcing him with the aid of a made pony to do so. He may be afraid of meeting another pony, but he will get over this if he be put into a ride, half of which is formed up at each end of the school with wide intervals between horses ; these half rides being practised in passing through one another, first at a walk and then at the trot and gallop, with gradually reduced intervals between the horses of each half side. If intelligent thought be exercised, practices can be invented to suit and rectify each fault, as it becomes evident in the course of play, all the ordinary ones having been previously guarded against. Everything has now been done to ensure success, and the only thing is to exercise patience. Many well-bred and excitable Australians take a very long time in the making, but when made are often the best. That great specialist and polo player, Colonel de Lisle, devoted two years to a thoroughbred Australian racing pony, by name "Mary Morrison," before she ever played in a game, and all who have seen her marvellous play will allow that he received a full reward.

The made polo pony, like the made pig-sticker, varies in price according to the demand at the time, and also according to the circumstances of the owner. It is curious to trace the careers of many ponies, as they show the truth of this point so clearly. I owned an Arab pony myself which I bought raw in Bombay for Rs.500, and, having played him for two years, sold just after a good tournament for Rs.1000. The man to whom I sold him went to an out-of-the-way station, where there was very little polo, and circumstances forced him to sell. Although advertised, no one even offered to buy him, because the owner's regiment was known at the time to be not playing tournaments, and, therefore, considered unlikely to have good animals. No one in that small place wanted him, so, failing to sell, he wrote to me towards the end of the hot weather, offering him for Rs. 500. I took him for an officer in my regiment, who played him in a local tournament within a month. Our team won; and he sold him on the spot for Rs. 1500 to a man who had seen him playing. He in turn, having won a first-class tournament, sold him within a month for Rs. 2000.

Within two months, then, this made polo pony had varied in price between Rs. 500 and Rs. 2000.

The moral is: If you want to buy a made pony, keep your eyes open and be ready to do so when the occasion offers, always bearing in mind that beaten teams have just as good ponies in them as winning ones, and that they often are much cheaper. During the tournament season a famous tournament pony will fetch almost any figure, but during the hot weather prices go down. A knowledgeable man could do a very good business by buying ponies out of season and selling them again in season; but to do this he must keep them before the eyes of the world and must be free to sell when he wants to, which he is not, if he is a member of a team, unless he keeps so large a number that, after selling, he is still capable of mounting himself well on the remainder, or unless the team is not playing any more tournaments for that season.

An experienced man and a good rider can often pick up a really good pony cheap, either because the owner is an indifferent or weak rider, or because he is either too ignorant to grasp the cure or too lazy to apply it. Many ponies, especially Australians, are very slow to learn the game, but grasp it eventually quite suddenly; and others, from among both Arabs and Australians, improve wonderfully in pace with time. A well-shaped pony of either of these breeds may often be bought cheap, because he is apparently too slow.

Generally, a would-be purchaser is allowed a trial in a game. Do not forget, if you are the purchaser, that no pony plays up to his form the first time with a strange rider, so do not expect too much when you are trying him, and judge rather from how you have seen him playing with his owner, always taking into consideration the owner's riding capacities and not over-estimating your own. A fine rider will play magnificently on a pony that is useless to a poor one. Handiness, staunchness and pace are a necessity; extreme speed is a luxury.

The price of a tournament polo pony is such a variable one that it is hard to say what it should be. But if I bought from advertisement a fairly young, practically sound weight-carrying Arab or Australian pony, up to tournament form, for Rs.1500, I should expect to get a thoroughly useful, handy, staunch pony with a turn of speed, but nothing more.

There is nothing peculiar as regards the special stable management of the polo pony in India, other than what was noted under the head of "Pig-sticking." One or two golden rules should, however, be observed.

1. Always inspect your ponies yourself the morning after a game, and before they have had any exercise at all. See them then and you will be able to detect and diagnose ailments better than when they have "warmed up."

2. Always look to see whether their mouths have been "cut" in the game, not forgetting to look under the tongue, a precaution often omitted. Take the tongue in the hand and pull it out to one side, and you will often find the sole of the mouth cut. Look at both sides. If the cut be a simple one, it will heal in a few days; but if a long-standing, neglected one, with splintered bone at the bottom, it may take months. "Cut mouths" are very common indeed, but are seldom noticed, except by the pony, unless the jaw bone is splintered. A bad case must be put out of work and treated, but the ordinary one will be saved if a tape be tied over the tongue and under the lower jaw, just before the pony is actually played. This keeps the tongue over the injured part, protecting it effectually. Neglected cut mouths are responsible for many pullers, and the man who wilfully neglects them is a barbarian.

Exactly the same saddles are required as for pig-sticking, and these have been described. The saddles may be a shade lighter, but the thing to look to is that the saddle is one you can reälly sit tight in, thus enabling you to give your pony every possible help and the least possible hindrance. You should be very careful as to the fit of the bit, which must be the correct width, and the double bridle, Liverpool driving bit and Segundo, combined with a judicious use of the tight nose-band, should hold anything that is worth playing.

This nose-band should be entirely separate from the head-stall, and should be worn under it. No interference with the head-stall is permissible, as it throws the working of the bit out of gear.

These should be used according to the special requirements of each pony. The "running" one is seldom useful. A standing martingale is necessary for almost every pony. In the ordinary pattern the length of this is altered by shortening or lengthening the loop through which the girth goes, entailing delay in undoing the girths and doing them up again. Most polo ponies are of very much the same size, and therefore the whole of the breastplate may be made of an average size. A strap connecting the nose-band and the breastplate ring can be shortened and lengthened in a second, which is useful when it is required to alter the adjustment of the martingale in a hurry. The "mul-mul," or "pugree," standing martingale, may be used if the pony chafes between the fore legs; but for quick and accurate adjustment it is better that the ordinary shape of the martingale be kept, substituting muslin for leather where it affects the legs, *i.e.* between the breast ring and the girths.

A good hat is a necessity, and that recommended for pig-sticking is the best. Spurs, if necessary at all, should be blunt or short-necked;

and a whip with a wrist-strap should always be carried. Breeches of white cord are ordinarily worn, and can be made in India from a good pattern. These stand the rough treatment of the Indian washerman better than the English article. Boots are generally worn; they may be black or brown leather or white canvas. Some teams, notably native ones, wear Jodpur breeches. The boot is, I think, preferable, as it saves many a knock from the ball and occasionally a kick from a pony.

Some sort of protection for the ponies' legs is necessary to save them against hits from the stick or ball. For this object "boots" of numnah are generally worn with strap attachments. These certainly afford the necessary protection, but they are clumsy things, which must, I think, affect the pony's pace, and, although giving protection, they do not afford the legs any support. Better than this is the "Newmarket bandage," properly applied. This bandage, made of very elastic material, if wrapped round the leg firmly from below the fetlock joint up to a point just below the knee, gives sufficient protection as well as great support. Leg bandages, thus put on to protect the fetlock, require a little skill in their adjustment, and consequently they are usually merely wrapped round the leg above the fetlock, thus leaving unprotected and unsupported the part most liable to injury from both hits and sprains. To minimise the chances of injury from the over-tightness of the "puttie" or the "tape," they should not be put on until the animal is likely to be required, and they should be removed when his play has finished.

Polo sticks vary in length, shape, and make, according to the inclination of the player, as well as to his position in the team. Nos. 1 and 2, who are more generally playing short, quick, and accurate strokes, can do so more easily with a short, stiff stick; while No. 3 and back, whose business lies more in long drives, do better with a more "whippy" cane; and, as they constantly have to hit back-handers round the pony's tail, a long reach is useful, and is much aided by the use of a long stick. The same player consequently would use a different stick at No. 2 from that which he would use at back.

The shape of the head is a matter of fancy, as well as the material of which it is made. A certain amount of bulk is required in the head, and if a man cannot wield a heavy head the material must be light. For these, willow is perhaps the best, but it is an unreliable wood. The strongest is bamboo root, but that, again, is somewhat heavy. As to the shape, it is almost entirely a matter of fancy; but there is this much to be said, that there is no necessity for the square section head in India, as the ground differs from English ground with its somewhat long grass and soft lumps, while it would seem that if the stick touches the hard ground in hitting, the round section head would not be impeded by it so much as the head with the sharp lower edge. Eroom & Co., Calcutta, make very good sticks at Rs.15 or £1 per dozen.

The tendency of everyone is to get the biggest ponies they can, and too much importance is, I think, attached to this point. Unless a pony be very perfect, the bigger he is, the less handy he will be. The point that determines the best possible height is the size of the ground and the "depth" of the going. If the ground were only as big as a croquet lawn, a big pony would have no scope for his pace; but if it were a mile long, size, with its accompanying pace, would become more important. A small pony, likely to get off quickly, is probably faster than a big one for 20 yards, though not for 200 yards. In India the going is light, and the strength that goes with size is not so important as in England. In a general way, 14.1 is big enough for anyone on an Indian ground. However, as the public prefers big ponies, if a man wants to get "long prices," he must get his ponies big. According to the measurement rules, every pony has to be measured before he plays in a tournament, and, provided the animal be six years old or over, the measuring certificate granted holds good for life. The pony may be measured whenever an official measurer is available, which is only occasionally at small stations, but frequently at big ones, and always at such places as Bombay and Calcutta. If, therefore, a man has a pony who stands perhaps as high as 14.2 and is six years old, for whom he requires a certificate, he feeds him low for some time, and keeps him in at slow, uninteresting work, thus getting him "slack." He will then probably succeed in "measuring" him. Given, then, that a very big pony is wanted, he can either be bought with a certificate at an enhanced price, or he may be bought "over height," being subsequently prepared and measured. If buying from the importers direct, the pony always lands very slack off the voyage, and the purchaser must bear this in mind, or else the 14.1 pony he buys will surprise him by being 14.2, or over, when he is fit and well. The best policy, therefore, is to have him measured at the port of disembarkation while he is yet poor and weak. As this can only be done provided the animal is six years old, the pony's condition must be considered, as well as the probable amount of his ordinary growth, when calculating the eventual height of any pony under the age of six at the time of purchase. There is also this to be borne in mind, that a newly-landed six-year-old will be seven years before he is "made" if he be an Arab or a made Australian, and eight years if he is a "raw" Australian. If, on the other hand, you buy a four or five-year-old, thus having a pony at his prime by the time he is made, you will either have to be content with one on the small side, or add to your calculation of the eventual cost of the made pony a very large item for "anxiety," as well as the actual one of depreciation in value owing to "failure in measurement."

Finally, it must be remembered, all the figures given, relating to the actual cost of producing a made pony, are based on purely business grounds. Many men take a vast pleasure in the training, and others consider it a labour. To the former only will the figures therefore not apply, because in their case against the debtor item of keep must be put the credit one of value received.

For a man who is content to have second-class ponies, it is not worth while buying raw Arabs or Australians, unless he live at the port of disembarkation, or else does so because he enjoys "making" them. To such a man a country-bred might afford much amusement. A fairly good country-bred might be obtained at a fair for Rs.200, but he would be not older than four years. If he grew over height, it would not matter for use in the ordinary station game. Good station game ponies are not difficult to come by, and can usually be bought as "failures" for first-class polo for about Rs.500.

The number of ponies necessary for a tournament depends on the "length of play" of each particular game, or the limit number of ponies allowed. The usual length of a match is thirty minutes' actual play, exclusive of any time during which the ball is not in play. Thus such a match beginning at 4 P.M. would probably not be concluded till 5.15 P.M. The number of ponies for this would be limited to eighteen per team, or four for each player, with two to spare. As casualties occur before the game, a man who mounted himself would require to keep at least six good ponies. Three ponies produced at the ground, fit and well, should be ample for such a game.

In polo the subject of paramount importance is the stud, and this differs according to the inclinations of the individual and the object which he has in view. If a man is preparing for first-class tournaments his best policy is to buy made ponies; if a player enjoys making ponies, and is an expert at it, has special facilities for buying raw ponies cheap, and is in a position to sell when opportunity offers, there is money and amusement to be got from the raw article; if, however, all these recommendations do not exist, he had better confine himself to made ponies. As to the best class of animals to buy, there are great differences of opinion. I personally think that when buying made ponies it is a case of "handsome is as handsome does," so try your pony and buy what suits you best. I prefer the Australian to the Arab, and both to the country-bred. When buying raw animals, much depends on what facilities you have for buying. Given equal opportunities for buying Australians or Arabs, I prefer the Arab.

To the beginner I would say, "Begin on perfectly made Arabs, easy to play, even if slow, and leave Australians, country-breds, and unmade ponies alone till you know the game." For men who desire only to play in a station game for exercise, and do not mind being outclassed by other players, much value can be got out of handy, slow ponies, and these can be readily bought cheap. The country-bred is usually very suitable for this purpose, if he is made and known. The raw country-bred is a very tricky animal, and an unknown quantity.

Finally, if treating the subject from a financial point of view, go carefully into figures before buying anything in the raw.

HUNTING

GENERAL

HUNTING, as we know it in England, has been given a trial in India, but, owing to the peculiarities of the climate, it has not become in any sense universal. The heat of that region during a large portion of the year is sufficient to prostrate any hounds which are not of the country, and there are no indigenous breeds that run by scent. Crosses of all sorts have been tried, but no satisfactory general result attained, so that "hunts" still have to call on the Mother Country for their pack. This incapacity to endure heat has very much curtailed the length of the hunting season, which is generally a very short one. Then, again, even when the climate admits of working the delicate, unacclimatised hound, and the temperature is fairly cool, there is still a hot sun, which, sucking up all the dew and moisture from the surface of the ground, obliterates scent. To obtain a longer season, if not a longer working day, it would be imagined that the hounds might perhaps be kept a year and acclimatised, like the imported horse, and that, although the lack of scent might close the hunt early in the day, yet at any rate the length of the season might be protracted. This, however, is prevented by the unfortunate fact that for some reason hounds gradually lose their "noses" in India, so that packs are obliged to have a strong "draft" imported from England every year. As the "seasons" vary in different places, packs generally pass on their hounds to other packs at the conclusion of their particular season. The only five regular packs are those of Madras and Ootacamund in the Madras presidency, Bombay and Poona in the Bombay presidency, and Peshawur in the Punjaub. The hunting season in Madras and Bombay is from November to the end of January, in Ootacamund and Poona from July to November, and at Peshawur from October to February.

For all these hunts much the same style of horse is required. He should be a sound, hard-working animal, handy, clever across country, and a good, safe jumper. A moderate amount of pace is all that is required. For Peshawur the speciality required is cleverness and a capacity for jumping the so-styled "gridiron." The "gridiron" consists of two, three, or even more fair-sized irrigation ditches running close together, with barely room to "change" in between them. In the Ootacamund country there is practically no fencing, since the run is over "downs"; hence the best sort of horse there is a compact, well-bred, sturdy animal about 15 hands high, with good shoulders, to enable him to go fast down the hills. A suitable horse for hunting should be procurable "made" for Rs.800, or for Rs.400 in the rough. The market is the same as described for the pig-sticker.

BOBBERY PACK

APART from hunting proper in the English sense, there is another form of hunting which has grown up to suit the needs of the lovers of dogs and horses, and the exigencies of the climate. This is the chase of the fox, jackal and hare, with a mixed, or, as it is called in India, a "bobbery pack." This is generally a very amateur kind of sport, but nevertheless it gives much amusement. The "pack" seldom belongs to one man, and, except when actually in the field, the members of it are not even under the charge of anyone in particular. A certain number of men meet for a hunt, each bringing any kind of dog he may happen to possess; terriers of all sorts, spaniels, Airedales, hounds, poodles, country-breds, and in fact any kind of dog, are welcome. With the aid of this so-called pack, they scour the country, pursuing anything they find. The "dogs" do not run by scent, except when in cover, and are "lifted" immediately anyone sees the quarry. The man who sees the game signals to the huntsman and rides in its direction. The dogs hunt and bark, and eventually the animal probably breaks into the open. Immediately the huntsman gallops after him, followed, in any order or disorder, by the dogs, who, viewing him, have a regular "course." The jackal, or whatever it may be, is perhaps caught in the open, or else makes good the next cover, in which latter case the "field" try and command the exits, and, the huntsman entering the cover with the dogs, the game is carried on as before. The number of brushes, as well as the trueness of the sport, varies according to the class of dog used. If the pack includes among them a greyhound or two, the bag is probably a good one numerically, but of little value to the sportsman. The jackal is very crafty, but not fast, and falls an easy prey to the greyhound in the open; the fox and the hare give even greyhounds a fine course. The pack, therefore, should not hold greyhounds, unless the country is not open, or unless hares and foxes are to be the main object. Given a somewhat difficult country the dogs may be as fast as can be got, even when the jackal is the object; and the fox and hare will give even imported English greyhounds a fine run over any type of ground.

The Indian fox is a very little fellow when his tail is left out of consideration, being in weight little more heavy than a good specimen of an

English ferret. He is a most graceful little creature, with any amount of assurance, while his pace and capacity for "jinking" is amazing. An Australian friend of mine, a "shipper," brought me over as a present a very fine pair of Australian greyhounds. We went out with the pair to see if we could find a fox for them. The day previously we had seen one on a large, open, sandy plain, and my friend maintained that it was unsporting to run a little fellow like him with anything larger than terriers. We went out, however, with the two hounds and were lucky enough to find our little fox fair in the middle of the plain, watching our approach from a small tuft of grass. He eventually went off with 20 yards start of the hounds, who gained on him hand over hand and getting within striking distance, dashed at him. A whisk of the tail was seen, and then there was the fox 20 yards away from the disappointed pair and on their flank. The fox went along quite steadily and the hounds had another try at him, their quarry repeating the manœuvre. This game continued for some minutes, when the fox, tiring of the fun, set his head for some cover half a mile off, and with flying brush, ran clean away from the baffled hounds.

A bobbery pack is, however, sometimes run on more business-like principles, and, given a fair country, the sport afforded is almost, if not quite, as good as pig-sticking, which indeed it resembles closely. The fight at the end is of course absent, but, to make up for this, there is the interest which the pack itself affords and the independence ensuing from being able to do without beaters.

Before the fullest enjoyment can be got out of such sport, it is, however, necessary to study the subject in every detail. If the dogs or the horses are too fast, the sport becomes tame; and if not good enough, disappointments are too frequent. Matters should be so arranged that the chances of a kill are well on the side of the hunt, but no more.

The pack should be divided into two classes of dogs, the "hunters" and the "runners." The hunters may be any breed that will work hard and give tongue, and they must be fast enough to be there or thereabouts in a run. A brother officer and myself owned a bobbery pack for fifteen years, and had all sorts of dogs through our hands. The best dogs for hunting that we ever had were spaniels of the fast, hard-working type, such as are used in England for hunting rabbits in hedgerows and brambles. We also had some real wonders of the fox terrier class, with a dash of the bull terrier in them; but the majority of the hunters were fox terriers proper. Then, too, we at one time had half-a-dozen fox-hounds who were excellent hunters and added tone to the music; but they felt the heat too much and were a source of anxiety in the hot weather.

The "hunters" are easy to obtain, as there

are always a selection in barracks, and Rs. 5 will generally tempt "Tommy." The "runners" are not so easy to come by, as both greyhounds and "rampurs" are too fast, and almost any dog of the running type has a tendency to "loaf," instead of joining in the "beat." We bred a class of our own, which, though fast enough to catch a jackal, were nevertheless workmen in cover, thereby giving a great dash to the whole pack, owing to their excellent noses and the pace at which they could carry a hot scent through cover.

Our best runners were the pups of a very staunch native greyhound, the father being a magnificent old tackler called "Joe." Joe, in turn, was a cross between a bull terrier and an ordinary "pye," or country-bred mother. Joe, himself, was in appearance an enormous yellow terrier, weighing 60 lbs., with a short tail; he was fairly fast, and an indefatigable workman—would tackle anything. The pups were very similar in appearance, only lighter in build and faster.

The hunt horses should be stout horses of any size, provided they are handy, bold, clever and good jumpers. If the horse be too fast, it becomes too easy to keep up in a run, and much of the enjoyment is lost. In our hunt, we used to ride our chargers, which thereby became ideal service horses, as they could and would negotiate any obstacle without hesitation; "over" or "into" or "through" they had to go, or else they were useless as hunters; and they very soon became keen, and learnt that where there was a will there was a way. At first we used to ride ponies, but they gave us so many falls that we took to riding horses, and never had reason to regret it.

The actual hunt, too, was run on regular principles. The pack went with the huntsman, while the whip kept well ahead. In open ground, he would be at least a quarter of a mile in front; and if a cover were being drawn, he would take up a position on the far side. In a wheat field, for instance, the master would notice the dogs begin hunting about more energetically than usual; then something would give tongue, and the whole pack would instantly join the speaker. Another whimper, then more, and the whole pack would push along as fast as the scent permitted. The jackal would, meanwhile, be sneaking along, 200 yards in front, at such a pace that the dogs would not be able to gain on him with the generally weak scent, the result being that "jack" would gain some cover from view. He would then make his way to his next cover so swiftly, that, by the time the pack gained the open, the jack would be out of view, and, the scent failing, he would escape without being pressed at all. Put your whip well ahead, however, and all is changed. He hears the first dog speak, and also probably sees the jack's head, as he peeps anxiously through the crop at the approaching pack. Then he sees the whip ahead of him, and wonders what he is doing, as he sits motionless on his horse, while a white handkerchief flutters from his upraised hand. The master, however, does not wonder, for he has been waiting for this signal. He immediately calls the dogs and gallops forward. Presently the jack hears him and begins sneaking along, but not unseen, for the whip keeps a keen eye on him, as he moves with the quarry. Suddenly, the jack sees the game, and, recognising that further concealment is useless, he makes a fair bid for his objective, taking the line which gives him the most cover and the hunt the most obstacles. By this time, the huntsman and pack have shortened the space which formerly separated them from the jack and the whip, and are still hoping to be able to get yet nearer before their approach is discovered. Vain hope! for when the "whip" and his signal are yet some way off, perhaps as much as 200 yards, the master sees the kerchief come down, and the whip start riding, as if for his life, with a wild tally-ho! The pack and the master's horse seem electrified by the joyful sound, for all immediately "lie down" to their work, and strain every nerve towards the sound, till, clearing the cover, they see their whip going in front, still screaming, while the master endeavours to go to his help, trusting to the pack to find its own way. This the dogs do as best they may, and each in his own manner. The "running" dogs, racing mute and doggedly, just keeping pace with the master; the music of the hound, the sharp yap-yap of the terrier, and the despairing screams of the excited spaniels, all becoming fainter and fainter as the hunters gradually lose ground, for the jack is making at present a straight run. Suddenly, however, the whip swerves sharply to his right and disappears, emerging almost at once from what is evidently a "nullah." The master knows that a man on each side is what is wanted; so, turning at once to his right, he aims to cut off the whip, while the yelling "hunters" behind make a still shorter course, all converging on the whip. On the bank of the nullah he turns again to the right, and sees the whip on the far side, and the jack in the stream bed, with the "runners" close up. The hunters, too, arrive in time to catch a brief glimpse of the prey, but soon they are left behind by the pace of the chase. The riders have done all they can for the moment, and now the "runners" are responsible for the result. They gain slightly, but not much. Now one gets closer, favoured by a good bit of going, only to fall back again as he strikes a rough piece, while another has a stroke of luck, and the jack only avoids death by a sharp "jink" at a turn in the nullah, and has gained a strip of thick reeds, into which he plunges, followed closely by the runners. The master instantly halts at the near end of the reeds, while the whip speeds to the far end, both master and whip commanding the nullah. By this time, the baffled runners are lying panting in a puddle of water, having been unable to keep touch with the jack. Within a minute, the hunters commence to arrive, streaming across country in twos and threes. They are immediately urged into the cover. For a time only the rustling of the reeds can be heard, then a whimper; another, and then a full chorus, as the quarry is pressed along through the reeds. In dash the refreshed runners, and soon the welcome "gone away" is heard, for the "jack" has broken across the open with a terrier close to him. He tries every trick known to foxes, but his time has come, for he is worn out, and he soon falls a victim to the trained "bobbery pack."

Such is the class of sport, and anyone can understand the sort of horse required for it; if the whip's horse hesitate a moment at an obstacle, the jack will surely become unsighted and lost, since, during the first phase of the run, there is no one to help him. It requires a clever and handy horse to follow the twists and turns of the wily jack or fox in the midst of a variety of bad going; trappy ditches, nullahs, walls, broken ground and what-not, all to be negotiated as the quarry directs and at top speed. The difference between the hunter and pig-sticker is that the former requires less speed, and can, and, generally speaking, should, be ridden on a snaffle, as the rider has two hands for his reins, and can manage on a snaffle a horse that requires a bit for pig-sticking where one hand is engaged with the spear. The season for hunting is during the cool weather, from October to March, because the dogs cannot hunt in the heat.

The keep of a pack varies with the number of

dogs, but for food alone, Rs. 2 per dog a month should be ample. One servant to ten dogs should be sufficient, and his wages would be about Rs. 7 a month. With all extras, a general charge of Rs. 3 per dog a month would be a fair calculation.

No matter what the quarry, the principle on which it is hunted is the same. There is some variety. The jackal, fox and hare, are the usual game; but in the course of our fifteen years' experience with our pack we compassed the death of the following species:—Jackal, fox, hare, blackbuck, ravine deer, hyena, wolf, pig, wild cat, sambhur stag and porcupine. Of these, the porcupine and pig must, if possible, be avoided, as they kill the dogs too frequently. There is no sport that is better training for a man's eye for country, riding, and quickness of sight, or that makes so well or thoroughly that most delightful of possessions, a really clever, handy horse.

Note on the Packs

The Bombay hounds are a subscription pack, kennelled at Santa Cruz, some fourteen miles from Bombay. A professional huntsman has charge of the kennels and returns to England every summer to purchase and import an entire fresh pack of drafts from the leading English kennels. In the selection of these drafts the huntsman is assisted by any prominent members of the Bombay Hunt who happen to be at home during that particular summer. The old pack is sold off each spring to other hunts and bobbery packs, and a considerable number find their way annually to Ootacamund.

The season opens in December and continues until March, when the hot weather puts an end to the sport. The jackal is the only quarry, and, although less speedy than the fox, it can show a clean pair of heels on occasion and thus furnishes really good runs. The country is terribly rough according to English ideas; the Marole and Andheri Hills are steep and in some places covered with thick jungle, while rocky ground, swamps and cactus are sufficiently plentiful to render the jackal's long swinging gallop fast enough for even the epicure. Sixteen to eighteen couple form a full pack, and fifty horsemen a large field; the weekly programme consists of a Sunday and a mid-week meet. At the end of the season the Jackal Club's point to point races compensate Bombay sportsmen for the lack of a steeplechase meeting. The principal events are:—

1. The Hunt Cup for horses. Point to point. Catch-weights, English and Australians, 12 st. 7 lbs. and over. C.B.'s, 10 st. 7 lbs. and over. Owners up. Distance, 3½ miles.
2. The Pony Hunt Cup for ponies 14.1 and under. Point to point. English and Australians, 14.1, 12 st. Arabs

and C.B.'s, 14.1, 11 st. Ponies, 13.3 and under, allowed 7 lbs. Distance, 3½ miles.

In addition to this meeting, Mr "Jack" Symons, one of the keenest sportsmen and best "spears" in Western India, has for some years past held a private point to point meet every March, giving prizes himself. The races attract much the same fields as the hunt events.

The Poona and Kirkee foxhounds do not confine their attention to the fox, and indeed have most of their best runs after jackal. The Indian fox is small and very fast, and in rocky country can laugh at a pack of English fox-hounds. The Poona season opens with cubbing in June, and continues until early October, when the growing crops, principally "jowari," impede both hounds and riders. In a fair season twenty to twenty-five brace of jackal are accounted for, and the pack is kept up to twenty or twenty-four couple by importation, purchase and breeding. The master must face fully as many difficulties as the average English M.F.H., and in addition to crops and barbed wire, stones and prickly pear obstruct good hunting. The record run of recent seasons lasted for forty-seven minutes in hilly country; and, under an Indian sun, the hardest rider in the Shires might count that gallop a hot thing. The season usually ends with a point to point meeting and a hunt dinner.

The Madras hounds hunt twice weekly from

December to March, principally on the Guindy side, and the hunting country lies within easier reach of Madras sportsmen than Santa Cruz or Bombay. The pack is well supported, and hunting holds its own against all rival sports. At Bangalore a private pack has existed for some seasons past, but, although known as the "Bangalore Hounds," and thrown open to the station, the hunt can hardly be reckoned a permanent institution.

The most celebrated pack in the Southern Presidency is undoubtedly the Ootacamund. Supported by European and native sportsmen, and fortunate in the possession of a fine hunting country, the Ootacamund holds the premier place in the sports of the summer capital. The jackals bred on the breezy downs give splendid runs, and a heavy-weight must find good horses to carry him up and down the steep banks within view of the hounds. The annual hunt races spread over two days, and are confined to horses that hold the Ootacamund Master's Certificate. The first day's programme consists of flat races of Rs.250 in value, the second of point to point events, of which the following are the most important. The hunt cup is an unique trophy in Indian sporting circles, and was first instituted in 1892 when Lord Wenlock, then Governor of Madras, rode second in the race.

THE OOTACAMUND HUNT CUP, value Rs.600, presented by Colonel the Honourable H. T. Lawley, with Rs.350 from the fund, of which

Rs.200 goes to the winner, Rs.100 to the second, and Rs.50 to the third. Point to point race for horses, the property of subscribers of not less than Rs.100 to the hunt, and that have been regularly hunted during the season. Certificates signed by the master to be lodged with entry. Australians and English catch-weights over 12 st., Arabs and country-breds, C.W., over 10 st. 7 lbs. Winner of any point to point race during the last four years to carry 10 lbs. extra for each race won. Riders other than owners to carry 7 lbs. extra. No owner to start more than three horses. The cup to become the absolute property of any owner winning three consecutive years. The cup may not be taken out of India until won outright. Not less than four miles over a fair hunting country.

THE PONY HUNT POINT TO POINT RACE. A cup, value Rs.150, to the winner, and Rs.50 to the second. For ponies that have been regularly hunted with the Ootacamund hounds throughout the season; master's certificate to accompany the entry. Australians and English ponies, 14.2, to carry 12 st. 7 lbs.; Arabs and country-breds, 14.2, to carry 11 st. 7 lbs.; W.I. with penalties. Distance, about two miles.

The lady members of the hunt have two special races at this meeting, one for horses and one for ponies, but big fields are seldom forthcoming.

With the exception of the Peshawar Vale Hounds, supported by the large garrison of that northern town, few other Indian packs have risen even temporarily to general notice. For several seasons a good pack hunted in the neighbourhood of Mozufferpore, with imported foxhounds, huntsmen in pink and all the usual formalities, but the hunt never became a permanent institution. In days gone by, a Calcutta hunt flourished in the capital, but a recent attempt made by the Earl of Suffolk to reinstate the sport in public favour has signally failed. Paper-chasing occupies the attention of those who should support a hunt, and a division of the riding contingent into paper-chasing and hunting sections imperils the chances of both sports.

It would seem that hunting cannot flourish in level and uninteresting country, and the flat plains of Bengal do not offer the variety and excitement obtainable at Santa Cruz, Poona, or on the downs of Ootacamund. From the point of view of the master of a small bobbery pack, however, flat country has the advantage of rendering hunting possible with a small pack. To any lover of horse and hound, the training and hunting of five or six couple of assorted dogs will afford the keenest enjoyment. Jackals abound; all that remains is to catch them. Two cautions can never be too often repeated. Don't ride over crops; and don't treat the native husbandman like a dumb beast of burden. Learn his language, treat him with ordinary tact, and he will probably prove a friend indeed.

RACING AND STEEPLE-CHASING

To render in concise form a complete account of racing in India is a task which presents no little difficulty, and on many points of interest the information contained in the following chapter must assume a very general character.

On the Indian turf the place of the Jockey Club is filled by the Calcutta and Western India Turf Clubs. The authority of the latter body is confined to the Bombay Presidency and adjacent districts under the civil or military authority of the Bombay Government, while the rest of India and Burma is subject to the rules of the Calcutta Club. But the rules of the two bodies are now identical, and since the stewards reciprocate in all matters of detail, racing may be considered as subject to one uniform jurisdiction. The members of these clubs are elected by ballot, and annually appoint five of their number to act as stewards. The handicappers, starters, and secretaries are paid officials, and the last-named, assisted by a clerical staff in Calcutta and Bombay, attend to the issue of fortnightly racing calendars, official notices, records, etc.

The entrance fee to the Turf Club is Rs.150, except for officers of His Majesty's regiments, who pay only Rs.50. Resident subscription is Rs.25 annually.

The enormous distances between the various racing centres tend to localise sport with a consequent limitation of gate-money and entries, and the inevitable corollary of small stakes.

(1) All race meetings in India must be sanctioned by the stewards of one or other of the turf clubs, except those at which no prize exceeds Rs.49 in value, and at which all the prizes are of fixed and published value. In order to avoid the trouble of obtaining such sanction, and to maintain a free hand in the management of all details, organisers of Gymkhanas and Skye races restrict the value of their stakes to Rs.49. Such unrecognised meetings are held in nearly every military district throughout India, and depend mainly on the shifting support of local garrisons. Hacks and polo ponies provide the bulk of the sport, and in this form racing is brought within the capacity of the most moderate incomes. Skye meetings and Gymkhanas flourish in the following stations :—

Bangalore.	Jalpaiguri.	Prome.
Bankipur.	Jullundur.	Rawalpindi.
Burdwan.	Kirkee.	Secunderabad.
Cawnpore.	Lucknow.	Shillong.
Coconada.	Maymyo.	Simla.
Darjeeling.	Meerut.	Sonepore.
Dehra Dun.	Mozufferpore.	Tollygunge (Calcutta).
Futteh Mardan.	Ootacamund.	
Fyzabad.	Peshawar.	Umballa.
Gorakhpur.		

The term Gymkhana is becoming restricted to the special class of entertainment known as "Bumblepuppy," the programmes at which consist of such events as hat trimming competitions, and potato and bucket races, with perhaps a polo scurry to conclude the card.

(2) The second class of meetings comprises those which, falling within the jurisdiction of the turf clubs, depend wholly or principally upon local support. Of these there were some thirty during 1902-3, as detailed in the list below. The class of animals catered for, and the value of the stakes offered vary from year to year on every course, and many of the meetings themselves cannot be regarded as annual fixtures.

(3) The official racing year extends from 1st April to 31st March, but the racing season proper from September to February only. The attraction of valuable stakes has overcome the difficulties of distance, and the racing army travels from Poona in September to Calcutta in December, and westward again to Bombay in February. Detachments halt by the way for the December and February meets in Lucknow, while the stewards at Bangalore in July and at Meerut in March endeavour with indifferent success to extend the limits of the season. Stakes, value Rs.1500 (£100) and over, are offered on these six courses alone, the steeplechases at Tollygunge being considered as an item in the January programme in Calcutta.

Photo] CALCUTTA RACE COURSE [*Kapp & Co., Calcutta*

With the exception of Bangalore and Poona, where some attempt can be made to imitate the elasticity of English turf, Indian race-courses are mostly level and very hard. The absence of "straight" courses is very noticeable. None of the larger courses can boast even a "straight five furlongs," and on the Bombay and Calcutta tracks the run in does not exceed three furlongs. For training purposes special tan or litter tracks are provided at all the principal centres, but can never be more than a makeshift, and few fore-legs can stand more than two or three seasons of racing.

Approximate Lengths of Indian Courses.

	M.	F.		M.	F.		M.	F.
Bangalore .	1	2	Karachi	1	3	Rawalpindi	1	3
Berhampore	1	3	Lucknow	1	6	Simla .	0	3
Bombay .	1	4	Madras	1	4	Umballa .	2	1
Calcutta .	1	5	Meerut	1	4	Wellington	0	5
Dacca .	1	3	Poona .	1	4			

The classification of horses, with its accompanying and intricate scale of weights, needs some explanation.

Rule No. 34 of the C.T.C. Rules of Racing reads :—

"Horses are of four classes—English, Australian, country-bred, and Arab. European and North American horses are classed with English, African and South American horses with Australian, Persian horses with Arab, and other Asiatic horses with country-bred. . . .

"A country-bred is a horse got, foaled, and kept in India until he first starts for a race."

The Australian race-horse has supplanted his English cousin on the Indian turf, and although a small number of English horses are still imported annually and annex a few of the more valuable stakes, the vast majority of fields consist of Australian horses. Experience tends to show that the Australian adapts himself more readily to the Indian climate than the English thoroughbred, whose brittle, "shelly" feet give endless trouble on the hard ground to which he is so unaccustomed. A good class Australian with staying power can be purchased much cheaper than a horse who has shown any form in long-distance events in England. On the other hand, a useful plater can sometimes be secured at a low figure in England who will outclass the fields in the valuable sprint races at Calcutta and Poona. On the Calcutta side, Arab and country-bred horses are practically unknown, and the attempts to foster these classes at Poona and Bombay have not as yet achieved any conspicuous success.

Complete scales of weights for age and class, differing for each month in the year, appear in every racing calendar, and the extremes, those for January and December, are as follows:—

JANUARY.

	¾ mile and under.								Over 1¼ miles and up to 1½ miles.							
	3 years.		4 years.		5 years.		6 and aged.		3 years.		4 years.		5 years.		6 and aged	
	st.	lbs.	st.	lbs.	st.	lbs.	st.	lbs.	st.	lbs.	st.	lbs.	st.	lbs.	st.	lbs.
English	7	13	9	1	9	3	9	3	6	12	8	10	9	1	9	3
Australasian	8	8	9	2	9	3	9	3	7	11	8	12	9	3	9	3
Country-bred	5	0	6	8	7	1	7	3	3	9	5	7	6	9	7	3
Arab	4	0	5	8	6	1	6	3	2	9	4	7	5	9	6	3
	Over ¾ mile and up to 1 mile.								Over 1½ miles and up to 2 miles.							
	st.	lbs.	st.	lbs.	st.	lbs.	st.	lbs.	st.	lbs.	st.	lbs.	st.	lbs.	st.	lbs.
English	7	9	9	0	9	3	9	3	6	9	8	9	9	1	9	3
Australasian	8	5	9	1	9	3	9	3	7	9	8	12	9	3	9	3
Country-bred	4	7	6	2	7	0	7	3	3	5	5	5	6	8	7	3
Arab	3	7	5	2	6	0	6	3	2	5	4	5	5	8	6	3
	Over 1 mile and up to 1¼ miles.								Over 2 miles.							
	st.	lbs.	st.	lbs.	st.	lbs.	st.	lbs.	st.	lbs.	st.	lbs.	st.	lbs.	st.	lbs.
English	7	5	8	13	9	3	9	3	6	3	8	7	9	0	9	3
Australasian	8	2	9	0	9	3	9	3	7	5	8	11	9	3	9	3
Country-bred	4	3	6	0	6	13	7	3	3	1	4	13	6	6	7	3
Arab	3	3	5	0	5	13	6	3	2	1	3	13	5	6	6	3

DECEMBER.

	¾ mile and under.								Over 1¼ miles and up to 1½ miles.							
	3 years.		4 years.		5 years.		6 and aged.		3 years.		4 years.		5 years.		6 and aged.	
	st.	lbs.	st.	lbs.	st.	lbs.	st.	lbs.	st.	lbs.	st.	lbs.	st.	lbs.	st.	lbs.
English	9	1	9	3	9	3	9	3	8	7	9	0	9	3	9	3
Australasian	8	6	9	2	9	3	9	3	7	8	8	12	9	2	9	3
Country-bred	6	3	7	1	7	3	7	3	5	5	6	8	7	2	7	3
Arab	5	3	6	1	6	3	6	3	4	5	5	8	6	2	6	3
	Over ¾ mile and up to 1 mile.								Over 1½ miles and up to 2 miles.							
	st.	lbs.	st.	lbs.	st.	lbs.	st.	lbs.	st.	lbs.	st.	lbs.	st.	lbs.	st.	lbs.
English	8	13	9	3	9	3	9	3	8	6	9	0	9	3	9	3
Australasian	8	3	9	1	9	3	9	3	7	6	8	11	9	2	9	3
Country-bred	6	0	6	13	7	3	7	3	5	3	6	7	7	2	7	3
Arab	5	0	5	13	6	3	6	3	4	3	5	7	6	2	6	3
	Over 1 mile and up to 1¼ miles.								Over 2 miles.							
	st.	lbs.	st.	lbs.	st.	lbs.	st.	lbs.	st.	lbs.	st.	lbs.	st.	lbs.	st.	lbs.
English	8	11	9	2	9	3	9	3	8	3	8	13	9	3	9	3
Australasian	8	0	9	0	9	3	9	3	7	2	8	10	9	2	9	3
Country-bred	5	12	6	12	7	3	7	3	4	11	6	5	7	2	7	3
Arab	4	12	5	12	6	3	6	3	3	11	5	5	6	1	6	3

No horse may carry less than 6 stone in a flat race, 9 stone in a hurdle race, and 9 stone 7 lbs in a steeplechase, and this rule is not interfered with by the above figures, lower weights being inserted in the scale only to show the relative weights of the different classes. The necessity for so much nicety is due to the fact that English horses date their ages from 1st January and Australians from 1st August in each year. Thus in January 1904, an English horse foaled in January 1901, and an Australian foaled in August 1900, must both run as three-year-olds, although the latter will then be six months older than his rival. In December the position is reversed, and the English horse has the advantage in age, which this carefully-adjusted scale attempts to neutralise.

At first sight, the concessions granted to Arabs and country-breds appear enormous; but practically they have no effect, since these classes cannot attempt to compete with English and Australian horses.

Of recent years some attempts have been made, notably at Patiala, to breed country-bred race-horses, and the Bombay programmes now include a number of special races closed to this class. Owners of Arab horses have been similarly encouraged by the W.I.T.C. Stewards, but Arabs are seen at their best among the pony classes.

A pony is defined as "a horse measuring 14 hands 2 inches or under." At the lowest estimate, two-thirds of the races run annually in India are confined to ponies; in many districts horse-racing does not exist at all, and the pony takes second place in Calcutta alone. The climate and other considerations tend to the prevalence of pony-racing; and, avoiding the vexed question of comparison with the more "legitimate" sport according to English ideas, it is sufficient for the purposes of this article to note that the racing pony appears to be growing rather than declining in public favour. All classes are catered for, from the 12 hands Indo-Burman to the 14.2 Australian, and the conditions are variously framed to bring the different heights and classes together.

Of recent years a marked improvement has taken place in the Australian racing pony, while the Englishman, once supreme on the Indian turf, now rarely secures a winning bracket. Occasionally a well-measured country-bred defies opposition in the open races, but such exceptions only prove the rule of Australian superiority.

Rule 88:—"In weight for inch races the allowance shall be 3 lbs. for every quarter of an inch; . . . no allowance for anything less than a quarter of an inch."

In Calcutta, Arabs and country-breds are not encouraged, and the pony races are divided between two classes:—(1) English and Australians 14.1, and others 14.2 and under; (2) English and Australians 13.3½, and others 14.1 and under.

The conditions of the Civil Service Cup at Lucknow, the principal pony race in India, are given elsewhere.

The long programmes of Poona and Bombay depend mainly upon the pony classes, and the Arab tends to improve his position at the expense of the country-bred. The Arab pony between 13.3 and 14.0 hands may be regarded as the mainstay of racing in Western India. The country-bred, whose improvement is asserted by several well-known authorities, has not hitherto ratified their good opinion in the pages of the Calendar.

The following lists comprise the principal races for horses and ponies, compiled from the programmes and prospectuses of 1903:—

HORSES.

	Name of Race.	Stakes.	Distances.	Terms of Race.	Class of Horse.
June—Mysore—		Rupees.			
	Arab Plate	1,500	1¼ miles	W.A.	Arabs
	Maharajah's Cup	2,500	1 m. 3 furls.	Handicap	,,
	Dewan's Cup	1,500	1¼ miles	,,	Country-breds
	Birthday Cup	2,000	1¼ ,,	,,	Horses
July—Bangalore—					
	Trial Stakes	1,500	1¼ ,,	W.A. and C.	,,
	Mysore Maharajah's Cup	4,000	1¼ ,,	Handicap	,,
	August Stakes	1,200	1¼ ,,	,,	,,
Sept.—Poona—					
1st day	Trial Stakes	3,000	1 mile	Special	,,
2nd day	Western India Stakes	7,500	1¼ miles	Handicap	,,
	The Criterion	2,000	7 furls.	Special	,,
3rd day	September Stakes	2,000	1 mile	,,	,,
4th day	Ganeshkind Stakes	4,000	6 furls.	Handicap	,,
	Steward's Purse	2,000	1¼ miles	,,	,,
5th day	Oriental Stakes	4,000	1½ ,,	,,	,,
	October Stakes	2,000	6 furls.	Special	,,
6th day	Poona Handicap	2,000	5 ,,	Handicap	,,
	Arabs and Country-breds.				
1st day	Aga Khan's Commem. Plate	2,000	1¼ miles	W.A. reduced 7 lbs.	Arabs

	Name of Race.	Stakes.	Distances.	Terms of Race.	Class of Horse.
Sept.—POONA—		Rupees.			
1st day . .	Breeders' Plate . . .	2,000	6 furls.	Handicap	Country-breds
2nd day . .	Poona Derby . . .	3,000	$1\frac{1}{2}$ miles	W.A. reduced 7 lbs.	Arabs
3rd day . .	Aga Khan's Purse . .	1,500	1 mile	Handicap	,,
4th day . .	Governor's Cup . . .	4,000	R. C. & Dist.	,,	,,
	Merchant's Cup . . .	2,000	1 mile	,,	Country-breds
5th day . .	Winner's Handicap . .	1,500	$1\frac{1}{2}$ miles	,,	Arabs
	Turf Club Cup . . .	2,000	$1\frac{1}{4}$,,	,,	Country-breds
Dec.—MADRAS—	Ampthill's Cup . . .	3,000	R. C.	,,	Horses
,, CALCUTTA—					
1st Extra . .	Maiden Horse Race . .	2,000	7 furls.	W.A. & C. reduced 7 lbs.	
	Club Plate	1,200	$1\frac{1}{4}$ miles	,,	,,
2nd Extra .	Fort Plate . . .	2,000	5 furls.	,,	,,
	December Plate . . .	2,000	$1\frac{1}{4}$ miles	,,	,,
	Corinthian Plate . .	1,300	R. C.	,,	,,
	First Meeting.				
1st day . .	THE TRIALS . . .	10,000	1 mile	W.A. and C.	,,
	Paddock Plate . . .	2,600	$1\frac{1}{4}$ miles	Handicap	,,
2nd day . .	THE VICEROY'S CUP (£100 Cup)	27,000	$1\frac{3}{4}$,,	W.A. and C.	,,
	Calcutta Plate . . .	3,700	7 furls.	Handicap	,,
3rd day . .	COOCH-BEHAR CUP (£100 Cup) . . .	6,000	$1\frac{1}{4}$ miles	,,	,,
	Sandown Park Plate . .	4,500	5 furls.	,,	,,

4th day . .	Lawn Plate . .	2,000	6 ,,	,,	,,
	MACPHERSON CUP . .	6,000	St Leger	,,	,,
	Chowringhee Plate .	4,000	6 furls.	,,	,,
	New Year Plate . .	2,000	R. C.	,,	,,
	Dealer's Plate . .	2,000	6 furls.	W.A.	Australian
	Second Meeting.				
1st day . .	THE KING'S PLATE .	13,000	R. C.	Handicap	Horses
	THE METROPOLITAN .	10,000	6 furls.	,,	,,
	Kidderpore Plate .	2,500	$1\frac{1}{4}$ miles	,,	,,
2nd day . .	Hooghly Plate . .	3,700	5 furls.	,,	,,
	Merchant's Plate .	6,000	$1\frac{1}{2}$ miles	,,	,,
Feb.—LUCKNOW—					
1st day . .	Steward's Cup . .	5,000	5 furls.	,,	Horses
2nd day . .	Calcutta Stakes . .	1,500	1 mile	,,	Special
3rd day . .	Dilkhusha Stakes .	1,800	$1\frac{1}{4}$ miles	,,	Horses
Feb.—BOMBAY—					
1st day . .	Mansfield Plate . .	3,000	6 furls.	Handicap	Horses
	Mahaluxhmi Stakes .	2,000	9 ,,	Special	,,
	Bombay Derby . .	3,000	1 m. 3 furls.	W.A. and C.	Arabs
2nd day . .	GRAND WESTERN H'CAP .	10,000	9 furls.	Handicap	Horses
	Importer's Plate . .	2,000	5 ,,	Special	,,
	Produce Stakes . .	2,000	1 mile	Handicap	Country-breds
3rd day . .	Colaba Plate . .	3,000	1 m. 3 furls.	Special	Horses
	Sir C. Jehangir's Purse .	2,000	9 furls.	Handicap	Arabs
	Stud Stakes . .	2,000	6 ,,	,,	Country-breds
4th day . .	Exeter Stakes . .	4,000	7 ,,	,,	Horses
	Stand Plate . .	2,000	5 ,,	Special	,,
	Champion Stakes .	2,000	1 m. 3 furls.	Handicap	Country-breds
5th day . .	BYCULLA CLUB CUP .	5,500	1 m. 5 ,,	,,	Horses
	Importer's Handicap .	1,500	6 furls.	Special	,,

	Name of Race.	Stakes.	Distances.	Terms of Race.	Class of Horse.
Feb.—BOMBAY—		Rupees.			
5th day . .	Turf Club Cup . . .	3,000	1 m. 5 furls.	Handicap	Arabs
	Second Dealers . . .	2,000	6 furls.	Special	,,
March—MEERUT—					
1st day . .	Turf Club Cup . . .	1,500	5 ,,	Handicap	Special
3rd day . .	Cambridgeshire Stakes .	1,300	1¼ miles.	,,	,,

PONIES.

	Name of Race.	Stakes.	Distances.	Terms of Race.	Class of Horse.
June—MYSORE— .	Installation Cup . . .	2,000	7 furls.	Handicap	Ponies 14.2
Sept.—POONA—					
1st day . .	Maiden Stakes . . .	2,000	7 ,,	W.I.	Arabs 14.0
	New Stakes . . .	2,000	6 ,,	,,	Ponies 14.2
	Stand Plate . . .	1,500	½ mile	,,	,, 14.0
2nd day . .	Dealers' Plate . . .	2,000	1 ,,	,,	Arabs 14.0
	Arab Pony Derby . .	2,500	6 furls.	,,	,, 13.3
	International Stakes . .	3,000	5 ,	Handicap	Ponies 14.1
3rd day . .	Wanowrie Stakes . .	3,000	6 ,,	W.I.	Arabs 14.0
	Lilliputs	1,500	½ mile	,,	,, 13.3
4th day . .	Coronation Stakes . .	3,000	7 furls.	Handicap	Ponies 14.2
	Lawn Stakes . . .	2,000	5 ,,	,,	Arabs 13.3
5th day . .	Paddock Stakes . . .	1,500	5 ,,	,,	Ponies 14.0
	Kirkee Cup . . .	1,500	5 ,,	,,	Arabs 14.0
	Ghorpuri Stakes . . .	1,500	7 ,,	,,	,, 13.3
6th day . .	Desert Handicap . .	1,500	1 mile	,,	,, 14.0
	Lilliput Handicap . .	1,500	½ mile	,,	,, 13.3
	Commissioners' Purse .	1,500	6 furls.	,,	,,	Ponies 14.1

Nov.—LUCKNOW—	ARMY CUP	2,000	7 ,,	Special	Arabs 14.0
Dec.—DACCA—	K.A.O. Purse	1,500	7 ,,	Handicap	Ponies 14.1
,, CALCUTTA—	*First Meeting.*				
1st day	Maiden Pony Plate	1,500	5 ,,	W.I.	Arabs and C.B.'s 14.1, and others 13.3½
	International Plate	4,000	7 ,,	,,	Arabs and C.B.'s 14.2, and others 14.1
2nd day	Eclipse Pony Plate	3,000	7 ,,	,,	Arabs and C.B.'s 14.1, and others 13.3½ and under
3rd day	Gunny Meah Cup	2,000	R.C.	Handicap	Ponies, 14.2
	Stand Cup	1,500	7 furls.	,,	Arabs and C.B.'s 14.1, and others 13.3½ and under
4th day	Innovation Handicap	1,600	1 mile	,,	Arabs and C.B.'s 14.2, and others 14.1 and under
	Pony Handicap	1,600	6 furls.	,,	Arabs and C.B.'s 14.1, and others 13.3½ and under
	Second Meeting.				
1st day	Belvedere Pony Plate	1,600	1 mile	,,	,, ,,
	New Plate	1,600	5 furls.	,,	Ponies 14.2
2nd day	Scurry Handicap	1,600	5 ,,	,,	Arabs and C.B.'s 14.1, and others 13.3½ and under
	Pony Purse	1,600	7 ,,	,,	Arabs and C.B.'s 14.2, and others 14.1 and under
Feb.—LUCKNOW—					
1st day	Great Oudh Handicap	4,500	6 ,,	,,	Arabs 14.1
2nd day	CIVIL SERVICE CUP	8,000	6 ,,	,,	C.B.'s 14.1 to carry 9 st.; Arabs 14.1 to carry 7 st. 10 lbs.; Aust. and English 13.3½ to carry 8 st. 10 lbs.; penalties and allowances

	Name of Race.	Stakes.	Distances.	Terms of Race.	Class of Horse.
Feb.—LUCKNOW—		Rupees.			
2nd day	Martiniere Plate	1,500	2 miles	,,	Arabs 14.1
3rd day	Goomtee Stakes	1,500	5 furls.	,,	Arabs and C.B.'s 14.1, others 13.3½ and under
	Desert Handicap	1,500	1000 yds.	,,	Arabs 14.1
	Lucknow Stakes	1,500	1 mile	Special	Ponies
Feb.—BOMBAY—					
1st day	The Mesurier Stakes	2,500	6 furls.	W.I.	Arabs 14.0
	Gaye Cup	2,000	7 ,,	,,	Ponies 14.2
	Lilliput Plate	2,000	5 ,,	,,	,, 14.0
2nd day	Imperial Stakes	4,000	6 ,,	Handicap	,, 14.1
	Dealer's Plate	2,000	1 mile	,,	Arabs 14.0
	Paddock Stakes	2,000	5 furls.	W.I.	,, 13.3
	New Stakes	1,500	½ mile	Special	,, ,,
3rd day	Steward's Purse	2,000	5 furls.	Handicap	Ponies 14.2
	Melton Stakes	2,000	6 ,,	Special	Arabs 14.0
	Asian Stakes	1,500	7 ,,	Handicap	,, 13.3
4th day	Lawn Stakes	1,500	5 ,,	,,	Ponies 14.1
	Town Plate	2,000	1¼ miles	,,	Arabs 14.0
	Midget Plate	1,500	5 furls.	,,	,, 13.3
5th day	Bedouin Stakes	1,500	6 ,,	,,	,, 14.0
	Innovation Plate	2,000	6 ,,	,,	Ponies 14.2
	Small Pony Plate	1,500	½ mile	,,	,, 14.0
March—MEERUT—					
1st day	Silver Cup	2,000	5 furls.	,,	Arabs 14.1
2nd day	Gold Cup	2,000	,,	,,	Eng. & Aust. 13.3½, others 14.1 and under

"A 'maiden' is a horse or (pony) which has never won a race (other than a match or private sweepstake) of the value of Rs.200 at any recognised meeting in India; or in any other country.

There are now two official measurers, Messrs Beresford and Gray, the secretaries of the race clubs. These gentlemen visit the principal racing centres during each year, and grant certificates of measurement to the owners of ponies brought before them. A register of all particulars certified in these measurements is kept by both clubs.

11. In the measurement of a pony the following rules shall be strictly observed:—

(*a*) The pony shall stand stripped on a perfectly level platform.

(*b*) The head shall be so held that a line from the poll to the wither would be parallel to the platform. The fore legs from the point of the shoulder, and the hind legs from the back downwards, shall be as perpendicular to the platform, and as parallel to each other, as the conformation of the horse allows.

(*c*) The wither may be shaved, but the mane must not be pulled down, or the skin of the neck or wither in any way interfered with.

(*d*) The pony shall not be held or touched by any person not approved by the Official Measurer.

(*e*) The measurement shall be made at the highest point of the wither with a measuring rod of a pattern approved by the Stewards, and no allowance shall be made for shoes.

The fees credited to a special fund are:—

For every pony presented for measurement, ... Rs. 30
For every measurement, . . Rs. 20
For every certified copy of an entry in the register, . . . Rs. 2

The following lists comprise the principal meets held under the rules of the Calcutta and Western Indian Turf Clubs during the season 1902-03:—

Class I.

Month.	Meeting.	No. of Days.	Value of Highest Stake.
			Rupees.
July.	Bangalore . .	3	3,500
Sept.	Poona . . .	8	6,500
Nov.	Lucknow . . .	3	2,000
Dec.	Madras . . .	3	3,000
”	Calcutta . . .	4	16,650
Jan.	Tollygunge . .	2	4,000
”	Calcutta . . .	3	10,000
Feb.	Lucknow . . .	3	8,000
”	Bombay . . .	5	10,000
March.	Meerut . . .	3	1,500

Class II.

Month.	Meeting.	No. of Days.	Value of Highest Stake.	
			Rupees.	
April.	Karachi . .	2	350	...
”	Peshawar . .	2	150	Ponies.
”	Rangoon . .	4	500	”
May.	Mahableswar .	2	100	”

Month.	Meeting.	No. of Days.	Value of Highest Stake.	
			Rupees.	
May.	Ootacamund . .	4	1,000	...
"	Wellington . .	3	900	...
"	Dibrugarh . .	1	200	Ponies.
"	Quetta . . .	2	200	...
"	Simla . . .	3	350	Ponies.
June.	Bangalore . .	4	200	...
"	Rangoon . .	1	200	Ponies.
July.	Poona (extra) .	2	200	...
Aug. & Sept.	Calcutta Monsoon	5	750	...
"	Poona extra . .	7	200	...
"	Secunderabad .	2	200	...
"	Ootacamund Hunt	2	200	...
"	Dehra . . .	2	200	Ponies.
Oct.	Quetta . . .	3	200	...
"	Meerut . . .	2	200	Ponies.
"	Poona Extra . .	1	200	...
"	Karachi . .	3	200	...
"	Lucknow . .	2	700	...
"	Maymyo . .	1	350	Ponies.
"	Rangoon . .	3	700	"
Nov.	Umballa . .	3	700	...
"	Bangalore . .	2	150	...
"	Rangoon . .	1	200	Ponies.
"	Fort Stedman .	3	100	"
"	Berhampore. .	2	500	...
"	Meerut . . .	3	200	...
"	Mandalay . .	3	100	Ponies.
Dec.	Dacca . . .	3	1,500	...
"	Tezpur . . .	2	300	Ponies.
"	Cachar . . .	2	200	"
"	Prome . . .	2	200	"
"	Calcutta Extra .	2	1,100	...
"	Bombay Extra .	2	200	...
Jan.	Calcutta Extra .	1	900	...
"	Rangoon . .	1	150	Ponies.
"	Dibrugarh . .	3	250	"
"	Rampore Boalia .	2	200	...
"	Bombay Extra .	4	200	...
"	Chittagong . .	3	1,300	Ponies.

Month.	Meeting.	No. of Days.	Value of Highest Stake.	
			Rupees.	
Jan.	Fort Stedman .	1	500	Ponies.
„	Calcutta Extra .	1	900	...
Feb.	Mozuffarpore .	2	99	...
„	Bombay Extra .	1	200	...
„	Calcutta Extra .	2	900	...
„	Bangalore . .	2	200	...
„	Bombay Extra .	1	200	...
„	Kathiawar . .	2	200	...
March.	Umballa . .	3	700	...
„	Jorhat . . .	2	200	...
„	Rawalpindi . .	3	500	...
„	Native Cavalry .	1	199	...
„	Bombay Extra .	3	200	...

The fluctuation of Indian racing is exemplified by the absence from the above list of such well-known meetings as Barrackpore, Cawnpore, Lahore, Midnapore, Mysore, Patiala, Raneegunge, and Sonepore, ancient strongholds of the sport.

At Mysore the Maharajah has offered Rs. 20,000 as a fresh impetus to racing in Southern India, and in June 1903 the first meeting was held under the management of H. Donne, Esq. All the races were Rs. 1000 in value, two reach Rs. 2000, and the Maharanee's Cup for Arabs Rs. 2500. These prizes place the meeting in the first class of my general classification, and should assist the entries at the subsequent and adjacent meeting at Bangalore.

Horses imported from England are subjected to neither quarantine nor veterinary inspection, but Australian shipments are "passed" by a Government V.S. before landing.

Freight from England averages £20 per horse, while a horse-box will cost about £10. For a single animal it will not usually be worth while to engage a special attendant for the voyage, and £5 to the ship's butcher will go far to ensure its comfort and safety.

The agents of the Anchor Line, Liverpool, now supply boxes at a fixed rate, "and undertake all shipping arrangements." The rate for insurance is about £4, 10s. per £100.

Import duty in all cases will be the usual 5 per cent. *ad valorem*.

Anyone desiring to purchase a race-horse in England for despatch to India could not do better than place himself in the hands of the International Horse Agency, whose representative in India is Mr H. E. Abbott, c/o Editor, *Indian Planters' Gazette*, Calcutta.

From Australia, whence large shipments of horses reach India throughout the summer and autumn, the freight is £8 per head. For this sum, however, a stall 9 feet long and only 2½ feet wide is provided, but valuable horses are usually allocated double width at a charge of £16. Insurance, 4½ to 5 per cent. Any importer would gladly include a single animal in his own shipment for a small commission.

Full directions for the management of horses on board ship are given in "The Transport of Horses by Sea," a handy little book by E. E.

Martin, A.V.D., published by Messrs Thacker, Spink, & Co., of Calcutta, at Rs.2. Horses should be shipped in fair working condition, having been placed on a laxative diet several days before embarkation, and on arrival at his destination it is most important to give an animal plenty of time to recover from the effects of the voyage before setting him to work, or even despatching him on a railway journey.

The amateur trainer still reigns supreme at the vast majority of smaller meetings, but the professional has ousted him completely from "first-class" racing. Some of the larger owners, such as Mr A. A. Apcar, the late Maharajah of Patiala, and Mr "J. B." employ their own trainers, but most of the others will gladly undertake the care of a horse or pony at Rs.80 per mensem during the racing season. Among the more prominent trainers are J. D. Scott, who himself owns a considerable string, and summers at Dehra Doon; Tom Scott of Patiala, perhaps the finest cross-country rider now in India; Heywood of Lucknow, who trains for Colonel Beaver and others; the veteran Oscar Dignum, Norton, Pearson, and Smallman, another fine cross-country and hurdle race rider, who trains in Calcutta. Poona, Bangalore, Lucknow, and Darjeeling are favourite stations for summering horses.

Jockeys' fees are Rs.50 losing and Rs.100 winning mounts in flat races value Rs.200 and over; half these sums in races of less value.

The fees in "jump" races are double those allowed in flat races.

"The fees to native jockeys shall be half the amount allowed to other jockeys."

The leading Australian and English riders are:—Ramshaw, Robinson, Cowell, Southall, Penton, Hoyt, and a few others; Murphy and Ames are exponents of the "American" seat, which has not yet become the fashion in India. Successful native jockeys are Heeroo, Kamad, Oomerkhan, Baichan, and C. B. Mahomed.

Among the cross-country division Tom Scott, Smallman, Burns, Lansdown, Morrison and Hoyt are the most conspicuous professionals.

The official list contains some fifty G.R.'s, but these in India are a kaleidoscopic community, here to-day, gone to-morrow. Amongst the best known performers are:—

Major Stisted, Captains Randall and Kennard, Messrs Barrow, Barton, Barrett, Courage, Deakin, Gresson, Hamilton, Lance, and Pallin.

Increasing cost has placed first-class racing beyond the scope of ordinary incomes, and the list of leading owners is comprised mainly of wealthy natives. Long prices are paid for imported horses, and the class of animals competing for the more valuable stakes steadily improves. No comparison is possible between Indian and Australian or English form. A study of book form might suggest the conclusion that the Viceroy's Cup or the Indian Grand National lie at the mercy of any moderate performer at Epsom or Aintree, but experience has proved that in these races victory is hardly less uncertain than in the classic events of the English racing season. The exhausting sea voyage and enervating climate produce widely different effects upon individual constitutions, and even between horses imported in the same steamer and trained in the same stable, a three-stone reversal of form would not be without precedent. A frequent cause of failure to confirm Australian or English running would appear to lie in the common practice of training and racing horses within a few months of their importation, and, with due respect to adverse and weighty opinion, it may be doubted whether the average imported thoroughbred can be acclimatised in less than eighteen months from his arrival in India. To despatch a horse from England in July to race in Calcutta during the following December is to court failure.

While deprecating the abuse of the stop-watch, it may be admitted that the uniformity of "going" on the majority of Indian courses increases the value of clocked gallops, and the following list of timings compiled from various sources will suggest an idea of the form requisite in an aspirant to "first-class" company on the Indian turf.[1]

[1] The Indian method of calculating pace will be strange to the new-comer, who may well be mystified by such an expression as an "eight-anna gallop." There are sixteen annas in a rupee, and the anna system having been introduced to impress the native riding-boy with some idea of speed has been universally adopted. A full-speed gallop is commonly called "sixteen annas," half-speed "eight annas," quarter-speed "four annas," etc.

AUSTRALIAN AND ENGLISH HORSES

VICEROY'S CUP, CALCUTTA. One and three-quarter miles.

1895.	B. Eng. g.	SPRIGHTLY	9st. 0lbs.	3m. $4\frac{2}{5}$s.
1900.	B. Eng. h.	UP GUARDS	9st. 3lbs.	3m. 7s.
1901.	B. Aust. h.	TUBAL CAIN	9st. 3lbs.	3m. $9\frac{2}{5}$s.
1902.	Br. Nth. Amer. g.	VASTO	9st. 0lbs.	3m. $9\frac{1}{5}$s.

MERCHANT'S CUP, CALCUTTA. One and a half miles.

1897.	B. Aust. m.	MONASTERY	7st. 4lbs.	2m. $38\frac{2}{5}$s.
1900.	Br. Nth. Am. h.	BRAVE HIMYAR	8st. 8lbs.	2m. 41s.
1901.	B. Aust. g.	CHERRY	9st. 10lbs.	2m. $40\frac{3}{5}$s.
1902.	B. Eng. h.	BENCHER	7st. 8lbs.	2m. 39s.
1903.	do.	STAND OFF	8st. 5lbs.	2m. 35s.

COOCH BEHAR CUP, CALCUTTA. One and a quarter miles.

1894.	Bk. Aust. g.	COLLEEN JUNA	8st. 7lbs.	2m. $7\frac{2}{5}$s.
1900.	B. Aust. g.	STAND OFF	8st. 13lbs.	2m. $12\frac{2}{5}$s.
1901.	do.	do.	9st. 6lbs.	2m. 10s.
1902.	do.	do.	8st. 13lbs.	2m. $10\frac{3}{5}$s.

TRIAL STAKES, CALCUTTA. One mile.

1883.	B. Aust. h.	TRANSFERRED	8st. 6lbs.	1m. $43\frac{3}{5}$s.
1901.	B. Aust. g.	CHERRY	9st. 3lbs.	1m. $43\frac{2}{5}$s.
1902.	do.	STAND OFF	9st. 3lbs.	1m. $43\frac{3}{5}$s.
1903.	do.	RECORD REIGN	9st. 3lbs.	1m. 43s.

METROPOLITAN STAKES. Six furlongs.

1891.	B. Aust. g.	LITTLE PRINCE	9st. 1lb.	1m. 15s.
1901.	do.	SECURITY	9st. 2lbs.	1m. 16s.
1902.	do.	do.	9st. 2lbs.	1m. $16\frac{1}{5}$s.
1903.	do.	MALTO	7st. 13lbs.	1m. 15s.

SANDOWN PARK STAKES. Five furlongs.

1888.	Br. Eng. h.	BLANCHLAND	8st. 4lbs.	1m. 2s.
1900.	B. Aust. g.	MALTO	7st. 7lbs.	1m. $2\frac{4}{5}$s.
1901.	do.	do.	8st. 1lb.	1m. 3s.
1902.	Ch. Aust. h.	VIGOROUS	9st. 5lbs.	1m. 3s.

ARABS AND COUNTRY-BREDS.

One and a quarter Miles.

1884.	Calcutta Trades Plate	Br. A. h.	SHERWOOD	10st. 2lbs.	2m.	18¼s.
1890.	do. Gunny Meah Plate	Ch. cb. g.	GOLD LEAF	8st. 7lbs.	2m.	16s.
1901.	Poona Aga Khan's Commemoration Plate	Ch. A. h.	ECLIPSE	10st. 6lbs.	2m.	25⅖s.
1902.	Poona Aga Khan's Commemoration Plate	B. A. h.	ARTHUR	8st. 13lbs.	2m.	24⅗s.

One Mile.

1874.	Madras Arab Handicap	G. A. h.	SARACEN	9st. 0lbs.	1m.	50½s.
1891.	Calcutta Martin Stakes	Ch. cb. m.	SUNSHINE	8st. 9lbs.	1m.	46⅗s.
1901.	Poona Aga Khans Purse	B. cb. m.	BIJLEY	9st. 9lbs.	1m.	50⅘s.
1902.	do. do.	Br. A. h.	NARUNJEE	9st. 3lbs.	2m.	5⅖s.

Six Furlongs.

1847.	Calcutta	B. A. h.	CHILD of the ISLANDS	8st. 7lbs.	1m.	21s.
1891.	do. Sensation Handicap	Ch. cb. h.	TANGRI	9st. 12lbs.	1m.	17½s.
1903.	Bombay Stud Stakes	B. cb. m.	GENTLE LADY	do.	1m.	18⅗s.

PONIES.

ECLIPSE STAKES, CALCUTTA. Seven Furlongs.

1900.	Ch. Aust. m.	LADY YETMAN	13h. 2ins.	9st. 1lb.	1m.	22s. (6 furls.)
1901.	B. cb. g.	UPSTART	14h. 1in.	9st. 7lbs.	1m.	34⅗s.
1902.	Br. Aust. m.	BESS	13h. 3ins.	9st. 0lbs.	1m.	35⅗s.

INTERNATIONAL PONY STAKES, CALCUTTA. Seven Furlongs.

1900.	Ch. Aust. h.	YANKEE BOY	14h. ¾in.	8st. 3lbs.	1m.	33⅘s.
1901.	B. cb. g.	UPSTART	14h. 1in.	8st. 6lbs.	1m.	34⅖s.
1902.	Ch. Aust. h.	YANKEE BOY	14h. ¾in.	9st. 7lbs.	1m.	34s.

CIVIL SERVICE CUP, LUCKNOW. Six Furlongs.

1898.	Br. Eng. g.	MULBERRY		8st. 9lbs.	1m.	19s.
1899.	B. Aust m.	NOT YET	13h. 3ins.	9st. 4lbs.	1m.	20s.
1903.	do.	HOUSE MAID II	13h. 2¾ins.	9st. 7lbs.	1m.	20s.

INTERNATIONAL PONY STAKES, POONA. Five Furlongs.

1900.	Ch. Aust. m.	REBECCA	14h. 0ins.	9st. 1lb.	1m.	5s.
1902.	B. Aust. m.	ANNIE LAURIE	14h. 0¾ins.	7st. 4lbs.	1m.	8⅘s.

ARAB PONIES.

ARAB PONY DERBY, POONA. Six Furlongs.

1900.	G. A. h.	Ptarmigan	13h. $1\frac{1}{2}$ins.	8st. 2lbs.	1m. $25\frac{1}{5}$s.
1902.	B. A. h.	Shaiboob	13h. 2ins.	8st. 8lbs.	1m. 25s.

LE MESURIER STAKES, BOMBAY.

1901.	B. A. h.	Brigand	13h. 3ins.	7st. 11lbs.	1m. $36\frac{4}{5}$s. (7 furls.).
1903.	B. A. h.	Rose		8st. 2lbs.	1m. $21\frac{3}{5}$s. (6 furls.).

ARMY CUP, LUCKNOW. Seven Furlongs.

1899.	Ch. A. h.	Parole	9st. 9lbs.	1m. 39s.
1900.	Ch. A. h.	Ruddigore	9st. 8lbs.	1m. $42\frac{2}{5}$s.
1901.	B. A. h.	Bin Curtas	10st. 0lbs.	1m. $42\frac{2}{5}$s.

A horse or pony may be taken over "on racing terms" for a specified period or for life with all its engagements. The real owner retains a share, usually 50 per cent. of the nett winnings, and the party taking the animal over assumes all responsibility of running, etc. Such a transaction must be notified to the Calcutta or Western India Turf Club, and will be published in the Racing Calendar. The exact terms of the agreement should be stated and preserved in writing.

A person desiring to use an assumed name must register such name annually in the office of one of the turf clubs and pay a fee of Rs. 30 for such registration, which will remain in force for the season only.

Racing colours may be registered on payment of a fee of Rs. 10, which will remain in force for two years. Colours not registered must be declared before the race at such time as the stewards of the meeting may direct, and will be rejected if they clash with registered colours declared by another owner for the same race.

At the larger centres strict regulations are enforced in the use of the tan or litter training tracks. Leave to use the track must be obtained from the secretary, and the customary fee for each horse or pony is Rs.20 for the season.

"In the absence of any agreement to the contrary, a horse shall be taken to be sold with his engagements." So if such a sale be not registered with the secretary of the turf club the seller will be held responsible for forfeits on default of the purchaser.

"Any gentleman wishing to ride in races on even terms with jockeys shall obtain a permission from the stewards of the turf club or from the stewards of the meeting at which he wishes to ride. The permission of the stewards of the turf club shall be current till revoked."

The Ceylon Turf Club, with headquarters at Colombo, is the ruling body on the Ceylon turf. At present it enforces a separate set of rules, but there is every prospect of an early assimilation to those of the Indian turf clubs.

The principal meeting is held in August, when the following prizes are offered :—

Governor's Cup . .	£50 and Rs.2000	1¼ miles	W.A. & C.
Turf Club Cup . .	2000	,,	Handicap.
Fort Plate . . .	3000	,,	,,

As in the majority of Indian districts, racing in Ceylon fluctuates between prosperity and depression, but at its lowest ebb the Colombo and Newara Eliya meetings find sufficient support among the residents in the island and the garrison. Horses owned by Ceylon sportsmen frequently appear on the Calcutta course, but hitherto Indian owners have not been attracted to the island.

Pony racing flourishes in Rangoon, and meetings are also held in Mandalay, Fort Stedman, Maymyo and Prome. The bulk of the sport is supplied by the Indo-Burman pony, whose height runs from 12 hands 2 inches upwards. For these diminutive racers native jockeys are in sole demand, and the Burmans are keen sportsmen and ardent race-goers. Australian ponies go down from Calcutta to Rangoon by steamer in order to compete for the Governor's Cup and other races in Burmah, and the colours of one or two Calcutta owners usually appear on the Rangoon course at the November meeting.

Horse shows flourish in the majority of the larger military stations, and among the more important shows are those at Bombay, Calcutta (Tollygunge Club), Madras, Murree, Lahore and Mian Mir, Poona, Simla, Shillong and Secunderabad.

Like the starting machine, which has proved a general success on Indian courses, the totalisator has been introduced from Australia. At the Calcutta meetings the betting machine is large and elaborate, being firmly established in popular favour. A separate building accommodates the boards, of which there are six for the "ten rupee" punters, three for win and three for place tickets, while two are reserved for the issue of fifty rupee tickets, win and place. In the issue of tickets each board works separately, displaying the number of tickets purchased on each horse, and also the total number of tickets issued. A clerk stands at a window beneath each board, and delivers to the bettor a ticket impressed with the number (as shown on the race-card) of the horse he wishes to back. While impressing the ticket, the machine works automatically, changing the numbers on the board. Thus, at the commencement of betting, if the first purchaser applies for a ticket on horse No. 2, the board will read:

Total No. of tickets, 1
Horse No. 1 0—No. 2 1—No. 3 0, etc.

Should a second bettor purchase a ticket on No. 3, the board will then read:

Total No. of tickets, 2
Horse No. 1 0—No. 2 1—No. 3 1, and so on.

Thus the odds obtainable on each board may be roughly reckoned, but since the figures change momentarily as the purchasers file past the window, and since all the boards are amalgamated to ascertain the dividend, even a careful calculation can only be approximate. A large and efficient staff is maintained to expedite the payment of dividends, which are posted on a conspicuous notice board, and the fortunate punters can obtain their winnings at a separate set of pigeon holes a few minutes after the "all right" signal has been hoisted. Dividends are calculated by dividing the total amount of takings by the number of tickets purchased on the winner, first deducting a percentage for expenses, etc.

The bookmakers flourish even in the shadow of their big rival, and statistics have shown that in the long-run there is little to choose between the "Bookie" and the "Tote" in the matter of odds, sometimes one, sometimes the other being more favourable to the punter. As a general rule the small bettor will find it more profitable to back a favourite with the bookmakers and the outsiders on the totalisator.

At the majority of smaller meetings and Gymkhana races, totalisator and bookmakers are replaced, or at least rivalled, by overnight lotteries. Before attending a lottery the new arrival in India, who may be attracted thither by virtue of ownership in a pony entered for one of the races, should obtain a clear understanding of its nature. Briefly the procedure is as follows:

The secretary of the lottery first sells a numbered list of tickets, of which there will be 25, 50, or 100, costing Rs. 5 or Rs. 10 as may best suit the company present. Anyone who wishes to bid in the subsequent auction must purchase at least one ticket. Tossing for tickets is a common practice, loser paying cost, but sharing equally with winner in the event of drawing a horse. The partnership is thus entered on the list : "James to Rawlins," and the secretary will collect the ticket price from the person first named, in this instance, "James," a rule worth noting.

All the tickets having been sold, numbered wads are placed in one hat, slips bearing the names of the horses left in for the first race in the other, and drawing proceeds in the usual manner. Each horse having been thus allotted, a compulsory auction is held of the winning tickets. It is here that the novice may come to grief, for the successful bidder will in each case have to pay *twice* the amount of his bid, once to the lottery fund, and once to the persons who drew the horse he has purchased in the drawing for tickets. The owner of a horse may claim the privilege of taking over a quarter or a half share from the highest bidder.

Bidding is often most spirited and the new hand should beware of attempts by the auctioneer and his friends to "rush" him, advice which is easier to give than to follow! The main objection to a lottery is the fact that odds cannot be ascertained until the auction is over, after which the following calculation will give the required result.

From the sum-total of the ticket prices and the prices realised at the auction, deduct the double price of your horse (and also the race fund percentage), and—As the balance is to the doubled price of your horse, so are the odds against him.

Steeplechasing does not at the present time

flourish in India as a separate form of sport. The number of bona-fide steeplechase meetings may be counted on the fingers of a single hand, and one at least of these results in a heavy annual deficit, which is defrayed out of the surplus profits accruing to the Calcutta Turf Club from the legitimate sport. Into the causes of this decline, or the remedies which it might be possible to apply in order to prevent its continuance, it is unnecessary to enter here. The number of courses which still exist in a more or less dilapidated condition throughout India furnish sufficient proof that the sport was formerly more popular, and supply a ready means to satisfy any future revival of public interest in cross-country racing.

During the past three seasons steeplechases have been run at the following stations :—Cawnpore, Dibrugarh, Fort Stedman, Mandalay, Meerut, Quetta, Rawalpindi, Secunderabad and Umballa. With one or two exceptions, these chases were closed to ponies of varying heights and all the stakes were of small value.

During the 1902-3 season stakes above Rs. 500 in value were offered on four courses only: — In August at Bangalore, where the stewards have experienced the greatest difficulty in attracting entries for their jump events; in September at Poona; in December and again in February at Lucknow; and in January at Tollygunge (Calcutta). The following meagre list represents the principal prizes offered to owners of steeplechasers in the course of the season :—

HORSES.

September—POONA.—POONA GRAND NATIONAL. Value Rs.2000. W. A. and C. raised 21 lbs. Distance 2½ miles.

GRAND ANNUAL CHASE. Value Rs.1800. Handicap for horses. Distance 2¼ miles.

January—CALCUTTA.—TRIAL CHASE. Value Rs.2000. W. A. and C. raised 21 lbs. Distance 2½ miles.

INDIAN GRAND NATIONAL. Value Rs.7000. W. A. and C. raised 21 lbs., with penalties and allowances. 3 miles.

MAIDEN STEEPLECHASE. Value Rs.2000. For maiden horses. W. A. and C. raised 21 lbs. Distance 2½ miles.

TOLLYGUNGE.—SUBURBAN PLATE. Value Rs.2000. Handicap for horses. Distance 2½ miles.

TOLLYGUNGE PLATE. Value Rs.3700. Handicap for horses. Distance 3 miles.

February—LUCKNOW.—HORSE CHASE. Value Rs.1500. Handicap for horses. Distance 2½ miles.

PONIES.

September—POONA.—KIRKEE CHASE. Value Rs.1500. For Arabs and Country-breds 14.2, other ponies 14.1 and under. Those heights to carry 1 stone 10 lbs. W. I.

Distance 2 miles. Allowances. Arabs 16 lbs., Country-breds 8 lbs., Maidens 7 lbs.

GANESHKIND CHASE.—Value Rs.1500. Handicap for ponies 14.2 and under. Distance 2 miles.

December—LUCKNOW.—PONY CHASE. Value Rs.700. Handicap for Arabs and Country-breds 14.2, and other ponies 14.0 and under. Distance 1¾ miles.

January—TOLLYGUNGE.—PONY CHASE. Value Rs.1500. Handicap for Arabs and Country-breds 14.2, other ponies 14.0 and under. Distance 1¾ miles.

PONY HANDICAP.—Value Rs.1500. Handicap for all ponies 14.2 and under. Distance 1¾ miles.

February—LUCKNOW.—PONY CHASE. Value Rs.1500. Handicap for Arabs and Country-breds 14.2, other ponies 14.1 and under. Distance 2 miles.

MEERUT.—PONY CHASE. Value Rs.1000. Same terms and distance.

The paucity of valuable stakes is due solely to lack of support from owners, and the turf clubs have shown their readiness to meet any demand for additional races which would draw a moderate field to the post.

How do the courses compare with those in England and Australia? This will be the first question of owners, trainers and riders alike. There has been some complaint that

Indian courses are not sufficiently "stiff" to protect the bona-fide steeplechasers from the illegitimate competition of the speedy flat-racer, and in comment it is sufficient to note that the favourite for the last Grand National—starting at the extraordinary price of 7 to 4 ON—went to the post without any schooling worthy of the name!

The following is a detailed description of the fences over which the Indian Grand National is run, taken from the programme published by the Calcutta Turf Club. Many of these follow the regulation dimensions of the National Hunt, but the bush fences are thin and weak compared with their prototypes on English courses.

DESCRIPTION OF JUMPS.

Horse Steeple-Chase Course.

Jumps Nos. 1 and 8.—A bush fence 4 feet 6 in. high with a guard rail 57 feet long, 2 feet high and 1 foot apart from the fence.

Jumps Nos. 2 and 9.—A bush fence 5 feet high with a guard rail 60 feet long, 3 feet high close against the fence.

Jumps Nos. 3 and 10.—A natural hedge 3 feet high, on the take-off side of a ditch 8 feet broad (no guard rails).

Jump No. 4.—A grassed bank 2 feet 6 in., 6 feet wide at base, bushed up to 5 feet, with a guard rail 50 feet long, 2 feet high and 1 foot apart from the bank.

STEEPLE CHASE COURSES

AT

TOLLYGUNGE

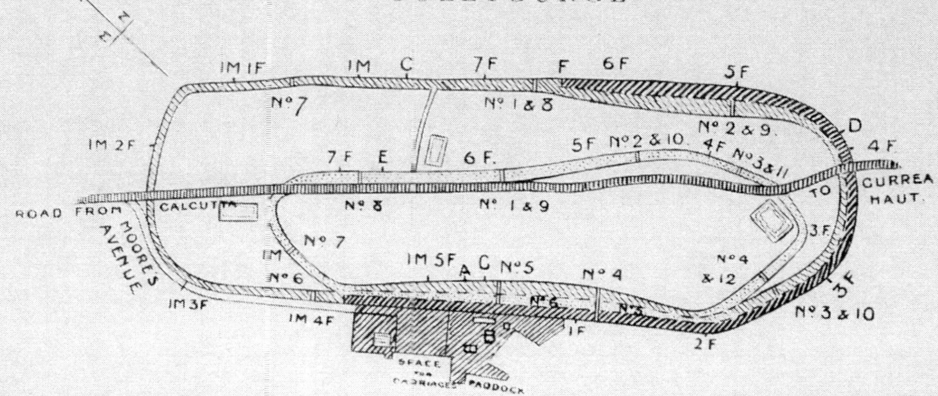

A.—Winning Post.
B.—Stand.
C.—Start for Horse Steeple Chases (Long Course).
D.— Do. do. (Short Course).
E.—Start for Pony Steeple Chases.
F.—Start for Flat Races.
G.—Start for the Indian Grand National.

Horse Steeple Chase Course
Pony do. do.
Flat Course . . .
Pucca Road . . .

Jump No. 5.—The "Water Jump," water 12 feet wide, 2 feet 6 in. deep with a bush fence on the take-off side 3 feet high (no guard rail).

Jump No. 6.—A bush fence 4 feet 6 in. high with a guard rail on the take-off side 90 feet long, 2 feet high and 2 feet from the fence.

Jump No. 7.—A bush fence 4 feet high with a ditch on the take-off side 6 feet wide and 3 feet deep, with a guard rail 60 feet long, 2 feet high in front of ditch and close against it.

Pony Steeple-Chase Course.

Jumps Nos. 1 and 9.—Thick hedge 4 feet high with a guard rail 50 feet long, 2 feet high and 1 foot apart from the hedge.

Jumps Nos. 2 and 10.—Natural hedge 3 feet high with a guard rail 46 feet long, 1 foot 6 in. high, 1 foot apart from the hedge, and a ditch 6 feet wide, 2 feet deep on far side.

Jumps Nos. 3 and 11.—Hedge 4 feet 6 in. high with a guard rail on take-off side 55 feet long and 2 feet 6 in. high, close against the hedge.

Jumps Nos. 4 and 12.—Natural hedge on a bank, whole 4 feet high with a guard rail 50 feet long, 1 foot 8 in. high and 1 foot apart from the bank.

Jump No. 5.—Grassed bank 2 feet high, 6 feet wide at base, bushed up to 4 feet 6 in. with a guard rail 40 feet long, 1 foot high and 1 foot apart from the bank.

Jump No. 6.—Water jump 10 feet wide, 2 feet

deep with a bush fence on the take-off side 2 feet 6 in. high (no guard rail).

Jump No. 7.—Grassed bank 2 feet high, 6 feet wide at base, bushed up to 4 feet, with a guard rail 54 feet long, 1 foot high and 1 foot apart from the bank.

Jump No. 8.—A bush fence 3 feet 6 in. high with a ditch on the take-off side 5 feet wide and 3 feet deep, with a guard rail 46 feet long, 1 foot 6 in. high in front of ditch and close against it.

The pony course runs inside the big course at Tollygunge, which is picturesquely situated in the country some three miles south of Calcutta.

The Lucknow course is perhaps the best in the country, at any rate for ponies, and the following description, for which I am indebted to the *Indian Planters' Gazette*, gives a fair idea of the pony course as recently amended :—

Fence No. 1.—Mud wall 3 feet high, and bushed to 4 feet, with a ditch on the landing side 6 feet wide and 2 feet deep.

Fence No. 2.—Water jump 10 feet wide, 2 feet deep, with a hedge on the take-off side 3 feet high, and a guard rail 2 feet high.

Fence No. 3.—Bush fence 4½ feet high, with a guard rail 2 feet high.

Fence No. 4.—Bush fence 3½ feet high, with a ditch on the take-off side 4½ feet wide, and a guard rail 1 foot high in front of the ditch.

Fence No. 5.—Mud wall 2½ feet, bushed up to 4 feet, with a 3-feet ditch on the landing side.

Fence No. 6.—Bush fence 4½ feet high, with a guard rail 2 feet high and 1½ feet from the fence.

Fence No. 7.—Mud wall bushed up to 3½ feet, and a ditch on the take-off side 6 feet wide and 2 feet deep.

Fence No. 8.—Mud wall 2 feet high, bushed up to 4½ feet, with a guard rail 2 feet high.

Fence Nos. 9 and 10.—Bush fence 4½ feet high, with a guard rail 2 feet high placed 1 foot away from the fence.

Point to point races hardly fall within the scope of this section, but this form of cross-country sport flourishes in Bombay, Quetta, Ootacamund and Poona.

The stewards of the Turf Club spare no expense to improve the fences and the going, but no amount of preparation can do more than thinly disguise the iron hardness of the sun-baked ground, which accounts for the breakdown of so many candidates for steeplechasing honours.

On the Poona course the fences are somewhat more formidable, the going is good, there is plenty of room at the jumps, and the course is in full view of the stands from start to finish.

There are no separate meetings in India devoted to hurdle racing, but the majority of flat-racing programmes include one or two jump events. The plan usually adopted is to commence proceedings each day with a hurdle race, after which the hurdles can be removed from the course and the flat-racing begun without delay. As shown by the list below, the most valuable stakes are offered at the cold weather meetings in Calcutta, where this form of sport retains its popularity. The hurdles are placed on the flat race-course, and are not very formidable obstacles. Black in colour, and constructed like the ordinary English sheep hurdle, they are very lightly planted in the ground, and not uncommonly the entire flight is flattened to the ground by the passage of a numerous field. These hurdles are not bushed, and although in some places, as at Umballa, the stewards have adopted this English custom, bushing is still the exception, not the rule. The influence of Australian methods can be detected in this matter also, although the stone wall policy of the colonials finds little favour among the racing authorities of India. Australian hurdles driven deep into the ground are almost unbreakable, and constitute formidable fences. Similarly their steeplechase courses are well calculated to prevent the appearance of any unschooled competitors, the fences being so stiff and unyielding that even among fields of magnificent jumpers, the annual casualty list assumes alarming proportions.

The following are the principal hurdle races run during the season 1902-03 :—

HORSES.

August and September—

CALCUTTA.—Four races value Rs.750, and three closed to hunters, value Rs.350 each. Distance 1½ miles. Handicaps.

October—

LUCKNOW.—Horse Hurdles. Handicap. Rs.1500. Handicap. R.C.

Photo] FIRST OVER [*Kapp & Co., Calcutta*

December and January—

		Value Rs.		Distance.
CALCUTTA .	Hurdle Race .	1500	W.A.& C. raised 1 st.	1½ miles.
	Elgin Stakes .	900	Handicap . .	1¾ ,,
	Burdwan Cup ,	4500	W.A.&C. raised 7lbs.	1¾ ,,
	Grand Annual	6000	Handicap . .	2 ,,
	Tally-Ho Plate	3700	,, . .	2 ,,
	Horse Hurdles	1200	,, . .	1¾ ,,

February—
LUCKNOW.—Horse Hurdles. Value Rs. 1200. Handicap. R.C.

PONIES.

December and January—
CALCUTTA.—Zeerut Stakes. Value Rs. 1000. Handicap. Arabs and Country-breds 14.2; others 14.1.
Pony Hurdles. Value Rs. 1500. Handicap. Ponies 14.2.

February—
LUCKNOW.—Pony Hurdles. Value Rs. 1500. Handicap. Arabs and Country-breds 14.2; others 14.1.
MEERUT.—Pony Hurdles. Value Rs. 1000. Handicap. Arabs and Country-breds 14.2; others 14.0.

Hurdle races of less value were also run for horses at Ootacamund, Bangalore, Poona, Quetta, and Karachi; and for ponies at Simla, Ootacamund, Bangalore, Poona, Quetta, Karachi, Umballa, etc.

PAPER-CHASING

IN India this popular game is played on horseback; but in the various districts, conditions of country, fences and "fields" differ so widely, that the sport in each station would really require a separate description. In Calcutta, Lucknow, Poona, Madras, Secunderabad, Shillong, Rawalpindi and twenty other places where Englishmen congregate, paper-chases are organised in the cool season of the year. Often they furnish a mere excuse for a gallop across country, winding up with a breakfast supplied by some hospitable regimental mess. The hares lay false tracks and leave blanks in the true trail in time-honoured fashion, while every available horse and pony in the station is turned out to join in the scramble.

In arranging a paper-chase of this nature, a careful survey of the ground is essential, in order to guard against unnecessary risks in the shape of nullahs, tanks, disused wells, and other dangerous pitfalls. The erection of artificial fences will, in many localities, be unnecessary; and, indeed, whenever these appear, the paper-chase must develop into a steeple-chase, since the paper trail becomes more or less superfluous while such fences are in sight.

But it is in a more advanced stage of development that paper-chasing has become a definite form of sport, capable of accurate description. In Poona, Lucknow and Madras, meets are of more or less regular occurrence, and cups are sometimes offered for competition. In Shillong, during last season, a committee arranged a series of chases much on the Calcutta model, but in the capital of India the paper-chase has long been an established institution.

The Calcutta Paper-chase Club is managed by a small committee of leading sportsmen, who extend the membership—entailing an annual subscription of only ten rupees—by invitation.

Such invitation is in practice extended to members of all recognised clubs in India, who reside in the Metropolis or visit the capital for the cold weather season. All the arrangements are in the hands of this committee, whose office is no sinecure. The chases are held weekly from mid-December to early March, and are run over the thickly-wooded country beyond Ballygunge, the south-eastern suburb of Calcutta.

The courses average three and a half miles in length, and lie for the most part along strips of light plough-land, in which artificial fences are erected at intervals. Mud walls and bushed hurdles form the usual obstacles, and average no more than four feet in height, but the going is rough, and the early morning light is often very treacherous, so that they suffice to bring about a long list of falls in the course of a season. Patches of jungle alternate with the cultivated lands, and to pass from one open stretch to another the course-makers utilise the narrow paths which intersect the woodland in every direction. The sharp turns necessitated by these form the one noticeable feature which distinguishes the sport from steeple-chasing, which in other respects it closely resembles. As a general rule, the hares lay the paper in profusion and complete the course before the starter sends the field away. False trails are obsolete, but "hounds" must keep a constant look-out for accidents due to a runaway horse, which throws one of the "hares" and lays scent on its own account, or mischievous native boys, who delight to confuse the "sahib-log" by moving the paper.

Fields are divided into two classes: horses, and ponies under 14.1 hands, which run separately. An "Average Cup" is awarded to the best performer in the season's chases, usually twelve in number. The leading six horses in every chase obtain one point each, and the cup goes to the horse which, with owner up, has secured most points at the end of the season. In the event of a tie, the better average of placings is preferred, but the horse that has run five times sixth excludes another that may have run four times first. This mode of reckoning prevents desperate finishes for places, and has been found satisfactory in practice.

The Paper-chase Cup, value Rs.500, to which is added a handsome Challenge Bowl presented by the officers of the Rifle Brigade, is the Club's premier trophy. For this, and for a Heavy-weight Cup, a separate chase is run in March under special conditions.

As in the Average Cup competition, members of the Club riding their own horse are alone eligible, and such horses must not have won a race of any description value Rs.550 or over, and must, further, have been regularly paper-chased throughout the season to the satisfaction of the committee. A minimum weight of 11 st. is imposed, and to compete for the Heavy-weight Cup, members must walk at least 11 st. 7 lbs. and ride 12 st. 7 lbs.

Photo] AN HISTORIC FINISH [*Kapp & Co., Calcutta*

An annual Ladies' Cup provides an exciting spectacle in a ladies' steeple-chase, and a large field of fair candidates always muster at the start. Cups for the pony class are run on similar lines, but only one was offered last season.

To compete in the first flight of a Calcutta paper-chase, the eleven-stone man must expect to pay at least a thousand rupees for his mount.

In addition to the above prizes, the Calcutta Turf Club offers annually a number of races for the hunter class, which provides a great incentive to owners of paper-chasers to pay high prices for their animals.

All these chases are run in the early morning, and thus necessitate early rising and well-strung nerves. As a test of endurance, bold horsemanship and presence of mind, a paper-chase cup race may be favourably compared with any steeple-chase in the world, and in no school can these qualities be more readily acquired.

The illustration shows an historic finish between two well-known riders, Mr Mayne, now settled in Yorkshire, and Mr Barrow of Calcutta. The third figure is Mr George Walker, familiarly known as the "Squire," who has for many years been the life and soul of the Calcutta Paper-chase Club.

In India there is usually a choice of but two methods of purchase; the one through advertisements in the *Pioneer* and other newspapers, the other from the yards in the Presidency towns. The first method is good only if an inspection of the animal advertised is possible prior to purchase, and, as a rule, distance will be found an insurmountable bar to this very necessary precaution. In other circumstances, purchase through press advertisements is not to be recommended, and it will be better to buy either personally or through a friend direct from the stables or yards in Calcutta, Bombay or Madras.

A similar system obtains for Australian horses in these three centres and for Arabs in Bombay. The majority of imported horses are taken to one or another of the different commission yards maintained by local firms, and thence sold to purchasers by the shipper direct. In Bombay, one of the best yards for the purchase of Arabs is that of Ali Bin Talib, while for Australians those of R. G. Baldock and The Bombay Stable Co. have an excellent reputation. In Madras, the firm of Kerouse, Madden & Co. is the most widely known, and imports all classes of Australian horses and ponies. In Calcutta there are half-a-dozen big yards and twice that number of well-known shippers. Of the former, Messrs Cook & Co., Messrs R. S. Hart Bros. and Messrs Milton & Co. may be mentioned, and of the latter Messrs Glasscock, Gilder, Ferry, Lamotte, Margrett, etc.

A few hints as to the actual purchase may be worth mentioning.

It is courting disaster to enter the market with any doubts as to the height and stamp of animal required; and, as a preliminary to a bargain, always state clearly the work he will be required to do, and also the limit of price which you mean to pay.

Avoid all appearance of cleverness, real or assumed. Remember that silence is golden; if the buyer does not comment on the horses under inspection the seller must, and this will suit your purpose better. Do not waste time in looking for vague symptoms of unsoundness; leave this to a "vet," for, if the animal is worth buying at all, he will be worth an extra guinea for a certificate of soundness. Confine your attention to make and shape; a well-bred, clever head and pleasant eye will be discernible by the veriest tyro. For saddle work, avoid a straight-shouldered animal, look especially for a long rein, big bone beneath the knee, and a well-ribbed up powerful back. Pasterns should not be too straight and short, nor yet too long and sloping. For harness, shoulders and back are of less moment, but quarters should be well developed, and hocks clean and well set. Have the horse led up and down the yard, watching him from before and behind. See that he steps well out with his hind feet, and picks up all four cleanly, putting them down true and level without crossing his fore-legs, or turning his toes in or out. From behind, see that he bends his hocks straight, and that they do not incline inward or outward as the weight comes upon them in motion.

By the time you have seen the first, the dealer will have made up his mind which horse he thinks he can sell you. This may or may not be the first shown, but, in any case, ask to see anything else he thinks suitable before going further.

Having made a choice, the next step is to obtain a trial; and, whether in harness or saddle, ask to see this outside the yard, when you will be better able to judge as to manners. If this outside trial prove satisfactory, you can close the bargain, subject to examination by a veterinary surgeon. If you cannot visit the stables yourself, and can find no suitable animal in your own district, commission a friend, whom you can trust to observe the above simple rules—even should you think he knows less about horses than yourself—to make the purchase on your behalf. Lastly, when once suited, avoid selling, even for a small profit; it may be long before you do so well again.

Though exceptions may exist to prove the rule, no owner can hope for success with his hacks unless he takes an intelligent and constant interest in their welfare. If your stud be limited to a single pony, it will still be worth while to purchase and study one or two books on the subject of horse-keeping in India. Such works as "Indian Horse Notes," by Major C——, price Rs. 2, and "Training and Horse Management in India," by Captain Hayes, price Rs. 6, both published by Messrs Thacker, Spink & Co., Calcutta, kept handy for daily reference, may save both trouble and loss. A smattering of knowledge is sometimes dangerous, but by applying the suggestions and remedies detailed in these books to the daily routine of your stable, however small, a valuable practical experience will soon be attained.

The new purchase having arrived in your compound, do not abandon him to the tender mercies of the first syce who presents himself with a bundle of "chits" (certificates, which may very possibly be hired for the occasion) and begs to be permitted to enter your service. In your first venture ask some more experienced friend to engage a man for you, but in whatever manner you engage him, and however excellent his testimonials, do not trust him until you have yourself proved him. Before settling with a new syce, ascertain the custom of the station or district as regards not only wages, but the supply of oats, grass, hay and straw. Whether you purchase these yourself or through your syce, examine them personally on arrival. Should you suspect, without being confident, that the quality is bad, ask the opinion of someone with experience.

Insist on obtaining the best quality of forage from the beginning, and occasional surprise surveys later will suffice to keep the supplies up to the mark. Observe the daily routine of a new syce—feeding, watering, grooming, bedding, etc. —but avoid unnecessary interference with his "dastur," or custom. Compare his practical methods with your own theoretical knowledge, and when they disagree, as they assuredly will in many instances, think the matter well out before harassing him with special instructions.

The Indian groom has fifty-and-one objectionable tricks, most of which are pointed out by Major C——, or Captain Hayes, while those which they do not pause to celebrate will be obvious to the meanest intellect. Having arrived at a conclusion, instruct your syce accordingly and listen to no argument or excuses.

The question of stable management has extensive limits, but without entering into details the following hints may be suggested.

Food.—Oats, gram, cooltee and barley are the staples of horse diet in India. Of these oats are the most expensive, but incomparably the best. Up country, gram forms the staple food; it is somewhat heating, so a proportion of bran—say one-third — should always be given with it. Barley should always be parched or boiled. Cooltee, which must always be boiled, is the staple food in Madras. Remember that an imported Waler or English horse is subject to the exigencies of a climate for which Nature has not prepared him, and his digestion becomes a matter of first importance. Carefully regulate the quantity of oats and other "hard" food supplied, and in health and full work give about one-fifth bran in each feed. Decrease the oats at once if the animal is thrown out of work, and at all times one "bran mash" weekly is advisable. This should always be well steamed, and a sprinkling of salt added. No rule can be laid down as to quantity; 3½ to 4 seers (*i.e.* 7 to 8 lbs.) will suffice for a small pony in light work, while a race-horse in hard training will sometimes comfortably digest as much as 9 seers, besides hay or "doob" grass practically *ad lib.* Vary the menu of dainty feeders. Occasionally mix with the evening feed a pound of barley or linseed, newly boiled until quite soft. Give carrots, Lucerne, etc., whenever available.

Simple laxatives are linseed oil, and in fever Epsom salts, while sweet spirits of nitre may be safely used in the common case of "hide-bound" animals, whose dull-staring coats proclaim their inability to sweat. Such symptoms should be treated without delay, but avoid if possible the regular use of laxatives.

Hay and Grass.—Even in the Presidency towns good hay is very difficult to obtain, but "doob" grass is as nutritious as the best hay. "Doob" is a peculiar root grass, which grows along the surface of the ground, very much like a creeper. See that your grass-cutter brings you real "doob" and not rank or coarse jungle grasses, as he will be very ready to do, should you fail to watch him.

Water.—Do not allow your syce to water after feeding; it is a good practice to have water always in the stall, but to renew half an hour before each feed.

The golden rules to be observed in feeding the horse are:—

1. Water before feeding.
2. Feed frequently a little at a time.
3. Water and feed at regular hours.
4. Do not work on a full stomach.

Grooming.—Natives, as a rule, are good grooms, but one point deserves special notice. Legs may perhaps be washed without ill effects, but should you discover a syce throwing water over his horse's body in order to save himself trouble in cleaning, avoid unnecessary violence, but eject the offender instantly from the premises and never permit him to show his face within your compound again.

Keep an attentive eye on your horses' feet. Imported, especially English, horses suffer much in this respect. The best preventive of all diseases of the feet is scrupulous cleanliness of the stable floor.

Stabling.—Observe by personal inspection that your stable is clean, sweet, and as cool as practicable. Exercise your ingenuity to baffle the rays of a tropical sun, and remember that a current of air is a boon unspeakable. In extremely hot weather a horse will often be cooler in the shade of a leafy tree than cooped up in a walled stable.

The cost of keeping hacks varies greatly in different stations and districts, but even in the Presidency towns a syce's monthly bill, with shoeing and veterinary and all minor charges included, should not exceed Rs.35. In mofussil districts, with free stabling, abundant grass, and no extras, the cost of keeping a country-bred pony will not much exceed Rs.15 a month. The monthly pay of a syce is Rs.7 to Rs.9; of a grass-cutter Rs.4 to Rs.6; and of a riding-boy Rs.20 to Rs.30.

PART IV

SOME MINOR SPORTS AND GAMES

TRAINING, CONDITION AND DIET

CRICKET

FOOTBALL

GOLF

HOCKEY

TENNIS AND RACQUETS

MISCELLANEOUS (ATHLETICS, BADMINTON, BICYCLING, BOXING, BOWLS AND CROQUET, MOTORING, PIGEON-SHOOTING, SWIMMING)

YACHTING

ROWING AND BOATING

GYMKHANAS

CHEETAH-HUNTING

TRAINING, CONDITION AND DIET

A GENERAL account of the minor games of India, as distinguished from the main branches of sport, is rendered not a little difficult by the varying conditions under which they are played in different presidencies and districts.

Polo is the Indian game par excellence, and as such is separately treated; the new arrival will find that in the vast majority of stations all other games are of secondary importance. As might be expected, however, the popular games of England, the games of public schools and village greens, have in turn spread throughout India, and every station of moderate size can show its cricket and football ground and its racquet court.

Conditions sometimes foster one game at the expense of others, but as a general rule the management of minor sports is in the hands of the committee of a single "gymkhana" or games club, to which all Europeans in the station belong as a matter of course. The committee constantly changes, as the garrison or civilian officials move on in rotation, but the club continues as a going concern, and with an unfailing supply of new members a small entrance fee and subscription suffice for the up-keep and repair of lawns, courts and buildings. By joining the station club, a step he will be expected to take immediately on arrival, the newcomer will at once find himself in the swim, with ample opportunity to take exercise in his own particular game.

Cricket, racquets, tennis, croquet, with possibly football and hockey, and such indoor amusements as billiards, badminton, cards and dancing, all fall within the scope of the ordinary station club, and with an energetic secretary the greater part of the year will be occupied by a succession of matches and tournaments in every possible game. This general rule applies only to the large number of stations in which the European community consists entirely or almost entirely of Government officials and the officers of the garrison.

Similar clubs exist, however, in many civil stations, and in "planting" districts such as Behar and Assam, where the unofficial element prevails. Particular exception must be made of those large towns, such as Bombay and Calcutta, in which the European population suffices to support a number of separate clubs, and where class distinctions add to the difficulty of union. In Calcutta, for instance, separate clubs exist for cricket and tennis, golf, football and hockey, racquets and rowing! With racing and social clubs in addition, prohibitive fees and subscriptions compel a new-comer to confine his attention to one or two particular amusements.

In all military stations, in addition to the station clubs, regimental teams form an important factor in the provision of matches, and their influence is especially felt in cricket, football and hockey. The last game in particular has of recent years become very popular among native regiments. With the single exception of Association football, regimental teams, both British and native, usually contain a fair sprinkling of officers, and in matches and tournaments inter-regimental contests serve to foster and encourage *esprit de corps.*

India has not escaped the modern mania for tournaments and competitions; prizes, cups, and medals are in constant demand; and in Association football trained regimental teams scour the country in search of sport. But the professional has not as yet secured any foothold in the country, and the amateur player can still enjoy a game in his leisure hours without the mortification of being out-classed by those who make it the special business of their life to excel in one special branch of sport.

In his endeavour to attain the perfection of physical condition the English athlete can find valuable advice in the pages of numerous books and pamphlets on the subject, but hitherto no writer has, so far as I am aware, attempted to record actual experiences of training in India with a view to assisting his fellow-athletes. Yet in a tropical climate the question develops great importance.

In England the average sportsman can sit in

the saddle or carry a gun for eight hours on a stretch without careful preparation or extensive self-denial, and still feel no ill effects at the close of the day. Training methods affect only the select band competing in races and championships, while the vast majority are content to enjoy their sport without troubling themselves at all in the matter of diet or regulated exercises. And this indifference remains the general rule, despite the development of new principles concerning hygiene and diet.

In India, hard condition is absolutely essential to the enjoyment of a day's shooting, a game of hockey, or even a single "chukker" on the polo ground. The fierce rays of the sun penetrate the widest helmet; the abnormal heat opens every pore in the body; enormous waste of tissue results, and the stomach promptly rebels against the slightest over-exertion unless it be held in complete subjection. Such subjection is indeed necessary to athletic success in any country, but a tropical climate enhances while altering the nature of the difficulty in its attainment. The English athlete will often be cautioned to guard against over-indulgence, especially in meat foods, a temptation occasioned by a healthy appetite induced by exercise and fresh air. In a tropical climate the need of a flesh diet is less sensibly felt, nor in India will the quality or appearance of such dishes usually afford much temptation to a jaded appetite. Vegetarian diet has been successfully tried in India by individuals, but there would seem to be even less reason in a tropical climate than in England for the adoption of a system involving entire abstinence from meat.

The maintenance of sufficient, rather than the removal of superfluous, tissue constitutes the difficulty which athletes must face in India. On emigrating to the tropics some Europeans no doubt tend to put on weight with alarming rapidity, but such cases are exceptional, and as a general rule few Englishmen in health and moderate exercise are troubled in India with superfluous tissue. Excessive perspiration causes a constant and considerable waste at ordinary times, but fast or continued exercise results in an abnormal depletion of tissue and necessitates a plentiful supply of fresh fuel.

Hard condition implies well-developed and hardened muscles, but muscle can no more be made without tissue than bricks without clay! The first question for solution is therefore how to regulate the diet in order to obtain a maximum of tissue.

Now, the futility of laying down any hard and fast rules for diet has been amply demonstrated in England, and the reasons that render such rules ineffective are common to all climates and countries. Men's digestions are no more alike than their faces, often considerably less so; and a peaceable digestion is the *sine qua non* of condition, if not indeed of all earthly happiness! In recent years, analysts have overwhelmed the reading public with statistics showing the exact constituents, nutritious and otherwise, of the various dishes commonly encountered on our breakfast and dinner tables, but the man of sense may safely avoid the examination of such intricate details. Hunger is older than the chemist; the sense of repletion is more subtle than the ablest physician; and an implicit confidence in these two natural guides will seldom, under ordinary circumstances, be misplaced.

It may be argued that an Englishman's circumstances in India are far from ordinary, but nevertheless the best advice experience can give is that every man should obey the dictates of his natural instincts. A fixed diet on which one man would thrive and prosper might easily reduce another to extreme exhaustion, and the danger of mistakes is aggravated by the unnatural severity of the climate. These principles seem to have a common-sense foundation, and, accepting them as a reasonable doctrine, advice on the subject of diet must be purely negative. First, then, do not persevere with any system that may be recommended to you, should you find it disagree in any way with your constitution. Second, and most important, do not continue severe exercise in the face of a failing appetite. As I have already observed, to maintain a sufficient amount of tissue—in other words, to keep up your strength—is of paramount importance, and if a man who indulges in hard exercise cannot take in a steady supply of fresh fuel, a breakdown must quickly follow, perhaps with disastrous and permanent effects upon his health. So much for the food question. Although the same principles apply, the matter of drink is not so easily disposed of. Again, no fixed rules will apply. One man will thrive on a quart of strong bottled beer daily, while a pint would suffice to upset a less powerful digestion. For training in India, as elsewhere, water is hard to beat, but boiled water has little attraction even for a considerable thirst, and as a beverage it is certainly unpopular! Brandy used at one time to be the ordinary drink among Europeans in India, but has been replaced to a great extent by whisky and soda. The majority of Anglo-Indians, more particularly those who take fast exercise, are content with a very weak mixture, and the newcomer will do well to imitate their caution in this respect. The Indian "thirst" has been glorified in a well-known song, but the athlete will find it somewhat of a trial. Even a couple of sets of tennis will raise a thirst inconceivable at an English garden party, but such thirst must be rationally treated. The whole body craves for liquid and absorbs it with great rapidity, but the stomach has a comparatively small capacity, insufficient to meet such an unusual demand. It will quickly resent any attempt to force it to do so, and assert its right for consideration in face of the most uncompromising thirst! Loss of appetite is the certain result of over indulgence in liquids, and after his game of polo, hockey or tennis, the player should content himself with a small supply, and suffer as much thirst as his endurance can support. As his condition improves his thirst will grow less imperative, until he can train himself to abstain from all liquids till a full hour after his game. A bath, best taken tepid, will reduce a thirst far more effectually than a water-logged stomach.

While on the subject of abstinence the tobacco question may be briefly touched upon. No one has attempted to argue that pipe, cigar or cigarette can have anything but a harmful effect on the "wind." The matter resolves itself, therefore, into a question of how far such harmful effect may be supported in order to avoid such counterbalancing discomforts as may arise from a total abstinence from tobacco. Unless a man is in hard training for some special effort, there is no necessity to deprive him entirely of so coveted a pleasure, but the rule still holds good—the less smoke, the better wind. The inveterate smoker urges that a stoppage of his daily allowance would surely be followed by loss of sleep, nerve and temper. The reply to such a plea is obvious. He is not master of himself, and, apart from the subject of training, would be well advised to break his bondage by gradual stages.

Having secured a full supply of tissue, it still remains to turn it into muscle by dint of proper exercise. For indoor exercises fixed systems, such as the Sandow or Macdonald-Smith, may be adopted, but have no peculiar application in India. Steadily adhered to, such exercises must produce similar muscles in different individuals, and no necessity arises for special treatment; but in India the disciple of such teachers should carefully avoid the least over-exertion. The tropical sun renders the question of out-door exercise rather more difficult, and again the best advice seems to be that each man should follow his natural instincts.

When the writer first landed in India, a "Quai hai" of the old school, for whose opinion he had a mistaken respect, impressed on his youthful mind that a sharp walk before breakfast was an absolute essential to permanent good health. He followed this advice for six months, with a result that the hard exercise in the sun on an empty stomach produced loss of appetite, weakness and heart palpitation. All these distressing complaints disappeared when he abandoned the system and postponed all severe open-air exercise until later in the day. After such experience I naturally refrain from recommending any particular method of exercise, and can only register a concluding caution against over-exertion in a high temperature.

Get slowly into condition before attempting a supreme effort. No game is worth the risk incurred by a man who is weak or in ill-health. To those whose careers are laid in India, health must ever be a primary consideration, for a breakdown, which in England a short rest would suffice to repair, may develop in the tropics into a permanent injury.

CRICKET

Cricket in India labours under serious disadvantages as compared with other forms of sport. The essential elements of the game are not easily procured. Ninety-nine per cent. of Europeans in India are busy men, or at any rate have regular daily duties to perform, and cannot easily find time for a two or three days' cricket match. Polo can be played for an hour in the evening, and, the ordinary station game being within the capacity of a subaltern's income, the cricket field in ordinary times is deserted for the polo-ground. Two players can enjoy a game at golf—even a solitary round possesses some attraction—and the increasing number of links have added to the difficulty of collecting a team of cricketers.

Both these drawbacks are partially avoided by the existence of native teams, but the native cricketer has not appeared in the majority of districts, and can only be reckoned an important factor in the game on the western side of the Peninsula.

Again, the tropical sun renders the maintenance of a respectable ground a matter of considerable labour and expense. During the dry season, which extends over the greater portion of the year, grass dies unless watered daily, and the method of watering is of necessity primitive. Except in Bombay and Calcutta, and perhaps one or two other large towns, water must be carried from rivers or tanks in skins or buckets (usually petroleum tins), and the coolies engaged in the work require strict supervision. The difficulty of obtaining a good grass wicket under these conditions hardly requires explanation. Even constant watering will not keep Indian grass alive more than two or three years, and pitches must be frequently raked up, so that permanent turf, as procurable in England, remains practically unknown. Those whom such difficulties overwhelm have recourse to matting, which can be well laid on a sun-baked soil, and in some hill stations, as Darjeeling and Mussoorie, no other pitch is possible. A very fair wicket can be thus obtained, but to the English cricketer a grass pitch, if not a green field, seems essential to his favourite game. Although good sport may be had out of a strip of matting laid on a sandy plateau, it is never quite the "real thing." Again, the establishment of a flourishing club with officials, ground men, pavilion, and other comforts is necessary to the full enjoyment of the game, and the shifting nature of the European community, garrisons and civilian officials continually moving on to some other station, renders the existence of such institutions very precarious. The polo club accompanies the regiment, but a moveable cricket club cannot retain its popularity.

The natural result follows that the arrangements on the ordinary station ground are primitive in the extreme. Professional umpires or players find no support, and details depend upon the energy or indifference of the honorary secretary who happens to be in temporary charge of affairs.

Lastly, it must be remembered that the ordinary Indian station is self-contained. The immense distances between cricketing centres increase the difficulties of visiting and touring teams, who can rarely break the monotony of return matches between every conceivable permutation of the same two-and-twenty players.

So many complaints might appear sufficient to kill any game, but the vitality of cricket survives them all, and week after week columns of the sporting papers are devoted to reports of matches which the editors consider worthy of record.

The game flourishes principally in the Bombay Presidency, where the Parsees assist materially to keep the ball rolling. Many of the latter are fine players, and the example of Mehta, who is now employed professionally at the Old Trafford ground in England, will suffice to show that individuals rise to even first-class form. The Europeans of the Presidency find it necessary to collect their strongest team to engage their rivals on equal terms.

A consideration of the 1903 tour made by a team of Oxford University Authentics, captained by Mr K. J. Key, affords a sufficiently accurate bird's-eye view of the location and quality of the best Indian cricket at the present time.

The members of the team, excluding F. G. H. Clayton and J. B. Aspinall, who played only eight and nine innings respectively, were :—

H. B. Chinnery, H. H. Hollins, A. H. Hornby, C. Headlam, F. Kershaw, K. J. Key, H. J. Powys-Keck, R. H. Raphael, J. N. Ridley, G. H. Simpson-Hayward, J. E. Tomkinson and R. A. Williams.

The majority of these names are not yet celebrated in English first-class cricket, but many are improving players, and it may well happen that the paper strength of the team will appear greater a few seasons hence. Critics in India generally agreed, at the end of the tour, that the Authentics were fully as strong in all departments of the game as Lord Hawke's more famous team, and, in spite of the long record of disaster, enthusiasts can assert with confidence that the standard of Indian cricket has improved rather than deteriorated in the interval. The following list shows the matches played and their results :—

Where Played.	Against.	Result.
Bombay	Bombay Presidency	Lost by 46 runs
Do.	Hindus	Drawn
Do.	Parsees	Lost by 8 wickets
Secunderabad	Secunderabad	Drawn
Bangalore	Mysore State	Won by 6 wickets
Madras	Madras Presidency	„ 110 runs
Trichinopoly	Southern India	„ innings and 95 runs
Calcutta	Bengal Presidency	Drawn
Do.	Calcutta C.C.	Won by innings and 333 runs

Where Played.	Against.	Result.
Delhi	Gents. of India	Won by 6 wickets
Peshawar	Peshawar	" innings and 320 runs
Rawalpindi	Northern Punjab	" innings and 194 runs
Lahore	Punjab	" 100 runs
Aligarh	Aligarh College	Drawn
Jhansi	Bundelkund	Won by innings and 9 runs
Allahabad	United Provinces	" innings and 40 runs
Mozufferpore	Behar Wanderers	" 345 runs
Lucknow	Oudh Province	" innings and 227 runs
Cawnpore	Cawnpore & District	Drawn

Glancing at this table the impression at once arises, subject to an examination of the drawn matches at Aligarh, Calcutta and Cawnpore, that the Bombay and Secunderabad teams were the only serious opponents of the visitors. Of these the two latter ended greatly in the Authentics' favour, and at Aligarh, on a bowlers' wicket, the home team required 180 in their second innings, 57 only having resulted from their first venture.

In modification of this impression, however, it must be remembered that in Bombay the visitors were not yet accustomed to the strange light and unusual conditions of the tropical climate, and the Western teams met them in the weakest period of their tour, and, further, unsupported by two of their strongest players.

In justice to Indian cricket, the additional fact must be noted that many of the best players in the country failed to take the field against the Authentics at any part of their tour. This may be accounted for by the fact that the great Durbar at Delhi drew military and civilian officials from every province, and thus threw increased work upon those who remained at their posts. The teams of Northern India, of Gentlemen of India, and of the Bengal Presidency suffered severely in this respect.

Taking all these matters into consideration, a fair idea may be obtained of first-class Indian cricket, which is, of course, well below English County form. The standard of station games varies locally from year to year, after the manner of country town and village cricket in England.

In one district or another, cricket continues in India nearly the whole year round, but in the plains play is confined to the cold weather months. November to February roughly covers the cold season, which varies, however, in extent and degree in different latitudes. The "rains" of June and July bring a general stoppage.

In the hill stations, such as Darjeeling, Mussoorie, Shillong, Ootacamund and Simla, the cricket season proper extends from mid-April until the rains break in June; and on the Annandale ground, in the Vice-regal summer capital, cricketers gather from all parts of India. In Madras the game is well supported, and the occasional visit of a Ceylon or Bombay team arouses keen interest in the game throughout the southern Presidency. In Calcutta, despite the large European population and a number of local clubs, cricket has for some years past declined steadily, and the premier club, with its beautiful grounds in the Eden Gardens, close to the river

Hooghly, is largely maintained by the support of the tennis-playing members.

The new arrival will require some little time to accustom himself to the fierce light which beats upon an Indian cricket ground, even in the coolest season of the year, and on this subject a word of warning may not be out of place. A new arrival is notoriously less sensible of the sun's rays, and often regards the precautions of older residents in protecting their heads and eyes—particularly their eyes—as over-cautious and even absurd. Bearing in mind, however, the terrible and life-long injury that might result from a neglect of such precautions, a zealous imitation of more experienced players is strongly to be recommended.

FOOTBALL

Many causes contribute to the greater popularity of the Association rules in India, but the enthusiasts of the senior game contrive to prolong its existence in a tropical climate, despite many adverse conditions. The same difficulties that beset the Indian cricketer suffice to overwhelm the supporter of the Rugby Union rules in the vast majority of stations and districts. The primary obstacle is occasioned by the iron hardness of the ground, which renders the Rugby game impossible during nine months of the year. For a few weeks only, after the annual "rains," is the ground sufficiently softened to reduce the danger of a heavy fall within reasonable limits. For the native, the Rugby game has little charm; few stations can produce thirty players; and, without the support of regimental teams, even this essential number can only be obtained in three or four large centres. In the great majority of regiments the Association game has secured the undivided attention of Thomas Atkins, and those battalions that maintain a strong Rugby team are now few and far between. During the past decade the regiments that have supported Rugby to any appreciable extent may be numbered on the fingers of one hand. Of these, the most notable are the Buffs, the Border Regiment, and the Welsh Regiment, of which the last-named can claim to have the finest fifteen at present in India. During 1902 they travelled in succession to Bombay, Madras and Calcutta, and defeated all-comers in the three Presidency towns. In these regiments the spirit of tradition more than suffices to keep the game alive, and as an example of the enthusiasm which may be engendered by success, I may relate the following incident in the experience of an officer of the Buffs.

The battalion Fifteen had carried off the Calcutta Cup on several occasions, but, when ordered to the front for the Tirah Expedition, football was sacrificed to the stern call to war. After two years' campaigning and outpost duty the battalion again assembled in a frontier station, and the officer afore-mentioned was requested by a corporal of his company for permission to play off the ties for the Annual Company Cup, which had been left unfinished *two years before*!

With the exception of such purely regimental sport, a consideration of the Rugby game in India resolves itself into small compass. In Madras and Rangoon, tournaments are held annually, and the "Gymkhana" in each of these towns includes a sufficient number of Rugby footballers to render them independent of military support. Madras and Calcutta teams have recently exchanged visits, and the Madras tournaments often attract other powerful visiting fifteens. In Bombay, every effort is made to sustain the game; naval officers render valuable aid to the Gymkhana, and the Bombay Tournament seldom fails to produce interesting matches. Of recent years, the Welsh Regiment have been constant and successful visitors, and the Rugby officials of the Gymkhana endeavour to arrange alternate visits with the Calcutta Football Club.

This, the premier football club in Calcutta, has extended its operations to Association and also to hockey, but the fostering of the Rugby Union game remains its primary object. Every possible means are adopted by the committee to increase the popularity of the game and to sustain public interest in the annual tournament. Other local clubs are supported, and a junior cup encourages school teams, which are coached and instructed by members of the Calcutta Club. Regimental teams within reach of Calcutta will find their way made financially and otherwise easy should they express any desire to compete in the tournament; and members of a visiting team may expect in addition a warm welcome and lavish entertainment from the officials and playing members of the Calcutta Football Club.

Without in any way disparaging the efforts of the Bombay and Madras Gymkhanas, the very existence of Rugby football in India may be said to depend upon the enthusiasm and labours of the successive honorary secretaries of the Calcutta Club. The names of Messrs Frank Carter, C. G. Newton and A. D. Pickford will live long in the grateful memories of Rugby enthusiasts throughout India.

As in the Old Country, so in India, the Association game has appealed directly to the masses. From Bombay to Calcutta, from Peshawar to Madras, a cup tie will attract Europeans and natives alike, and in large centres the latter invest the ground in their tens of thousands. Association football is the game nearest to the heart of the British soldier, and nearly every regiment in India boasts its team of trained players. To these distance presents no insuperable difficulty, and the crack regimental elevens will travel many days' journey to compete for the cups and medals which are now offered in most large stations. In the tournament held at Delhi during the great Durbar, so many British regiments entered teams that the preliminary ties were played off beforehand, and only the winning team in each "command" competed at Delhi itself.

The strict regulations against rough and unnecessary charging, necessitated by the modern development of the game, have rendered play possible even upon ground baked to a brick-like consistency. Each centre has its particular football season, but so greatly do these vary that in one district or another tournaments are in progress nearly the whole year round. By a strange reverse, the cold weather months form the off-season for football in India. Regiments are engaged in manœuvres and route-marching, and civilians of all ranks work at double pressure. The days are short, twilight is unknown, and few offices empty until the lamps have long been lit.

The busiest period extends from June to October, when the rains have softened the ground and cooled the atmosphere, but in some stations, as for example Calcutta, the season proper begins in May, the hottest month of the whole year!

The Durand Cup, played for in Simla during September, long held its position as the premier trophy of India. Having been won outright, a challenge cup is now offered annually in its place, but the Bombay Rovers' annual tournament, held in the same month, attracts entries equal or superior in number and quality to those received at Simla. In point of both time and importance, the Harris Tournament in Poona follows these two annual fixtures, and also attracts the majority of first-class regimental teams. Civilian clubs rarely figure in the final rounds of these tournaments. Great exertions in a foreign climate naturally necessitate careful physical preparation, and want of strict training, together with lack of continual practice, suffice effectually to handicap the more or less scratch elevens of civilian clubs.

The Murree Tournament held early in June perhaps comes next in importance, and in Calcutta a handsome challenge shield is thrown open to all comers in the same month. In the capital of India the game finds strong support, and a sufficient number of local clubs have sprung up to constitute a "league" run on English lines. This league and the annual tournament are subject to the jurisdiction of the council of the "Indian Football Association," a title which requires comment, as likely to mislead a stranger. This council—as the latest annual report confirms—has little if any jurisdiction beyond the suburbs of Calcutta, and the officials have hitherto failed to attract any considerable number of visiting teams to their open tournament. Its latest offspring, the Calcutta Referees' Association, while suggesting a more suitable name for the parent body, testifies to the flourishing condition of the game in India. The Western India Football Association has been recently formed in Bombay to control football and to act as a court of appeal for clubs and leagues in the

Bombay Presidency, and, since its jurisdiction extends to Poona, Karachi and Quetta, this body at once attains to considerable importance.

Among other tournaments may be noted those of Bangalore, Lahore, Madras, Mandalay, Rangoon and Secunderabad.

With regard to the form displayed in the Durand, Bombay Rovers and Harris Tournaments, no satisfactory comparison with English standards is possible. Under such trying climatic conditions, a hard game of football is a severe strain on the strongest constitution, and few players can maintain their form longer than three or four seasons. Even regimental teams change so rapidly that the champions of 1900 may find themselves unable to survive the preliminary rounds of tournaments in 1903. But the places of those who fall out are filled by an unfailing supply of new recruits, and year after year the popularity of the game increases. This popularity is the more extraordinary when we recollect that football is the winter game of England, and apparently quite unsuited to the fierce heat of a summer evening in the tropics. The question whether football is a rational exercise for Europeans recently arrived in India may be left to individuals and their medical advisers, but the fact remains that Association flourishes, despite every disadvantage, throughout the length and breadth of India.

In many districts the natives have taken kindly to the game, and tournaments confined to native clubs multiply apace, but their form shows little promise of rising to the European level.

GOLF

In Bombay and Calcutta, clubs of long-standing exist, but even in those centres the game attracted little attention until a very recent date. Fifteen, even ten, years ago, golf was confined to a handful of devotees ; to-day the links of the Presidency towns are overcrowded with enthusiasts. Wherever links have been constructed, and a permanent club established, the game has prospered amazingly, and courses are slowly but steadily increasing throughout the Peninsula.

As a game adaptable to the rigours of a tropical climate, the merits of golf are undeniable, and its advantages over other ball games manifold. The golfer obtains steady exercise without too much exertion, and the football or hockey player, who finds that he can no longer keep pace with his younger rivals, turns gladly to devote his entire energies to the slower, but more scientific, game. In comparison with polo, racing and even ordinary riding, golf is a very inexpensive amusement, and on the links the poor man struggles against no such overwhelming odds as he must be prepared to face on the polo ground.

Again, the golfer requires but a single opponent, and can enjoy a round during a leisure hour at any time of the day; the cricketer must first consult the convenience of twenty-one players, and then devote a whole day to a single match. No wonder, then, that golf is popular, and the question at once arises — Why are there not links in every station? To this query the answer is easily found. It must be granted that little difficulty arises in the matter of location, for, with the exception of hill stations, space can usually be found on which to construct links, even though they may not approach the golfer's ideal. But in the ordinary Indian station, military or civil, the European population is temporary and transient. The benefit of their labour in preparing links would be reaped by new-comers, perhaps the new garrison would neglect the greens and allow the course to revert to its primitive jungle state. Temporary occupiers of Government quarters have no guarantee that their reliefs will take over the capital outlay involved, and, in fact, they may well have serious doubts as to the willingness of their successors to accept such liability. Indian labour, though cheap, is not so cheap that the construction of even a nine-hole course can be undertaken without careful consideration of the cost. And so it happens that, despite the popularity of existing courses, golf links are still but sparsely scattered over the country.

The principal centres and best links will generally be found in those places which contain a non-official European community — business men, as in Bombay and Calcutta; or retired settlers, as at Ootacamund. These constitute a sufficient nucleus to guarantee the labour and expenditure involved in the foundation of a golf club, and afterwards provide a committee and secretary, whose interest in the welfare of the club is not terminated by the vagaries of the Government Gazette.

Like all other games, the conditions under which golf is played vary immensely in different parts of India. English links differ considerably in aspect, but those in India differ so widely that the whole character of the game is affected. According to English ideas, a "putting green" seems almost as essential to the game of golf as a ball or clubs, but in India many links exist on ground innocent of a single blade of grass. The holes are placed on carefully rolled patches of sand, and at a first trial the lightning speed of these "browns" might even puzzle Vardon himself. The difficulty of cultivating grass, and of preserving it from destruction in the long Indian summer, diminishes the number of grass courses to a small proportion, and, needless to add, the best golf and most interesting competitions take place over these courses.

No professional players have as yet reached India, and the native "caddies" and "malis" (gardeners) still confine themselves to their humble duties. At cricket, racquets and billiards, individual native players have excelled in first-class company, as the names of Ranjitsinhji,

Jamsetjee, Jayaram and Mehta abundantly testify; and, perhaps, an Indian golfer may yet astonish the natives of Bideford or St Andrews.

At present, only two or three clubs in India show any signs of attaining a financial position of sufficient strength to warrant the engagement of a permanent professional from home.

Among the best Indian links are those at Calcutta and Barrackpore, Bombay, Madras, Bangalore, Gulmarg, Ootacamund, Nasik and Yerrowda (Poona). To commence with the capital of India, no less than five separate courses have been laid out in and around Calcutta. The Calcutta Golf Club is perhaps the strongest club in the country, and the programme for 1902-03, given in full below, testifies to the flourishing condition of the game in the metropolis. Some of these competitions draw more than seventy entries! The club links lie over the maidan, or park, which is bounded on one side by the river Hooghly and Fort William, on the other by the European quarter of the town. The pride and delight of the ordinary resident, the maidan is rather disappointing from a golfer's point of view. The section on which the military authorities permit golf to be played extends to less than a mile in length and about four hundred yards in breadth. No permanent bunkers may be constructed, and the only natural obstacles are four "tanks," or artificial ponds, and the ornamental trees with which the park is studded. Certainly the grass grows green throughout the year, but during eight or ten months of the cold and dry seasons the brick-like consistency of the ground places fine golf at a discount. From a miserable drive, that would scarce suffice to cover thirty yards over springy turf, the Indian "duffer" may see his ball run on and on over the top of the hard ground until the advantage due to his opponent's cleaner shot is almost nullified. Over these flat courses the rubber ball has recently produced startling effects on the scores of handicap players, and the absence of the "scratch" men from the lists of winners will probably result in an all-round reduction of the handicaps. This fact has been quickly recognised, and all the leading players in the last amateur championship of India used the Haskell or Kempshall balls.

Pathways cross the Calcutta maidan in every direction, and the ceaseless processions of native wayfarers constitute another grave nuisance to the golfer; but the links are within easy reach of both the business and residential quarters of the city, and, despite the uninteresting character of the sport obtainable, the course is crowded with players throughout the year.

Barrackpore lies on the river Hooghly, some fifteen miles by rail from Calcutta, and contains a small garrison of field artillery and infantry. On the river bank the Viceroy has a country residence, which he occupies only during the cold weather months and then only for a few days at a time. The beautiful park surrounding the bungalow he has thrown open to golfers and an excellent eighteen hole grass course attracts many week-end visitors from the capital. The garrison and suburban residents support a local club, but the Calcutta Golf Club contributes to the maintenance of the links and has a separate bungalow for its own members near the course. With a free hand an energetic committee might construct splendid links at Barrackpore, but the enforced absence of bunkers and a superfluity of ornamental trees constitute serious defects in the eye of a golfer. For these drawbacks the superior turf and ample space hardly compensate, and the smaller links at Tollygunge have ousted both the maidan and Barrackpore links from the pride of place in the esteem of Calcutta golfers.

The Tollygunge Club lies some four miles south of Calcutta, but an electric tramway has brought it within easy reach of residents in town. The founders of the club intended to promote all manner of sports, principally racing and gymkhanas, but improved links and the tramway have attracted a golfing element that outweighs all other interests. An excellent race-course still exists, but the park surrounding the two club houses is dotted with greens and bunkers, and the golfer reigns supreme. Sunday play is still prohibited on the Calcutta maidan, and thus the business man is attracted to Tollygunge in ever increasing numbers. A nine-hole course is quickly overcrowded, and the Calcutta golfer will soon be forced to seek pastures new.

The amateur championship of India so-called—and with perhaps as good a right to that high sounding title as any other competition in India—is played during Christmas week over the Tollygunge links.

Rangoon golfers, and occasionally a Bombay player, are attracted to this open meeting, but the championship usually falls to a local "crack" familiar with every rut and hillock on the links.

The championship meeting begins with an open handicap over the Barrackpore course, to which a challenge cup and other valuable prizes are attached. For the championship itself a qualifying test of thirty-six holes over the Tollygunge links under medal rules leaves eight competitors to contest the issue by match play. The semi-final rounds are decided over eighteen holes and the final over thirty-six, a trying conclusion to a very severe test comprising three full days of play. The competition record for the Tollygunge green stands at eighty-one, and, considering the difficulties of the course, this figure represents very good golf.

While on the subject of match play, the effect of a tropical climate on both the physique and morale of the golfer may be remarked. Even in the cold season a European cannot expect to play thirty-six or even eighteen holes under a tropical sun without putting his staying powers to a severe test. A three days' tournament cannot be lightly undertaken, and the player who is not in hard condition may relinquish hope of seeing the final rounds. Again the discomfort of an Indian hot weather acts as a rare stimulant to irritability and impatience, feelings that are fatal to steady golf. An imperturbable temper is of immense service to a golfer in any country, but in the tropics its rarity increases its value to an extent that can hardly be expressed in too extravagant terms.

In addition to these three links, a ladies' club flourishes under the lee of the big club, and a miniature course has been laid out in a corner of the maidan. A neat little moveable bungalow provides a centre from which the ladies contest a programme that is only surpassed in length and variety by that of the Calcutta club itself.

Good links exist at Dum-Dum, celebrated for its small-arms ammunition factories, which lies some five miles out of Calcutta. An electric tramway is alone needed to render this course a welcome rival to that at Tollygunge and to relieve the present overcrowding of that popular green. The Calcutta season proper extends from early November to the end of June, when the "rains" put a stop to competitions. In the off-season, however, the links are by no means deserted and the uninitiated observer might fail to notice any marked difference between the two periods. The following list of cups, bowls, medals and competitions may be permitted to speak for itself, and the Bombay and Madras clubs can boast programmes little inferior in length and value to that of Calcutta.

Calcutta Golf Club.

List of Fixtures, Season 1902-03.

November	Opening Day. Handicap Competition with two prizes for Senior and "Duffer" divisions.
December	Open Handicap at Barrackpore and "Asian" Challenge Bowl.
	AMATEUR CHAMPIONSHIP OF INDIA.
	Visitors *vs.* Calcutta.
January	Handicap Tournament by holes for the Penan Silver Medal.
	Lansdowne Gold Medal.
February	The Ladies' Bowl.
March	Club Gold Medal (scratch).
	Captain's Cup.
April	Foursomes Tournament.
	Blackheath Gold Medal and Cup.
	Easter Handicap at Barrackpore.
	Madras Silver Medal.
May	Bogey Competition.
June	St Andrew's Silver Tankard.
	A Cup.
	Bogey Competition.
	Bombay Silver Medal.
	Colombo Medal.

Cashmere Silver Challenge Cup.
Ormiston do. do.

In addition to these competitions, for the most part annual fixtures, a number of special prizes are offered from time to time by past or present members of the club, and additional competitions over the Barrackpore and Tollygunge links attract all the premier golfers of the Calcutta Club.

In Bombay golfers labour under greater difficulties than their brethren of Calcutta. The links lie over the maidan and marine lines within the town, which are cramped, enclosed, and infested by swarms of pedestrians. The Government or municipal authorities naturally object to the construction of permanent bunkers, and so flat and uneventful are the links that many players find that a cleek and a putter form a sufficient armament, and seldom call their other clubs into requisition. Screen bunkers have lately been adopted to vary the monotony of the course, and if conducive to worse temper and language, these substitutes for the real article certainly necessitate better golf. Despite every obstacle, however, the game flourishes in Bombay, and the links are quite inadequate to the demands of an increasing band of golfers.

The Royal Bombay Golf Club organises a long series of competitions, and their principal tournament is held in October. In that month the atmosphere is humid and muggy in the extreme, but the greens are in fine condition after the rains, and the turf—if any Indian grass deserves the name—is sufficiently soft and springy to resemble its English prototype. Among the principal events of the Bombay golfing season are the club handicap and scratch competitions in October, the St Andrews gold medal and handicap and the Calcutta silver challenge medal in December, the Blackheath gold medal and the Forty-two medal in January, the St George's and Wimbledon medals in February, all with handicaps attached, and the Bombay Golfers' Cup in April.

A curious little course has been constructed on the sea-shore at Bandra, a northern suburb of Bombay. These links are frequented by residents, for the most part business men, who escape each evening from the confined atmosphere of the city, and also by regular players of the Bombay Club, who visit Bandra in the character of week-end trippers. The course is devoid of grass, very rough and precipitous, and the little "browns" poised on the edge of a cliff or carved out of a steep hillside demand very considerable skill in approach and the utmost caution in putting.

But Bombay golfers can obtain better sport at Nasik, which lies within a few hours by rail to the north-east. The Western India Golf Club (of Poona) have erected a club-house at this station, and the Western India championship is played over their links in September. A gymkhana club has been formed to provide residential accommodation close to the course for visitors, and an annual subscription of Rs. 10 entitles "country" members to a share in this convenience.

The head-quarters of the Poona club are at Yerrowda, but golf has not obtained the same firm hold on public favour as in Bombay, principally owing to the paucity of non-official European residents, who must always form the mainstay of golf in India.

In the Madras Presidency there are several good links, the principal centres being Bangalore,

Ootacamund, and the presidency town itself. Golfers in the capital have the choice of two links, one at Guindy, five miles out of town, and the other within the city itself. The latter are on the "Island," which is also utilised as a race-course and a parade-ground. The links are flat and uninteresting and boast but one or two artificial bunkers. The natural obstacles consist of sandy patches and the water that surrounds the course on three sides. The links at Guindy lie on the site of an old race-course, lately abandoned by the race club. Most of the tournaments and the annual match against Bangalore take place on this course, but competitions are also held over the Island links. Among the principal annual fixtures are the following:—

The April handicap at Guindy opens the Madras season, and is followed by a series of competitions for the Guindy cup. The Calcutta medal and handicap over the Island links in May, the Guthrie medal and handicap in June, and, after the usual break caused by the rains, a series of monthly medals extend to November when the captain's prize is played for. The Ootacamund links rival the best links in India, but, as at Bangalore, local support alone maintains the course, and the club competitions attract little outside interest. The links were re-modelled in 1899 and 1900, after considerable bickering with the riding and hunting contingent, who strongly object to any encroachment on their sacred "Downs." A pavilion now stands on the links, and many efforts have been made to coax the "browns" into a semblance of real putting greens and otherwise to improve the course. A few artificial bunkers have been erected, but the steep slopes, swampy bottoms, and patches of scrub provide sufficient obstacles in themselves. The season at Ootacamund is comparatively a short one, for the Downs are exposed to the full blast of the south-west monsoon, when wind and rain render golf practically impossible.

The admirers of the Peshawar Vale links declare them without exception the finest in the East; "the turf through the greens is soft and springy, and the putting greens equal to those of any inland course in England!"

Alas, that so few Indian golfers can enjoy so glorious a prospect! The open meeting of April 1903, the Peshawar Vale open championship, attracted only seven entries, and even of this tiny band more than one declined the contest. This lamentable fact exactly illustrates the principal difficulties that beset golf in India, the distances that prevent busy men from journeying to scattered centres in search of sport, and the Government gazettes that move military and civil officials from station to station and from district to district, regardless of their personal inclinations. The non-official community collects in a few trade centres, and without its support even good links like those of Peshawar cannot greatly flourish.

The Mahomed Bagh Club at Lucknow has

recently constructed an improved course, the holes varying in length from 220 to 360 yards, and in this large station the game has of recent years advanced rapidly in popularity. The finest links, however, in Northern India, perhaps in all India, despite the predilection of local golfers for Tollygunge, Peshawar, or Ootacamund, are those at Gulmarg in Kashmir. They lie in a cup-like hollow, surrounded by mountains, at a height of 10,000 feet above sea level. With the advantage of a perfect climate and beautiful surroundings, they have also splendid turf and fine greens, and space sufficient for a full course of eighteen holes. The Northern India Tournament is played at Gulmarg in the autumn, and attracts all the Punjab golfers who can tear themselves away from their duties in the plains.

Rangoon is another great golfing centre, and a Rangoon player usually finds his way through the qualifying rounds of the Amateur Championship in Calcutta. Among other courses may be mentioned those at Waltair, Mount Abu, Shillong and Kolar, but on links other than those here mentioned play seldom attracts more than local attention.

HOCKEY

Although comparatively a new game in India, the popularity of hockey has of recent years advanced with rapid strides. In some districts of Assam and Bengal the term "hockey" is applied to the local polo which is played on very small ponies, but we are now considering the game of hockey as popularly known in England.

The first feature calling for notice is the remarkable aptitude for the game displayed by natives, whose speed and agility enable them to compete on equal terms with European teams more physically powerful. Led by their British officers, most of the native infantry regiments can place a strong hockey team in the field, and the tournament at the Delhi Durbar, confined to the native army, drew a great number of entries. The men take a deep interest in inter-regimental contests, and during the last China expedition several exciting matches took place under the walls of Pekin before an admiring throng of imperturbable Chinamen.

In British regiments the British officers take a personal interest in the game, and many military elevens, like the successful team of the Royal Irish Rifles, contain four or five subalterns.

Such extensive support from among the military would alone suffice to render a hockey match a familiar sight in the majority of stations, and tournaments have multiplied rapidly during the last few years. Among the more important of these may be mentioned :—

The "Aga Khan" at Bombay in May, the "Poona" in December, the "Punjab Native

Army" at Mian Mir in February, the "Madras Army" in September, the "All-India" at Allahabad in January, the "Beighton" at Calcutta and the "Madras" in April and May, the "All-Burma" at Rangoon in March, and the "Finney" at Rawalpindi in February.

From this list it might seem that the hockey season has no limits in India, but, speaking generally, hockey is a "hot-weather" game, not by reason of its suitability to extreme heat, but of necessity, as governed by the same conditions as Association football.

In addition to military elevens, civilian clubs abound in all large centres, schools and colleges can produce first-class teams, and the following twenty entries for the 1903 Aga Khan Tournament in Bombay speak eloquently for the wide-spread popularity of the game:—

British Army.	Native Army.	Civilians—European & Native.
Royal Scots	17th Bombay Inf.	Bombay Gymkhana
North Staffords	19th do.	Elphinstone College
The Buffs	21st do.	Cathedral Old Boys
Oxford L. I. Band	Pioneers	Esplanade Wanderers
E. & F. Coys. The Staffords	1st Inf., Hyderabad Cont.	Bombay Education Society
62nd Batt. R. F. A.		Byculla do.
R. G. A., Bombay		Government Telegraph Recreation Club
R. A., Colaba		

The Buffs, after hard struggles with the 19th Bombay Infantry and the Byculla Education Society, suffered defeat in the final after three drawn matches, at the hands of the Cathedral Old Boys. This result illustrates the sufficiency of native and civilian combinations to encounter the teams of British regiments on equal terms.

In Bengal, the native and College teams have proved themselves even more capable in this respect than on the Bombay side. The Royal Irish Rifles, champions of the 1903 "All-India" Tournament at Allahabad, succumbed shortly afterwards in Calcutta to a team of school-boys from Ranchi, who also outplayed all the best civilian teams in the capital.

Again, no comparison with English form is practicable, but the hard, dry ground, often, indeed usually, innocent of grass, tends to make the Indian game very fast and not a little dangerous.

The reason why hockey should be a less exhausting form of exercise than Association football is not quite clear, but the absence of "charging" may perhaps supply the explanation. The testimony of a pugilist is not required to affirm the exhausting effect of any description of body blow, and a series of the most innocent "charges" test the footballer's staying power to its very depths. This immunity may account for the comparative success of half-trained civilian teams, and that success suffices to explain the rapid advance of hockey in popular esteem.

If polo is the *national* game, hockey, after all a sister sport, may fairly be called the *popular* game of India.

TENNIS AND RACQUETS

One of the first to be introduced into India, lawn tennis is perhaps the best suited of all English games to a tropical climate, and to the conditions of European life in the East.

A set of tennis affords exercise without exhaustion, a negative quality which the majority of Anglo - Indians highly appreciate. Golf surpasses it in this respect, but stations possessing links are still the exception rather than the rule. Labour is cheap, courts can easily be constructed, and the requisite players are usually ready to hand. Houses and bungalows have their private courts, the cost of racquets and balls is comparatively low, and the necessity and disadvantages of a club are avoided.

The prefix "lawn," retained with effort even in England, loses its meaning and is unknown in India. Grass courts are the exception, and those that exist have no pretensions to the title of "lawn." Hard and dry, the Indian grass court plays, after a three months' drought, faster than the driest lawn in England. The ordinary sand court, well-rolled and level as a billiard table, plays faster still, and this fact constitutes the main difference that will strike the English player. He will soon grow accustomed to the strange light, and in other respects the Indian game presents few peculiarities. A host of servants to collect the balls will astonish and gratify the new arrival, who may have memories of long and tiresome searches in the shrubberies and cabbage beds of his country friends.

Tennis continues during the whole year, although the "rains" provide a brief interruption, but the cold weather is naturally the favourite season for tournaments.

Where every station, civil and military, organizes its annual tournament, a selection of the principal fixtures becomes an invidious task, but the following attract considerably more than mere local attention.

In February, the Bengal championships are played on the grass courts of the Calcutta Cricket Club, and the entries often include players from Burma and the Punjab. The Western India championships and the Marryat cup are March fixtures in Bombay, and the Southern India championships are held at Madras in the same month. The September tournament at Poona, and the "Rangoon" in January also call for mention, while those at Allahabad, Bangalore, Lucknow, and Lahore all draw the best players of their respective provinces.

The introduction of other games, such as golf and hockey, has led to many desertions from the ranks of regular tennis players, but the general popularity of a pastime so suited to the requirements of Europeans in a hot climate is likely to continue long.

In three hill stations, Simla, Darjeeling and

Dalhousie, covered courts have been erected on the model of the original at Cooch-Behar, the winter residence of the Maharajah of that name. The present Maharajah of Cooch-Behar and his son are both well-known on the polo-grounds of England and India, and the former is an unequalled exponent of this particular game.

The court consists of an ordinary stone or cement tennis court, enclosed by side and back walls. One side wall is perpendicular to the height of six feet only and thence slopes outward, forming a broad "pent" or slope running the entire length of the court. The other side runs straight up, like the back wall of a racquet court, to the spectators' gallery. Ordinary tennis bats and balls are used and scoring proceeds as at lawn tennis. This game, like "real" tennis, has a peculiar fascination for the veriest tyro, and a match will draw a crowded gallery of spectators, but the cost of building prevents it from developing into a popular pastime.

The same objection applies to racquets, but custom long decreed that a military station was incomplete without its racquet court, and the game is consequently far more general than in England. Nevertheless, racquets can never become a popular game, partly by reason of its cost, partly because a single court serves to accommodate so few players. In the plains men take their exercise regularly and within specified hours in the morning or evening of each day; how many courts would be required to accommodate one hundred regular racquet players! The enormous European population of Calcutta rests content with two courts, another way of saying that, with the exception of a mere handful, they do not care to play racquets at all! Throughout the north-west and the United Provinces the game is more popular, and in some of the older stations enthusiasts still utilize the huge and antiquated courts built in the sixties and seventies or maybe earlier. With regard to tournaments, racquets may be called a "station" game, and such contests rarely engage other than purely local interest. For the last open tournament in Bombay, but three entries were received, and those at Calcutta and Murree attract a handful of local players.

Some of the native markers attain to great skill, and the brilliant success in London of "Jamsetjee" the Bombay professional affords sufficient testimony to their capabilities. With a few notable exceptions, European players in India can show but moderate form.

MISCELLANEOUS

The sprinter and the hurdler find in India some few opportunities of showing their heels on the running track, and some very smart records are put up from time to time. The few grass tracks are of course abnormally fast, a fact which should not be forgotten in comparing times. The principal meetings are those of the Burma Athletic Association in Rangoon, the Southern India Athletic Association in Madras, the Presidency Athletic Association in Calcutta, and those at Bombay and Bangalore.

In Calcutta "British Army" and "Native Army" championships attract distant entries, but not in sufficient numbers to give the winners any substantial claim to the championship of all India. Similarly open events at other meetings seldom rise above the level of local or at most provincial contests, and the form displayed at the different centres, though variable, averages nearly equal.

Those who require fuller information regarding records and times, as also those who have occasion to organise regimental or other athletic meetings will obtain valuable information from a little book entitled "Athletic Sports and how to run them." The author, Mr W. S. Burke, has long experience and a thorough knowledge of his subject, and copies of the work may be obtained at the moderate price of eight annas from the office of the *Indian Field*, Calcutta, or any bookseller.

As a substitute for tennis during the rainy season, if not as a rival to that game, badminton is by no means to be despised. A keen set calls for a degree of skill and endurance to which the practised player alone can attain, and the game is deservedly popular throughout India. Though often attempted on a lawn, badminton can only rank as an indoor amusement, for the shuttlecock is over-sensitive to the least disturbing element in the weather.

The programmes of the larger athletic meetings include bicycling events, but good fields have hitherto proved the exception. The Bengal Cyclists' Association, organised in Calcutta, supports one, three, and twenty-five mile championships, but the hopes of its founders have hardly been realised. The Ramblers' Cycle Club sustains the sport in Bangalore, and races are also held in Bombay. Racing, however affects but a very small percentage of bicyclists and as a mode of exercise and of locomotion the safety bicycle has proved an inestimable boon to many thousands of Anglo-Indians. Not only are the streets and main roads in and about the large towns and stations thronged with bicyclists but in the remotest districts and wildest jungles the astonished native has already grown familiar with the curious machine, another strange device of the impatient "sahib-log." All the leading makers have agents in the presidency and other large towns, but nothing is lost by purchase in England, and a good bicycle forms no mean addition to an up-to-date Indian outfit.

The "noble art" is assiduously cultivated among British regiments in India, and military discipline ensures the orderly conduct of contests and the maintenance of a proper spirit among the competitors. The school of gymnasia at Poona under the able management of Captain Lewis has done much to encourage the sport, and the annual naval and military tournament draws a large entry from all parts of India. Soldiers predominate in the four open classes, and the officer's class alone fails to fill well. Other boxing contests are held annually in Bombay, Bangalore and Wellington, if sufficient entries are forthcoming.

The civilian element consists mainly of stray pugilists from Australia or New Zealand, and an occasional touring prize-fighter from England. From time to time individuals announce their claim in the daily press to such titles as "champion of India" or "of the East," but their challenges seldom lead to a serious contest.

Neither of those lawn games, bowls and croquet, can take deep root in India owing to the difficulties attending the cultivation of good greens. Calcutta is one of the few towns in the plains where these difficulties are surmounted, and the Calcutta Golf Club boasts a permanent bowling-green upon which at regular intervals matches are played against the Howrah Bowling Club, perhaps the only bona-fide bowling club in the country. Croquet clubs have not yet reached India, and the characteristics of the game are not such as to render their appearance probable.

Several well-known Indian princes have fallen victims to the fascinations of the motor-car, and among these may be mentioned His Highness the Aga Khan, and his brother sportsman, the wealthy potentate of Mysore. The inhabitants of the presidency towns have already learned to see, hear and smell the latest product of Western genius without surprise, but promoters (of the Indian trade) have yet to gain for their cars the confidence and popularity which prevail among the wealthy classes of France and England.

The costly amusement of pigeon-shooting finds few supporters in India, but a club of many years' standing still exists in Calcutta, where the great merchant firms maintain a small but regular supply of new members.

Twenty years ago, the majority of Anglo-Indians resorted daily to the station swimming bath, but the custom is no longer general, owing perhaps to the development of altered ideas and more careful management in matters of hygiene. A large percentage of Europeans, however, still indulge in the luxury of a daily swim, and many find that the exercise benefits their general health. In accordance with the fashion of Englishmen all the world over, the opportunity of obtaining sport is not neglected even in an Indian swimming bath. Races, diving competitions and water-polo matches are arranged on every possible occasion, and such entertainments seldom fail to fill the spectators' gallery to overflowing.

YACHTING

In the Royal Bombay Yacht Club the European residents of Bombay possess one of the finest clubs in India, and, although the yachting members form but a small minority, interest in the sport is well sustained. The club-house has a magnificent situation facing the harbour; its verandahs welcome the sea-breezes, and its lawns extend to the sea-wall, beyond which lie yachts at their moorings, and further out the white cruisers and gunboats of the East Indian Squadron.

The Bombay harbour and the sheltered bay on which it lies offer an ideal racing or cruising ground. During the greater part of the year a steady breeze blows across the bay from dawn until past sundown, variable in strength, of course, but always dependable. The south-west monsoon, however, sweeping the rain-clouds across the Indian Ocean, bursts with unbroken fury on the Bombay coast, and its storms drive the trim yachts into "winter quarters" early in June. Several islands break the smooth expanse of the bay, and on one of these, Hog Island, the yacht club owns a bungalow devoted to the use of week-end cruisers, who can thus obtain a pleasant change from the confined atmosphere of the city.

Despite many natural advantages, yachting is too costly a sport to develop into a popular pastime, and the number of bona-fide yachtsmen in the Royal Bombay Yacht Club has shown no sign of appreciable increase during recent years. In the seventies and early eighties the racing boats of Bombay carried lateen sails like the native "buggela" boats of to-day; the run of the hull was somewhat different, however, and their bows were spooned like modern racing craft. To-day the racers are divided into three classes, in each of which sufficient entries are forthcoming to provide material for weekly races throughout the long season, Recently the interest taken by the Governor of Bombay and the enterprise of the club commodore, Mr Scovell, have attracted considerable attention to the doings of yachtsmen in Bombay. Mr Scovell's 1903 cruise from England in his 45-ton yawl, *The Godwit*, created great interest in yachting circles, and his safe arrival in Bombay on the successful conclusion of his voyage gave a timely stimulus to the sport. For the weekly handicaps an aggregate cup is given in each class, and at the close of the season more important regattas are held. Lord Curzon's challenge cup, over a fifteen-mile course, and the club challenge cup are among the most coveted trophies.

Among the naval officers of the station the commodore obtains some little support, but the abolition of the Indian Defence Squadron has put a stop to races for ships' boats, formerly a regular item in the regatta programme. The sailing committee of the yacht club hope to induce vessels of the merchant service to supply this deficiency.

At Naini Tal, a "hill station" in the Himalayas, there is a little lake of prodigious depth, the bottom of which is popularly supposed to be covered by at least one layer of little yachts that have raced and sailed on its surface. The treacherous squalls whirling down upon the lake through the openings in the surrounding hills cause frequent accidents, and the list of fatalities is far from a short one.

Visitors to the hill station, however, still continue the sport, undeterred by the mishaps of their forerunners; and the little craft race desperately against each other in the summer regattas, that also include rowing events. Like the Bombay Yacht Club, the importance of the Naini Tal Boat Club arises mainly from its social functions. So long as the rank and fashion of the gay hill station flock down to the waterside in the afternoons, just so long will sailing and rowing flourish on the Naini Tal lake.

The Kashmir lakes lie somewhat beyond the beat of the ordinary Indian sportsman, but the number of visitors from the plains increases yearly, and in another decade a flourishing yacht club may exist at Ningal, and then the white sails of its cruisers will cover the Woollar lake. If enthusiasts can be found to brave the waters of Naini Tal, the Manisbal and Dal lakes in Kashmir should attract the yachtsman, while the Woollar is out and away the finest stretch of inland water anywhere in India. This lake is formed by the Jhelum, one of the great rivers that rise in Kashmir, and lies some twenty-five miles south of Srinagar. It extends to nearly

Photo] NAINI TAL LAKE AND BOAT HOUSE [*Laurie, Naini Tal*

ten miles in length and six in breadth. At Ningal lies a tiny fleet of pleasure craft, including a racing cutter, an American-designed "Una," a jolly-boat, and a steam launch, a variety that gives promise of increasing numbers in the future. The ponderous house-boat, creeping laboriously from port to port, is a more familiar sight, and makes an excellent moveable pivot for a sporting cruise. The fisherman has deserted Ningal for more profitable waters, but the finest chikor shooting in Kashmir can be obtained along the shores of the Woollar lake. To indulge in this sport a license must be taken out from the Kashmir Government; this permit costs less than thirty shillings, and covers chikor, pheasant and partridge from September to February; duck, geese, snipe and teal from September until April. Sailing from point to point the sportsman can obtain variety, not only of sport, but of wind and water, for on the Woollar a breeze freshens into a squall or dies away to a calm with glorious uncertainty and astonishing speed.

What a healthy prospect for the jaded dweller in the plains, and how insipid in comparison are the costly delights of Simla, Mussoorie or Darjeeling. A centre-board cutter, old, but reasonably seaworthy, can be hired at a moderate figure, and will provide an amateur crew with excitement and experience galore. Even such a boat, however, will only be found to-day after persistent enquiry, and Kashmir yachting, so far as the short-leave plainsman is concerned, is a sport of the future, not of the present; of the near future perhaps, but still of the future.

ROWING AND BOATING

ROWING and boating do not flourish in India. The reasons are various; some obvious, others less easy to determine. As a general rule, it may be said that anything approaching serious rowing and its attendant training and preparation, as understood in England, is carried out under conditions so unfavourable that none but an enthusiastic few are found willing to undertake it, or having done so, to continue it for any length of time. The anxieties, troubles, hard labour and disappointments that constantly overshadow the efforts of those who earnestly try to save the sport of boat-racing from dying of sheer inanition are very real. Rowing at home is not unassociated with trials to those who promote it and those who indulge in it, but no one who has not had experience of Indian rowing can have any idea of the difficulties with which it is beset. To enumerate a few of them. The immense distances between rowing centres militates against the appearance of visiting crews at the regattas. In these days of strenuous competition, rowing men find leave hard to get. Climatic conditions deter all but the most enthusiastic and fittest from taking up a sport which makes such calls upon their time and strength. The migratory character of the European population is another drawback; constant transfers, frequently resulting in astonishing fluctuations in the energy and enterprise of most clubs. The absence of twilight is a tremendous handicap, for, between ordinary office hours and the darkness, we have but a couple of hours of light, and, as in many cases, the boat-houses are miles away from the business or residential quarters of the towns, rowing men are often rushed in a way that ultimately cools their enthusiasm.

Still, there are ten rowing and boating clubs scattered over the Peninsula from Karachi in the north-west to Colombo in the south, and Rangoon in the extreme east, with the clubs of the Presidency towns and hill stations dotted in between the immense triangular area enclosed by these three points. Rowing is kept alive mainly by the efforts of old Varsity and public school men, from whose ranks the committees and the most prominent of the active members are recruited. Of old rowing Blues there are a few; of men who have rowed for their schools and colleges there are many. When the fates are kind, and a fair number of such men find themselves in close association and willing to co-operate in the promotion of their favourite sport, rowing booms for a while; under less happy conditions it languishes sadly.

1. The Calcutta Rowing Club.

Founded in 1859 by a few enthusiastic rowing exiles, the club had attained a membership of twenty-six and a fleet of four boats when the great cyclone and tidal wave of 1864 totally wrecked the club-house and reduced the boats to firewood. Rebuilt the following year on the Strand Road, the club flourished in its wooden boat-house till 1884, when it was removed to its present site; and when the improvements in modern racing-craft rendered operations on the Hooghly dangerous, two boat-houses were built on the south bank of the Kidderpore Docks backwater, and here all the serious rowing of the club is carried out, the old house opposite the band-stand being relegated to the "picnickers," the evening loungers and the patrons of pleasure craft.

The entrance fee is Rs.25, and the annual subscription Rs.50, payable in quarterly instalments. The colours are blue and white, blue coat piped with white and club badge on breast; and all members of the civil and military services, professions and those received in general society are eligible for membership, which is by ballot. Temporary members pay no entrance fee, but cannot remain as such for a period longer than six months. The absent fee is Rs.3 per quarter. The C.R.C. is affiliated to the A.R.A. and has one vote; its affairs are managed by a committee of six, of which the captain and honorary secretary are *ex officio* members, and there is a president and vice-president. The annual general meeting is held in January.

The fleet comprises five clinker-built racing fours, two ditto pairs, four clinker-built racing double-sculling boats, four ditto single-sculling skiffs, four carvel-built racing skiffs, two whiffs, ten coaching and double-sculling tubs, three tub fours, three dinghies and three canoes, chiefly by Clasper, Biffen and Salter.

The rowing season is from March to November, and regattas are held in March, May, August and October, every class of boat, oarsman, or sculler being provided for. The courses are from three-quarter mile for senior events, to quarter-mile for bumble-puppy items. There are three challenge cups—the Hooghly Cup for senior fours, the Hoare Cup for junior fours, and the Power Cup for senior sculls, each tenable for a year.

Throughout the year pleasure rowing is indulged in, and in the cold season—November to March — the Strand Road boat-house is particularly patronised by the devotees of Sunday and holiday river trips, and by those who use the reading-room, the bar and the verandahs overlooking the Eden Gardens and the Hooghly.

2. The Madras Boat Club.

Founded in 1870, this club has the largest membership of any rowing club in the Peninsula, there being usually over 300 members on the roll. It is open to the services, the professions and non-official gentlemen. Admission is by ballot. There is no entrance fee, and the subscription is Rs.10 per quarter. Visitors to Madras are eligible for honorary membership. Its colours are dark blue and gold. The affairs of the club are managed by a committee of seven, consisting of a president, captain, honorary secretary and four members, and the annual general meeting is held early in the year. The club-house is permanently situated on the river Adyar, about five miles out of the city of Madras; but during the cold weather, when the principal regatta is held, a large tank, called the "Long Tank," opposite the Cathedral of Madras, fills and gives a stretch of water 3 miles by 2 miles. A temporary boat-house is erected there while the water lasts, and the big regatta is generally held in this tank. The roads leading to the club are shaded by magnificent avenues, the drive being one of the best in Madras.

The fleet numbers about fifty craft, and comprises racing fours, pairs, double sculls and skiffs, together with the usual pleasure boats in the shape of tubs, canoes and whiffs, while there are several small sailing-boats, chiefly canoes. At the big regattas, should there be visiting crews, the fours are rowed over a mile course, and the pairs and sculls over three-quarter mile. The senior club events are rowed over three-quarter mile and the junior events over half mile. The

Opposite Eund Hill, Poona

course is straight, with a depth ranging from 6 to 12 ft. During the hot weather, regattas are held on the Adyar, the three-quarter-mile course being from "The Palms" to "The Mound," and the half-mile course from "The Lock" in; the course has one bend, and the water is shallower than in the Long Tank. The hot-weather regatta is held in August, and the cold-weather regatta in January, while pleasure-boating on the Adyar goes on throughout the year. The club has no special cups, but the Challenge Fours, Pairs and Sculls at the cold-weather regatta are open to all recognised boat clubs in India and the East, and cups are given to members of the winning crews.

3. The Poona Royal Connaught Boat Club.

This club, originally called the Poona Boat Club, started in rather a small way in 1868, and in 1889 linked up with itself the Kirkee Boat Club, the amalgamation being styled as above. It has an average membership of 170, admission is by ballot; the usually recognised class of gentlemen amateur oarsmen are eligible to join. There is an entrance donation of Rs. 25, and the quarterly subscription is Rs. 12. Temporary members may be elected for a period not exceeding four months on payment of a monthly subscription of Rs. 5; honorary membership cannot exceed ten days, and for this there is neither entrance fee nor subscription. The committee number eleven, including the usual club officials. The colours of the club are dark blue. The coat, dark blue with crimson edging; the badge, Tudor crown and rose; the cap, dark blue. "Rosherville," where the club-house is built, is on the north bank of the Mulla river, or rather at the confluence of the rivers Mutha and Mulla. There is a water-way of about 5 or 6 miles, which is formed by a bund, or embankment, built in 1859 to supply Poona with water.

Occasionally the river is dangerous, owing to the flow of water over the bund, but it is seldom that it cannot be used. There are two straight reaches of about a mile, the rest of the river being winding and picturesque. There is practically no tide. There is a main boat-shed at Poona near the bund, the club-house at "Rosherville" near Kirkee, being about 3½ miles distant. There are boats at both places, and "Rosherville" is reached by an excellent driving road. The fleet is maintained at about seventy assorted craft, almost every description of racing and pleasure boat being represented. There are racing eights and fours, pair and sculling boats; clinker-built tub fours, pairs and dinghies, barges, randans, whiffs, canoes and several sailing boats.

Rowing is practically continuous throughout the year, but the activity of the club is subject to fluctuations. Sometimes the presence in the station of several enthusiastic oarsmen results in regattas with visiting crews and excellent racing; at other times the club finds itself unable to bring off any regattas. Recently the policy has been to attempt modest monthly scratch regattas with an important fixture in September. The Poona season lasts from June to October, and during that time the river is extensively used.

4. The Naini Tal Boat Club.

There seems to be some doubt as to when this club came into existence, for its earlier records have perished; with Anglo-Indian vagueness the date is put "about forty years ago," and at that we must leave it; but there can be little doubt as to its situation being the most charming of any similar club in India. The boat-house stands at the head of the beautiful Naini Tal Lake, which is about 1500 yds. long by 400 yds. broad, the average depth being about 40 ft. Besides the accommodation for the boats, there is a big dining-room, a ladies' room, a bar and the usual dressing-rooms, and sailing is quite as popular as rowing. Membership is open to members of the Naini Tal Club, which is recruited from the services, for Naini Tal is a holiday resort, and its European population is very largely made up of officials on leave or duty. The average roll of membership is about 100. Membership of the Naini Tal Club entails a donation of Rs. 100, and a monthly subscription of Rs. 12, and to this must be added an entrance fee of Rs. 10 and a monthly subscription of Rs. 5 for the Boat Club. The rowing craft (exclusively by Searle of Henley) are maintained at about twenty-four boats, racing fours, pairs and skiffs dividing favouritism with tubs, wherries and canoes. There are also several half-rater sailing boats, some belonging to members, some club property, and others which can be hired from Messrs Murray & Co. and Mr Reynolds at Rs.50 or Rs.60 a month.

The rowing courses are half-mile, 600 yds. and quarter-mile, and there are no tides or bends. The club is open all the year round, but practically hibernates during the cold weather, and bursts into activity from April to October, or, in other words, during the "leave season."

Rowing and sailing regattas are held fortnightly during the hot weather and at long intervals in the rains, and the two principal fixtures come off during the "Ranikhet week" in May and the "Civil Service week" in September. On these festive occasions the Rampur Cup for fours and the Bulrampar Cup for pair oars, the gifts of the sporting potentates who rule those states, and open to crews representing clubs, regiments and Government departments, are offered for competition.

The sailing fleet comprises three half-raters, built by Mr Reynolds of local celebrity, and three imported from Belfast by Messrs Murray & Co.—these for hire—and three others the property of club members. The sailing course is about six miles round buoys beating up to S.S.E. with a run home to N.N.W. There are sailing races every Wednesday, starting at

Photo] NAINI TAL [*Laurie, Naini Tal*

10.30 A.M. The Baker-Russell Challenge Cup is competed for annually at the September regatta and is awarded to the competitor who comes out best of three heats.

5. The Karachi Boat Club.

For a comparatively small town like Karachi the boat club may be called a flourishing one. It was founded in 1872; it has over fifty members, and is situated on the banks of the Karachi harbour backwater, locally known as Chinna Creek. Members of the Sind Club and Karachi Gymkhana are eligible for membership of the boat club, and others are elected by the committee. The entrance fee for permanent members is Rs.30, and the subscription Rs.4 per month. Temporary members pay no entrance fee but a subscription of Rs.6 per month; non-rowing members pay Rs.30 entrance fee and Rs.2 per month subscription. There is a committee of five, including the captain and honorary secretary. The annual general meeting is held in August, and the annual regatta during the second week in October, though some years there is one in June as well. The rowing season extends from March to October.

The club boats, ten in number, are furnished by Salter Brothers, Oxford, and comprise the ordinary clinker-built light fours, pairs and single sculls, with a boat or two for those who do not aspire to race. The course over which the races are rowed is a straight stretch of about three-quarters of a mile from the Chinna Creek railway bridge to the boat-house, and the races are usually rowed with the tide.

At the annual regatta two challenge cups are offered—the "Boyce-Combe Cup" for fours, tenable for a year, and the "Hart Davies Cup" for double scull, also tenable for a year. Lady coxswains are *de rigueur* in both races, and the cups can be held outright if won by the same crew three years running.

The colours of the club are red and white, narrow stripes.

6. The Colombo Rowing Club.

An active little club, the C.R.C. was founded in 1864, and has enjoyed a vigorous existence ever since. Not only does it foster rowing in Ceylon itself, but it has enterprise sufficient to send crews into foreign waters, even to distant Calcutta and Poona; and every time its representatives have ventured abroad they have returned bearing the palm. The club-house is on the Colombo lake, a shallow and tortuous stretch of water close to the heart of the town, surrounded by European residences and approached by ideal roads. The membership fluctuates between 100 and 150; all Europeans received in general society are eligible to join; the entrance fee is

Rs.20, and the annual subscription is only Rs.20. The colours are blue and white; a white jersey and blue jacket piped with white, with the club badge, a traveller's palm on the breast pocket; blue and white riband with the club badge worked thereon.

The racing craft consist of sliding and fixed seat fours, sliding seat racing pairs, and racing skiffs, with the addition of the ordinary pleasure boats, numbering about thirty, all by English builders, and the racing boats by Clasper. There is no tide on the lake and only one slight bend; there is ample room for five fours to race abreast; and the full course is a mile and a quarter. They row all the year round and hold their annual regatta usually in August. The only challenge cup is for sculls. It can never be won outright, but the winner receives a presentation cup.

Other Clubs.

There is a boat club, or rather there are boats, in Lucknow available to members of the Chutter Munzil Club (entrance Rs.50, and subscription Rs.5 per month) and the Mahomed Bagh Club. (For the services: entrance Rs.30, and subscription Rs.10 a month.) There are, as a rule, about twenty boats, mostly pleasure craft, but there are whiffs, fours and double sculling boats, and in some years a regatta is held during the rains.

The Bombay Gymkhana, an athletic club which embraces almost every class of sport and pastime, from polo to bowls, places a certain number of craft at the disposal of its rowing members; but rowing in Bombay is now practically a dead letter. The boats are located at Bandora, nine miles by rail from Church Gate Street station in the fort; the backwater on which rowing is attempted is most uninviting, not to say dangerous, with its shoals, its shifting mud banks, hidden snags and rocks, all of which necessitate the course being marked out somewhat after the manner of the pilot signals and marks on that treacherous river, the Hooghly. Small wonder that interest in rowing is practically non-existent, and that the chances of reviving the successes of former years are remote.

Rangoon has the best boat club in India, with a splendid club-house situated on the banks of the Royal Lakes, just out of Rangoon. There is an entrance fee of Rs. 20, and a monthly subscription of only Rs. 2. The fleet embraces almost every style of boat, and all these considerations render it a popular institution, and have secured for it a very large membership, for almost all the European population of Rangoon are members. Serious rowing, however, is not a prominent feature, for, though an annual regatta is held about October, beyond the race for fours against the German club and a spectacular event in which a four take on, and usually beat, a crew of Burmans in one of their wonderful racing canoes, there is not much activity as far as racing is concerned.

Ootacamund also has a boat club, its members confining themselves almost entirely to pleasure rowing, relieved by an occasional bumble-puppy meeting, in the programme of which "affinity" races figure prominently.

GYMKHANAS

THE "Bumble-puppy," or "Skittle," as distinguished from the Skye racing, Gymkhana, is a very popular institution in the majority of larger stations. The unqualified support of the fair sex suffices to account for this popularity, and a very moderate outlay in silver trinkets or other trifling prizes will attract a host of fair nominators or competitors. The demand for novelty is never satiated, and to appease it all manner of devices are adopted; even moonlight or torchlight gymkhanas have been organised to this end, but seldom achieve conspicuous success. The ingenuity of harassed secretaries has evolved a strange diversity of curious competitions, but these entertainments are often arranged at very short notice, and individual officials lack either the leisure or the inclination to search the scattered records of such gymkhanas for new and interesting events.

The following collection of competitions suitable for a bumble-puppy gymkhana may suggest some new idea to individuals, but, since all are confirmed by actual experiment, they put forward no claim to absolute novelty. Many are old and well-worn, but if familiarity breeds contempt, it also, in this instance, affords clear proof of success.

Affinity Stakes—(*A*) Gentlemen to ride a distance, dismount, and hand lady nominator sealed envelope, in which the name of an animal will be written. Lady to draw on paper the animal mentioned; gentlemen to guess the animal, mount and finish a course. First in with correct answer to win.

(*B*) Tent-pegging and tilting; gentlemen to take a peg; ladies to take three rings. Points for style and pace.

(*C*) Telegram race. Gentlemen to ride a distance, dismount, hand lady a telegram and reply form. Lady to fill in answer according to instructions attached, and hand back to gentleman, who remounts and finishes course. First in with correct form to win.

Aunt Sally—To gallop past a stuffed figure, or a lance supporting a chatty, and to break a clay pipe placed therein by throwing a small stick. For ladies or gentlemen.

Bareback Pony Race—Ladies nomination. Competitors to saddle up, ride a short course, dismount, unsaddle and return bareback.

Battledore and Shuttlecock—For ladies mounted or dismounted. Fifty yards, round a post and back.

Bending Race—Ladies or gentlemen. To ride in and out between flags or lances placed eight yards apart.

Bran Tub Stakes—Gentlemen with ponies run to ladies with sealed envelope containing coloured ribbon. Lady opens envelope and matches ribbon from other ribbons placed near by. Gentleman runs on to bran tub, where he again matches ribbon, mounts and rides to winning post. First in with three correctly matched ribbons to win.

Bullock Gharry Race—Ladies nomination. Two furlongs straight for pair-bullock gharries, hakries or recklas. European drivers.

Chatty Race—Competitors to ride a distance, pick up a chatty with a stick and return to starting point. First in with unbroken chatty to win.

Circus Stakes—Gentlemen to start on properly-saddled ponies, and to pass post carrying their saddles. Ponies not to be pulled up, and any competitor dismounting disqualified.

Coin Race—Competitors to gallop round course, holding a coin between each knee and the saddle. First in with both coins to win.

Costume Race—Ladies nomination. Gentlemen to ride bareback to a point, where ladies hand them costumes and help them to put them on. Gentlemen remount and finish. First in correctly dressed to win.

Distance Handicap—For ponies and horses. (Handicappers should recollect that ponies are very quick at starting, and also that in a scurry the scratch horses have but a scanty chance of getting through a big field.)

Dressing-room Stakes—Gentlemen to ride a distance without coats, ties or collars; dismount, dress and return.

Driving Competition—For ladies. Between chatties with prizes for driving and turn-out; or varied, as, for example: Lady to drive gentleman to a table, where he dismounts and drinks a cup of tea and remounts, when lady finishes course.

Education Stakes—Gentlemen to ride a distance with sealed envelopes containing simple arithmetical problem, historical or geographical questions. Dismount, hand envelope to lady, who replies and returns. Gentlemen ride back to starting post. First in with correct answers to win.

Egg-and-Spoon Race—For ladies mounted. Gentlemen attend to pick up egg if dropped.

Excelsior Stakes—Competitors (mounted) to pick up a lance stuck in the ground, break a cocoa-nut on a pole, 3 ft. high, take a hurdle, a ring, another hurdle, and lastly a peg at full gallop.

First-Aid Competition—Ladies nomination. Competitors to ride over two fences to nominatrix, carrying triangular bandages and safety pins. Lady will bandage his head with triangular bandage for imaginary scalp wound, after which he will ride back over the fences. First in with head correctly bandaged to win.

Go-Easy Stakes—Ladies to ride carrying tennis ball and racquet. Gentlemen to attend to pick up ball if it falls. First past the post with ball on racquet to win.

Gretna Green Stakes—Gentlemen to ride a distance leading lady's horse, dismount, mount lady, and the pair to ride back to winning post.

Heavenly Twins Stakes—For pairs. Lady and gentleman to ride round course, holding together a stick 3 ft. long.

Housekeeper Stakes—Gentlemen to ride a distance with a sealed envelope containing a list of vegetables, and also a basket. Ladies to fill basket with vegetables mentioned on list, and to hand it when filled to gentlemen, who remount and gallop back to starting post. First in with correctly filled basket to win.

Judgment of Paris Stakes—Ladies nomination. Gentlemen to ride at full gallop past their nominatrix and throw a tennis ball, which she is to catch.

Knock-me-down Scurry—Bare-back race for ponies, round two posts. It is advisable to run in heats of two.

Know-all Stakes—Similar to Education Stakes. Marks for time and correctness of answer.

Lightning Putter Competition—Gentleman to ride a distance carrying golf putter. Lady to hole-out two golf balls lying at opposite sides of the green.

Loyd-Lindsay—For pairs. Lady and gentleman to ride over a hurdle, gallop to a fixed point and dismount. A pile of small stones will be provided for each pair, and two chatties, fixed on stakes at a distance of 30 ft. Both chatties to be broken, after which pairs remount and finish the course together. This popular competition is capable of endless variations.

Menagerie Stakes—(In all animal races, domestic pets should be barred.)

Money-changer's Race—Gentleman to ride a distance to his partner, who will give him change for a certain sum; five-eighths to be in silver, one quarter in half-anna pieces, one-eighth in pice. First in with correct change to win, prize to lady.

Musical Lances—For ladies mounted. Played on the same principle as musical chairs. Lances one short of the number of competitors, and one of the latter falls out in each bout.

Not-at-Home Stakes—Competitors to ride a distance, leave their cards in specified "Not-at-Home" boxes, and finish round a course. First in with cards correctly left to win.

Poet's Scurry—Gentlemen to ride a distance, dismount and receive from lady-partner paper and pencil and a sealed envelope containing a given word. A four-line verse containing this word must be written in collaboration, and gentleman must reach winning-post mounted and carrying verse within a given time. Prize for best verse.

Picnic Stakes—For pairs. Gentlemen ride a distance, dismount and hand lady partners their cards. The lady then writes an invitation to a picnic on the card; both mount and ride off together to another given point, where lady eats chocolate or biscuit and gentleman drinks a "peg." Finish together round the course.

Pig-sticking—For gentlemen or ladies. A waterskin stuffed with straw represents the pig, and is dragged at the end of a long rope by a man on an active pony. Competitors run in heats of four carrying dummy spears furnished with a padded and chalked point. "First spear" wins.

Polo Ball Race—(*a*) Gentlemen to ride at full gallop and throw polo ball into a bucket of water, then ride to his lady partner, who throws another ball at him, which he must catch and throw into another bucket. Points for pace and style.

(*b*) To hit a polo ball round a flag and back between two posts, 10 ft. apart, placed near the starting-point. Each heat should be limited to four competitors. Many varieties of this competition will readily suggest themselves.

Pony and Chair Race—Competitors to ride twenty yards on a chair, mount horse or pony and ride a short course, dismount and finish course on chair.

Postillion Stakes—For ponies, to ride one and drive the other. A turn in the course usually creates diversion.

Potato Race—(*a*) Partners to stand facing each other ten yards away. Lady to throw six potatoes to partner who throws them into a bucket. First in with correct number wins.

(*b*) Ladies nomination. Gentlemen to ride a distance, dismount and take a potato from a bucket of water without using hands and to finish mounted with potato in mouth.

Rap-knuckle Stakes—To pick balls off cricket stumps while riding at full gallop, and to throw them into buckets.

Rumble-Tumble Stakes—For ponies nominated by ladies and ridden by men, the latter drawing lots at the post for their mounts. The rider of the winner takes the men's prize, the nominator of the last pony the ladies' prize.

Saddle and Off-saddle Race—Competitors to saddle their own ponies at the starting-point, ride a course and unsaddle.

Screen Race—Scurry for ponies through a white paper screen stretched across the course.

Skill at arms—Competitors to take a Turk's head, a ring, and a peg with a sword. Three runs. Points for style and pace.

Snatcher Stakes—For pairs. Gentlemen to take cricket balls off three stumps and to throw them into a bucket, ladies to take tennis balls off posts and throw them into sacks. Marks for style and pace.

Soda-water and Biscuit Race—For pairs, who will ride a distance together, dismount and dispose of a bottle of soda and a biscuit, mount and finish the course together.

Tent-pegging and Tilting require no description.

Time Race—For pairs. To ride a given course in a specified time, no watches allowed.

Trotting Race—For ladies; always a popular event.

Ulta Pulta Race—Run on the same principle as the English donkey race. Competitors change horses, and the last pony home takes the prize.

V.C. Race—Ladies nomination. Competitors ride over two flights of hurdles, pick up dummy, and return to starting-post.

Whistling Race—Gentlemen to ride a distance; dismount and receive from lady partner a sealed envelope containing name of a simple tune. Gentlemen to whistle this tune and ladies to guess its name. Gentlemen then remount and return to starting-point carrying envelope, contents of which must not be shown to partners.

White Tie Race—Gentlemen to ride a distance to lady partners, who adjust a white tie in a bow, after which they return to starting-point. First in with well-tied bow to win.

CHEETAH HUNTING

CHEETAH hunting is a sport but little known to Europeans, who prefer, as a rule, to take an active, rather than a passive, part in the pursuit of game of any description. In India, however, many of the native princes indulge in the pastime, and take a great pride in their cheetahs, or hunting-leopards as they are sometimes called. These animals are carefully trained for their work, which consists in running down deer, and are sufficiently tame to be easily handled by their keepers, though a stranger would do well to keep at a respectful distance from their formidable teeth and claws. The sport is usually carried on in the cold weather, as later on the grass and jungle become so dense that it is impossible for the spectator to obtain a good view of the chase. The hunting is not carried out on fixed days of the week, and very little preparation is required,

Cheetah Hunting

beyond starving the cheetahs for twenty-four hours or so, in order to make them keen, for, unless hungry, they will not trouble themselves to chase the deer. The sport usually takes place in jungles specially reserved for the purpose, and the *modus operandi* is as follows :—Two cheetahs are driven up on country carts in charge of their keepers, who hold them in leash and hooded, so as to prevent their sighting the deer before the time comes to slip them in pursuit. The spectators, who are generally few in number, as only two can conveniently go in each cart, and a large number of carts would frighten the game, then take their places just behind the bullock-driver and in close proximity to the cheetah's tail, and the carts set off, working in and out of the patches of jungle until a herd of deer is approached sufficiently close to give the cheetah a fair chance. The keeper then slips off the hood and lets go the leash, and the animal bounds off the cart and races after the deer which scatter in all directions. Soon he singles out one particular victim, redoubles his speed, crouches for a moment, and then springs on to the back of his prey, seizes it by the throat. He then bears it to the ground, where he sucks its blood. The keeper then runs up, cuts the poor beast's throat and allows the cheetah to drink deeply of its blood, after which he cuts off a strip of meat for him, replaces his hood, and leads him back to the cart. Sometimes the cheetah misses his spring, and then he throws himself in disgust under the shade of the nearest tree and waits patiently for the keeper to recapture him. The sport has not, of course, the same charm as shooting, or fishing, or pig-sticking, for one is a spectator merely, and takes no active part in the performance; but, all the same, it is exciting, and it is a pretty sight to watch the graceful, cat-like movements of the cheetah, the stealthy stalk and the sudden spring by which he approaches and seizes his prey.

The best sport is probably shown by the various rajahs of the Punjab Native States, though in Central India, Rajputana, and certain states in Southern India it is also practised by various princes and large landowners. There is usually no difficulty in obtaining an invitation to view the sport, for, if stationed in the neighbourhood, it is easy to make the acquaintance of the local rajah, and so obtain a personal invitation, while, if merely travelling through the district, a letter of introduction from the local civil officer in charge of the state will generally be sufficient. The rajahs are, as a rule, extremely sporting themselves, and are always glad to help visitors of good standing to see the sports of the country. Having obtained an invitation to see a cheetah hunt, the next thing is to get out to the meet, and, if the host does not himself drive you out, he will probably depute one of his officers to do so, and he will look after you well and tell you exactly what you are expected to do when you arrive at the scene of action. As already mentioned, you will see the hunt from a bullock cart, and all you have to do is to sit still and keep quiet till the cheetah is let slip, when, if you like, you may jump down and follow the run on foot, as the carts can only follow slowly and often have to make wide detours to avoid patches of jungle. You must on no account offer any sort of tip or present to your host or any of his higher officials, as such might give considerable offence ; but, of course, you are perfectly at liberty to give a few rupees to the huntsman and bullock drivers. It is not, however, absolutely necessary to do so. You had better not take any rifle or gun with you, unless specially asked to do so, for, as a rule, no shooting is allowed in the jungles reserved for the cheetah-hunting for fear of scaring away the game.

INDEX

ABBOTABAD, 132, 134, 173
Abbott, Mr H. E., 443
Abdal, 173
Achabal, 187
Aden, Fishing at, 295
Affinity Stakes, 542
Afghan Mountains, Oorial in the, 206
Ahmedabad, Fishing near, 285
Akloo (a Kashmir shikari), 138
Akyab, Fishing at, 292
Alampi La Pass, 168, 172
Alchori, 161, 165
Ali Bin Talib, 468
Ali Malik Mar, 144, 160
Almora, 269
Alpenstock, 91
Alcon, 174, 183
Alwas, 98, 107, 113, 119, 124, 128
Amethysts, 110
Amirgund, 187
Amritsar, 88, 268
Andaman Islands, Fishing at the, 296
Antelope, Four-horned, 194, 199
—— Indian, 196
—— Thibetan, 135, 142, 147, 151, 152, 153
Apcar, Mr A. A., 444
Arab Horses and Ponies, 332, 333, 339, 340, 344-346, 387, 389-394, 428, 448, 449
arctos, 58, 142
Argus Pheasant, 103
Asan, 265, 267, 274
Ashdari, 107, 113, 115, 129
Askole, 168, 181
Askora Nullah, 161, 166
Ass, Wild, 126
Assam, Fishing in, 235, 258, 259, 260, 264, 282; Rhinoceros in, 59, 66; Swamp Deer in, 203; Thamin in, 204; Tiger in, 5, 9
Association Football, 495
Assumed Names in Racing, 449
Astore, 142, 168, 169, 170, 171, 172, 176, 185, 187, 206
Atawat, 181
Athletics, 519, 520
"Athletic Sports and how to run them," (Burke), 520
Ating, 110, 111, 129
Atroto, 143, 144, 181
Attoli, 109
Aunt Sally, 542
Australia, Freight of Horses to India from, 443
Australian Horses and Ponies, 314-332, 339-344, 386, 391, 428, 447
"Average Cup," 466
Azizza (a Kashmir shikari), 138, 165

BABAR KACH, 286, 287
Babusar, 173
Bachwa, 226
Badminton, 520
Badrawar, 96, 102, 103, 130, 178, 183
Bagai, 98
Bagesur, 269, 273
Bagnell, Major, on Fishing in Madras, 284
Bahadur, Sir Jung, 31
Bahmin or Bhamin, 226, 285, 289, 290-293, 297, 298, 303, 304
Baira, 102, 124, 128
Bakloh, 280
Balakot, 173
Baldock, R. G., 468
Balesh, 98, 102, 123
Ballygunge, Paper-chasing at, 465
Baloochi Nullah, 172
Baltal, 148
Balti Dogs, 163
Baltistan, 98, 138, 142, 149, 153, 154, 161, 167, 168, 169, 170, 176, 181, 182, 186, 190, 206, 220
Baluchistan, Fishing in, 264, 286; Chikore in, 213; Oorial in, 206;

Ravine Deer in, 198; Sand-grouse in, 215
Banas River, 262, 285
Banbassa, 268
Bandipur, 138, 143, 156, 157, 167, 170, 172, 174
Bandra, Golf at, 509
Bangalore Hounds, 421; Race Meeting, 425, 426, 427, 433, 440, 441, 442
Barak River, 286
Baralacha Pass, 94, 127
Baramulla, 134, 143, 169, 176, 177, 187
Barangda Reserve, 74, 75
Barara, 98
Bara Singh, 71, 95, 120, 123, 141, 144, 147, 148, 178-180, 185, 205
Barbus, 246
Bareback Pony Race, 542
Bareilly, Fishing near, 268-273
Barepolay, 278
Baril, 226
Barilius, 225, 262
Barmoar, 94, 111, 112, 121, 123, 124, 126
Barrackpore, Golf at, 503; Raimgat, 442
Barracuda, 303
Basel Mission (Canara), 22
Basha Nullah and River, 162, 168, 171
Bashgo, 150
Basul, 173
Batoti, 130
Battledore and Shuttlecock, 543
Batwas, 108, 109, 113, 115, 129
Bawanni River, 228, 284
Bear, Black, 54, 79, 81, 98, 99, 101, 102, 103, 107, 113, 119, 120, 121, 126, 135, 141, 142, 143, 167, 176, 177, 186, 188, 190
—— Red, 58, 86, 95, 99, 107, 108, 109, 112, 114, 116, 117, 118, 119, 120, 121-3, 126, 129, 135, 141, 142, 144, 147, 149, 157, 158, 159, 160, 161, 167, 176, 186, 188, 189
Beaters, Pay of, 45
Beating for Panthers, 50; for Tigers, 37
Beaver, Colonel, 444
Beema, Fishing in the, 262, 281, 283
Begti, 289, 297, 298
Bellapatam River, 304
Bending Race, 543
Bengal, Fishing in, 260, 298; Lancers (14th), 329; Large Bags of Snipe in, 209; Panther in, 49
Beni Singh, 267
Berhampore Racecourse, 427
Betwa River, 262
Bhagia (a Chamba shikari), 89, 116
Bhamo, 264
Bhandal, 96, 130
Bhaji River, 286
"Bheestie," 26
Bhimber, 132
Bhimgoda, 276
Bhim-Tal, 287
Bhurie Singh, 89, 93, 112, 129
Bhutan Duars, Bison in the, 79, 80; Rhinoceros in the, 59, 65, 66
Bhutna Nullah and River, 96, 97, 109, 125, 129
Bias, 228, 268
Bicycling, 521
Bikanir, Black-buck in, 197; Tiger unknown in, 5
Billikal, 285
Bison, 67-80
Bits, 399
Black Bear, *see* Bear
Black-buck, 195, 196-8, 418
Boating, 528-541
Bobbery Pack, 409-418
Bodraj (Aurungabad), 23, 359
bola, 225, 262
Bola Falls, 276
"Bomalo," 291
Bombay, Black Partridge in, 212; Duck, 291; Fishing in, 260, 261, 285, 290, 297, 298; Golf in, 499, 507; Great Bustard in, 216; Gymkhana, 540; Hounds, 418, 419; Racecourse, 427; Racing at, 435, 436, 438, 440, 441, 442; Spears for Pig-sticking, 357; Stable Co., 468; Tiger in, 5; Yachting in, 523
Bonito, 303
Bo Nullah, 141, 157, 179
Boonjie, 170, 172
Books and Maps for Kashmir, 193
Boots for Himalayan Shooting, 91, 118; for Kashmir, 140; for Pig-sticking, 361, 384; for Polo, 401; for Tiger-shooting, 23
Boput (Nagpore), 24

Bora, Fishing in the, 282
Bos, 67, f.n.
Bowls, 522
Boxing, 521
Brabonti, 102, 103, 122
Brahmini Duck, 210
Braldhoo Nullah, 161, 162, 164, 176
Bran Tub Stakes, 542
Breeches, 361, 401
Breeding Seasons of Birds, 188
Bridles, 356
bubalis, 67, f.n.
Buck, Sir E., on Mahseer-fishing, 257
Buffalo, 70
Bugna, 96
Buldar River and Nullah, 171, 172
Bullets for Tiger, 15 (*see* also Rifles and Ammunition)
Bullock Gharry Race, 543
Bullock-Workman, Mr and Mrs, 168, f.n.
"Bumblepuppy," 426, 541
Bundar, 174
"Bundobust," 213
Bunjar Reserve, 76, 77, 79
Bunji, 187
Burdwan Race Meeting, 425
Burgi La Pass, 159, 160
Burhel, 95, 111, 120, 125, 126, 127, 135, 142, 147, 150, 151, 152, 180, 181, 185, 187, 188, 189
Burmah, Fishing in, 235, 263; Gaur in, 79; Mountains on the Frontier of, 229; Racing in, 451; Snipe in, 209; Tiger in, 59
Burnfoot Lake, 283
Burzil, 157, 158, 168, 172
Bustards, 216, 217
Butal, 115
Butnai, 174
Butter-fish, 303
Bygars, 67, 77

CABULI Horses, 398
Calcutta, Angling Club at, 255; Angling for Rohu at, 272; Football in, 494, 497; Games at, 478; Golf at, 502, 507; Paper-chase Club, 464, 467; Polo at, 385; Racing at, 434, 437, 440, 441, 442, 447, 462; Rowing Club, 530; Turf Club, 455, 458
Calicut, Fishing at, 291, 297
Camel Transport, 26
Camp-bed, 365
Cannanore, Fishing at, 291, 297, 303, 304
Caranx, 289
Carnatic Carp, 226, 278
Catla, 226
Cavery (or Cauvery) River, 228, 277, 278, 284
Caves, Bears in, 56
Cawnpore Race Meeting, 425; Saddles, 355; Tent Club, 22
Central India, Bison in, 67, 71, 86; Great Bustard in, 216; Pig-sticking in, 309; Swamp Deer in, 203; Tiger in, 5; "Trout" in, 225
Central Provinces, Black-buck in the, 197; Fishing in the, 260, 261, 281; Game Laws of the, 68, 69; Great Bustard in the, 216; Sambhur in the, 200; Swamp Deer in the, 203; Tiger in the, 5, 11
Ceylon, Angling Associations in, 255; Fishing in, 288, 295; Panther in, 49; Racing in, 450; Rowing in, 538; Tigers absent from, 5
"Chaguls," 25, 39
Chakla, 267
Chakor, 183
Chakoti, 134
Chamb, 267
Chambal River, 228, 262
Chamba State, Rajah of, 89, 93, 106, 112; Shikari, 138; Shooting in, 4, 82-130, 131, 146, 152, 178, 183, 185
Chanda, Bison Shooting near, 70, 78, 79
Chanderkut, 144, 159
Chandra Bagh, 106, 107, 111, 113, 115, 127
Chanegand, 149, 155
Changchenmo Valley, 150, 153, 169
Changla Pass, 151
"Chaplies," 91, 137, 139, 153
Charging of Wounded Animals, 118-120
Chashma Shahi, 186
Chathar, 263
Chatty Race, 543
Cheetah, 54, 181, 548-551
Cheetal or Cheetul, 68, 76, 181, 195, 202

Chenab River, 266, 267
Chikara, 198
Chikor, 135, 136, 207, 213
Chilas, 132, 138, 142, 153, 157, 170, 172, 173, 174, 175
Chillam, 172
Chilwa, 226, 284
Chindwara, The, 282
Chindwin Valley, 204
Chin Hills, 229
Chingham, 130
Chirroo, 263, 279
Chishoti, 129
Chitor, 262
Chittingul, 141, 148, 179
Chorinemus, 289
Chota Deosai, 158
Chota Nagpur, 79
Chukkurkoot, 171
Chukkur Talao, 151, 152
Chumathung, 152
Chutter Munzil Club (Lucknow), 539
Circus Stakes, 543
Clothing for Fishing, 257; for Himalayan Shooting, 83; for Kashmir, 133; for Pig-sticking, 361; for Tiger-shooting, 21-23
Cochin, Fishing at, 291, 297
"Cock-up," 298
Cockburn's Kashmir Agency, 135, 136, 139
Coconada Race Meeting, 425
Coin Race, 543
Colombo, Fishing at, 293; Rowing Club, 538
Colours, Racing, 449
Cooking Utensils, 84
Cooltee, 472
Coonoor, 284
Coorg, Fishing in, 277, 278, 283
Coracles, 278, 284
Coromandel Coast, Fishing on the, 292
Cost, *see* Expense
Costume Race, 543
Cotton Fishing Lines, 301
Country-Bred Horses, 332, 346, 428
Cranes, *see* Koolen and Sarus
Cricket, 478, 486-492
Crode, 284
Curlew, 219
Cutch, Gulf of, 4
Cybium, 289
Dacca Racecourse, 427; Race Meetings, 437, 441
Dachan, 187
Dachigam, 186
Dadupur, 266
Dak Bungalows, 70, 75, 88, 93, 127, 129, 133, 134, 150
Dalhousie, 81, 82, 83, 88, 90, 92, 95, 112, 123, 280, 518
Dal Lake, 526
Damon, Fishing in, 282
Danai Nullah, 113, 114
Dangara, 289, 297, 298
Darcha, 94, 126, 127
Darel, 170
Darjeeling, Cricket at, 487, 491; Race Meeting at, 425; Tennis Courts at, 517
Darwas, 108, 129
Day, Dr, 225, 298
Debring, 127
De Lisle, Colonel, 396
Deccan, Great Bustard in the, 216; Panther in the, 51, 52; Tiger in the, 5
Deer, Barking, 187, 203
—— Eld's, 204
—— Four-horned, 68, 79
—— Hog, 203
—— Mouse, 204
—— Musk, 186
—— Ravine, 195, 198
—— Spotted, 76, 202
—— Swamp, 71, 76, 77, 202
Deesa, 285
Dehra Doon, 203, 255, 265, 275, 276, 425, 441, 444
Delhi, Fishing near, 266
Dembra, 174, 175
Demgor La Pass, 151
Deoli, Fishing near, 263
Deosai Plateau, The, 144, 149, 155, 156, 160, 167, 168, 172, 176
"Dersi," 140
Dhalipur, 265
Dharmsala, 268
Dharra, 281
Distance Handicap, 543
Dibrugarh Race Meetings, 441, 455
Diet in India, 482, 483
Ditchell Nullah, 171
Dogfish, 285
Dogs, Panthers and, 53; Used in a Bobbery Pack, 412
Domel, 132, 134, 263

Donne, Mr H., 442
Dooni, 171
Doon, The Western, 274
Doyan, 172
Dras, 111, 147, 148, 149, 155
Dressing-Room Stakes, 543
"Drey," 268
Drinking-cup, 23
Drinking in India, 483
Driving Competition, 543
Drogmula, 186
Dubarri, 278
Duchkoot Nullah, 171
Duck, 136, 183, 207, 210, 211, 527
Dulai, 133, 134
Dum-Dum Bullet, 15; Golf at, 506
Dumoot Nullah, 171
Dunai, 129
Dunaitru Nullah, 107, 113, 115, 117, 119, 122, 124
Dunera, 88
"Dunga" Boat, 156
Durand Cup (Football), 496
Dushkin, 172
Dussaun, The, 281

Ecka or Ekka, 269, 367
Eden Gardens (Calcutta), 491
Education Stakes, 544
Egg-and-Spoon Race, 544
Elephants used in Shooting, 9, 59, 73
Elgin Mills Company (Cawnpore), 62, 365
Erin Nullah, 141, 157, 178, 179
Eroom & Co. (Calcutta), 359, 403
Excelsior Stakes, 544
Expenses of Hunting, 418; of Paper-chasing, 474; of Pig-Sticking, 366, 367; of Polo, 382, 383, 386-388, 392-394, 397, 398, 405; of Tiger Shooting, 28
Express Rifle, 85
Eye-fringes, 363

Feed, Horse, 370, 371
Felis, 3, 49, 181
Ferozepore, 197
Fever (horses), 317, 323, 375; (men), 73
"Finney" Tournament (Hockey), 514
First-Aid Competition, 544
"First Spear," 353, 379
Fishing, 223-305
"Fishing in the Kumaon Lakes" (Walker), 224, 274
Fitzwigram Girths, 356
Flies for Mahseer, 274, 277, 288
Fly-fishing, 252, 269, 276
Foklyan, 267
Football, 492-499
Forage, 471
Foreign Sportsmen in India, 131
Forest Department, The, 68
Fort Kangra, 268
Fort Stedman Race Meetings, 441, 442, 451, 455
Fottu La Pass, 149
Foxes, 186, 410
—— Flying, 220
Fox Terriers, 412
Fraserpet, 278
Freight of Horses, 443
Frog used for Bait, 273
Futteh Mardan Race Meeting, 425
Fyzabad Race Meeting, 425

Gadhai, 168, 172
Gadwell, 210
Gaff, Use of the, 256
Gagai, 144, 157, 178, 182
Gairsoppa Falls, 262
Gaiters, 22, 361
Galle Harbour, Seer Fishing off, 293
Game Laws (Central Provinces), 68; Jammu and Kashmir, 131, 186-192
Games Clubs, 477
Ganderbal, 148, 155
Gandla, 128
Ganganjir, 148
Ganges, The, 5, 65, 225, 232, 233, 265, 274, 276, 297, 298
Garepirs, 262
Garhi, 134
Garo Hills, 229
Gaur, 67, f.n., 79
Gazelle, Indian, 198; Thibetan, 95, 120, 125, 126
Geese, Wild, 136, 183, 211
Geldings, 390
Gentlemen Riders, 445, 450
Ghauts, Ibex, in the, 205; Rivers of the, 228; Sambhur in the, 200
Gibson, Captain, on Sea Fishing, 303
Gilgit, 141, 142, 144, 154, 155, 157, 158, 168, 169, 172, 173, 175, 178, 179, 206

Giri River, 266
Gistrie, 115
Gobra, 289, 300
Godavery, The, 5, 228, 261, 262
Godwin Austin, Mount, 160
Go-Easy Stakes, 544
Gol, 156
Golf, 499-512
Gomal River, 264
Gondal, 267
Gondari Nullah, 108, 109, 113, 115, 129
Gonds, 67, 75
Goonch, 226
Goond, 148
Gopipur Dera, 268
Gorai, 157, 178
Gorakhpur, Racing at, 425
Gorital Nullah, 178
Goural or Goral, 107, 120, 123, 124, 126, 128, 135, 186, 187
Government and Horse-dealing, 315, 331
Graham, Captain, on Fishing in Kashmir, 279
Grand National, The Indian, 445, 456, 458
Gram, 472
Grass Shoes, 91, 139
Grayling, 225
Gretna Green Stakes, 544
Grey Horses, 341
Greyhounds, 410
"Gridiron," 408
Ground-baiting for Rohu, 272
Guindy, 421, 510
"Gujar-logue," 106, 119, 144
Gujerat, 132, 197, 216, 260
Gulabgarh, 96, 97, 115, 125, 126, 129, 130
Gulf Arabs, 333
"Gullara," 269
Gulli, 174
Gulmarg, 131; Golf Links at, 502, 512
Gurais, 158, 182
Gurkha Methods of Fishing, 280
Gwalior, 381
Gwentred Nullah, 107, 113, 117, 118, 119
Gya, 95, 125, 126, 127, 153
Gymkhanas, 425, 426, 477, 541-548

Hanle, 152
Haramouk, Mount, 157
Haramoush, 170, 171, 176
Har Dras, 155
Hardwar, Fishing near, 265, 275
Hare, 207, 208, 220, 418
Harpodon, 291
Harris Tournament (Football), 496
Hassan Abdal, 132, 173
Hats for Pig-sticking, 360; for Tiger-shooting, 22
Hatti River, 263, 277
Hayes, Captain, 470
Head in Horses, Importance of, 337, 338, 339
Heavenly Twins Stakes, 544
Hermit-crab as Bait, 299
Himalayas, Fishing in the, 228; Gaur in the, 79; Ibex in the, 205; Leopards in the, 181; Partridges in the, 212; Pheasants in the, 218; Shooting Big Game in the, 80-130; Tiger at the foot of the, 4; Woodcock in the, 217; Yachting in the, 525
Hobbs, Major B., on Fishing, 27
Hockey, 512
Holeri, 278
Holland & Holland, Rifle by, 86
Hooghly, The, 503, 530
Hooks for Fishing, 243
Horses and Horse Markets, 313-474
Horton Plains, Fishing in the, 288
Hoshungabad, Fishing in, 282
Hotels, 74, 88, 133
Houbara, 207
Hounds, 407-413
Housekeeper Stakes, 544
Howdah, Shooting from the, 9, 13
Howrah Bowling Club, 522
Hunting, 407-423
Hunting Leopard, *see* Cheetah
Hunza Nagar, 168, f.n., 171
Hurdle Racing, 461-463
Hushu, 161, 162, 164, 165
Hutta, Fishing at, 282
Hyderabad, Tiger Shooting in, 9, 29
Hyena, Hunting the, 418

Ibex, 91, 97, 107, 109, 110, 111, 112, 113, 114, 115, 117, 120, 123, 124, 125, 126, 127, 129 135, 141, 142, 144, 148 149, 150, 154-169, 195
Ice-axe, 92
"Iley," 305

Indian Field, 520
"Indian Fishes" (Day), 225
Indian Football Association, 497
"Indian Horse Notes" (Major C——), 470
Indian Planters' Gazette, 443, 460
Indus, The, 95, 150, 152, 153, 155, 160, 161, 171, 228, 261, 264, 297
International Horse Agency, The, 443
Irawaddy, Fishing in the, 282
Islamabad, 95, 96, 130, 141, 143

JACKAL-HUNTING, 410, 414
Jallandhar, 268
Jalpaiguri Race Meeting, 425
Jammu, 96, 101, 132, 266
Jamsetjee, 502, 519
Jangaiwar, 96, 130
Jaora, 96, 130
Jared, 173
Java Rhinoceros, 65
"Jawasa Tatties," 365
Jayaram, 502
Jeffrey's Solid Bullet, 86
Jeypore Hills, Fishing in the, 262
Jhansi, 167, 263
Jhelum, The, 134, 177, 183, 228, 255, 263, 265, 266, 279, 280, 526
Jhula, 280
Jockeys, 444
Jodhpore, Breeches, 361, 401; Tiger absent from, 5
Jogwa, 267
Joonaghur, Nawabs of, 5
Jorhat Race Meeting, 442
Jubbulpore, Bison-shooting near, 68, 69, 74, 79; Fishing near, 281
Judgment of Paris Stakes, 545
Jullundur Race Meeting, 425
Jumna, The, 225, 228, 232, 233, 265, 266, 274, 275
Jumps in the Indian Grand National, 458-460
Jungle Fowl, 218
Jungoo Pool, 280

KABUL Tent, 24, 83
Kaghan, 173
Kail, 99
Kailang, 94, 126, 127, 128
Kajiar, 95
Kajinag, 134, 169, 176, 177, 183
Kalabans, 272
Kala Nadi, Fishing in the, 282
Kalemgo, Fishing near, 282
Kalgooni Nullah, 102
Kali Pani, 158, 159
Kalpe Jungle, 68, 75
Kanani, 96, 130
Kanara (or Canara), Bison in, 79; Fishing in, 262
Kangam, 148
Kansrae, 274
Kanzalwan, 144, 157, 178
Kapurthala, Pig-sticking in, 381
Karachi, Fishing at, 229, 293, 295, 298, 302; Football at, 498; Race Meeting, 427, 440, 441, 463; Rowing Club, 537
Karakwasla, 262
Kargil, 149
Karkitchu, 149, 155
Karmang, 155
Kashmir Agency (Cockburn's), 135, 192; Big Game of, 195; Black Bear in, 55; Curlews in, 219; Fishing in, 260, 263, 279; Game Preservation Department, 135, 136; Rainbow Trout acclimatised in, 255; Red Bear in, 58; Shooting in, 82, 130, 131-193; Stag in, 95, 135; Woodcock in, 217; Yachting in, 526
Katai, 177, 178
Katema, 269
Kathgodam, 273
Kattiawar, Black buck in, 197; Houbara in, 216; Lion in, 5; Panther in, 51; Race Meeting, 442
Kawaie, 173
Kerouse, Madden & Co., Messrs, 468
Khakur, 79, 120
Khalse, 168
Khapaloo, 168
Khassia Hills, 229
Khatsura, 168
Khel, 174
"Khitmatgar," 26, 84, 88
Khoja Chak, 267
Khokari, 289, 295
"Khubbar," 99, 113, 143
Khudstick, 9
Khulsi, 150
Kiang, 120, 126
Kidderpore Docks, 530
Kilar, 106, 107, 108, 111, 112, 113 115, 127, 128

"Kill," Shooting Tiger over a, 10
"Kiltas," 93, 138
King in India, H.M. the, 31
Kinloch, General A. A. A., on the Gaur, 79, 80
Kirgar Nullah, 170
Kirkee Race Meeting, 425
Kishengunga, 134, 157, 178
Kishtwar, 96, 103, 106, 107, 108, 123, 129, 130, 141, 144, 178, 187
Kistna River, 228, 283
Knock-me-down Scurry, 545
Know-all Stakes, 545
Kohala, 133
Kohat, 217
Koksen, 128
Kolar, Golf Links at, 512
Kolub, 262
Koolen, 211
Koorthoocoondi, Fishing near, 284
Korang River, 232
Krishna, Tiger south of the, 5
Kukti Pass, 94, 95, 111, 112, 124, 126
Kulang, 94, 95, 111
Kulu, 128, 217
Kulzum Pass, 128
Kumaon Lakes, Fishing in the, 260, 274
Kunas, 183
Kuram River, 264
Kushumel Nullah, 161
Kuttum Hole, 278

Labeo, 253, 264
Laccadive Islands, Fishing off the, 293
Lachalang Pass, 95, 127
Ladakh, 106, 111, 138, 142, 146, 147, 153, 155, 169, 181, 183, 206
Lahore, 261; Horse Show at, 451; Racing at, 442; Tennis at, 517
Lahoul, 94, 106, 111, 112, 125, 126, 183
Lalitpur, Fishing near, 263
Lalpura, 174
Lamayuru, 129, 149, 150, 180
Lanak, 112, 128
Langera, 95, 96, 130
Lee-Metford rifle and carbine, 20, 207
Leh, 95, 111, 125, 126, 127, 129, 142, 147, 149, 150, 151, 152, 168, 180
"*Lela*," 289
Leopard, 135, 181
—— Snow-, 94, 127, 166, 181
Lesser Indian Rhinoceros, 65
Licenses, Fishing, 280; Shooting (Chamba), 90; (Kashmir), 96, 135, 147
Lidapur, 278
Liddar Valley, 181, 280
Ligatures for Horses, 374
Lightning Putter Competition, 545
Limbar Nullah, 177
Lindsay Gordon, 73
Line Gear, 362
Lines, Fishing, 242
Lion, The Indian, 5
Live-bait Fishing, 269
"Liverpool Driving-bit," 356
Lolab Valley, 143, 173
Loralai, 286
Lotteries, Race, 453, 454
Loyd-Lindsay, 545
Luchipura, 177
Lucknow, Golf at, 511; Paper-chasing at, 464; Racing at, 425, 426, 427, 432, 435, 437, 438, 440, 441, 444, 448, 449, 455, 456, 457, 462, 463; Tennis at, 517
Luddyar River, 269
Lukang, 151
Luscombe (Allahabad), 25, 366

MACHAIL, 96, 97, 109, 110, 129
Machan, Shooting tigers from the, 39, 46; Shooting Panther from the, 52, 74
Machi Bawan, 267
Machigora, 282
Machkandu River, 262
Mackerel, 305
Maclaren, Lieut.-Col., on Fishing, 274
Madras, Absence of Black Partridge from, 212; Black-buck in, 197; Boat Club, 531; Carnatic Carp in, 226; Fishing in, 235, 260, 277, 283, 284, 294, 295, 301, 302; Football in, 498; Golf in, 509-511; Hockey in, 514; Hunting in, 408, 420, 421; Jungle-fowl in, 218; Paper-chasing in, 463; Pig-sticking in, 309; Racing in, 427, 434, 440; Sambhur in, 201; Tennis in, 517
Magi, 302
Mahableswar, Racing at, 440

Mahad, 98, 102
Mahé, Fishing at, 291, 297, 304
Mahl River, 255, 263
Mahomed Bagh Club (Lucknow), 511, 539
Mahseer, 223-288
Maidan Nullah, 178
"Maiden," Definition of a (Racing), 439
Makhan Nullah, 98, 99, 102, 121, 123
—— Pass, 107
Malabar Coast, Fishing on the, 291, 305
Malangan Nullah, 177, 178
Malaria, 287
Malik Kadal, 157
Mallard, 210
Malloch's Casting Reel, 242, 258
Malwa Tal, 287
Managuch, 174
Manaar, 284
Manaul Pheasant, 103, 183
Mandalay, Fishing at, 264; Football at, 498; Racing at, 441, 455
Mandi, 269
Mandla, 68, 69, 73, 74, 75, 76, 78, 79, 281
Mangalore, Fishing off, 293, 295
Mangli Nullah, 107, 108
Manipur, 204, 282, 286
Manisbal Lake, 526
Manjera, 96, 130
Mannlicher Action, 86
Manoo, 102, 103
Mansera, 138, 173
Mansu, 119
Manton & Co. (Calcutta), 85, 305
Maral, 248
Markhor, 91, 124, 132, 135, 142, 169-178
Marmots, 159, 167
Marsalong, 127
Marsemik Pass, 151
Martin, F. E., 444
Martingale, 356, 357, 400
Martini-Henry Rifle and Carbine, 206
—— -Metford Carbine, 85
"Mary Morrison" (Australian Pony), 396
Masulipatam, Fishing at, 292
Matayan, 148
Maula Chamba, 149
Maymyo, Racing at, 425, 441
Maynard Rifle, 206
Mayne, Mr, 467
Meade Shell, 20
Measurements of Black Bear, 58; of Cheetah, 54; of Panther, 53; of Racehorses, 439; of Tiger, 407
Medicine Chest, 63, 83; (for horses), 373
Meengoondi, 278
Meerut, Fishing near, 276; Polo at, 385; Racing at, 425, 426, 427, 436, 438, 440, 441, 455, 457, 463
Mehta, 502
Menagerie Stakes, 545
Mercara, 277, 278
Mettapollium, 278, 284
Mian Mir Hockey Tournament, 514
Midnapore, Racing at, 442
Minicoy, Fishing off, 293
Minimarg, 158
Minnow, 285, 291
Mirgal, 272
"Mogan" Beat, 55
Moimin, 303, 304
Money-changers' Race, 545
Moomsurry Berry, 271
Moonga Line, 271
Mosquitoes, 66, 156, 159, 160
Motinala Jungle, 76
Motoring, 522
Mount Abu Golf Links, 512
Mountain Sickness, 114
Moyan, 284
Mozufferpore, Hunting near, 423; Racing at, 425, 442
Mughal Maidan, 130
Mullah (a Chamba shikari), 89, 102, 104, 105
Muller, 289, 302
Mulley, 226
Mul-mul, 356
Multan, 260
Mundipla, 284
Munnahs, 355
Muntjac, 203
Muri, 174
Murray & Co. (Lahore), 360
Murree, 131, 132, 133, 134; Football Tournament, 497; Racquets at, 519
Murrell, 226, 272, 273, 281, 286
Musical Lances, 545
Musk Deer, 108, 120, 126, 186
Musroond, 97, 128

Mussoorie, 81, 153, 181, 201; Cricket at, 487, 491
Mustargh Range, 160
Mutchsil, 174
Muti Mula River, 262
Myiltha, 282
Myitkyina, 282
Mysore, 200, 216; Racing in, 433, 436, 442

NAGERKOT, Tiger in, 4
Nagpur (or Nagpore), Bison Shooting near, 7; Fishing in, 282; Game-laws in, 69; Railway from, 78
nahura, 136
Naini Tal, Boating at, 525, 526, 535; Fishing at, 225, 273, 287
Nainpur, 79
"Nair Min," 298
Names, Native (Fishes), 289, 298; (Oorial), 206; (Tiger), 48; (Various Game), 185-6, 196, 198, 203, 204, 206, 208, 210, 211, 212, 214, 216, 217, 218, 219, 220
Namika La Pass, 149
Namli River, 264
Nampoung River, 264, 282
Namsiri River, 264
Nanga Parbat, Mount, 169, 174
Naoshera, 266, 267
Naraingunge, 281
Narang, 173
Narangwari Nullah, 107, 113, 119, 122
Nari River, 286
Nasik, Golf at, 502, 509
Naukachia Lake, 287
Neali Nullah, 162
Negapatam, Sea-fishing off, 301
nehereus, 291
Neilgherry (or Nilgiri) Hills, Bison in the, 79; Fishing in the, 228, 255, 284; Ibex in the, 205; Sambhur in the, 200; Tiger in the, 10; Woodcock in the, 217
Nepaul Terai, Gaur in the, 79; Rhinoceros in the, 59, 61; Shooting generally in the, 8; Swamp Deer in the, 203
Nerbudda (or Narbadda) River, 80, 228, 261, 281, 282
Net, Use of the Landing, 256
Neve's Tourists' Guide, Dr, 173, 193
Newara Eliya, Racing at, 451
"Newmarket Bandage," 401
Newton, Mr C. G., 495
Nilghai (or Nilgai), 68, 194, 199
Nimmoo, 150
Nimur, Fishing in, 282
Ningal, Fishing near, 263; Yachting at, 526, 527
Ning Rhi Nullah, 150
Nizampatam, Seer Fishing at, 292
North - West Provinces, Tannery (Cawnpore), 355
Nose-band, 400
Not-at-Home Stakes, 545
Nowboog, 130
Nowgong, Fishing near, 263
Nullahs closed to Sportsmen, 189
Numbers of Animals allowed on each License (Kashmir), 189, 190

OKHLA, 266
Olthing Thang, 155
Oorial (*see* also Sharpu), 205
Ootacamund, Boating at, 541; Cricket at, 491; Fishing at, 285; Golf at, 502, 510; Hunting at, 408, 409, 419, 421, 423; Racing at, 425, 441, 461, 463
—— Tiger near, 10
Ordnance Survey Maps, 193, 257
Orissa, Fishing in, 260, 261
—— Tiger in, 5
Ovis ammon, 95, 120, 125, 126, 127, 142, 146-154
—— *hodgsoni*, 135
—— *nahura*, 135
—— *poli*, 154
—— *vignei*, 126

PACHESAR, 269
Pachmarhi Hills, 72, 73
Padam, 110, 111, 126, 127, 128, 129, 150
Padar, 96, 106, 108, 113, 115, 122, 125
Padri Pass, 95, 96, 97, 123, 130
Pagla, 273
Painted Partridge, 212
"Painted Snipe," 209
Palamin, 285, 303, 304
Paloi, 174
Pamirs, The, 154
Pangi, 94, 101, 102, 106, 108, 111, 112, 113, 125, 127, 129
Pangong Lake, 150, 151, 152

Panther, 48-54, 68, 79
Panwell River, 297
Paper-chase Cup, The, 466
Paper-chasing, 463-474
Parah, 289, 300
Parangla Pass, 128
"Paras," 35
pardus, 181
Parhun, 281
Parkuta, 156
Parsee Cricketers, 488
Parsons, Colonel, 250
Partridges, 135, 136, 207, 208, 212
"Parwana," 7
Pashkim, 149
Pass, Shooting (Central Provinces), 68 (*see* also Licenses)
Paste, Fishing with, 253, 280
Pathanket, 88, 268
Patiala, Horse-breeding at, 430; Racing at, 442
Paumben Pass, 291, 295
Peafowl, 207, 216
Pench River, 282
Pense La Pass, 110, 125
Periophthalmus, 299
Peshawar, Hunting at, 408, 422; Racing at, 425, 444
—— Vale Golf Links, 511, 512
—— Valley, 4, 229
Peshwari, 158, 172
Pestonjee's Store, 138
Phantom Baits, 250, 291
Pheasants, 135, 136, 183, 207, 217, 218
Phyang, 150
Pias, 96
Picnic Stakes, 546
Pigeon, Blue Rock, 207, 219; Green, 207, 219; Snow, 115; Wood, 219
Pigeon-Shooting, 523
Pig-sticking, 309-381
—— Competition, 546
Pilibhit, 269, 270
Pindobal, 160
Pintail, 210
Pioneer, The, 467
Pir Panjal, 132, 134, 169, 266
Pith Helmet, 22
Plovers, 219
Pobrang, 151
Pochard, 210
Pocket-saw, 23
Poet's Scurry, 546
Polo, 381-407
Polo Ball Race, 546
Polynemus, 289
Pony and Chain Race, 546
Pony Hunt Cup (Bombay), 419
—— Point to Point (Ootacamund), 422
Poona, Boating at, 533; Boxing at, 521; Fishing near, 262, 285; Football at, 496, 498; Golf at, 502, 509; Hockey at, 513; Hunting at, 408, 420; Racing at, 427, 432, 433, 434, 436, 440, 441, 444, 448, 449, 455, 456, 461, 463; Royal Connaught Boat Club, 533; Tennis at, 517
Poonch, 121, 134, 255, 263, 265
Porcupine, Hunting the, 418
"Poshteen," 140, 150
Postillion Stakes, 546
Potato Race, 546
Prankeeta River, 282
Prawn-bait, 272, 290, 291, 299
Professionals in India, 479
Prome, Racing at, 425, 451
Protection, Need of further, 208; of Fish, 254
Provisions, 90, 91, 93, 102, 103, 106, 138, 148, 155, 174, 175, 185
Puch Nullah, 178
Pulney Hills, 228
Pulwar Nullah, 141, 144, 158, 167, 179, 181
Punjab, The, 11, 81, 196, 205, 209, 215, 216, 235, 254, 259, 281, 408, 550

QUAIL, 207, 208, 214
Queensland, Horses from, 334
Quetta, Fishing near, 264; Hurdle-races at, 463; Point-to-Point Racing at, 461; Steeplechases at, 455
Quinine, Use of, 73

RACING, 424-463
Racing Colours, 449; Terms, 449
Racquets, 518
Rail, Taking Horses by, 368
Railway Communication, 11, 78, 88
Raiwala, Fishing near, 265, 274
Rajghat, 265, 274
Rajputana, Cheetah - hunting in, 550; Fishing in, 260; Great and Lesser Bustard in, 216; Pig-sticking in, 381; Tiger in, 5

Ramasamy Kame, 278
"Ram Chikore," 218
Ramesar, 269
Ramgunga, 269
Ramnuggur, 281
Rampore, 76, 134, 141, 177
Rampura Nullah, 176
Rampur Mundi, 274, 275
Raneegunge, Racing at, 442
Rangoon, Football at, 494, 498; Golf at, 512; Hockey at, 514; Racing at, 440, 441, 451; Rowing at, 540; Tennis at, 517
Ranjitsinhji, 501
Raos, 289, 290
Rap-knuckle Stakes, 547
"Rassad," 137, 147
Rasul, 280
Ratyal, 266
Ravi, 228, 261, 280
Ravine Deer, Hunting, 418
Rawal Pindi, 131, 132, 133, 134, 232, 281, 385, 425, 427, 442, 455, 463
Rayasam, Fishing at, 285
Red Bear, *see* Bear
Reels, Fishing, 241, 292
Regattas, 531, 533, 535, 536, 538, 539
Regimental Teams, 479
Registration of G.R.'s, 450
Reroo, 127
Rewards, Government — Panther, 69; Tiger, 68; Wild Dog, 69
Rhinoceros, 59-66
Rifles and Ammunition for Bear, 116; for Bison, 70; for Himalayan Shooting, 84 - 87; for Panther, 49; for Small Deer, 206; for Tiger, 13-20
Rigby, Rifle by, 64
Ringal Rods, 254
Ringdum, 110, 125
Rings for Fishing Rods, 241
Rivett Carnac, Capt. (on Fly-fishing), 276
Roan Horses, 341
Roarers, 317
Rock Cod, 289, 300
Rods, Fishing, 239, 292, 296
Rohu (or Rohoo), 226, 271, 281, 286
Rondu, 171, 176
Rope Galls, 369
Royal Irish Rifles (Hockey), 513
Ruddy Sheldrake, 210
Rudok, 151, 152
Rugby Football, 492
Rukchen, 95, 125, 126, 127, 128
"Rukhs," Preserved, 181
Rumble-tumble Stakes, 547
"Runners" in a Bobbery Pack, 412
Rupshu, 94, 111, 120, 125, 126, 152
Rurkee (or Rurki), 275
Russian Camp in Madras, 285

SABERMATI River, 285
Sach Nullah, 122, 124
Sach Pass, 97, 98, 101, 106, 113, 117, 122, 129, 130
Saddle and Off-saddle Race, 547
Saddles, 355
"Safed Cheetah," 181
Sagonia, 75
Sai, 99, 119
Salawa Falls, 276
Sale with Engagements (Racing), 450
Saligram (Dalhousie), 90
Salmo, 284, 285
Salt Range, 205, 206, 213
Sambhur (or Sambur), 68, 74, 75, 76, 77, 195, 200-202, 418
Sanch, 127
Sand-grouse, 207, 215
Santa Cruz, Kennels at, 418, 421
Sardah River, 268, 269, 270
Sari Sangor Pass, 159
"Sarnai," 267, 268
Sarus, 212
Saspul, 150
Sath-Tal, 287
Satpura Range, 80
Saugor, 281
Sauli, 226
Scinde (or Sind), Fishing in, 260, 298; Tigers in, 5; Valley and River, 141, 142, 147, 148, 155, 178, 179, 181, 182, 262
Scovell, Mr, 525
Screen Race, 547
Sea-Fishing, 289-305
Season for Bara Singh, 179; Birds, 208; Bison, 71, 72; Black Bear, 143; Cricket, 491; Deer, 194; Fishing, 230-236, 263, 270, 273, 274, 276, 280, 281, 283, 286, 287, 290, 304; Himalayan Shooting, 102, 106, 107, 109, 129; Hockey, 514; Hunting, 408, 417, 419;

Ibex, 125; Kashmir, 132, 148, 155, 156, 173; Pig-sticking, 314; Red Bear, 122, 144, 146; Rhinoceros, 62; Rowing, 531, 534; Sambhur, 201; Small Game Shooting, 135, 136; Snipe, 209; Tiger, 12, 30
Seasons, How imported Horses feel the Indian, 322, 323, 324
Secunderabad, Cricket at, 489; Football at, 498; Paper-chasing at, 463; Racing at, 425, 441, 451, 455
Seer, 285, 289, 293, 303, 304
Seetal, 226
Seoni, Railway at, 78
Serle, 127
Serow, 120, 135, 144, 180, 181
Servants, *see* Wages
Shadipur, Fishing near, 263, 279
Shan States, Rivers in the, 282
Sharks, Fresh-water, 264
Sharks, Marine, 285, 303
Sharoand, 97, 98, 124, 128
Sharpu (or Sharpoo), 120, 126, 135, 142, 147, 153, 160, 162, 180, 206
Shayok River, 156, 168, 169
Shelter Nullah, 171
Shigar, 161, 164, 168, 169, 171, 176
Shigathang, 168
Shikari (in Chamba), 89; (in Kashmir), 136, 138; Licensing of, 191; for Pig-sticking, 367
Shillong, Cricket at, 491; Golf at, 512; Paper-chasing 463, 464; Racing at, 425, 451
Shimshiberi Range, 169, 177
Shingo Nullah, 149, 159
Shingye Nullah, 170
Shot-gun, Use of (in big game shooting), 64, 87
Shoulders in Horses, 336
Shoveller, 210
Shushoti, 127
Sialkot, 266, 267
Siam, 204
Sights for Rifles, 15, 52
Sikhim, 181, 205
Simla, 4, 81, 217, 266, 425, 427, 441, 451, 463, 491, 496, 517, 527
Singa La Pass, 149
Singapore, Tiger near, 5
Singhurpoor, 281
Sintham, 130
Sirin River, 279
Sisi, 213
Sisu, 128
Siwalik Hills, 200
Skardu, 149, 155, 156, 160, 161, 164, 168, 172
Skill at Arms, 547
Skinning Bears, 145
Skipjack, 289, 300
"Skittle," 541
Skye Races, 425, 541
Sloth Bear, 54
Smoking, 114, 484
Snatcher Stakes, 547
Snipe, 136, 207, 208-210
Snowdon Lake, 285
Snow-leopard, *see* Leopard
—— Pheasant, *see* Pheasant
—— Pigeon, *see* Pigeon
Snurla, 150
Soda Water and Biscuit Race, 547
Sola, 109
Solah Topee, 22
Sonamarg, 148
Sonar, 281
sondaicus, 65
Sonepore, Racing at, 425, 442
Soonderbuns, Fishing in the, 298; Gaur in the, 79; Rhinoceros in the, 65; Tiger in the, 5, 10, 47, 66
Sopor, 177, 263
Sore back in Horses, 370
Souter's Saddles, 355
Southern India, Cheetah Hunting in, 550
South Phen Country, The, 76
Sowl, 272
Spaniels, 412
Spavin, 316
Spearing Tigers, 47
Spears for Pig-sticking, 357-360
Spinner & Co. (Manchester), 63
Spinners & Spinning Tackles, 249
Spitak, 150
"Splashed" Horses, 341
Spoon Baits, 250, 269, 276, 291, 296
Spoonbill, 210
"Sportsman's Guide to Kashmir, The" (Ward), 110
Spotted Deer, *see* Deer
Spurs, 362, 490
Squirrel, Flying, 220
Srinagar, 81, 96, 111, 125, 126,

127, 130, 131, 132, 133, 134, 135, 136, 139, 140, 141, 142, 143, 145, 146, 147, 148, 156, 172, 176, 183, 184, 527
Stables and Stable Management, 368-373, 398, 470-474
Stalking Black-buck, 197; Ibex, 162, 163
Stallions, Drawbacks of, 345, 389
Starting Machine, The, 451
Stedman, Fort, 441, 442, 451, 455
Steeple-chasing, 454-461
Sticks, Polo, 402
Stock Horses, 320
Suela, 98, 102, 107
Suez, Fishing off, 296
Suffolk, The Earl of, 423
Suhej, Fishing at, 281
Suliman Mountains, 269
Sullivan, Colonel, 109
Sultanpoor, 128
Surchu, 127
Surjoo River, 269, 273
Surmi, 289, 293
Suru, 110, 111, 125, 129, 149, 154, 155
Suswa, The, 274, 275
Sutal, 108
Sutlej, The, 228, 261
Swamp Deer, *see* Deer
Swimming, 523

TACKLE Shops in India, 254
Tæping, The, 282
Tagalang Pass, 95, 127, 153
Tanail, 99
Tanduri, 286
Tangrot River, 255, 265, 280
"Tank Angling" (Thomas), 224, 254
Tankse, 151, 152
Tanks, Fishing in, 253, 261, 262, 271
Tanuchpur, 269
Tapti, Fishing in the, 261
Tarkuti, 155
Tarn, 289, 302
"Tatties," 365
Tawi Rivers, 255, 263, 266, 267
Teal, 136, 210, 211
Tellicherry, Sea-fishing at, 291, 297
Tench, 285
Tennasserim, 204
Tent Clubs, 317
Tent-pegging, 547
Tents, 24, 27, 62, 83
Terai, Malaria in the, 235, 271; Sambhur in the, 200; Tiger in the, 5, 13, 30
Tezpur, Racing at, 441
Thamin, 204
Thanala, 95, 96, 130
Thanna Mundi, 132
—— River, 297
Thar, 91, 103, 107, 116, 123, 126, 135
Thassa, 151
"The Angler's Handbook," 224, 232
"The Highlands of Central India" (Forsyth), 67
"The Rod in India" (Thomas), 224, 258, 264
"The Transport of Horses by Sea" (Martin), 443
Thibet, 81, 111, 146, 185 (*see* also Antelope and Gazelle)
Thomas, Mr H. S. (quoted), 224, 229, 232, 237, 239, 240, 242, 252, 253, 254, 298
Thrush in Horses, 370
Tiari, 116
Tides for Sea-fishing, 290, 304
Tiger, 3-48, 68, 74, 75, 77, 79, 101,
tigris, 3
Tikri, 98, 112, 123, 124
Tilel, 141, 154, 158, 182
Tilting, 547
Time Race, 547
Timing, Indian Method of (Racing), 446
Tindi, 112, 127
Tips to Natives, 184, 551
Tissa, 89, 97, 98, 99, 101, 102, 106, 112, 113, 119, 121, 124, 128
Tollygunge, Golf at, 504; Racing at, 425, 440, 455, 456, 457
Tolti, 155, 156
Tongas, 88, 131, 132, 133
tor, 246
Torbela, 266, 279
torquatus, 142
Totalisator, The, 451-453
Tournaments, Hockey, 513-4: Football, 494-8; Polo, 382, 384
Tragbal, 141, 144, 157, 167, 172, 178
Training for Athletes, 480-486; for Horses, 351, 394, 444
Trang, 286
Transport, 26, 28, 70, 78, 83, 88,

127, 132, 133, 134, 147, 148, 151, 153, 184, 185, 269, 287, 367, 372
Travancore, Gaur in, 79; Sea-fishing on the coast of, 295
Tree, Shooting Tiger from a, 39
Triloknath, 94, 112, 124, 127
Trisingham Nullah, 141, 143, 181
Trotting Race, 547
Trout, 225, 262, 263, 269, 284, 285, 288
Tso Morari Lake, 95, 112, 113, 126, 127, 128
Tunny, 303
Tussar Line, 271
"Tying up" for Tiger, 34, 69

ULTA PULTA Race, 547
Umasi La Pass, 97, 109, 110, 125, 126, 129
Umballa, Polo at, 385; Racing at, 425, 427, 441, 442, 455, 462, 463
uncia, 181
unicornis, 59
United Provinces, Fishing in the, 260, 265
Upshi, 95, 127, 153
Uri, 132, 134, 177
Ursus, 58, 142

V.C. RACE, 547
Veterinary, 373-375
vignei, 136
Vindhya Range, Rivers of the, 228
Vizagapatam District, Fishing in the, 262, 295

WADERS for Fishing, 256
Wages of Native Servants—for Kashmir, 137, 184; for Pig-sticking, 367; for Tiger shooting, 26, 27
Waingunga, 282
Waist-belt, 23
Waitar, 173
Wake, Captain (on Fishing), 286
Walker, Dr, 224, 274
Wambi, 158
Wangat, 141, 148, 179, 182
Wanla, 126, 149
Ward, Colonel, 110, 130, 151, 170, 180, 193
Wardha, 282
Wardwan, 111, 141, 154, 178
Warora, 70
Water, Clear or Thick (for Fishing), 232, 274, 275
Watering Horses, 473
Weight of Cheetah, 54; of Panther, 53
Wellington, Boxing at, 522; Racing at, 427, 441
Welsh Regiment, 493, 494
Wenlock, Lord, 421
Whistling Race, 548
White, Fort, 282
White Tie Race, 548
Wigram, Major, 135, 136, 139 f.n., 192
Wildfowl, 135
Wilson, The late Fred, 275
Woodcock, 207, 217
Wular (or Woolar) Lake, 141, 143, 156, 157, 173, 179, 183, 526

YACHTING, 523-528
Yak, 127, 136, 147
"Yakdans," 138
Yerrowda, Golf Links at, 502, 509

ZASKAR (or Zanskar), 97, 106, 109, 110, 111, 126, 128, 129, 149, 153, 183
Zhob River, 264
Zingzingbir, 127
Zoji La Pass, 111, 147, 148